Textus

English Studies in Italy

volume XXXVI (2023), No. 1
(January-April)

Carocci editore

Textus: English Studies in Italy. First published in 1988, *Textus* is the leading journal of English studies in Italy and the official review of the AIA – Associazione Italiana di Anglistica (Italian Association for English Studies). Double blind peer reviewed and indexed by the main international databases, it is dedicated to promoting scholarly exchange among Italian and international researchers. Each issue is jointly edited by an Italian and a foreign scholar of international standing and addresses a topical area of language, literature and cultural studies. With its unique coverage of English studies in Italy, *Textus* is a forum for new critical and theoretical approaches and an invaluable resource for academic research and teaching.

Editore
Carocci S.p.a., Viale di Villa Massimo 47, 00161 Roma
Tel. 0642818417, e-mail: riviste@carocci.it

Abbonamenti 2023: per l'Italia € 60,00 (per i soci AIA € 42,00), per l'estero € 101,00. Prezzo fascicolo singolo € 21,50.

Il versamento va effettuato a favore di Carocci editore S.p.a., Viale di Villa Massimo 47, 00161 Roma con una delle seguenti modalità: – a mezzo di bollettino postale sul c.c.n. 000063545651 – tramite assegno bancario (anche internazionale) non trasferibile – con bonifico bancario sul conto corrente 000001409096 del Monte dei Paschi di Siena, filiale cod. 8650, Via Abruzzi 6, 00187 Roma; codici bancari: CIN C, ABI 01030, CAB 03301 IBAN IT40V0103003250000063545651 – SWIFT BIC: PASCITMMXXX.
La sottoscrizione degli abbonamenti può essere effettuata anche attraverso il sito Internet dell'editore www.carocci.it, con pagamento mediante carta di credito.
Gli abbonamenti decorrono dall'inizio dell'anno e danno diritto a tutti i numeri dell'annata. Le richieste di abbonamento e/o di numeri arretrati, le variazioni di dati (indirizzo civico per spedizione, indirizzo e-mail ecc.) e le informazioni utili alla gestione della rivista devono essere comunicate direttamente a Carocci editore (riviste@carocci.it).

Impaginazione: Studio Editoriale Cafagna, Barletta
Copertina: Giulia Rossi

Autorizzazione del Tribunale di Roma n. 234 del 27 luglio 2012
Direttore responsabile: Lilla Maria Crisafulli

Finito di stampare nel mese di ottobre 2023 presso la Litografia Varo, Pisa

ISSN: 1824-3967
ISBN: 978-88-290-1960-1

Contents

**Dimensions of framing:
representation, cognition, interaction
edited by Paola Catenaccio, Giuliana Garzone and Martin Reisigl**

Paola Catenaccio, Giuliana Garzone, and Martin Reisigl
Introduction. Dimensions of Framing:
Representation, Cognition, Interaction   7

Stefania Consonni, Michele Sala
Towards a Heuristic Typology of Frames qua Frames:
Operationalising Frame Analysis across Domains,
Media and Modes   25

Alessandro Aru
Frame Shifting and Satirical Reading   51

Sergio Pizziconi
Frames in a Meta-analytical Perspective:
The Case of a Pre-survey on Queer Studies   71

Anna Mongibello
How Political Deepfakes Shape Reality:
A Visual Framing Analysis   91

Jekaterina Nikitina
Discursive Duelling in International Criminal Justice:
Dialogical Framing in Opening and Closing Statements
at the International Criminal Court   113

Francesco Nacchia
Feminine and Masculine Wines: A Corpus-assisted
Critical Specialised Discourse Analysis of Gender Framing
in Promotional Tasting-Notes   135

Maria Cristina Nisco
Framing Disability and Sexuality:
An Analysis of Instagram Users' Comments   157

Jacqueline Aiello
(Re)framing Climate Change
in a Climate Sceptic Online News Outlet   179

Lorenzo Buonvivere
"Te Awa Tupua is a legal person": The Framing of Nature
in the Whanganui River Deed of Settlement   199

Maria Grazia Guido, Pietro Luigi Iaia
The Metaphysical Reframing of Sustainable
and Inclusive Tourism in the Post-pandemic Digital Era:
An ELF-mediated Approach   219

Piergiorgio Trevisan, Eric Louis Russell
Layering in Frames, Frames in Layers:
Dreaming of Naples   237

Elisa Mattiello
Metaphor and Framing in Cognition and Discourse:
'War' and 'Journey' Metaphors for COVID-19   261

Denise Milizia
Framing the Pandemic in the UK and in the US:
The war, the Science and the Herd   281

Maria Cristina Paganoni
'Living with Covid': Boris Johnson's Communication
in Post-Pandemic Times   309

Walter Giordano, Katerina Mandenaki
Framing the COVID-19 Pandemic Crisis in Financial Discourse.
A Sentence Embeddings Approach   331

Contributors   355

Introduction
Dimensions of Framing:
Representation, Cognition, Interaction

Paola Catenaccio, Giuliana Garzone and Martin Reisigl

1. Dimensions of framing

This issue of *Textus* offers a multi-faceted approach to the linguistic, semiotic, critical and cognitive notion of frame, one of the most influential concepts in linguistics and discourse studies. The original idea at the heart of the project was to investigate and (re)assess this theoretical construct by discussing several of today's most productive critical models of framing, both in theoretical terms and through examples of their use, as key interpretive tools in the analysis of discourses in a wide variety of domains, genres and contexts.

The related concepts of frame and framing have been around for over half a century now, and have been applied in the most diverse disciplines and research areas – sociology, and in particular social movement research, cognitive sciences, anthropology, psychology, sociology, political science, artificial intelligence and, of course, linguistics and discourse analysis, communication and media studies.

While – as will be illustrated shortly – the notion of frame has been used with some continuity in the last few decades, recent times have seen a remarkable surge in scholarly interest in it, in terms of both theory and applications. In the same period when this thematic issue was being designed, prepared and edited, a special issue of *Discourse Studies* was also in preparation dealing in particular with the application of frame analysis in social movement research, and at the time of writing of this introduction (April 2023) the issue has just been published. This coincidence in timing testifies to the relevance and topicality of the concepts of frame and framing in discourse-related research and the interest it is currently attracting. Of course, there are important differences in the perspectives adopted in the

ISSN 1824-3967
© Carocci Editore S.p.A.

issues of *Discourse Studies* and of *Textus* respectively. Although both have frames and frame analysis as their main subject matter, in the case of *Discourse Studies* the focus is on their application to social movement research, and the research discussed has a strong sociological orientation, whereas in this issue of *Textus* the analytical perspective is specifically linguistic and particularly based on text linguistics and linguistic discourse analysis. Within this broad distinction, the issue features studies which vary in method and approach, thus bringing to the fore the richness, flexibility and adaptability of the concept. This wide semantic scope of the frame concept has certainly been a factor in its fortune, but – at the same time – has also contributed to its often underdetermined status, and occasionally vague use in research as well as on occasions even non-scientific use in public media discourse, for instance in German speaking countries, where Elisabeth Wehling's (2016) work on strategic "political framing" and her media presence as language advisor and critic led to controversy (see, Kuck 2022, Wengeler 2022, Ziem 2022). Before going on to examine the aspects and topics explored in the contributions collected in this issue, a brief discussion of the polysemic notion of frame is therefore in order.

Ervin Goffman was one of the first authors to bring the notion of frame to the attention of sociologists, linguists, and discourse analysts, crediting it as an important analytical tool when it comes to analysing the organization of everyday experiences and especially with respect to communication, interaction and cognition. In his *Frame Analysis* (1974), however, the author made it clear that the notion had already been introduced, and traced its origins back to a line of thought running from William James, through Alfred Schutz, Harold Garfinkel to Gregory Bateson and himself. In particular, he pointed out that in Bateson's seminal paper "A Theory of Play and Fantasy" (Bateson 1954/1972) the term "frame" appeared in the sense in which Goffman himself intended to use it, i.e. as inherently metacommunicative and "involv[ing] the evaluation of the message it contains, or merely assist[ing] the mind in understanding the contained message"[1]. Goffman's own definition boils down to the fundamental question that all individuals face when they need to

---

[1] It is to be noted that Bateson discussed frame as a manipulative tool in psychotherapy.

make sense of an experience in a specific situation: "What is it that's going on here?". Any event can be described "in terms of a focus that is close-up or distant", adopting the perspective of one or another of the actors involved, or in case of a retrospective look, taking different views with different evaluative assessments of how to interpret the specific undertaking (Goffman 1974: 8). In particular, he is interested in "the basic frameworks of understanding available in our society for making sense out of events and to analyze the special vulnerabilities to which these frames of reference are subject" (Goffman 1974: 10), which he also defines "schemata of interpretation" (Goffman 1974: 45).

Goffman distinguishes between *natural* and *social frames*. For him, *natural frames* are merely physical events that have purely "natural" causes or determinants and do not depend on the will or any intentions of human actors. In contrast, *social frames* depend on social actions that result from human intentions and conventions. Important social frames include – according to Goffman – the *frame of pretending* (as imitation in play or joke), the *frame of competition*, the *frame of ceremony*, the *frame of special performing* (e.g., as rehearsal, exercise, or demonstration), and the *frame of (transmedial) recontextualization* (e.g., if a novel is reworked into a play). Further important frames Goffman is interested in from his sociological perspective are the *theater frame,* the *broadcasting frame,* the *novel frame, the film frame* and the *frame of conversation*. Social frames are modulated by keys. *Keys* function as systems of conventions that transform an activity so that it is placed in a new frame (Goffman 1974).

Since its establishment as an instrument for conceptualization and as an analytical tool, the concept of framing has been the object of numerous theoretical articulations over time, mostly in broad terms related to each other, but characterized by important conceptual differences and perspectives. More specifically grounded in cognitive theory is the notion of semantic frames, related to the structures of knowledge, which Fillmore (1976) relied on for the study of word meanings and subsequently of linguistic patterns, thereby opening up a research paradigm called *Frame Semantics* within which he also used the terms "scenario" and "schema". Tannen (1993: 16) traces the use of the term *schema* with more or less this meaning as far back as to Bartlett (1932), and sees it used also by Chafe (1977), who describes the verbalization of an event as consisting of the determination of a schema followed by the determination of a frame, and by Hymes (1974), who includes frames as one of the "means of speaking".[2]

In the same period, the notion of frame was also relied on in research on artificial intelligence, which at the time – in Shank and Abelson's words – meant work intended "to lead towards the eventual computer understanding of natural language" (1977: 20). In a seminal paper in which he is pursuing both "a theory of human thinking and a scheme for making an intelligent machine", Minsky provides a definition of frame as "a data-structure for representing a stereotyped situation", i.e. a *remembered* framework that is selected from memory whenever one encounters a new situation to be used "to fit reality by changing details as necessary" (Minsky 1974: 111). In a similar vein, working on "how concepts are structured in the human mind" with a view to computer programming, Shank and Abelson (1977: 41) preferred the term *script* to refer to structured representations of knowledge, and in particular of specific knowledge, i.e. our knowledge about recurrent events, consisting of "a pre-determined, stereotyped sequence of actions that defines a well-known situation" in a particular context.

The work on Artificial Intelligence inspired Van Dijk (1977), who saw a frame as an organizational principle denoting "a conceptual structure in semantic memory" (1977: 159), and more specifically, "[t]he set of propositions characterizing our conventional knowledge of some more or less autonomous situation (activity, course of events, state)" (1977: 99). According to this view, in terms of cognition, frames guide information processing by providing cognitive scaffoldings, or pre-existing data structures stored in our memory, against which to evaluate new data.

The idea of frame as a mechanism in the individual's cognition process discussed so far is also taken up by Tannen (1993), but with a difference: as an interactional sociolinguist inspired by Gumperz (e.g. 1982), she is especially interested in frames in the context of interaction; for their analysis, an "interactive notion of frame" is necessary providing "a definition of what is going on in interaction,

---

[2] For a very extensive history of the various frame concepts cf. Busse (2012).

without which no utterance (or movement or gesture) could be interpreted" (Tannen and Wallat 1987: 206). Examining all the different conceptualizations of the notion of frame given until then, Tannen saw them as amounting to the simple concept of "structure of expectation" (borrowed from R.N. Ross 1975), and attributed a twofold function to them: first, they "make it possible to perceive and interpret objects and events in the world"; but at the same time they "shape those perceptions to the model of the world provided by them" (Tannen 1993: 21).

While most of the conceptualizations discussed so far are centered on the role of frames in cognition, the other important line of research on frame and framing focuses on the use of this same mechanism in discourse. The cognitive relevance of frames in the individuals' processes of understanding and interpreting events and activities lends itself to being exploited for the purpose of shaping people's perceptions, as described by Tannen, orienting the way they understand and evaluate events, facts and activities.

Under this perspective, in relation to discourse, frames have been characterized as resources by which it is possible "to select some aspects of a perceived reality and make them more salient in a communicating text, in such a way as to promote a particular problem definition, causal interpretation, moral evaluation, and/or treatment recommendation for the item described" (Entman 1993: 52). This is Entman's fundamental understanding of the function of frames in discourse. It is in line with Goffman's original specification of frames as mechanisms that enable people to make sense of "what is it that's going on" in a given discourse episode, thus influencing how it is understood by participants.

In accordance with this, although Goffman's influence is not always explicitly acknowledged (for this critique see, for example, Matthes 2014: 24-25), the notion of framing is used in studies of communication, news, media, politics, etc., to refer to the way in which discourse mechanisms and strategies can be deployed to affect the cognitive representations with which people approach issues, episodes and information (cf. e.g. Gamson and Modigliani 2004). This approach to framing focuses on how a content producer constructs a message. It is especially interesting for linguists, as salience mainly relies on linguistic "cues and markers" (Goffman 1981: 156) that signal the presence of specific frames.

This use of the notion of framing has been instrumental in research on a large number of topics in a variety of domains: social movement research (as in the special issue of *Discourse Studies* mentioned above), communication on climate change (Ansari et al. 2013; Lefsrud and Meyer 2012), sustainability and globalization (Fiss and Hirsch 2005), conflict and negotiation research (Dewulf et al 2009), making sense of new technologies (Orlikowski and Gash 1994; Kaplan and Tripsas 2008; Barrett, Heracleous and Walsham 2013), Public Relations and legitimation strategies in multinational corporations (Vaara and Tienari 2008), news discourse (Greco and Tribastone 2018; von Sikorski and Matthes 2020) and the representation of evolutions in science, technology and society (Garzone 2019; Archibald, Catenaccio, Garzone 2019), to name but some. What makes the study of frames and framing even more interesting and relevant is the fact that – from a social constructionist perspective (Berger and Luckman, 1966) – frameworks that are extensively and pervasively disseminated through the press, television and other mass media, as well as political communication, become social constructs and are incorporated into a community's culture. In this respect, D'Angelo and Kuypers's (2010) edited collection of studies of framing in news discourse, and more generally in the media, is especially important, with contributions by leading 'frame scholars' such as B.T. Scheufele (Scheufele and Scheufele 2010) and R. Entman (2010).

The rich and highly influential literature briefly outlined above testifies to the importance of investigating the role of discourse framing in all forms of communication, and in particular in public communication. Such a research effort is deemed to be especially critical because of the usually covert character of framing. By its very nature, framing tends to go undetected even while strongly influencing, and indeed often constraining, interpretation: an in-depth linguistic analysis can contribute to exposing biased representations and "influenced" understandings of certain issues, its effectiveness being enhanced by the fact that our research relies on objective linguistic data.

Which brings us to one of the key reasons why we thought that devoting an issue of *Textus* to framing was especially important – and indeed, as highlighted above, both timely and long overdue. In spite of the considerable amount of research into framing, most of the studies produced in this area do not have linguistic and rhetorical aspects as their main focus of interest. Often, rather than by linguists, they have been authored by scholars in other disciplines, e.g. sociology, anthropology, researchers in social movement research or communication and media studies. Within this scenario, the studies collected in this thematic issue are especially topical and can offer a comprehensive picture of possible applications of the notion of framing in a linguistic and discourse-based perspective, exploring the linguistic and discursive resources used in the framing of discourse (semantics) at all levels, in lexico-grammatical and phraseological choices, and in the deployment of communicative and rhetorical strategies – including definitions, repetitions, analogies and metaphors.

In this respect, recourse to metaphors is especially significant. The framing effects of metaphors are widely recognized (e.g. Gibbs 2017; Landau and Keefer 2014; Semino 2021) on account of their crucial role in conceptual structures and processes. Metaphorical expressions are the linguistic manifestation of conceptual metaphors. In Kövecses' well-known definition, "a conceptual metaphor consists of two conceptual domains, in which one domain is understood in terms of another" (Kövecses 2010: 4). This means that certain aspects of the source domain are mapped onto aspects of the target domain, thus activating different ways of understanding and making sense of it – in other words, framing certain aspects of the objects or experience being represented (cf. Semino 2008). This mechanism had already been pointed out by Lakoff and Johnson themselves in their first, seminal book, when they noted that the choice of the source domain highlights some aspects of the target domain and tends to obfuscate others (Lakoff and Johnson 1980: 10-13 and passim). This selective use of the features of a given metaphorical domain has been shown to be in the service of framing as a process aimed at both reflecting and activating different ways of understanding and reasoning about things (Semino, Demjén and Demmen, 2018). It has been proved experimentally (Thibodeau and Boroditsky 2011) and observed in public debates (Schön 1993, Ritchie and Cameron 2014) that this function of introducing a selective focus is a fact, with metaphors having been shown to influence readers' and hearers' responses even when recipients are not aware of them, and indeed being even more influential when this is the case (Gibbs 2006).

So, for instance, in the case of social issues "the perspective that is taken ... is determined by the way that it is metaphorically represented" (Charteris-Black 2004: 22-24), e.g. in the media. Hence the wide debate on the use of bellicose metaphors in dealing with disease, e.g. with cancer and more recently with COVID-19, which some researchers saw as likely to have an impact on people's perception of and reaction to the medical condition (Semino, Demjén and Demmen 2018; Semino 2021; Garzone 2021). There can be no doubt that the deployment of metaphors in public debates is often aimed at influencing people's views of facts, problems, issues.

Against this background, the studies collected in this issue tackle complementary facets of framing as a key meaning-making system within specific linguistic, discursive and communicative dimensions. They analyse exemplary samples of discourse in multiple domains and in diversified genres and modes.

2. Outline of issue

The popularity, as well as productivity, of frames and frame analysis in their multiple forms and manifestations is also testified by the sheer number of proposals submitted for this issue of *Textus*. The process of selection was difficult not only because of the high quality of the submissions, but also on account of their scope, which covered a very broad array of approaches, methods, themes and materials. The decision to publish a double issue descends from the recognition that sticking to the number of articles originally planned would have resulted in the exclusion of entire strands of research which deserved to be featured. The ensuing collection is therefore rich and varied, and offers an extremely interesting overview of the numerous ways in which the concept of framing can be used in linguistic and especially discourse-analytical research.

The first volume opens with an article by Michele Sala and Stefania Consonni. It addresses the problem of operationalising the notion of frames in linguistic terms. Sala and Consonni argue that while frames have been widely studied in terms of conceptual units, scarcer attention has been devoted to their surface features, i.e. to the metatextually explicit (as opposed to subtle and implicit) semiotic features which are foregrounded in different forms and media of communication to raise expectations against which texts and meanings are interpreted. To refer to these mechanisms of frame instantiation, they propose the label 'Frames qua Frames' (FqFs), and explore when, in what way and for what purposes they are used as *economic* (or adaptive) resources and as *energetic* (or attractive) resources for text interpretation.

The exploration of the way in which textual elements trigger frames – and consequently expectations as to the way a text is (or indeed, as the case may be, may be expected) to be interpreted – is at the heart of the two articles that follow, authored by Alessandro Aru and by Sergio Pizziconi. Alessandro Aru's study focuses on the role of framing in satire. It investigates the effect of frame shifting on text interpretation respectively in satire and in humour, where it is known to play a crucial role. His findings suggest that frame shifting is perceived as stronger in humorous texts with respect to satirical ones: Aru's hypothesis is that in humorous texts frame shifting contributes to the general effect of amusement and entertainment by introducing incongruous and unexpected materials, whereas in satirical texts the represented materials trigger further inferences that determine a shift in attitudes, turning the general effect into criticism and moral condemnation.

An experimental design also characterizes the following article, by Sergio Pizziconi, whose contribution discusses frames from a meta-analytical perspective and reports on an experiment aimed at assessing the power of frames in triggering audience responses. Pizziconi's experiment involved administering a pre-survey to students who attended a seminar on queer studies at the University for Foreigners of Siena and recording their reactions to a set of stimuli linked to the topic of the seminar. To ensure that the recorded reactions were as spontaneous as possible, students were asked to self-record them in spoken form, a departure from conventional ways of collecting student data in educational settings designed to weaken the academic frame, which might have encouraged them to provide "right", as opposed to honest, answers. The findings showed that responses to the pre-seminar survey were at least in part affected by the conceptual frames activated by the seminar topic, leading to the conclusion that procedures and phrasing that are prototypical of a given setting are likely to trigger responses influenced by the frames associated with such setting. This has important implications for social research and should be taken into consideration in experiment design.

One of the takeaways of Pizziconi's article is that an awareness of the potential of frames for influencing (either inadvertently or deliberately) understanding and response is needed in order to critically interpret text and discourse. Indeed, critical awareness of framing strategies and their effects is extremely important, especially if one is faced with forms of discourse which are either manipulative by design, as is the case with the political deepfakes analysed by Anna Mongibello in the fourth article in this volume, or aimed at (re)constructing facts and characters so as to establish the truth about a contested reality, as described in the following text, authored by Jekaterina Nikitina and featuring an analysis of opening and closing statements at the International Criminal Court.

Anna Mongibello's study investigates the role of visual framing in enhancing the credibility of political deepfakes – both "real" (i.e. fake videos designed to manipulate public opinion) and "fake" (i.e. created with the expressed intention to expose them as deepfakes, with the aim to educate the public to recognise them). Mongibello shows that the credibility of the videos relies on artful visual framing combined with linguistic and rhetorical likelihood. She concludes that for the creation of successful forgeries both visual and rhetorical features are essential, which confirms the power of language as an effective tool for reaching ideological aims, first and foremost through the manipulation of authenticity.

The power of language to create an impression of authenticity is central to Jekaterina Nikitina's investigation, which explores the role of framing and counterframing in the depiction of characters and events in the statements made respectively by the Prosecution and the Defence at the beginning and at the end of international criminal trials involving defendants accused of genocide. Nikitina finds that when depicting the defendants or rebutting each other's stories, the parties use a paradoxical combination of humanising and dehumanising (stereotypical) frames, and notices that such frames evolve dialogically with the unravelling of proceedings even within statements by the same party, as framing appears to be used as a key semiotic resource for the discursive reconstruction and negotiation of reality.

Mongibello's and Nikitina's articles show the working of a conscious and deliberate (and, it may be argued, unscrupulous, or at least potentially so) use of framing in strategic communication. However, framing can work in much subtler ways, producing, reproducing and reinforcing conventionalised ways of looking at and interpreting reality. Stereotypes, for instance, can be seen as ready-made frames which limit our understanding of reality. In this respect, gender stereotypes can be especially constraining, as is shown in Francesco Nacchia's analysis of promotional wine-tasting notes, where gender stereotypes abound and show no signs of abating. Persisting stereotypes are also identified by Maria Cristina Nisco in her study of the framing of disability and sexuality in Instagram users' comments on a lingerie campaign featuring models with disabilities. Despite evidence of a widespread willingness and readiness to welcome diversity, some of the comments show that representations of disabled bodies framed in the light of positive sexuality continue to attract aversion from some users and are often stubbornly resisted. In her conclusions, Nisco calls for greater active participation in debates concerning representations of disability so as to gradually erode taboos and normalize portrayals of people with disabilities.

The next two articles in the collection are concerned with framings of nature or of phenomena linked to it.

Jaqueline Aiello's article is devoted to the analysis of the way in which climate change is framed in a climate-change-skeptic online news outlet. Aiello's investigation shows that despite an appearance of objective coverage (testified by a consistent presence of climate-change related topics and themes), when reporting on such themes the news outlet analysed made extensive use of framings which clearly belied climate change scepticism. Among the strategies used were the identification of environmentalism with religion (or rather religious extremism), and recurrent representations of climate activists, especially women, as flawed and inadequate. As Aiello points out, a focus on framing, and in particular on the linguistic resources relied on for this purpose, can greatly contribute to a better understanding of the way in which climate change scepticism and other antagonistic ideological representations are – often surreptitiously – advanced even in the face of ostensibly objective coverage.

The framings identified by Aiello are functional to discourses of resistance which advocate change in the way mankind relates to the natural environment. In sharp contrast to this, Lorenzo Buonvivere's paper analyses the implications of recognising legal personhood to the Whanganui River, in New Zealand. Drawing on ecolinguistics and Positive Discourse Analysis, Buonvivere shows that by applying a legal framing to the representation of the river it is possible to assign nature an agentive role, thereby not only promoting a favourable understanding of the environment, but also allowing the allocation of responsibility for harmful actions against it.

A shift in framing – this time aimed at fostering more sustainable and inclusive practices – is also featured in Maria Grazia Guido and Pietro Iaia's article, which presents a case study of communicative strategies deployed in the conceptualisation, design and realisation of an advertisement aimed at promoting sustainable and inclusive tourism in the Southern Italian area of Salento. The article highlights that sustainability and inclusion – despite their ideal appeal – are hardly uncontroversial, and demand extensive discursive negotiation and an effective reframing of conventional ideas of tourism in order to be made acceptable to the various groups of stakeholders involved in the tourist economy. With specific reference to the Salento area, planned sustainability policies due to be implemented soon are seen by many as representing a threat to traditional local tourist economies. On the one hand, these policies include the installation of a huge wind farm off the coast, spoiling natural landscapes and heritage/art sites; on the other hand, the political plans relate the reception and integration of migrants who have arrived in large numbers on the Salento coasts. The advertisement discussed in the article exploits the affordances – both technological and, more broadly, cultural and communicative – of the metaverse to create a form of communication capable of activating typologically-hybrid cognitive and communicative framing processes suited to the effective representation of new forms of tourism.

In contrast to the reframing of tourism proposed by Guido and Iaia, Piergiorgio Trevisan and Eric Louis Russel's contribution reverts to more conventional representations of tourist destinations and experiences. Trevisan and Russel's analysis of the depiction of Naples and Amalfi in a US travel documentary shows that the use of conventional frames in the portrayal of the two locations (with

Naples being framed through the lens of danger, and Amalfi through that of rurality) is geared exclusively at fostering an impression of authenticity which can be commodified and offered to the viewers for consumption. They argue that such framing oversimplifies the representation of the two destinations, and gives rise to yet another manifestation of banal globalisation.

With the following article, the focus shifts to the COVID-19 pandemic and its framings in various contexts. The ways in which the pandemic – an event, for the present generations, of an unprecedented magnitude, which made it inevitably difficult to grasp – has been represented have been analysed in extensive research both during and in the period immediately following it. Much of this research has focused on metaphors, which were particularly productive in public discourse, and which – as highlighted in the first part of this introduction – are known to have a strong framing power. It comes as no surprise, therefore, that the first two articles focus on the use of metaphors. Elisa Mattiello's essays analyses the 'war' and the 'journey' metaphors in COVID-19 news discourse. While both metaphors are well known and have been discussed in the literature, Mattiello's treatment of the topic is original in that it highlights the way in which war- and journey-related conceptual metaphors can present different scenarios depending on the context in which they are used. This calls for further exploration of how metaphors function contextually, as well as for a more precise definition of framing.

In the following article, Denise Milizia also discusses the framing effects of the war metaphor, as well as those of references to science and to "the herd effects". She adopts a comparative perspective which examines and compares UK and US discourses. An interesting aspect of the use of the war metaphor in political discourse in the two countries that Milizia highlights is the preference for the lemma *fight* in the British corpus and for *war* in the American one. Milizia also emphasises the strategic recourse to the science frame – especially in the US corpus – as a way of deflecting responsibility for unpopular choices from politics to science, and notices the productivity of the lemma *herd*, which, starting from the expression *herd immunity* (initially advocated by both US and UK politicians), came then to be used in the US in derogatory expressions, such as *herd mentality*. Milizia concludes that the trajectory of the *herd* metaphor suggests that further investigation of novel and creative metaphors may be a particularly promising objective to pursue.

Political discourse is also the focus of Maria Cristina Paganoni's study of Boris Johnson's COVID-related communication during the final part of his term, from January to September 2022, a time when the pandemic was largely subsiding. Paganoni shows that over the period considered the warfare frame that had characterised the previous two years was de-emphasised and largely replaced with a 'living with COVID' narrative set against a changed background and a different timescale. In this mutated scenario, Johnson's rhetorical focus shifted to emphasising the full restoration of civil liberties to keep the country and its economy open, with economic recovery being prioritised at all costs without taking stock of the nation's feeling of exhaustion, particularly as regards the strain put on the NHS. Paganoni concludes that the prime minister's predominantly economic framing in his post-pandemic COVID-related communication largely ignores the complexity of the "new normal".

The final article of the collection, authored by Walter Giordano and Katerina Mandenaki, marks a shift – both in terms of the type of discourse analysed, and in terms of methodology adopted. Giordano and Mendenaki investigate the framings of the economic impact of the pandemic in a set of CEO letters featured in corporate annual reports issued respectively by companies that suffered financially in the pandemic (the 'losers') and by companies that benefited from it (the 'winners'). The study, which combines insights from discourse analysis and text analytics based on large language models (LLMs), uses sentence embedding techniques to calculate similarity scores among frame-cueing sentences occurring in the letters. The analysis identifies a number of recurring frames – more specifically, conflict, morality, human factor and opportunity –, with differences in their use for 'winners' and 'losers'. In particular, 'losers' were found to tend to bend their communication towards morality and to use the opportunity frame to talk about an envisaged recovery. By contrast, the opportunity frame is not exploited by 'winners', who seem to prefer to show themselves as sympathetic. Differences are detectable also in the use of the conflict frame, with 'losers' emphasising their 'local' fight to maintain safety and continuity of operation in the difficult conjuncture they had to face, and 'winners' emphasising, by contrast, the global scale of the problem.

The sheer variety of approaches and domains of application covered in the studies collected in this double issue of *Textus* demonstrates the complexity of the notions of *frame* and *framing* and the multiplicity of their applications in a variety of domains. The multifaceted contributions show many methodological challenges researchers are faced with if they try to respond to the various needs of diversified research on frames and framing. They provide critical insights into how framing works in processing empirical reality, and show that it can be used to codify phenomena into meanings and (conversely) to detect and interpret meanings when processing texts, codes and modes. Thus, this collection can be seen as a casebook about *frames* and *framing*, where each single contribution, besides being self-standing in exploring framing as a theoretical notion and as a key analytical concept, also contributes to outlining an overall picture of framing as a heuristic discourse-analytical tool.

References

ANSARI, SHAHZAD, WIJEN, FRANK, GRAY, BARBARA, 2013, "Constructing a Climate Change Logic: An Institutional Perspective on the 'Tragedy of the Commons'", *Organization Science* 24 (4), July-August 2013, pp. 1014-1040.

ARCHIBALD, JAMES, CATENACCIO, PAOLA, GARZONE, GIULIANA, 2020, "Debating evolutions in science, technology and society: ethical and ideological perspectives. An Introduction", *Lingue e Linguaggi, Special Issue: Debating Evolutions in Science, Technology and Society: Ethical and Ideological Perspectives* 34, pp. 5-15.

BARRETT, MICHAEL, HERACLEOUS, LOISOS AND WALSHAM, GEOFF, 2013, "A Rhetorical Approach to IT Diffusion: Reconceptualizing the Ideology-Framing Relationship in Computerization Movements", MIS Quarterly 37, pp. 201-220.

BARTLETT, FREDERIC, 1932, *Remembering: A Study in Experimental and Social Psychology*, Cambridge University Press, Cambridge, UK.

BATESON, GREGORY, 1954/1972, *Steps to an Ecology of Mind. Collected Essays in Anthropology, Psychiatry, Evolution, and Epistemology*, Jason Aronson Inc., Northvale, N.J. and London.

BERGER, PETER L. and LUCKMANN, THOMAS, 1966, *The Social Construction of Reality: A Treatise in the Sociology of Knowledge*, Anchor Books, Garden City, NY.

BUSSE, DIETRICH, 2012, *Frame-Semantik. Ein Kompendium*, de Gruyter, Berlin and New York.

CHAFE, WILLIAM, 1977, "The recall and verbalization of past experience", in Roger W. Cole (ed.), *Current Issues in Linguistic Theory*, Indiana University Press, Bloomington Ind., pp. 215-246.

CHARTERIS-BLACK, JONATHAN, 2004, *Corpus Approaches to Critical Metaphor Analysis*, Palgrave Macmillan, London.

D'ANGELO, PAUL and KUYPERS, JIM A. (eds), 2010, *Doing News Framing Analysis. Empirical and Theoretical Perspectives,* Routledge, London and New York.

DEWULF, ART, GRAY, BARBARA, PUTNAM, LINDA, LEWICKI, ROY, AARTS, NOELLE, BOWEN, RENÉ AND VAN WOERKUM, CEES, 2005, "Disentangling approaches to framing in conflict and negotiation research: A meta-paradigmatic perspective", *Human Relations* 62 (2), pp. 155-193.

ENTMAN, ROBERT, 1993, "Framing: toward clarification of a fractured paradigm", *Journal of Communication* 43, 4, pp. 51-8.

ENTMAN, ROBERT, 2010, "Framing Media Power", in P. D'Angelo and J. A. Kuypers (eds), *Doing News Framing Analysis. Empirical and Theoretical Perspectives,* Routledge, London and New York, pp. 331-355.

FILLMORE, CHARLES J., 1976, "Frame semantics and the nature of language", *Annals of the New York Academy of Sciences* 280 (1): *Origins and Evolution of Language and Speech*, pp. 20-32.

FISS, PEER C. AND HIRSCH, PAUL M., 2005, "The Discourse of Globalization: Framing and Sensemaking of an Emerging Concept", *American Sociological Review* 70, February, pp. 29-52.

GAMSON, WILLIAM A. and MODIGLIANI, ANDRE, 1987, "The changing culture of affirmative action", in R. G. Braungat and M. M. Braungart (eds), *Research in Political Sociology*. JAI Press, Greenwich, CT, pp. 137-177.

GARZONE, GIULIANA E., 2019, New biomedical practices and discourses: Focus on surrogacy, *Text & Talk*, Vol. 39, n. 3, pp. 363-387.

GARZONE, GIULIANA E., 2021, "Rethinking Metaphors in COVID Communication", *Lingue e Linguaggi* 44, pp. 159-181.

GIBBS, RAYMOND W. JR., 2006, "Metaphor interpretation as embodied simulation", *Mind and Language* 21, pp. 434-458.

GIBBS, RAYMOND W. JR., 2017, *Metaphor wars: Conceptual metaphors in human life*. Cambridge University Press, Cambridge.

GOFFMAN, ERVING, 1974, *Frame Analysis: An Essay on the Organization of Experience*, Harper and Row, London.

GOFFMAN, ERVING, 1981, *Forms of talk*, Blackwell, Oxford.

GRECO, SARA and TRIBASTONE. MIRIAM, 2018, "Framing in News Discourse: The Case of the Charlie Hebdo Attack Miriam Tribastone", in M. Danesi (ed.), *Empirical Research in Semiotics and Visual Rhetoric*, IGI Global, Hershey PA, pp. 71-85.

GUMPERZ, JOHN H., 1982, *Discourse Strategies*, Cambridge University Press, Cambridge.

HYMES, DELL H., 1974, *Foundations in Sociolinguistics: An Ethnographic Approach*, University of Pennsylvania Press, Philadelphia.

KAPLAN, SARAH AND TRIPSAS, MARY, 2008, "Thinking About Technology: Applying A Cognitive Lens To Technical Change", *Research Policy*, 37 (5), 790-805.

KÖVECSES, ZOLTÁN, 2010, *Metaphor: A Practical Introduction. Second edition*, Oxford University Press, New York.

KUCK, KRISTIN, 2022, "Framing im öffentlichen Diskurs. Eine Analyse des Diskurses um Elisabeth Wehlings Framing-Gutachten für die ARD", in K. S. Roth and M. Wengeler (eds.), *Diesseits und jenseits von Framing. Politikspracheforschung im medialen Diskurs,* Buske, Hamburg, pp. 31-53.

LAKOFF, GEORGE and JOHNSON, MARK, 1980, *Metaphors We Live By*, Chicago University Press, Chicago.

LANDAU, MARK J. and KEEFER, LUCAS A., 2014, "This is like that: Metaphors in public discourse shape attitudes", *Social and Personality Psychology Compass* 8 (8), pp. 463-473. https://doi.org/10.1111/spc3.12125.

LEFSRUD, LIANNE M. AND MEYER, RENATE, 2012, "Science or Science Fiction? Professionals' Discursive Construction of Climate Change", *Organization Studies* 33 (11), pp. 1477-1506.

LEONARDI, PAUL M., 2011, "When Flexible Routines Meet Flexible Technologies: Affordance, Constraint, and the Imbrication of Human and Material Agencies", *MIS Quarterly* 35 (1), 147-67.

MATTHES, JÖRG, 2014, *Framing*, Nomos, Baden-Baden.

MINSKY, MARVIN, 1974, *A framework for representing knowledge*, MIT-AI Laboratory Memo 306.

ORLIKOWSKI, WANDA AND GASH, DEBRA, "Technology Frames: Making Sense of Information Technology in Organizations," *ACM Transactions on Information Systems* 12 (2), pp. 174-207.

RITCHIE, L. DAVID and CAMERON, LYNNE, 2014, "Open Hearts or Smoke and Mirrors: Metaphorical Framing and Frame Conflicts in a Public Meeting", *Metaphor and Symbol* 29, pp. 204-223.

ROSS, ROBERT N., 1975, "Ellipsis and the Structure of Expectation", *San José State Occasional Papers in Linguistics* 1, pp. 183-191.

SCHANK ROGER C. and ABELSON, ROBERT P., 1977, *Scripts, Plans, Goals and Understanding: An Inquiry into Human Knowledge Structures,* Erlbaum, Hillsdale, NJ..

SCHEUFELE, BERTRAM and SCHEUFELE, DIETRAM A., 2010, "Of Spreading Activation, Applicability, and Schemas: Conceptual Distinctions and Their Operational Implications for Measuring Frames and Framing Effects", in P. D'Angelo and J. A. Kuypers (eds), 2010, *Doing News Framing Analysis. Empirical and Tehoretical Perspectives.* London and New York: Routledge, pp. 110-134.

SCHÖN, DAVID A., 1993, "Generative metaphor: A perspective on problem-setting in social policy", in A. Ortony (ed.), *Metaphor and thought,* 2nd ed., Cambridge University Press, Cambridge, pp. 137-163.

SEMINO, ELENA, 2008, *Metaphor in Discourse*, Cambridge University Press, Cambridge.

SEMINO, ELENA, 2021, "'Not Soldiers but Fire-fighters' – Metaphors and Covid-19", *Health Communication* 36 (1), pp. 50-58.

VON SIKORSKI, CHRISTINA, and MATTHES, JÖRG, 2020, "Framing and Journalism", *Oxford Research Encyclopedia of Communication*. Retrieved 15 Apr. 2023, from https://oxfordre.com/communication/view/ 10.1093/ acrefore/9780190228613.001.0001/acrefore-9780190228613-e-817.

TANNEN, DEBORAH, 1993, "What's in a Frame?: Surface Evidence for Underlying Expectations", in Tannen, Deborah (ed.), *Framing in Discourse, Oxford University Press*, New York NY, pp. 14-56.

TANNEN, DEBORAH and WALLAT, CHYNTHIA, 1987, "Interactive frames and knowledge schemas in interaction: examples from a medical examination/interview", *Social Psychology Quarterly* 50 (2), pp. 205-216.

THIBODEAU, PAUL H. and BORODITSKY, LERA, 2011, "Metaphors we think with: The role of metaphor in reasoning", *PLoS ONE* 6 (2), pp. e16782.

VAARA, EERO AND TIENARI, JANNE, 2008, "A Discursive Perspective on Legitimation Strategies in Multinational Corporations", *Academy of Management Review* 33 (4), pp. 985-993.

VAN DIJK, TEUN A., 1977, *Text and Context. Explorations in the Semantics and Pragmatics of Discourse*, Longman, London and New York.

WEHLING, ELISABETH, 2016, *Politisches Framing. Wie eine Nation sich ihr denken einredet – und daraus Politik macht*, Herbert von Halem Verlag, Köln.

WENGELER, MARTIN, 2022, "Warnung vor *Framing*? Kritische Überlegungen zu Frames und Framing aus polito- und diskurslinguistischer Perspektive", in K. S. Roth and M. Wengeler (eds.), *Diesseits und jenseits von Framing. Politikspracheforschung im medialen Diskurs,* Buske, Hamburg, pp. 9-29.

ZIEM, ALEXANDER, 2022, "Framing: Genese, Struktur und Problematisierung eines kognitionswissenschaftlichen Konzepts", in K. S. Roth and M. Wengeler (eds.), *Diesseits und jenseits von Framing. Politikspracheforschung im medialen Diskurs,* Buske, Hamburg, pp. 55-76.

Towards a Heuristic Typology of Frames qua Frames: Operationalising Frame Analysis across Domains, Media and Modes

Stefania Consonni, Michele Sala

Abstract

Frames have extensively been studied as perceptual and representational categories whereby humans make sense of the world and are able to share meanings. They also function as handles, or activators of ideational contents: it is precisely through frames that ideation becomes processable and sharable. Scarcer attention, however, has been devoted to the surface features of those handles, and how they contribute to establishing sets of expectations against which texts and meanings are interpreted and exchanged. This contribution focusses on the latter realisation of frames and, more specifically, looks at something we propose to label 'Frames qua Frames' (FqFs). Typically, frames are triggered by semiotic elements made available in the early stages of the processing of the text – or easily retrievable from skimming its surface presentation. They favour textual interpretation and social interaction but, once they are active, they are backgrounded in one's perception and cognition. In the case of FqFs, instead, the semiotic mechanisms of frame instantiation are foregrounded and made metatextually explicit as FqFs reflecting the recipient's expectations in regard to textualisation of the communicative act. In this paper, we look at how FqFs are exploited differently in different domains, communication types, media and modes. More specifically, we will see when, in what way and for what purposes FqFs are used as *economic* (or adaptive) resources and as *energetic* (or attractive) resources.

Key-words: framing, frame analysis, textualisation, cognitive linguistics, semiotic analysis.

1. Introduction: A rationale for Frames qua Frames

Frames have extensively been studied as perceptual and representational categories through which humans make sense of the world and are able to communicate meanings (Goffman 1974): triggered by lexical, notional or semiotic handles, sets of meanings

ISSN 1824-3967

become available by which it is possible to scan, organise and interpret specific stretches of reality (Fillmore 1976; Minsky 1975; Schank and Abelson 1977; Chafe 1977). Scarcer attention, however, has been devoted to the formal aspects (i.e. surface features, like the textual patterning or various visual configurations) of those handles, and to how formalisation contributes to establishing sets of expectations against which texts and meanings are interpreted and exchanged in various ways (Sala 2005; Consonni 2018). This contribution focusses on the latter realisation of frames, that is, the idea of formal (or morphological) frames and, more specifically, looks at something we propose labelling *Frames qua Frames* (FqFs). The assumption at the basis of this study is that communication is realised through shared codes which make it possible to "recognise coherent sequences of [language] activities" (Ensink 2003: 63; van Dijk 2008; 2009) and distinguish them from (otherwise) random series of semiotic signs, whereby the functioning of these codes as framing devices *de facto* unlocks the communicative act and, at the same time, posits forms of textual coherence and cohesion (Halliday and Hasan 1976). Our purpose is, firstly, to illustrate the functioning of such textual structures as cognitive resources for both meaning representation and decodification, and, secondly, to provide workable criteria – namely, sequential processing, structural patterning and semiotic encoding – by which to assess their efficiency and effectiveness in general communication, as well as, from a different angle, through which to produce texts that are appealing for an ideal audience, and by which to anticipate and control the recipient's response.

We base our study on four presuppositions. First of all, Kristeva's idea of intertextuality (1977), by which a text is not a self-sufficient or hermetic whole (cf. Worton and Still 1990: 1) but rather "a link in a chain of texts, reacting to, drawing on, and transforming other texts" (Fairclough, Mulderring, Wodak 2011: 361). This textual interrelatedness is also reflected in the concept of interdiscursivity (or 'constitutive intertextuality'), introduced by Critical Discourse Analysis to refer to the "heterogeneous constitution of texts out of elements (types of conventions) of orders of discourse" (Fairclough 1992a: 82), on the assumption that, contents being instantiated by particular forms, and precisely because different contents imply different forms, "the form is therefore part of the content" (Titscher, Meyer, Wodak, Vetter 2007: 150; cf. Fairclough 1992b: 93).

A second and interlinked perspective is Even-Zohar's socio-semiotic idea of repertoires as sets of materials and rules or codes, from which any cultural product – from talk to text, from artefacts to images, events, etc. – is always selected, negotiated and consumed on the basis of its usability constraints within specific material and historical contexts (1997: 20; cf. Blommaert 2005: 253). In this view, text-making is hardly a form of unconstrained production but rather the outcome of "the producer's capacity to successfully implement [existing] models" (1997: 24). As a consequence, model implementation – i.e. the association of materials and codes – makes repertoires recognisable and, as such, cognitively processable by their alignment to linguistic and textual norms, as well as layout regularities.

Thirdly, we are indebted to Teun van Dijk's socio-cognitive model theory (2008; 2009; 2011), and more precisely to the notion of context models, which "are formed from the current, ongoing experience of interaction and communication defining the context of text and talk" (2011: 391) and, as such, they "control *what* we say and especially *how* we say it (style, register) in a specific communicative situation" (p. 392, emphasis in the original).

The fourth perspective stems from Systemic Functional Grammar (Halliday 2002; 2004) and is related to the textual metafunction, which is taken to account for the structural and discursive strategies available to language users for "the presentation of ideational and interpersonal meanings as information that can be shared by speaker and listener in text unfolding in context" (Matthiessen and Halliday 1997: 10). Such metafunction provides the underlying organising formal principle (Eggins 1994: 302ff), by which "we link and relate individual propositions so that they form a cohesive and coherent text [and] make sense in conjunction with other elements of the text" (Vande Kopple 1985: 87).

These classical studies indicate that, be it in terms of dialogic resonance, pre-existing cultural repertoires or situational models, the formalisation of texts may be considered as a vessel for the effective elaboration, negotiation and transmission of individual and collective contents in terms of communicative structures. We hypothesise that this happens in reason of a key metacognition function that is triggered and deployed by some formal aspects of language and communication – namely, FqFs – which this study intends to break down, conceptualise and operationalise in typological terms, thereby outlining a micro-model for multimedia discourse analysis that might hopefully be conversant with extant research on framing and its social, semiotic and possibly creative functions. We believe that genres and text types, but also formats, visual conventions, constraints, styles, registers, etc. (Sala 2005) are the manifest result of such interaction between shared repertoires and individual outputs, as much as between producers and consumers of meanings. By putting emphasis on the vessel itself (i.e. form) rather than its content, we therefore aim at further exploring some formal aspects of social discourse in terms of – as we wish to put forward – FqFs.

2. Methods: Towards a modelisation of Frames qua Frames

As configurational structures, frames draw discernible and continuous boundaries around communicative acts of various kinds (Goffman 1974). In so doing, they trace the contours (and cut the edges) of representation, set up a material space for the signification process, and – by providing structural finiteness, stability and predictability to human experience – they assist in establishing a logic of systemic correlation among the elements that stand within the margins of that semiotic space, thus *de facto* shaping the organisation of experience into social discourse. Their metacognitive function stems precisely from their ability to provide a sense of symbolic mediation, and of material – in many cases empirically visible – infrastructure (with respect to text-external reality) to the flow of semiosis.

Frames typically spawn from semiotic elements made available in the early stages of the processing of a text, or easily retrievable from skimming its surface presentation. In oral communication, for instance, they may be instantiated by indexical elements working as frame triggers, such as greetings, opening sequences (Schlegloff 1968) or other pointers like "lexical expressions, intonation, gestures or facework" (van Dijk 2014: 57). Written communication may resort to specific formal arrangements – typically, the rhetorical structure for text-types (Graesser and Mills 2011) or the move structure for established genres (Trosborg 2000; Bhatia 2004). Visual communication may use configurational elements such as salience, size of frame and perspective devices, information patterning, etc. (O' Toole 2011; Reynolds and Niedt 2021). Regardless of the mode they serve, frames favour textual interpretation and social interaction, by making it possible to distinguish such diverse semiotic artefacts as an emergency phone call, a medical prescription or a medical research paper, even without the need for contextual cues. They enable the processing of a text, by which the likelihood of each incoming piece of information can be predicted or accommodated, not only on the basis of all prior (semantic or textual) information but also in reason of the range of potential meanings that are made available by recognisable repertoires and codes.

Once they are activated, however, frames are generally backgrounded – albeit remaining always available and retrievable – in one's perception and cognition. To put it in heuristic terms, what happens with them is similar to the process of *dealing with a door*: once we recognise it as such (for its conventional shape, size, and distinctive features, e.g. a door frame, handle, hinges, etc.), and once we identify its typical function and open it, the door vanishes (both perceptually and cognitively) into the naturalisation of its function. In most cases, as it were, the 'objectivity' of frames – i.e. their discernible materiality as formal objects – is indeed dissolved. We call these *naturalised* frames, where recognisable configurational conventions are typically activated at the very outset of the hermeneutic process, and remain implicitly active, without any text-internal or text-external interferences, interruptions, intermittencies or incursions, until the process comes to an end. In other words, we recognise the configuration of a message (as an email, a poem, a prescription, an essay, etc.) and we process the text accordingly.

In the case of FqFs, however, such configurational conventions are foregrounded and made metatextually explicit and relevant. FqFs activate by materialising – presenting, or sometimes even flaunting – the conventions of meaning-making and textualisation, thereby controlling the recipient's expectations in regard to the socialisation of the communicative act itself. An example that is familiar to linguists and analysts, especially in written communication, may be the case of endophorics ('in the first paragraph, 'in the table below', 'to conclude', etc.), whose non-referential purpose is to make the cohesive tenets of the text actually visible (Hyland 2005); or the use of opening and closing conventions (and chapter segmenting) in prose (Dames 2014). In visual artefacts, examples may include the frame enclosing the edges of a picture; film frames, opening and closing credits, cross fades (signalling dream or flashback sequences; cf. Jacobs 2011); in sculpture, the presence of a pedestal and the design of surfaces that signal the borders of the artwork "and the space excluded from it" (Lotman 1971: 210); in architecture, the peristyle-like elements that circumscribe the perimeter of a building; in graphic genres (e.g. infographics, visual synopses, etc.), the geometric shapes and vectors that function as logical scaffolding to the argumentation. We tag this an *economy* (or *adaptive*) model of the FqF. Its general function is to help recipients "to mentally connect ideas in the text" (Graesser and Mills 2011: 131-132) and can be conceptualised as a *map*, providing cohesive and directional chartings of given regions, thus being a resource for making sense of and navigating the reality beyond the text.

In other cases, however, configurational conventions are made explicit not to confirm but to complexify – and possibly interfere with, or even violate – the recipient's expectations as to the processing of the text. In this model, which we tag as *energy* (or *attractive*), FqFs are not responsible for facilitating one's understanding of the communicative act, but are instead part and parcel of the content itself. In the role of "the boundary separating the [text] from the non-text" (Lotman 1971: 209), *the frame itself* takes on a specific perceptual, semiotic and cognitive relevance (cf. Kiilerich 2001). Examples range across media and modes, typically in creative domains: reflexive frames in literary metafiction (e.g. J.L. Borges's tales, Laurence Sterne's *Tristram Shandy*; cf. Alter 1975; Waugh 1984); structural frame-play in film narrativity (e.g. Quentin Tarantino's *Pulp Fiction* [1994], Christopher Nolan's *Memento* [2000] and *Tenet* [2020]); the use of artistic frames no longer meant as "enclosing and focusing the viewer's gaze onto the scene which unfolds within its boundaries", but as more complex *parerga* (Derrida 1979; Duro 2019) that speculate on the ambiguity of that liminal portion of discursive artefacts "where 'real space' ends and representation space begins" (Carter 1990: 73; cf. Platt and Squire 2017). Examples of the latter category include Salvador Dalì's *Couple aux têtes pleines de nuages* (1936), where the frame metatextually replicates the morphology of the painted subject; the infringed continuity in the framing configuration in Réné Magritte's *L'évidence eternelle* (1930); the *trompe l'oeuil* of Borrell Del Caso's *Huyendo de la crítica* (1874), in which a feigned, painted frame is being illusionistically clambered over by a curious character that escapes into the 'real' world; or the literalisation of door frames as such in the *Bible* (cf. Smith 2022) and in classical mythology (cf. Ogle 1911); in narrative (e.g. *Dr Jekyll and Mr Hyde* [1886], Franz Kafka's *Vor dem Gesetz* [1919], Umberto Eco's *Il nome della rosa* [1980]), painting (e.g. Banksy's *Mobile Lovers* in Bristol [2014]), sculpture (e.g. Michelangelo Pistoletto's *Door* at Tate [1976, 1997] and film (e.g. Peter Greenaway's *The Draughtsman's Contract* [1982], Pixar's *Monsters, Inc.* [2001]), etc. In this respect, energy FqFs may be conceptualised as *jigsaw puzzles*, where each piece is part of the whole, but the fragmented structure is essential for grasping the overall meaning, and coherence is eminently text-internal, rather than purely dependent on the relation between "linguistic/ discourse characteristics and world knowledge" (Graesser and Mills 2011: 131-132).

On the basis of the above, it is now possible to hypothesise a workable definition of FqFs and their functions. Firstly, as the label indicates, FqFs are frames whose being in place is made metatextually explicit and significant (i.e. they are exploited *qua frames*), in that they display surface features which are perceived as:

a) noticeable (i.e. they stand out, or are markedly different) with respect to those of naturalised frames, and/or
b) distinctive of (and coherent with) a given communicative act, i.e. dissimilar from the one implied by a naturalised frame.

As a consequence, FqFs activate a three-step cognitive assessment process:

i) the morphology of the FqF is recognised (i.e. a formal dis-alignment is acknowledged between a naturalised frame and one used *qua frame*);
ii) the potential meaningfulness of the FqF is established (i.e. the type of communicative act presupposed by the FqF is identified);
iii) the implied cognitive processing of the FqF is activated (i.e. the content of the FqF is processed according to the conventions of the related communicative act).

We can therefore say that, by being noticeable, i.e. materially impossible not to notice, FqFs are highly recognisable formal structures through which the (standard) linear processing of communication's ideational contents is momentarily hindered by the recipient's awareness of the frame's very morphology, so that s/he is forced to consider *how* information and/or messages of various types are configured within a specific communicative act, rather than just *what* the information/message type communicates. For this reason, the cognitive processing of FqFs generally results in either *cognitive adjustment* (or *re-alignment*) or *cognitive displacement* (or *alienation*).

The former is the case of economy FqFs, where specific markers, structures or textures (Fairclough 1992b) are recognised and exploited as pointers to a different but recognisable range of meanings (with respect to naturalised ones), and how they are to be dealt with. For example, within an anthology of literary texts, some structural and discursive features – like frequent line breaks, rhythm and rhyme patterns, unconventional syntax, lack of punctuation, figurative language, etc. – help recognize a text on a page as a poem, rather than an excerpt from a novel. As such, the FqF posits the coherence of that particular communicative act, whereby we appreciate even a highly unconventional use of language and a way of presenting contents which is otherwise unlikely to be accepted in novels, media communication or everyday language. On the other hand, displacement, alienation, disorientation and defamiliarisation (Sklovskij 1929), can (at least at first) be produced by energy FqFs, which impose nonconventional, 'artificial' forms of coherence and cognition upon discursive constructions, whereby the FqF does not liaise but disrupts and supplants the recipient's grasping of ideation, thus 'ungluing' textuality and reality. An example can be the *Jabberwocky* in Lewis Carroll's *Alice* (1865), a lookalike poem with no recognisable words or referents: the morphological incongruity of this text is to be taken as part and parcel of the informative content itself, as an integral part of the 'jigsaw puzzle' that is *Alice in Wonderland* (Frye 1957).

In the light of all this, our paper looks at a heuristic typology of FqFs in different domains, communication types, media and modes. In what follows, we will operationalise the three-step cognitive processing outlined above, and analyse the *sequential processing*, *structural patterning* and *semiotic encoding* of FqFs. We will see when, in what way and for what purposes they are used as economic (or adaptive) resources – i.e. as maps to external territories, or doors to rooms – and as energetic (or attractive) resources – i.e. as jigsaw puzzles, or as doors in their reflexive function of architectural artefacts, or artistic pieces of interior design (cf. The Met 2011).

3. Analysis: Towards a typology of Frames qua Frames

3.1. Economy frames

Economy FqFs are used to facilitate access to ideation with little cognitive expenditure. Although, as seen above, they are (or are made) deliberately noticeable in the embedding naturalised frame – i.e. they stand out (typographically, as we will see) or are pointed at (through metadiscourse) – their use has become so conventional in referential communication that noticing them does not disrupt the interpretive process. On the contrary, it signals the switch between the naturalised and the FqF, and, as a consequence, liaises the transition between the two frames.

Economy FqFs are typically instantiated in terms of *sequential processing*, *structural patterning* and *semiotic encoding*.

3.1.1. Sequential processing

At this level, FqFs can be identified when a large text is divided into clearly distinguishable blocks (i.e. parts, paragraphs, sections, sub-sections, etc.), for instance through double spacing, indentation, etc. By identifying these separate blocks – which, on the one hand, are presented as potentially self-standing conceptual units, yet, on the other, cannot but be part of the larger text –, FqFs help the cognitive harmonisation between the parts and the whole, which conventionally can be explained in terms of:

a) emphasis (the content of the separated unit is made to synoptically stand out to mark its relevance with respect to the given information and surrounding text);
b) addition or juxtaposition (the content of the various blocks is to be interpreted in terms of correlation – the meaning of Unit Y is meant to parallel, complete or just be separated from that of Unit X);

c) causation (the meaning of Unit X introduces and explains that of Unit Y).

In some cases, though not necessarily, the FqF function of such units is also signalled metadiscursively (Hyland 2005) through titles (anticipating their content or the function, e.g. 'Introduction', 'Methods', 'Concluding remarks'), numbering or lettering (indicating the sequencing of the various blocks, e.g. 1.2, 3.1.a, etc.), thus explicitating the ways the information of various blocks is to be integrated. In these cases, metadiscourse may be said to function as a specific actualisation – probably the most familiar example from the standpoint of linguists and analysts – of the wider textual process of formal grasping that is typical of FqFs. As we see, the outline of the information sequencing provides varyingly detailed textual maps which help locate information, understand its contextual relevance and facilitate its processing.

3.1.2. Structural patterning

At this level, FqFs can be found in noticeable and highly conventionalised structures like indented quotations and bulleted sentences.

Either when used as evidentials (to validate a claim through the voice of an authoritative source), as glosses (to clarify meaning) or as examples, quotations are signalled as FqFs through quotation marks and, notably, indentation which typographically introduce heteroglossia or polyphony (Bakhtin 1979) – the presence of different voices. As such, they justify potential idiosyncrasies which are otherwise not very common in monoglossic texts, namely:

a) semantic redundancy, especially in the case of quotation used as glosses (where information already given is then replicated through a cited author's words);

b) style, tone and register shifts (the quoted text may display different rhetorical features with respect to the one it is embedded in) – note, for instance, the shift from a depersonalised tone (third person pronouns) to a personalised (first person pronouns) and emphatic one in the following excerpts: "*Her* advice is to use other partial synonyms or eliminate some of the references […] altogether. One possible solution might be as follows: '… what *I* see now is the reflection of the soul. *Ah! Vityenka's good!'"* (in Katan 2004: 184, emphasis added);

c) lack of morpho-syntactic coherence (although integrated in the larger text, quoted excerpts may be expected to display different grammatical subjects or pronominal indexes, tense, mode, punctuation, etc.) – note the shift in the subjects (*they* vs. *I*) and tense (past vs. present perfect) in the following example: "*They*'d both left school at 16, both were working-class wunderkind with an innate belief *they* had some 'genius' to offer. '*I*'ve read just about all of [Wilson's] early books. And some of them are pretty hard to find. But *I*'d rather find them by browsing around than order them from a library or anything – it's a lot more fun'" (in Blanchard 2021: 108, emphasis added).

As we can see, once the 'quotation' FqF is active, these semantic and formal irregularities do not hinder interpretation.

Likewise, bulleted sentences work as FqFs in that they are easily recognised as strategies meant to break down complex information into manageable units. Bulleting re-aligns interpretation by anticipating and legitimising:

a) emphasis (even extreme) conferred to a specific informative element in each entry of the bulleted list (whose relation to the others is then to be worked out, likely in either additive, sequential, or chronological terms);

b) content simplification and schematisation, and parallel constructions among entries (in terms of length and structure), which allow comparison between the various elements in the list, thus facilitating comprehension and memorisation;

c) "block language" (Firth 1957) or non-standard syntax, i.e. expressions consisting of nominal or verbless clauses, prepositional phrases in isolation (Quirk, Greenbaum, Swartvik, Leech 1985: 846), omission of articles, determiners, prepositions, auxiliary verbs, the verb *be*, etc.

Some of these features can be observed in all bulleted lists in this very article, whereby the FqF can justify relatively long entries starting with the subject complement without the replica of the related subject and verb (cf. § 2), or with the grammatical object (without the replica of the related verb and subject, as would be advisable in Standard English).

3.1.3. Semiotic encoding

At this level, FqFs can be instantiated by texts which are semiotised through non-verbal symbolisation systems which avoid, minimise, substitute or complete the scriptural mode – namely, the numerical mode (numbers, formulae, or tables with data expressed through numbers), the graphical one (graphs, diagrams, charts, maps, etc.) or the figurative one (pictures, images, conventional symbols, etc.) (Consonni 2018). By exiting the usually dominant and standard scriptural mode, these alternative representation systems work as FqFs in that, on the one hand, they require interpretive re-alignment (from words to numbers, structures and visuals) and, on the other, they activate preferred ways of interpreting information, namely:

a) the numerical mode is expected to represent quantities and quantity-related relations between objects (i.e. occurrences, distribution, frequencies, etc.);

b) the graphical mode points to trends, lines of development, incidence, relevance, re-occurrence, etc. obtained by filtering complex realities through a limited number of parameters (represented along two axes in graphs, calculated in percentages in charts, etc.);

c) the figurative mode has both a glossing and an evidential function, picturing and visually reproducing elements of the external reality in order to corroborate given meanings and facilitate their comprehension.

On the basis of these sets of expectations, the switch presupposed by intersemiotic FqFs, far from being cognitively disruptive, has the function of a cognitive facilitator.

We may conceptualise economy FqFs through the following blueprint (which is indeed a FqF itself):

FIGURE I. A SCHEMATISATION OF ECONOMY FqFs, WHERE □ = IDEATIONAL CONTENT(S)

In this model of communication, the frame is a transparent vector – because of its high conventionality – that is designed for easily navigating the text from A to B (where A and B are the ideational contents of the communication); cognitively, it allows effortless (or effort-saving) processing of the text on the part of the recipient; the hermeneutic effect is one of domestication, or adaptation.

3.2. Energy frames

This model pivots on markers that are made materially visible in such ways as to reflexively reveal what is indeed framing's metacognitive function, i.e. the infrastructural design of semiosis. As shown in Fig. 2, the morphology of energy FqFs no longer serves as a linear vessel for (de)codification, but becomes embedded in a more complex (and less transparent) cognitive process. As the recipient acknowledges and systematises the formal eccentricity of the FqF, the frame itself becomes part of ideation, displacing (or even disrupting) the grasping thereof. This typically discards conventions and expectations, producing hermeneutic non-linearity or even semiological arrest, but also interpersonally intriguing recipients.

FIGURE 2. A SCHEMATISATION OF ENERGY FQFS, WHERE □ = IDEATIONAL CONTENT(S)

Energy FqFs function as offer structures in which expectations are experience-driven (rather than experience being expectation-driven), and they occur in communication types which are designed to attract and entice the recipient. This is achieved through the violation-of-expectations effect of the FqF, as shown by examples such as advertising discourse and creative, aesthetic or artistic communication in general (Danesi 2015; Goddard 1998 [2002]; Jakobson 1960). A significant amount of collateral cognitive expenditure is needed to process the message, as the FqF does not decrease or smoothen but intensifies one's interpretive labour, the opacity of their configuration actually placing them among the most productive semantic engines of today's communication (Sala 2005).

Energy FqFs, too, can be instantiated in terms of *sequential processing*, *structural patterning* and *semiotic encoding*.

3.2.1. Sequential processing

At this level, FqFs activate while the text as a whole is sequentially perused by the recipient. As the text is read, looked at or listened to, salient textual or interpersonal elements are progressively perceived that – precisely because they interfere with the expected naturalised sequence of that communicative act – have to be assessed and 'digested' for the recipient to make sense of the text as a whole. The result is generally cognitive dis-homogeneisation and (at least at first) dis-harmonisation between the parts and the whole, producing effects of:

a) stasis (the sequencing of discrete units does not immediately translate into any noticeable cognitive saturation with respect to a given ideational core);
b) circularity (the units' lack of progression may result in iteration);
c) accumulation (the processing of units may converge on the same ideational core, producing redundancy or, in contrast, ellipsis or lack of semantic coherence among the units).

In particular, FqFs can function at the level of text-type or genre (e.g. satire, parody, spoof), whereby the acknowledgment of incongruous formal markers may point to a shift from more conservative (or imitative) to parodistic practices (e.g. the interspersing of actual songs and fake commercials in the album *The Who Sell Out,* 1967; the contrapuntal use of statistical data in Jonathan Swift's *A Modest Proposal,* 1729; Marcel Duchamp's moustached *Gioconda*; 'Kafka breaks' in Coen Brothers films). At the macro-linguistic level, they can be triggered by configurational elements that displace the naturalised order of time, logic and language. For instance, the non-linear signposting in Laurence Sterne's *Tristram Shandy*, John Fowles' *The Collector* (1963) or Martin Amis' *Time's Arrow* (1991) signals the direction changes, roundabouts, U-turns, obstructions or dead ends that must be navigated as one makes sense of time shifts and reversal of causal order[1]. FqFs can also be found at the micro-

---

[1] Cinematic examples include the looping sequence of Akira Kurosawa's *Rashomon* (1950); Quentin Tarantino's poetics of sequential misplacement, whereby the time frame is a substantial piece of content, which is brought to its logical consequences

linguistic level, where minimal markers such as the use (or non-use) of punctuation, personal pronouns, modes, tenses, etc., may indicate the transition from classical narrativity to free association, stream of consciousness, mythopoeia, etc.

3.2.2. Structural patterning

At this level, FqFs impact on the synoptic grasping together of the communicative act as a structural whole. By disrupting the seamless continuity of texts, FqFs steer (and intensify) the recipient's apprehension of the discursive artefact's external contours and internal patterning, i.e. its spatial modelling. For this reason, FqFs tend to sharpen one's sense of structure, i.e. one's awareness that form and meaning have deeper margins for mutual interaction and interference than normally expected within commonly shared codes and genres. This process is typically based on the FqF's potential to materialise – i.e. expose or visualise, typically not motivate or legitimise – the semantic productivity of spatial phenomena such as:

a) intertextuality, or dialogism (frames cannot liaise – as would be the case of economy FqFs – but mark off or problematise the conceptual transition from text to text, and/or from textuality to reality and *vice versa*; cf. Bakhtin 1979; de Man 1982);
b) metatextuality, or text reflexivity (the recipient's self-aware relationship with the structure itself, obtained by means of various *mise-en-abyme* framing strategies, can be used to destabilise the notion of referentiality; cf. Derrida 1979);
c) discreteness and segmentation (the patterning of solids and voids within the space of the artefact can expose the centripetal relationship between discourse and reality; cf. Lotman 1971).

Structural FqFs can easily be found across different media and modes, often covering more than one such function, from overarching story frames in *One Thousand and One Nights*, the *Decameron*, the *Canterbury Tales*, to the 'Chinese box' patterning of Mary Shelley's *Frankenstein* (1818) and Joseph Conrad's *Heart*

---

by Christopher Nolan's films, where the opposite framing vectors of *fabula* and *plot* are presented as the film's very thematic core.

of Darkness (1899) and metafiction in general (Alter 1975; Waugh 1984). Reflexive examples abound in visual language, from the pioneering meta-frame of Jan Van Eyck's *Portrait of Margareta* (1439) to frames behaving not as boundaries of artworks but as part of their representational content[2], to frames that disappear from paintings (e.g. Mondrian, Monet's *Water Lilies* series). While the use of chapters in prose may be an example of naturalised segmentation (or, in specific cases, of economic sequential segmentation, cf. section 3.1.1), since it works like a network of 'resting places' for textual wayfarers, as Henry Fielding would have it in *Joseph Andrews* (1742), energy FqFs can be found in *Tristram Shandy*'s (non-existent) 'chapter on chapters', the twentieth chapter of Ronald Firbank's *Inclinations* (1916), and the unconventional structuring of Julio Cortázar's *Hopscotch* (1966) and B.S. Johnson's *The Unfortunates* (1969) (cf. Dames 2014). In all these examples, the spatial artificiality imposed by FqFs reflects and emphasises the configurational reification of experience that is typical of any frame (naturalised frames included).

3.2.3. Semiotic encoding

At this level, FqFs mainly operate on the hybridity of intersemiotic communication. The acknowledgement of formal shifts in the encoding of texts through different symbolisation systems (cf. section 3.1.3) does not always result in a functional ecology of words, pictures, numbers and graphics. Transitioning across the different affordances (and expectations) associated with different modes can in fact trigger cognitive effects that are far from the fluidity of automatic collaboration, such as:

  a) semantic hampering (a 'funnel effect' can be produced by the multimodal intricacy of FqFs);
  b) densification (a growing concentration of formal signifiers, and matching complexification of meanings, typically occurring when different modes are incorporated, e.g. *Konkrete Poesie* experiments);
  c) cannibalisation (forms of competition and conflict among modes can be generated by multisemiotic FqFs).

---

[2] Cf. the *parerga* mentioned in section 2 above.

In all these cases, FqFs deviate the linearity of "intersemiotic translation or transmutation" (Jakobson 1959), complicating – instead of facilitating – the interpretation of meanings. An example of hampering is *Tristram Shandy*'s 'description' of Widow Wadman, i.e. a blank page that readers must sketch on by their own hand, which is likely to confound them and suspend their hermeneutic activity, at least for a while. (A counterexample being procedural discourse, like 'think-aloud' verbal protocols or illustrated building instructions, which is typically mono – or paucisemiotic). Ideologically propagative hybrid genres, such as for instance copy-art advertising billboards (e.g. the 1959 'Think Small' Volkswagen Beetle campaign), visual synopses and infographic genres, and intermedia animated documentary films (e.g. J.P. Rasmussen's *Flee*, 2021), may show how FqFs can densify the communicative affordances of multisemiotic products. FqFs can also trigger code competition and cannibalisation, as shown for instance by experimentation in the language of film opening credits: while Paolo Sorrentino's *Il divo* (2008) features a semiotic guerrilla between verbal language and the grammar of moving images, those of the TV show *Lost* (2004-10) – a fourteen-second vision of a tilted white inscription on a black background – would appear as a concise interrogation of today's image-centricity.

4. Discussion and conclusion

4.1. Applicability of the model and limitations of the study

Needless to say, this is an exploration of discursive and media phenomena that is biased by its very choice of domains and examples; nevertheless, what we wish to put forward is simply the heuristic potential that future research on framing may derive from considering the morphological and cognitive effects produced by formalisation. It therefore seems appropriate to present some critical reflections concerning the theoretical limitations and analytical potential of the exploratory model we have so far set out to outline. To what extent, one may legitimately wonder, could the notion of FqF fit in and contribute to the widely reified field of framing studies? Does our model offer any applications to discourse and communication analysis in general? Is it employable with more homogeneous data sets, other than the spectrum of examples from different domains, media and modes we have presented in this paper?

To address these crucial issues, we should remember that the notion of FqF and, in particular, the distinction between the *economy* and the *energy* model, is not to be intended as purely formal, or a mere matter of classification. Indeed, the relevance of such resources resides in the different metacognitive function they play in different communicative contexts, which in turn depends, firstly, on the domain of the communicative exchange and, secondly, on the type of communication itself.

If we define a domain as the site where cultural products (and texts as such) are constructed and consumed for given purposes, then these sites can be distinguished in (at least) two macro-groups that represent the apexes of a wide spectrum within which discursive forms may develop, that we have tried to render through the multisemiotic diversity of the disparate examples we have collected throughout the paper. On the one hand, *mimetic* domains (either speculative – i.e. philosophy, literary studies, etc. – or applied – i.e. medicine, science, politics, media communication, linguistics, etc.) are those in which the representation and communication of meanings is meant to make reality manageable, either cognitively or operatively. These domains are aimed at expanding people's knowledge about some external reality, with the purpose of allowing in-depth understanding, control or modification of the mechanisms governing it. By hinging on a 'centripetal' principle relating textuality and reality, these domains provide an 'adhesive' model of communication, thus cognitively 'gluing' together meanings and experiences. Users in these domains have specific needs: senders have interests and stakes, and information to offer; receivers have informative gaps to be filled.

On the other hand, *anti-mimetic* (or *creative*) domains are those non-applied discursive environments that are neither (primarily) aimed at a better understanding or command of some external reality, nor meant to single out or govern that reality's commonalities, recognisable trends or expectable mechanics. These domains rather revolve around the perception and symbolisation of irregularities, idiosyncrasies and/or violations to some expected order of phenomena (Lotman 1971: 96). Creative domains have no utilitarian purpose, as exemplified by recreational, leisure-oriented, aesthetic or ludic texts, or by eminently symbolic texts, like religious or artistic ones. By promoting a 'centrifugal' relationship between textuality and reality, they provide a detachment model of communication, thus somewhat 'ungluing' meanings and empirical reality. Users in these domains may not be said to have specific needs, but rather symbolic or epistemological ones.

Each domain has its own preferred communicative mode, meant to make meanings and their processing contextually relevant. In mimetic domains, communication is mainly referential or transactional (cf. Brown and Yule 1983), that is, factual, ideation-based, message-oriented and aimed at "the efficient transference of information" (1983: 2). To boost communicative efficiency, discursive and semiotic regularities are favoured, as is alignment to given formal expectations in terms of linearity and transparency, precision, objectivity, economy (i.e. minimax effect), clarity and appropriateness (cf. Grice 1975, Snell-Hornby 1988). Anti-mimetic (or creative) domains hinge instead on non-transactional, reflexive communication types that are maximally impactful, cognitively engaging or even challenging or destabilising, in reason of their misalignment with given formal expectations, due to their speculating on opacity (cf. Jakobson 1958) and their being not necessarily linear (or utterly non-linear) or even openly ambiguous. These texts primarily aim at providing an engaging message, handling cues as to how to make sense of their internal semantic economy, rather than its relevance to an external reality.

4.2. Potential for future research

It is precisely in relation to these (only apparently unrelated) texts, domains and communication types that the perceptual and hermeneutic notion of FqF – and, more specifically, its contrastive and fairly specular modelisation in terms of *economy* vs. *energy* frames – acquires its relevance and may eventually show its potential for future research.

Active in mimetic domains, transactional communication types and maximally efficient texts, economy FqFs are in fact mainly instantiated as *demand*-based structures, i.e. structures which respond to an informative need on the part of the recipient, and in which experience is expectation-driven (for formal expectations govern the receiver's experience of the text). In this instantiation of the model there is a strategic reduction of the cognitive load expected from the recipient: owing to its formal recognisability, conventionality and social shareability, once opened (or unfolded), the *FqF-as-map* at the same time flaunts and aligns to its functional and representational role. For this reason, we have described economy FqFs in terms of *adaptive* resources, producing morphological effects of cognitive adjustment.

In this respect, we believe that economy FqFs may be a useful concept around which different disciplines and models studying communication in mimetic domains – as diverse a pragmatics, argumentation research, LSP, and all those focussing on the mechanisms regulating felicitous exchanges – may cohere. In fact, what in those approaches is understood as being standard, normalised, conventional, typical, unmarked, appropriate or easily recognisable (and, as such, likely to be favoured, preferable or at least resorted to as a reference parameter for efficient communication) falls within our classification of economy FqF, in that related to (or the effect of) the application of representation models that are used precisely because easily recognisable as representation models (i.e. exploited *qua* such). On this basis, the notion of FqF may be fruitful for future research in order to observe configurational variation over time and contexts, and possibly pinpoint the sequential, structural or semantic elements of the frame which can be exploited *qua* frame and those which have lost (or are progressively losing) such representational dimension.

In contrast, being operative in anti-mimetic domains, reflexive communication types and maximally effective texts, energy FqFs are instantiated as *offer* structures, i.e. structures which do not come in response to any informative need, in which expectations are experience-driven, for formal expectations are governed and reformed by the experience of the text itself. In this instantiation of the model, there may be an indefinite increase of cognitive work on the part of the recipient. The outcome of such a process – regardless of its being creative, symbolic, aesthetic or artistic – is the flaunting of the *FqF-as-jigsaw-puzzle* itself, for it is precisely the formal joining of pieces that makes a jigsaw puzzle what it is: a semiotic artefact, whose *raison d'être* is not its referential content but its internal fragmentation and articulation. For this reason, we have defined these frames in terms of *attractive* resources, pivoting on morphological effects of cognitive displacement. We think that energy FqFs might in turn prove a helpful resource for structurally deconstructing and functionally analysing anti-mimetic (or creative, or artistic) discourse beyond, and in friction with, the – indeed not trouble-free – aesthetic metafunction of language. They may actually offer workable parameters by which to assess, on the one hand, how and under what conditions FqFs may lose their attractive potential, i.e. when (formerly creative) sequential, structural and semantic configurations become gradually naturalised, possibly due to replication and recursiveness of given models, thus ending up reflecting, rather than discarding or playing with, the receiver's expectations. On the other hand, they may help scholars analyse the mechanics of creative communication in a (non-obvious) dialogical continuum with transactional communication, thus assisting them in understanding why and along which lines (with respect to what naturalised expectations, and in what contexts and modes) new 'energising' FqFs may emerge across different discourses and media.

On the basis of the above, we would finally like to suggest that, by underpinning and revealing the cognitive economy of demand vs. offer communication, as well as the ecology of experience – vs. expectation-driven hermeneutics, the configurational productivity of *Frames qua Frames* may be a valuable tool for researchers to further focalise (and empirically materialise) the key function of framing itself, that is, the infrastructural design of human experience into diverse, and yet interconnected, forms of semiosis and social discourse.

References

ALTER, ROBERT, 1975, *Partial Magic: The Novel as a Self-Conscious Genre*, U. of California P., Berkeley.

BAKHTIN, MIKHAIL M., Éstetika slovesnogo tvorchestva, 1979, Engl. trans. *Speech Genres and Other Late Essays*, by V.W. McGee, U. of Texas P., Austin, TX, 1986.

BHATIA, VIJAY K., 2016, *Critical Genre Analysis: Investigating Interdiscursive Performance in Professional Practice*, Routledge, London.

BLANCHARD, TIM, 2021, *Like Magic in the Streets*, Crakle + Hiss, London.

BLOOMMAERT, JAN, 2005, *Discourse*, C.U.P., Cambridge.

BROWN, GILLIAN and YULE, GEORGE, 1983, *Discourse Analysis*, C.U.P., Cambridge.

CARTER, MICHAEL, 1990, *Framing Art: Introducing Theory and the Visual Image*, Hale & Iremonger, Sidney.

CHAFE, WALLACE L., 1977, "Creativity in Verbalization and Its Implications for the Nature of Stored Knowledge", in Roy O. Freedle (ed.), *Discourse Production and Comprehension*, Ablex, Norwood, NJ, pp. 41-55.

CONSONNI, STEFANIA, 2018, "Multimodal Literacy in Academic Environments: PowerPoint as a Motivational Genre", *Language Value* 10 (1), pp. 1-28.

DAMES, NICHOLAS, 2014, "The Chapter: A History", *New Yorker*, 29 October, https://www.newyorker.com/books/page-turner/chapter-history, last accessed June 11, 2022.

DANESI, MARCEL, 2015, "Advertising Discourse", in K. Tracy, C. Ilie, T. Sandel (eds), *The International Encyclopedia of Language and Social Interaction*, Wiley & Sons, Hoboken, NJ. doi/10.1002/9781118611463. wbielsi137.

DE MAN, PAUL, 1982, "Dialogue and Dialogism", *Poetics Today* 4 (1), pp. 99-107.

DERRIDA, JACQUES, *Parergon*, 1979, Engl. trans. *Parergon*, by C. Owens, *October* 9, pp. 3-41.

DURO, PAUL, 2019, "What Is A Parergon?", *Journal of Aesthetics and Art Criticism* 77 (1), pp. 23-33.

EGGINS, SUZANNE, 1994, *An Introduction to Systemic Functional Linguistics*, Pinter, London.

ENSINK, TITUS, 2003, "Transformational Frames: Interpretative Consequences of Frame Shifts and Frame Embeddings", in T. Ensink and C. Sauer (eds), *Framing and Perspectivising in Discourse*, John Benjamins, Amsterdamo-Philadelphia, pp. 63-90.

EVEN-ZOHAR, ITAMAR, 1997, "Factors and Dependencies in Cultures: A Revised Outline for Polysystem Culture Research", *Canadian Review of Comparative Literature* 26 (1), pp. 15-34.

FAIRCLOUGH, NORMAN, 1992a, *Discourse and Social Change*, Polity, London.

FAIRCLOUGH, NORMAN, 1992b, "Discourse and Text: Linguistic and Intertextual Analysis within Discourse Analysis", *Discourse and Society* 3, pp. 193-219.

FAIRCLOUGH, NORMAN, MULDERRING, JANE, WODAK, RUTH, 2011, "Critical Discourse Analysis", in T. van Dijk (ed.), *Discourse Studies*, Sage, London, pp. 359-78.

FILLMORE, CHARLES J., 1976, "The Need for a Frame Semantics within Linguistics", *Statistical Methods in Linguistics* 12 pp. 5-29.

FIRTH, JOHN, 1957, *Papers in Linguistics*, O.U.P., Oxford.

FRYE, NORTHROP, 1957, *Anatomy of Criticism: Four Essays*, O.U.P., Oxford.

GODDARD, ANGELA [1998] 2002, *The Language of Advertising: Written Texts*, Routledge, London.

GOFFMAN, ERVING, 1974, *Frame Analysis: An Essay on the Organization of Experience*, Harvard U.P., Cambridge, MA.

GRAESSER, ARTHUR and MILLS, KEITH, 2011, "Discourse and Cognition", in T. van Dijk (ed.), *Discourse Studies: A Multidisciplinary Introduction*, Sage, London, pp. 126-42.

GRICE, PAUL, 1975, "Logic and Conversation", in P. Cole and J.J. Morgan (eds), *Syntax and Semantics*, Vol. 3: *Speech Acts*, New York, Academic Press, pp. 41-58.

HALLIDAY, M.A.K., 2002, *On Grammar*, Continuum, London.

HALLIDAY, M.A.K., 2004, *An Introduction to Functional Grammar: Third Edition*, Hodder Arnold, London.

HALLIDAY, M.A.K., 2009, "Methods, Techniques, Problems", in M.A.K. Halliday and Jonathan J. Webster (eds), *Continuum Companion to Systemic Functional Linguistics*, Continuum, London, pp. 59-86.

HALLIDAY, M.A.K., HASAN, RUQAIYA, 1976, *Cohesion in English*, Longman, London.

HYLAND, KEN, 2005, *Metadiscourse: Exploring Interaction in Writing*, Continuum, London.

JACOBS, STEVEN, 2011, *Framing Pictures: Film and the Visual Arts*, Edinburgh U.P., Edinburgh.

JAKOBSON, ROMAN, 1958, "Closing Statement: Linguistics and Poetics", in V. Leitc, W. Cain, L.A. Finke, B. Johnson (eds), *The Norton Anthology of Theory and Criticism*, Norton, New York, 2001, pp. 1258-65.

JAKOBSON, ROMAN, 1959, "On Linguistic Aspects of Translation", in R.A. Brower (ed.), *On Translation*, Harvard U.P., Cambridge, MA, pp. 232-39.

JAKOBSON, ROMAN, 1960, "Linguistics and Poetics", in D. Lodge and N. Wood (eds), *Modern Criticism and Theory: A Reader*, Longman, London, pp. 32-57.

KATAN, DAVID, 2004, *Translating Cultures*, St. Jerome, Manchester.

KIILERICH, BENTE, 2001, "Savedoff, Frames and Parergonality", *Journal of Aesthetics and Art Criticism* 59 (3), pp. 320-33.

KRISTEVA, JULIA, *Se-meio-tike-. Recherches pour une sémanalyse*, 1977, Engl. trans. *Desire in Language: A Semiotic Approach to Literature and Art*, by T. Gora, A. Jardine, L.S. Roudiez, Columbia U.P., New York, 1980.

LOTMAN, JURIJ, *Struktura khudozhestvennogo teksta*, 1971, Engl. trans. *The Structure of the Artistic Text*, by R. Vroon, U. of Michigan P., Ann Arbor, MI, 1977.

MATTHIESSEN, CHRISTIAN M.I.M. and HALLIDAY, M.A.K., 1997, *Systemic Functional Grammar: A First Step into the Theory*, Routledge, Oxon.

THE MET (METROPOLITAN MUSEUM OF ART), 2011, *Connections/Doors*, feature by Dan Kershaw, https://www.metmuseum.org/connections/doors#/Feature/, last accessed June 15, 2022.

MINSKY, MARVIN, 1975, "A Framework for Representing Knowledge", in P.H. Winston (ed.), *The Psychology of Computer Vision*, McGraw Hill, New York, pp. 211-77.

O'TOOLE, MICHAEL, 2011, *The Language of Displayed Art*, Routledge, London.

OGLE, MARBURY B., 1911, "The House-Door in Greek and Roman Religion and Folk-Lore", *American Journal of Philology* 32 (3), pp. 251-71.

PLATT, VERITY and SQUIRE, MICHAEL, 2017, *The Frame in Classical Art: A Cultural History*, Cambridge U.P., Cambridge.

QUIRK, RANDOLPH, GREENBAUM, SIDNEY, SWARTVIK, JAN, LEECH, GEOFFREY, 1985, *A Comprehensive Grammar of the English Language*, Longman, London.

REYNOLDS, RACHEL R. and NIEDT, GREG, 2021, *Essentials of Visual Interpretation*, Routledge, London.

SALA, MICHELE, 2005, "Formal Scripts and Meaning: A Script-Based Approach to Textual Forms and Their Relevance towards Interpretation", *Linguistica e Filologia* 20, pp. 101-26.

SCHEGLOFF, EMANUEL A., 1968, "Sequencing in Conversational Openings", *American Anthropologist* 70 (6), pp. 1075-95.

SCHANK, ROGER C. and ABELSON, ROBERT P., 1977, *Scripts, Plans, Goals, and Understanding: An Inquiry into Human Knowledge Structures*, Lawrence Erlbaum, Hillsdale, NJ.

SKLOVSKIJ, VIKTOR, *O teorii prozy*, 1929, Engl. trans. *Theory of Prose*, by B. Sher, Dalkey Archive Press, Normal, IL, 1990.

SMITH, STEPHEN, 2022, *What Does the Bible Say about Doors*, https://www.openbible.info/topics/doors, last accessed June 15, 2022.

SNELL-HORNBY, MARY, 1988, *Translation Studies: An Integrated Approach*, John Benjamins, Amsterdam-Philadelphia.

TITSCHER, STEFAN, MEYER, MICHAEL, WODAK, RUTH, VETTER, EVA, 2007, *Methods of Text and Discourse Analysis*, Sage, London.

TROSBORG, ANNA (ed.), 2000, *Analysing Professional Genres*, John Benjamins, Amsterdam-Philadelphia.

VAN DIJK, TEUN A., 2008, *Discourse and Context: A Socio-Cognitive Approach*, Cambridge U.P., Cambridge.

VAN DIJK, TEUN A., 2009, *Society and Discourse: How Social Contexts Influence Text and Talk*, Cambridge U.P., Cambridge.

VAN DIJK, TEUN A., 2011, "Discourse and Ideology", in T.A. van Dijk (ed.), *Discourse Studies*, Sage, London, pp. 379-406.

VAN DIJK, TEUN A., 2014, *Discourse and Knowledge: A Sociocognitive Approach*, Cambridge U.P., Cambridge.

VANDE KOPPLE, WILLIAM, 1985, "Some Exploratory Discourse on Metadiscourse", *College Composition and Communication* 36, pp. 82-93.

WAUGH, PATRICIA, 1984, *Metafiction: The Theory and Practice of Self-Conscious Fiction*, Routledge, London.

WORTON, MICHAEL and STILL, JUDITH, 1990, "Introduction", in M. Worton and J. Still (eds), *Intertextuality: Theories and Practices*, Manchester U.P., Manchester, pp. 1-44.

Frame Shifting and Satirical Reading

Alessandro Aru

Abstract

The study aims at analysing the impact of frame shifting on the recognition of a text as satirical. Frame shifting is a characteristic feature of both humour and irony, which, in turn, are often found in satire. However, what leads a text to be identified as satire is not just the presence of humour or irony. Several features, in fact, interact together to let the satirical interpretation emerge. A behavioural test containing two satirical texts and two jokes was presented to 40 English native speakers in order to verify the influence of frame shifting, along with other parameters, on the perception of a text as either humorous or satirical. Results showed that frame shifting is perceived as stronger in humorous texts with respect to satirical ones. This may be due to the fact that in humorous texts the frame shift gets the slots to be filled with material that is just incongruous and unexpected thus contributing to the general effect of amusement and entertainment. In contrast, in satirical texts, the materials introduced trigger further inferences that determine a shift in attitudes, turning the general effect into criticism and moral condemnation.

Key-words: satire; frame shifting; joke; irony; humour.

1. Introduction

Understood as basic cognitive structures which guide the perception and representation of reality, semantic frames are widely recognized as instruments for organizing knowledge and motivating inferences. Typically, the structured knowledge they represent makes use of slots for expected objects. When a sudden deviation from the expected object triggers the search for another frame of knowledge in which the unexpected object can find a coherent place, we have the phenomenon of frame shifting. This operation of reanalysis of lexical meaning is one of the mechanisms which are responsible for

ISSN 1824-3967

humour and irony. In turn, humour and irony are part of a range of linguistic and rhetorical devices which characterise satire as a genre and interact in different ways to dynamically bring about specifically intended effects (Bertuccelli Papi 2018).

Within this perspective, the present study investigates the contribution of frames to the understanding of satire. Frame shifting is undoubtedly one of the main features of humorous effect, but is it sufficient by itself to produce a satirical reading? Even though I am aware that each of the notions involved in this study (humour, irony, satire) has been extensively explored from several theoretical perspectives, this is the specific research question my study will be focused on. A total of 40 participants were asked to perform different tasks in order to evaluate their expectations for a given text and were asked to answer some questions which evaluated their opinions towards the texts.

The article is structured as follows: section 2 provides an overview on the concept of frame and how it contributes to creating expectations; in section 3, a view of satire as a genre emerging from the interaction of several parameters is presented; in section 4, I describe how I set up the test; finally, results are discussed in section 5.

2. Frames and expectations

Within the framework of cognitive linguistics, meaning is viewed as encyclopaedic in nature. It is conceived of as a structured system of knowledge, organized as a network, whose composition has been investigated from several perspectives.

A highly influential proposal focuses on the notion of a frame against which word meanings are understood. This idea was developed in linguistics by Charles Fillmore (1975; 1977; 1982; 1985), who argued that a frame is a schematisation of experience (a knowledge structure), which is represented at the conceptual level and held in long-term memory. The frame relates the elements and entities associated with a particular culturally embedded scene from human experience.

In other words, frames are detailed knowledge structures or schemas emerging from everyday experiences (Evans and Green 2006: 222). Therefore, knowing the meaning of a word is, in part, knowing the individual frames with which a word is associated.

For instance, consider the related group of words "buy", "sell", "pay", "spend", "cost", "charge", "tender", "change". In order to understand them, we need access to a COMMERCIAL EVENT frame which provides 'the background and motivation for the categories which these words represent' (Fillmore 1982: 116-17). Frames have *slots*, i.e. when conceptual objects are called up, they can be more precisely specified using various (but not arbitrary) knowledge features (Ziem 2014: 9).

Once a frame is activated (i.e. evoked or invoked), language users perform the semantic construction work themselves by filling the slots of a frame with "details". Slots are, thus, bound to *fillers*, or representations of the particulars of a situation.

Minsky (1975) described the example of a birthday party frame, which includes slots, such as food, games, and presents, that specify general features of the event (Coulson 2001: 19). In a process called *slot-filling*, slots such as food are bound to fillers such as cake or ice cream.

According to Fillmore, slots either stem from the linguistically given data ("information in the rest of the text"), from para- or non-verbal information sources ("the current situation"), from general world knowledge ("system of beliefs"), or – in the case of oral communication – from conversation partners who provide further "details" (Ziem 2014: 244).

Within this perspective, we do not treat every new person, object or event as unique and separate. Seeing the connections between things, and between present things and things we have experienced before or heard about, is what helps us make sense of the world. When we measure a new perception against what we know of the world from prior experience, we are dealing with expectations (Tannen 1979: 137). Expectations are based on our experience of the world; they help us organise the world and predict interpretations and relationships regarding new information, events and experiences.

In sum, activating a frame creates expectations about important aspects of the context by directing the agent to fill the slots with available information. Moreover, the real power of frames derives from the use of *default values*, which consist of the most typical and/or frequent filler for each slot. If information about the actual slot-filler is unavailable, a slot is assumed to be filled by the default (Coulson 2001: 19).

However, when normal expectations are violated, we are forced to reorganise existing information into a new frame. This process of conceptual revision is called *frame-shifting* and it is involved in the interpretation of utterance (1):

> (1) By the time Mary had had her fourteenth child, she'd finally run out of names to call her husband (Coulson 2001: 49).

In this case, the reader initially interprets "names" as referring to the name given to a baby. This is determined by our world knowledge about actions associated with childbirth, which include also naming. This expectation is strengthened by the idea (retrieved from our world knowledge) that fourteen is an unusually large number of children and a mother might have difficulty in finding a name that she would like to give to her fourteenth child. However, the presence of "husband" in the final part of the sentence upsets our expectations, by introducing an inconsistent element which prompts lexical reinterpretation of "names" as "derogatory epithets". In order to process this unexpected element, we need to retrieve previously suppressed information involving our knowledge of events surrounding childbirth, including the pain and discomfort associated with giving birth, the subsequent hard work associated with caring for an additional child, and the husband's role in the pregnancy (Ritchie 2005: 5).

This shows how meaning construction depends on the dynamic activation of frames, which are flexible – i.e. may select and include variable segments of knowledge to cope with specific contexts – and, therefore, economic instruments, because, by a simple shifting mechanism, we do not need to process all the information (for instance, all the information about childbirth) potentially available in long-term memory.

Some of the most obvious examples of frame-shifting can be found in jokes:

> (2) After successfully delivering the first child of a Canadian couple visiting Scotland, the doctor popped into the waiting room to tell the anxious husband the good news.
> "It's a boy – eight pounds exactly!"
> "Oh," replied the flustered father. "Will you take a check?"
> (Reader's Digest, Jan. 1984: 89, quoted in Liu 1995: 179).

Most extant theories of jokes, and of humour in general, rely on one or more of three explanatory mechanisms: aggression (Freud 1960; Zillmann and Cantor 1976), incongruity and unexpectedness (Raskin 1985; Attardo and Raskin 1991; Attardo 2001; Giora 2003), and arousal-safety (Rothbart 1972; Forabosco 1992). Each of these approaches explains some important aspects of humour, but none seems complete on its own (Ritchie 2005: 5). For reasons of space, I cannot review here the rich literature on humour: as Chiaro has repeatedly pointed out (cf. Chiaro 2008), humour is not a simple phenomenon and indeed several theories have highlighted its complex nature. Here I will only briefly recall that incongruity-based theories are the ones which are most consistent with the frame-shifting approach. Incongruity theories argue that humorous effect is obtained through a cognitive dissonance between the immediately accessible information and the subsequent stretch of discourse, an incongruity that has to be resolved by the surprised hearer.

Another interesting perspective is found in Giora's (2003) Graded Salience Hypothesis, according to which we invariably access the most salient meaning first. In this view, humour provides an initial highly salient interpretation, which is then revisited when the punch-line forces us to retrieve the initially suppressed information.

Frame-shifting is, therefore, tightly linked to incongruity, unexpectedness and surprise, which are properties also present in a majority of ironic statements and situations (Bertuccelli Papi and Aru 2020: 30). Humour and irony do not coincide, but irony can have a humorous effect, for instance in cases of surrealistic ironies:

(3) Are you going to school tomorrow?
    No, I am riding my unicorn to Alaska! (Kapogianni 2013: 1)

On the other hand, we can have irony without humour, as in:

(4) [Angry mother to her son, who did not clean up his room] "I love children who keep their room clean"

In other words, humour is not a necessary component of irony (Bertuccelli Papi and Aru 2020). Unexpectedness, surprise, detection and resolution of an incongruity may produce humour as a side-effect of irony. However, as Dynel remarks, the incongruity itself must not be completely resolved if we want humorous ironies to be successful:

Humorous irony must leave some of the incongruity unresolved, which allows the hearer to alternate between the cognitive model of reference and the ironic utterance, as well as appreciate the contrast between the speaker meaning and the literal meaning (Dynel 2013: 304).

Despite being different phenomena, both humour and irony involve a contrast of frames. They both underline connections that may have previously gone unnoticed, or at the least raise the salience of previously ignored or suppressed aspects of a situation. Thus, humour or irony may lead to a new understanding of a situation, or reinforce one set of meanings at the expense of other competing meanings (Ritchie 2005: 30). In turn, humour and irony are elements which are often used in satire, together with a series of linguistic and rhetorical devices which influence the recognition of satire as a genre. This relationship between humour, irony and satire will be briefly described in the following section.

3. The complexities of satire

Bertuccelli Papi (2018) highlights the complexities of satire, pointing out the difficulties of defining it as a genre given the various forms it can take (all the more so, if looked at diachronically), as evidenced by the different opinions of scholars who dealt with it: some researchers argue that "Satire is not a genre of discourse but a discursive practice that does things to and with genres of discourse" (Simpson 2003: 76); others that satire is a "technique", a "spirit", the "use of" wit along with a list of other literary and rhetorical devices (Kuyper 2012: 169).

Bertuccelli Papi (2018) tackles this challenge from a different perspective. Her idea is to adopt a cognitivist approach to genres in order to explain if and to what extent satire can nowadays be considered a genre. Contrary to the traditional classification of genre as taxonomic categories (where texts are grouped on the basis of shared structural and thematic properties), the view of genre as a cognitive construct focuses on the "flexibility of the human mind that allows us to deal with the almost infinite variety associated with genre forms manifested in discourse" (Stukker, Spooren and Steen 2016: 1). According to Steen (2011: 25), "genre is [...] a complex knowledge schema that individual language users have at their disposal to engage in discourse". Moreover, Stukker, Sporen and Steen urge to consider genre "as the multi-faceted, multidimensional and dynamic concept it appears to be, including linguistic, social, and content-related knowledge and is somehow stored in cognition" (Stukker, Spooren and Steen 2016: 1).

Within this perspective, satire can be conceived of as a genre if "the latter are conceived not so much as watertight containers but as dynamic categories that emerge out of a complex interplay of heterogeneous factors which cluster differently under the effect of different contextual and cotextual attractors" (Bertuccelli Papi and Aru 2020: 61).

In satire, these factors include several linguistic and rhetorical devices which combine and cumulate to convey the intention of shaming or exposing individual or social ills, along with a general purpose of improvement or reformation. Among these devices, an important role is played by irony and sarcasm, which share with satire the capability of implicitly conveying a critical attitude (Bertuccelli Papi and Aru 2020). Satire is also typically (but not necessarily) humorous and humour crucially hinges on frame-shifting: consequently, we assume that frame-shifting is also a mechanism involved in satire. However, I will argue below that understanding satire involves more than the linear sum of its individual components (humour and criticism). More specifically, I will assume that understanding satire is a context-sensitive operation, where the reader/listener is supposed to set up and maintain multiple mental representations and draw several types of pragmatic inferences. Frame-shifting is partly responsible for some aspects of the operation, but the global meaning of satire emerges as a function of the type of information that fills the slots of the underlying frame.

4. The study

In order to give empirical substance to my claim, I have set up an experiment, whose general format was inspired by Colston (1997), which I will illustrate in the following sections.

4.1. Participants and materials

A total of 40 English native speakers (27 females and 13 males) were selected for the test, through the online platform Prolific.co. Their age varied from 21 to 77 years old.

They were presented with two texts taken from the satirical magazines *The Onion* and *The Newyorker*. An exhaustive frame and mental spaces analysis of the texts was not possible here for space reasons. However, both are comprehensively examined in Bertuccelli Papi's (2018) work on satire as a genre. The texts are reported in the Appendices.

In Text 1 (*Cancer Researchers: 'Don't Get Cancer'* – see appendix A), we can detect a clash between frame expectations and what is actually said: the frame of cancer research creates expectations, including medical experts bringing new ideas, new experiments, clinical trials, hopes for the future, etc., which are all actually mentioned, but then the material that should fill the slots of the frame is consistently contradicted by information that is completely irrelevant to the reader.

The false presupposition underlying the whole text is that people are free to choose whether to get or not to get cancer. This presupposition reflects the belief of those people who believe that they can control everything in their bodies.

Due to the incongruous and unexpected material that fills the slots of the cancer research frame, the reader may be initially both surprised and amused by the text. These feelings are soon replaced by scorn and indignation for the lack of respect toward such a sensitive topic. In fact, the slots of the cancer frame are filled with information that is completely irrelevant or uninformative: for example, the obvious but irrelevant and uninformative truths in passages such as *"Top cancer researchers throughout the country urged individuals to think of the benefits of not having cancer, such as being alive for a much longer period of time, feeling healthy, etc.".*

The aim of the author is clearly to criticise researchers for being so clinical in interactions with patients, without improving our knowledge of cancer or providing clear information about the methods for treating it. The intention to condemn their behaviour, capitalizing on the specific mechanism of humour and irony and on the associated critical attitudes, turns the text into a satire (Bertuccelli Papi and Aru 2020: 85).

Text 2 (*Trump Signs Executive Order Giving Him Control of Weather* – see appendix C) is characterised by the presence of humour, hyperbole and irony whose interaction contributes to conveying the critical attitudes necessary for satirical purposes. Again, a clash can be detected between our conceptual knowledge of the political charge of U.S. President (and its powers) and the situation described in the text. The irony/sarcasm conveys a critical attitude towards Donald Trump's aggressive and reckless politics. Hyperbole contributes to highlighting the mocking attitude conveyed by the irony.

4.2. Procedure

Both texts were uploaded on Google Forms. The first part of the test consisted of a Fill in the Blanks exercise: key parts of the original texts were erased, and participants were asked to type in the blanks the words or expressions they thought best fit within that specific context. The texts were manipulated by removing the more strictly satirical material, thus creating empty slots and retaining the portion of text that serves to identify the knowledge frame (see appendices B and D).

In the second part of the test, participants were asked to read two texts: the original one (reported in appendices A and C) and a similar text which differed from the original in some aspects. More specifically, the satirical texts were modified in order to make them lose their satirical tone and appear as jokes playing on nonsense. For example, in the text about cancer, I wrote that in order to avoid cancer, people should avoid persons born under the sign of Cancer. Here, I report a brief extract of the joke: *"The panel, which consisted of medical experts at the top of their respective fields in cancer research, education, surgery, chemotherapy, and radiotherapy, addressed the media for 45 minutes, saying that people's best hope in terms of living a long, cancer-free life is to avoid people born between 22nd of June and 22nd of July"*.

After reading the two texts, participants were presented with multiple choice questions. In particular, they were asked which of the two texts (the satirical one or the joke) offered a critical perspective of cancer research and they were asked to briefly motivate their answers. Then, they were asked which of the two texts they found funnier; which of the two texts was closer to what they wrote in the Fill the Blank exercise; and to rate how humorous the two texts were, along a 5-point Likert Scale, with 1 indicating "non-humorous" and 5 "very humorous". The same procedure was repeated for the text on Donald Trump, where the slots relative to "weather" were replaced with "chickens", as in *WASHINGTON (The Borowitz Report) – In what some congressional Democrats are calling a flagrant example of Presidential overreach, Donald Trump on Tuesday signed an executive order giving him total control of chickens"*.

5. Results

5.1. Text 1

In the Fill in the Blanks test, the participants' answers matched the expectations. Slots were filled with expressions containing solutions for cancer prevention (*"not smoking"*; *"vaping instead of smoking"*); funding cancer research (*"do not stop funding research against cancer"*); or advice regarding how to behave when diagnosed with the disease (*"do not panic"*).

In the second part of the test, 97.5% of participants identified the satirical text as the one offering a critical perspective on cancer research. When asked to motivate their answers, several participants argued that they recognised the satirical tone in the first text, while the second one was just a joke based on nonsense. However, several participants also tried to provide a different explanation: *"the satirical text is supported more by scientific language"*; *"it has more research-based information"*; *"seems to give a more medical explanation than Text 2"*.

95% of participants considered the joke as funnier than the satirical text. Generally, Text 2 was perceived as more humorous than Text 1. Finally, 95% of participants considered Text 1 as closer to their expectations.

5.2. Text 2

Similarly to the text on cancer, in the Fill in the Blanks exercise, participants' answers matched the expectations but were more heterogeneous. The empty slots were filled with expressions regarding taking control of institutions (*Government, democracy, banking system, the Senate, the Congress*, etc.); social issues topics (*women's bodies, laws, people's lives* or *immigration*); military forces (*army, nukes*); territories (*U.S.A., the world, Mars*); and the media. A minority of participants, maybe conditioned by the text on cancer, gave unexpected answers regarding food (*McDonald's, hamburgers* and *sweets*) and Covid-19.

The results in the second part of the test were similar to Text 1, although with less striking percentages. In fact, 65% of participants indicated Text 1 (the satirical text) as the one offering a critical perspective over Trump's politics. When asked to motivate their answers, several participants recognised the intent of the writer to mock Trump's need for power and control.

The majority (65%) of participants found that Text 2 was funnier than Text 1, which was considered closer to their expectations by 65% of participants. Finally, when asked to rate how humorous the texts were (along a 5-Points Likert Scale), participants' answers were more balanced, with 50% of them rating Text 2 with 4 (40%) or 5 (10%), against 37.5% of 4 (22,5%) or 5 (15%) for Text 1. A score of 1 and 2 was given to Text 1 by 25% of participants (15% rated it with 1; 10% with 2); the same percentage attributed a value of 1 or 2 to Text 2 (10% with 1; 15% with 2).

6. Discussion

Within the limits of reliability that are always associated to experiments conducted with online participants, it seems to me that the results obtained enable us to draw some plausible conclusions. In particular, the results show that frame shifting is crucial to understanding these satirical texts, but it is not sufficient by itself to characterise the texts as satirical. For one thing, the role of humour in satire needs to be considered. The jokes based on nonsense were perceived as more humorous for both the cancer and Trump texts (although for the latter, percentages were more balanced). Nonetheless, a good percentage of participants could distinguish the satirical texts from the simply humorous ones. This means that in satire there is something more than simply humour: humour is one component, possibly a necessary one, but not sufficient by itself to trigger the satirical reading.

Also hyperbole can influence the interpretation of the reader. For instance, the satirical text on Donald Trump was perceived as more humorous if compared to the one on cancer. This may be due to the sensitivity of the latter topic but also to the presence of hyperbole which emphasises and exaggerates Trump's aggressive and reckless politics, thus increasing the humorous and ironic effects of the text. Therefore, it is not by chance, in my opinion, that the text on Trump was generally perceived as more humorous than the text on cancer. In Bertuccelli Papi and Aru's (2020) work on irony, in line with other researchers (Kreuz and Roberts, 1995; Wilson, 2017), hyperbole is considered as a cue which contributes to highlighting the speaker's ironic attitude. Its presence in the text on Trump may work as one of the parameters which let the satirical interpretation emerge.

As shown by the participants' answers to the test, also the register adopted in the satirical texts emphasised the critical perspective offered by the writers, in particular in the text on cancer research. In fact, several participants argued that the language used in the satirical text was supported by a "more medical explanation". This is in line with participants' answers on which of the texts (the satirical one or the joke) was closer to their expectations. The cancer research satirical text still adopted a scientific language, thus keeping itself closer to people's expectations in this respect. Nonetheless, it was able to surprise the reader by upsetting their assumptions through the falseness of the presuppositions according to which people can control everything in their bodies. From this, an inference is triggered that somehow places humour in the background and foregrounds a critical judgment towards the researchers. In other words, the frame shifting at stake in satire involves more than simply moving from one semantic domain to another: it involves the attitudes that are associated with some conceptual domains, and which are implicitly generated by the interrelations among the text components. It is from these interrelations that attitudes and intentions are inferred, and the further force of the texts as criticisms toward cancer researchers' behaviour or Donald Trump's politics emerges. Participants perceived a strong frame shifting in the humorous texts, as the material inserted was less close to their expectations. However, in satire, frame shifting may have a stronger effect, as the material inserted into the slot also carries a rather prominent attitude, which allows the reader/listener to infer the real intentions of his/her interlocutor.

The transition from the serious to the humorous text is perceived more lightly: it is so incongruous and unexpected that it can surprise and make one laugh. Whereas the shift from the serious to the satirical text is closer (in terms of language, semantic area, etc.), but it is more semantically loaded, because there is a shifting involved that is perhaps less striking but changes the attitudes conveyed.

7. Conclusions

In sum, understanding that a text is satirical involves more than the identification and cumulation of linguistic and rhetorical devices. Within a perspective in which genres are conceived of as emergent patterns resulting from interactions among several components of the text (each of them a parameter potentially subject to quantitative and qualitative variability), none of them is individually responsible for the emergence of the pattern (Bertuccelli Papi and Aru, 2020: 74).

All in all, the experiments prove that frame shifting is a powerful instrument in triggering humour but is not sufficient on its own to account for the satirical quality of a text. Rather, the latter seems to emerge from the interrelations/clash between expectations, types of information that fill the slots and inferences that these interrelations are able to trigger in the mind of the reader. More specifically, the material which fills the slots of the satirical texts is not only capable of surprising as a consequence of the frame shift, but it is also capable of conveying attitudes that cumulate to arouse feelings of indignation or critical judgments, which is what primarily makes a text a satire.

APPENDICES

A. Text 1

Cancer Researchers: 'Don't Get Cancer' (The Onion, November 18, 2013)

PHILADELPHIA – Calling the contraction of the disease "not good," and saying that not having the illness is highly preferable to having it, oncologists representing the American Association for Cancer Research urged the U.S. populace Monday not to get cancer. The panel, which consisted of medical experts at the top of their respective fields in cancer research, education, surgery, chemotherapy, and radiotherapy, addressed the media for 45 minutes, saying that people's best hope in terms of living a long, cancer-free life is to never develop cancerous cells in any part of the body, ever.

"After years of closely studying this illness and learning about how it grows and arbitrarily attacks vital organs throughout the body at an uncontrollable rate until one eventually dies, we have concluded that not having cancer is the best way to go," said Dr. Robert Bertino, who specializes in molecular biology at Memorial Sloan-Kettering Cancer Center. "If you are going to contract a harmful illness, get diagnosed with Crohn's disease, meningitis, or even Type 2 diabetes. Anything but cancer. Cancer is just the worst."

"A lot of people die from it," he added. "It's bad." According to specialists, people should not contract colon cancer, breast cancer, pancreatic cancer, stage IV lung cancer, esophageal cancer, liver cancer, non-Hodgkin's lymphoma, or any one of the roughly 200 other known forms of cancer. In addition, researchers confirmed that if it comes down to having terminal vs. non-terminal cancer, both are undesirable, but non-terminal is recommended.

However, oncologists said that even less threatening forms of the illness, such as non-melanoma skin cancer, should be steered clear of, with Bertino explaining that, "You have the surgery, you think it's gone, it comes back for some reason, God knows why, and then it spreads to your lymph nodes, and that's that."

AACR officials went on to recommend that individuals should avoid having a family history of cancer, and that if people must grow tumors, they should make sure to only develop benign ones.

"When a patient comes in to visit me because they have malignant tissue in their breast or under their arm, the first thing I say is 'It would be much better if this hadn't happened,'" said Dr. Sydney Drysdale, head of oncology at Johns Hopkins Medical Center. "I tell them I have studied this illness for decades, I'm the foremost expert when it comes to the spread of cancer, and then I look them in the eye and say cancer is literally the last thing I'd want in my body. I tell them it's not a death sentence, but that it certainly could be. It's cancer. You shouldn't get it."

"Sometimes patients will ask about clinical trials and I'll say clinical trials wouldn't even be an issue if you hadn't gotten cancer in the first place," Drysdale continued. "My best advice: Don't have abnormal cells that uncontrollably divide and invade other tissues."

Top cancer researchers throughout the country urged individuals to think of the benefits of not having cancer, such as being alive for a much longer period of time, feeling healthy, not putting your family through what will easily be the most difficult period of their entire lives, never feeling like you're at the mercy of near impossible and hopeless science, and being able to die of natural causes and not cancer. Moreover, while 10 out of 10 oncologists recommended never having cancer, 100 percent of people who do not currently have cancer reportedly said they are much happier because of it.

"If I could do it all over again, I would not have gotten cancer," said 46-year-old Kevin Glanville, who is currently battling chronic myeloid leukemia. "Getting chemotherapy two times per week and constantly feeling weak and nauseous when there is a good chance the treatment won't even work is much less attractive to me than, say, not dealing with those circumstances."

"My doctor contacted some colleagues of his who work in the cancer research lab at the Mayo Clinic," he continued, "and they said that, for the foreseeable future, if there is any way I cannot have cancer anymore I should do that."

B. Fill in the Blanks exercise

Cancer Researchers: 'Don't [...]'

PHILADELPHIA – Calling the contraction of the disease "not good," and saying that [...] is highly preferable to [...], oncologists representing the American Association for Cancer Research urged the U.S. populace Monday not to [...]. The panel, which consisted of medical experts at the top of their respective fields in cancer research, education, surgery, chemotherapy, and radiotherapy, addressed the media for 45 minutes, saying that people's best hope in terms of living a long, cancer-free life is [...].

"After years of closely studying this illness and learning about how it grows and arbitrarily attacks vital organs throughout the body at an uncontrollable rate until one eventually dies, we have concluded that not [...] is the best way to go," said Dr. Robert Bertino, who specializes in molecular biology at Memorial Sloan-Kettering Cancer Center. "If you are going to contract a harmful illness, get diagnosed with Crohn's disease, meningitis, or even Type 2 diabetes. Anything but cancer. Cancer is just the worst."

"A lot of people die from it," he added. "It's bad." According to specialists, people should [...] colon cancer, breast cancer, pancreatic cancer, stage IV lung cancer, esophageal cancer, liver cancer, non-Hodgkin's lymphoma, or any one of the roughly 200 other known forms of cancer. In addition, researchers confirmed that if it comes down to having terminal vs. non-terminal cancer, both are [...], but [...] is recommended.

However, oncologists said that even less threatening forms of the illness, such as non-melanoma skin cancer, should be [...], with Bertino explaining that, "You have the surgery, you think it's gone, it comes back for some reason, God knows why, and then it spreads to your lymph nodes, and that's that."

AACR officials went on to recommend that individuals should [...] family history of cancer, and that if people must [...], they should make sure to only [...].

"When a patient comes in to visit me because they have malignant tissue in their breast or under their arm, the first thing I say is 'It would be much better if [...],'" said Dr. Sydney Drysdale, head of oncology at Johns Hopkins Medical Center. "I tell them I have studied this illness for decades, I'm the foremost expert when it comes to the spread of cancer, and then I look them in the eye and say cancer [...]. I tell them it's not a death sentence, but that it certainly could be. It's cancer. You shouldn't [...]."

"Sometimes patients will ask about clinical trials and I'll say clinical trials wouldn't even be an issue if you hadn't [...] in the first place," Drysdale continued. "My best advice: Don't [...]."

Top cancer researchers throughout the country urged individuals to think of the benefits of not [...], such as being alive for a much longer period of time, feeling healthy, not putting your family through what will easily be the most difficult period of their entire lives, never feeling like you're at the mercy of near impossible and hopeless science, and being able to die of natural causes and not cancer. Moreover, while 10 out of 10 oncologists recommended never [...], 100 percent of people who do not [...] reportedly said they are much happier because of it.

"If I could do it all over again, I would not have [...]," said 46-year-old Kevin Glanville, who is currently battling chronic myeloid leukemia. "Getting chemotherapy two times per week and constantly feeling weak and nauseous when there is a good chance the treatment won't even work is much less attractive to me than, say, [...]."

"My doctor contacted some colleagues of his who work in the cancer research lab at the Mayo Clinic," he continued, "and they said that, for the foreseeable future, if there is any way I [...] I should do that."

C. Text 2

Trump Signs Executive Order Giving Him Control of Weather (The Newyorker, September 10, 2019)

WASHINGTON (The Borowitz Report) – In what some congressional Democrats are calling a flagrant example of Presidential overreach, Donald Trump on Tuesday signed an executive order giving him total control of the weather.

Under the terms of the order, Trump would assume the unilateral power to create all meteorological conditions, including but not limited to hurricanes, tornadoes, tsunamis, hail, sleet, and wintry mix.

After signing the order, a beaming Trump pronounced "total victory" over the weather, which he called "the enemy of the people."

"I have been treated very unfairly by the weather," Trump said. "The weather is a horrible person."

On Fox News, Sean Hannity praised Trump's decision to seize control of the weather and compared it favorably to former President Barack Obama's weather policy, which he called "a trainwreck." "Obama just let the weather run wild," Hannity said.

Although Trump's executive order is certain to face legal challenges, White House sources indicated that the President was ready to press forward with an additional order giving him dominion over all living things, the planets, and the stars.

D. Fill in the Blanks exercise

Trump Signs Executive Order Giving Him Control of [...]

WASHINGTON (The Borowitz Report) – In what some congressional Democrats are calling a flagrant example of Presidential overreach, Donald Trump on Tuesday signed an executive order giving him total control of [...].

Under the terms of the order, Trump would assume the unilateral power to [...], including but not limited to [...] and [...].

After signing the order, a beaming Trump pronounced "total victory" over [...], which he called "the enemy of the people."

"I have been treated very unfairly by [...]," Trump said. "[...] is a horrible [...]."

On Fox News, Sean Hannity praised Trump's decision to seize control of [...] and compared it favorably to former President Barack Obama's [...] policy, which he called "a trainwreck." "Obama just let [...] run wild," Hannity said.

Although Trump's executive order is certain to face legal challenges, White House sources indicated that the President was ready to press forward with an additional order giving him dominion over [...].

References

ATTARDO, SALVATORE, 2001, *Humorous texts: A semantic and pragmatic analysis*, Mouton de Gruyter, New York.

ATTARDO, SALVATORE and RASKIN, VIKTOR, 1991, "Script theory revis(it)ed: joke similarity and joke representation model", *Humor* 4-3/4, pp. 293-348.

BERTUCCELLI PAPI, MARCELLA, 2018, "Satire as a genre", *Pragmatics and cognition* 2, pp. 459-82.

BERTUCCELLI PAPI, MARCELLA and ARU, ALESSANDRO, 2020, *Lecture notes on irony and satire*, Pisa University Press, Pisa.

CHIARO, DELIA, 2008, "Humour", in *The Routledge Companion to Translation Studies*, Routledge, London, pp. 195-196.

COLSTON, HERBERT L., 1997, "Salting a Wound or Sugaring a Pill: The Pragmatic Functions of Ironic Criticism", *Discourse Processes* 23 (1), pp. 25-46.

COULSON, SEANA, 2001, *Semantic leaps: Frame-shifting and conceptual blending in meaning construction*, Cambridge University Press, Cambridge.

DYNEL, MARTHA, 2013, "Irony from a neo-gricean perspective: On untruthfulness and evaluative implicature", *Intercultural Pragmatics* 10, pp. 403-32.

EVANS, VYVYAN and GREEN, MELANIE, 2006, *Cognitive linguistics: An introduction*, Mahwah, NJ and Edinburgh.

FILLMORE, CHARLES, 1975, "An alternative to checklist theories of meaning", *Proceedings of the First Annual Meeting of the Berkeley Linguistics Society*, North Holland, Amsterdam, pp. 123-31.

FILLMORE, CHARLES, 1977, "Scenes-and-frames semantics", in A. Zampolli (ed.), *Linguistic Structures Processing*, North Holland, Amsterdam, pp. 55-82.

FILLMORE, CHARLES, 1982, "Frame semantics", in Linguistic Society of Korea (ed.), *Linguistics in the Morning Calm*, Hanshin, Seoul, pp. 111-35.

FILLMORE, CHARLES, 1985, "Frames and the semantics of understanding", *Quaderni di Semantica* 6, pp. 222-54.

FORABOSCO, GIOVANNANTONIO, 1992, "Cognitive aspects of the humor process: the concept of incongruity", *Humor* 5 (1-2), pp. 45-68.

FREUD, SIGMUND, [1905] 1960, *Jokes and their relation to the unconscious*, Norton, New York.

GIORA, RACHEL, 2003, *On our mind: Salience, context, and figurative language* Oxford University Press, Oxford.

KAPOGIANNI, ELENI, 2013, "Irony via surrealism: the humorous side of irony", in M. Dynel (ed.), *The pragmatics of humour across discourse domains*, Benjamins, Amsterdam.

KREUZ, ROGER and ROBERTS, RICHARD, 1995, "Two cues for verbal irony: hyper bole and the ironic tone of voice", *Metaphor and Symbol* 10, pp. 21-31.

KUYPER, KATHLEEN (ed.), 2012, *Prose literary terms and concepts*, Britannica Guide to Literary Elements, Britannica Educational Publishing, New York.

LIU, FUCHANG, 1995, "Humor as violations of the reality principle", *Humor* 8 (2), pp. 177-90.

MINSKY, MARVIN, 1975, "A framework for representing knowledge", in Patrick H. Winston (ed.), *The psychology of computer vision*, McGraw-Hill, New York, pp. 211-77.

RASKIN, VICTOR, 1985, *Semantic mechanisms of humor*, D. Reidel, Boston.

RITCHIE, David, 2005, "Frame shifting in humour and irony", *Metaphor and Symbol* 20, pp. 275-94.

ROTHBART, MARY K., 1972, "Psychological approaches to the study of humour", in J.A. Chapman and H.C. Foot, (eds.), *It's a funny thing, humour*, Pergamonpp, Oxford, pp. 87-94.

SIMPSON, PAUL, 2003, *On the discourse of satire*, Benjamins, Amsterdam.

STEEN, GERARD, 2011, "Genre between the humanities and the science", in M. Callies, W.R. Keller, A. Lohoefer (eds.), *Bi-directionality in the cognitive science: Examining the interdisciplinary potential of cognitive approaches in linguistics and literary studies*, John Benjamins, Amsterdam, pp. 21-41.

STUKKER, NINKE, SPOOREN, WILBERT, STEEN, GERARD, 2016, *Genre in language, discourse and cognition*, Mouton de Gruyter, Berlin.

TANNEN, DEBORAH, 1979, "What's in a frame? Surface evidence for underlying expectations", in R. Freedle (ed.), *Discourse production and comprehension*, Ablex, Norwood, pp. 137-81.

WILSON, DEIDRE, 2017, "Irony, Hyperbole, Jokes and Banter", in J. Blochowiak, C. Grisot, S. Durrleman, C. Laenzlinger (eds.), *Formal Models in the Study of Language*, Springer, Cham, pp. 201-19.

ZIEM, ALEXANDER, 2014, *Frames of Understanding in Text and Discourse: Theoretical foundations and descriptive applications*, John Benjamins Publishing Company, Amsterdam.

ZILLMANN, DOLFF and CANTOR, JOANNE R., 1976, "A disposition theory of humor and mirth", in T. Chapman and H. Foot (eds.), *Humor and laughter: Theory, research, and applications*, Wiley, London, pp. 93-115.

Frames in a Meta-analytical Perspective: The Case of a Pre-survey on Queer Studies

Sergio Pizziconi

Abstract
As with several other construals in the cognitive sciences, frames can be used in a meta-analytical perspective to analyse and reformulate the causes and effects of mechanisms affecting methods of inquiry in human and social sciences. A pre-survey administered before a seminar in queer studies at the University for Foreigners of Siena is used as a case study. The paper shows how conceptual frames, derived from topics connected to the seminar and highly ranked in the agendas of politics, media, and public opinion, triggered consistent reactions to the stimuli in two of the four major items of the questionnaire.

Key-words: semantic frames; puns; meta-analytical function; Queer Studies; emotions; survey design.

1. Introduction: Frames in the social sciences

The definition of frames that best fits in with the elaboration below is Fillmore's idea of frame semantics as a theory of understanding. In his own words:

> By the term 'frame' I have in mind any system of concepts related in such a way that to understand any one of them you have to understand the whole structure in which it fits; when one of the things in such a structure is introduced into a text, or into a conversation, all of the others are automatically made available. (Fillmore 1982: 111)

As a theory of understanding, frames and cognate cognitive construals, such as mental spaces (Fauconnier 1994) and scripts (Schank and Abelson 1977), have also been used to analyse rituals and other cultural practices. For instance, Croft and Cruse (2004) observe that psychologists developed the theory of categorisation to explain that in order to construe meaning, shared knowledge

ISSN 1824-3967

of basic facts about the categories through which we classify entities in our reality is needed rather than sheer perceptual features of those entities (p. 16-17). Moreover, Croft and Cruse point out that sociologists have made semantic values dependent on the communities in which concepts are used. They also explain how researchers in artificial intelligence elaborated the notion of "script", parallelling semantic frames, to analyse practices that encompass a sequence of events (Croft and Cruse 2004: 17-18). Birdsell (2014: 86), among many other examples, underlines how Fauconnier and Turner's mental spaces can help decrypt meanings in religious and folk rituals, as did Sweetser (2000), and conceptual blending "can be applied to social interaction and collaborative discourse using corpora, interviews and audio transcripts" (Birdsell 2014: 87), as did Oakley and Hougaard (2008).

One last example of the use of frames outside cognitive linguistics is Ervin Goffman's prodromous work on the way human beings experience social interaction that he collected in the volume *Frame Analysis. An Essay on the Organization of Experience* ([1974]1986). Goffman meant and used "frames" as a term complementing the one of "strip". Below, the definitions of the two concepts clarify why in this paper a connection between Fillmore's semantic frames and the social sciences is in order:

The term "strip" will be used to refer to any arbitrary slice or cut from the stream of ongoing activity, including here sequences of happenings, real or fictive, as seen from the perspective of those subjectively involved in sustaining an interest in them. A strip is not meant to reflect a natural division made by the subjects of inquiry or an analytical division made by students who inquire; it will be used only to refer to any raw batch of occurrences (of whatever status in reality) that one wants to draw attention to as a starting point for analysis.

And of course much use will be made of Bateson's use of the term "frame." I assume that definitions of a situation are built up in accordance with principles of organization which govern events – at least social ones – and our subjective involvement in them; frame is the word I use to refer to such of these basic elements as I am able to identify. That is my definition of frame. My phrase "frame analysis" is a slogan to refer to the examination in these terms of the organization of experience. (Goffman 1986: 10-11)

Although Goffman does not refer to linguistic activity proper, he sets a sign-function (Eco [1975]1994: 48-50) that combines "any raw batch of occurrences" with "definitions of a situation". Moreover, in the cases studied in *Frame analysis* and the essays collected in *Forms of talk* (1981), Goffman consistently refers to verbal language as one symbolic system to show how social interaction builds. More important for the sake of this paper is the explicit mention of the analyst in the definition of "strip" and the implicit one in the definition of "frame" when Goffman refers to the "basic elements" that the observer is able to identify. These statements pave the way for researchers to use frames to study their own analytical endeavours.

This paper explores the possibility of using frames on a meta-analytical plane, where "meta-" refers to the use of a concept to analyse the concept itself and, more widely, other concepts used to analyse the object of study of a given discipline. For instance, while the semantics of prototypes originated as a perspective to study how human beings categorise entities in their worldly experience (Rosch 1973; 1975), cognitive linguists have also used it to revise many conceptualisations about grammar categories[1].

The specific hypothesis is that Fillmore's semantic frames and their development into the "speech event frames" (Evans and Green 2006: 228-230), which are very close to scripts (Schank and Abelson 1977), can shed a different light on aspects of experiment and survey designs in the social and human sciences. In the literature on social and human research methodology, different types of response sets of the informants are discussed, pointing out that they can alter the data collection and experimental results. "Response set" is an umbrella term (Ruane 2005: 140) that refers to informants' responses that are not dependent on the contents of the stimulus but on other conditioning variables.

After a closer look at two cases in which scholars use frames with this meta-analytical perspective, the following section will describe the hypothesis and its application to the so-called experimenter effect in experimental design (Bailey 1994: 220) and acquiescence and social desirability in questionnaire administration (Ruame 2005: 72-73; Bailey 1994: 134f). Finally, the section before the closing remarks will show data extracted from a part of a survey administered to

---

[1] For this application of prototypes and many other uses in the language sciences, see Taylor 1995: 173ff.

university students before they started a seminar in queer studies at the University for Foreigners of Siena.

2. Two examples of meta-analytical use of frames

The first example refers to the work of anthropologist David G. Casagrande, who explains how different systems of classification affect interactions between the scientist and the communities studied in field research:

The informational and cognitive load of conversation and learning are reduced significantly by establishing discourse frames using category typicality (Casagrande 2000, 2002: 238-242). This is what was happening during my trail encounters with the Tzeltal. A plant that best represents the category (*V. litoralis*) was used to efficiently instantiate a discourse frame – a tacit understanding that we all have some knowledge in common that makes any subsequent meaningful exchange possible (Fillmore 1982). (Casagrande 2017: 59)

Casagrande's main point is the importance of using prototypical instances of a category to start an interaction with the community an anthropologist is studying. If the observer and the observee share enough knowledge about the instance at hand, that prototype can work as an access point to the discursive frame on which the interaction will build. Put differently: the typical example selects the area of the broader conceptual network connected to the category at hand in a given moment of the interaction. Circumscribing a specific area of the frame helps the anthropologist and the informants who belong to the community under observation understand each other.

The second example of frames used as a meta-analytical device deals with a renowned study by Stanley Schachter and Jerome Singer (Schachter and Singer 1962) about the two-factor theory of emotion. The five-year time between 1955 and 1960 saw the cognitive turn in many disciplines: psychology, linguistics, cybernetics, and anthropology (Mandler 1985: 7-9). Therefore, in the early sixties, many experimental designs in social psychology exploited the tenets of cognitivism, often at a pre-theoretical level, which is the case of frames in the Schachter and Singer experiment. In this discussion, their multilayered hypothesis is reduced to the first proposition:

Given a state of physiological arousal for which an individual has no immediate explanation, he will "label" this state and describe his feelings in terms of *the cognitions available to him*. To the extent that cognitive factors are potent determiners of emotional states, it could be anticipated that precisely the same state of physiological arousal could be labeled "joy" or "fury" or "jealousy" or any of a great diversity of emotional labels *depending on the cognitive aspects of the situation*. (Schachter and Singer 1962: 381-382 *emphasis added*)

The passage describes the two factors that determine emotions: first, we perceive an unspecified physiological arousal, then, we name it according to available pieces of information cognitively processed.

In order to verify their hypothesis, the two psychologists designed an experiment with college student participants, who were told that the research team wanted to test the effects on their vision of a vitamin supplement injection. Participants were divided into four groups: three were injected with epinephrine to engender the "state of physiological arousal" without knowing it was epinephrine, while the fourth received a placebo. Before and during the injection, the three epinephrine groups received different sets of information about the side effects of the substance. The researcher who gave the jab told the participants in the first group the effect epinephrine usually causes; those in the second group were informed about completely different effects; those in the third group and those who received the placebo were told nothing about side effects. After the injection, all groups were asked to wait for the vitamin supplement to enter the bloodstream before the researchers could run tests. During the waiting time, the researchers produced the emotion-inducing cognition; to do so, they procedurally applied the notion of frames. They let a stooge enter the waiting room and start one of two scripts: one meant to be interpreted as euphoria by the participant, and the other as anger. The expectation was that in a subsequent questionnaire, participants who received epinephrine and were informed of wrong side effects or not informed at all would report that their emotional status was either euphoria or anger, according to the script played by the stooge. In their article, Schachter and Singer provided a detailed report of the script the stooge followed with the specification of actions, attitudes, and lines to be said.

To induce euphoria, the stooge was instructed to play with scrap paper in the room, then to make paper planes and fly them, and finally to play with hula hoops. This is the way Schacter and Singer describe the script and how the frame is verbally enacted:

2. "This scrap paper isn't even much good for doodling" and crumples paper and attempts to throw it into wastebasket in far corner of the room. He misses but this leads him into a "basketball game." He crumples up other sheets of paper, shoots a few baskets, says "Two points" occasionally. He gets up and does a jump shot saying, "The old jump shot is really on today." [...]
5. Stooge continues basketball, then gives it up saying, "This is one of my good days. I feel like a kid again. I think I'll make a plane." He makes a paper airplane saying, "I guess I'll make one of the longer ones." [...]
14. Stooge twirls hoop wildly on arm, saying, "Hey, look at this – this is great." [...] (Schachter and Singer 1962: 384)

In all three activities that the stooge starts, through blended mental spaces, he generates a win-lose situation which can cheer him up when hitting the wastebasket or knocking down a tower of manila folders with his aeroplanes or rotating the hula hoop around his arm. His lines highlight his funny actions. Therefore, the whole scene has ties with frames typically connected to euphoric attitudes and emotions.

To induce anger, the researchers set the scene for a questionnaire to be filled out. The stooge comments aloud on many questions getting ever more boisterous and angry. The following are a selection of lines the stooge had in his script to trigger the frame of anger:

3. Question 9 asks, "Do you ever hear bells? How often_____ ?" The stooge remarks, "Look at Question 9. How ridiculous can you get? I hear bells every time I change classes."
4. [...] "I get annoyed at this childhood disease question. I can't remember what childhood diseases I had, and especially at what age. Can you?"
5. Question 17 asks "What is your father's average annual income?" and the stooge says, "This really irritates me. It's none of their business what my father makes. I'm leaving that blank."
6. [...] The stooge says, "I'll be damned if I'll fill out Number 25. 'Does not bathe or wash regularly' – that's a real insult." He then angrily crosses out the entire item.
7. Question 28 reads: "How many times each week do you have sexual intercourse?" 0-1 ____ 2-3 ____ 4-6 ____ 7 and over ____. The stooge bites out, "The hell with it! I don't have to tell them all this."

The frame of anger is built on a crescendo of harshness in words and actions: The series "ridiculous – annoyed – irritates – insult" about the stooge's appreciation of the questionnaire items, the exclamations "none of their business," "I'll be damned if" and "the hell with it" and his crossing out a whole item all contribute to the script of a person's angry reaction to some unpleasant input. Moreover, the stooge tries to get the participant in the room involved in his irritated reaction.

The accuracy Schachter and Singer employed to set the scene and define word by word the lines of the stooge's script are evidence that although Fillmore's theoretical elaboration was still to come,[2] they relied on the same cognitive processes and variables which semantic frames build on. They will be discussed in the next section, including the meta-analytical framework that I have hypothesised in this paper.

3. The hypothesis of the meta-analytical strength of frames

The cornerstone of the hypothesis is Fillmore's definition of frames reported above as a theory of understanding. The meaning of any text depends on the semantic network that the text as a whole and each expression within it generates by interacting with other concepts of the semiotic codes used and the context – for now, without any specification – in which the text is used. Parts (a), (b), and (c) in Fig. 1 represent different types of contexts that determine the frames.

In Fig. 1(a), the central icon of the text and the conceptual semantic frame show how the text is the access point to a network of related and presupposed concepts, directly or implicitly mentioned in the text. Therefore, drawing on Fillmore's discussion of the commercial frame, the sentence "Becky bought the wine in Paris," directly mentions a BUYER and the GOODS while indirectly entailing a

---

[2] Fillmore (1982) recognised that "the concept of 'frame' in various fields within cognitive psychology appears to have origins quite independent of linguistics" (p. 115). In 1977, he also stated that in linguistics, his case frame was the first use of the word, but "the idea, under various names, goes back at least as far as the schemata idea of Bartlett" in *Remembering: A Study in Experimental and Social Psychology*, published in 1932 (Fillmore 1977: 58).

SELLER who RECEIVED the MONEY from the buyer. Whether the location of the exchange is relevant depends on what other conceptual networks the text and other contexts allow the hearer/ reader to access. Fillmore (1977) discusses the way text analysis deals with this textual dimension and pushes the line beyond:

Successful text analysis has got to provide an understanding of the development on the part of the interpreter of an image or scene or picture of the world that gets created and filled out between the beginning and the end of the text-interpretation experience.... In other words what happens when one comprehends a text is that one mentally creates a kind of world; the properties of this world may depend quite a bit on the individual interpreter's own private experiences – a reality which should account for part of the fact that different people construct different interpretations of the same text (Fillmore 1977: 61).

Fig 1(b) depicts this larger frame in which "words represent categorizations of experience, and each of these categories is underlain by a motivating situation occurring against a background of knowledge and experience" (Fillmore 1982: 112). In this way, he expanded the concept of "scene" from the one determining grammatical cases around a verb to the situation in which the text is generated, shared and understood. In other words, the concepts with their meanings in the network activated by the text were dependent on the situational setting. At this level, cognitive linguists licensed the extension of frames to include also routinised exchanges in frequently occurring situations with sequences of actions and more or less fixed formulaic expressions. They are "speech event frames" similar to Schank and Abelson's scripts mentioned above.

This setting is the new layer in Fig. 1(b) and includes the context of the specific situation and the cultural contexts within which the text is used as a cultural practice. In order to introduce the successive two layers in the graphical representation of frames, a remark on the meaning of "cultural context" is in order. The concept of "culture" has undergone a comprehensive revision in the last decades triggered by the post- prefixed movements, particularly post-structuralism and post-modernism. Atkinson (2004) summarises the critical aspect of the concept and suggests that when considering the cultural context, attention must be paid to scale effects that can overturn expectations, presuppositions and entailments even when the interaction is carried out between people who allegedly belong to the same culture because a smaller culture is necessarily closer to an individual. The rhetorician explains that we need to look at small cultures as well:

The idea behind the notion of small cultures, then, is that when we break our analysis down into complexly interacting small, medium-sized, and large cultures, we get a much more complex (if still probably somewhat structuralistic) notion of the interactions of different cultural forces. (Atkinson 2004: 286)

Especially after the explosion of the Internet and social media, the notion of small cultures also applies to the next layer of context, the one represented in Fig 1(c). It refers to the framework that the agendas of mass media, politics, and public opinion activate. The conceptual networks that compose this frame are naturally affected by the cultural and small cultural context; nonetheless, they tend to have an overarching influence because not only do they set the agenda in terms of contents that must be brought to the attention of society, they are also able to define a hierarchy among the many topics and among possible facets of the same topic. For example, for several months in 2021 in Italy, the LGBTQ+ debate centred on the themes tackled by the so-called Zan's bill and the hardships of having the bill approved in the Italian parliament. The bill aimed to fight intolerant actions against the LGBTQ+ community and people living with disabilities. Therefore, concepts such as "non-binary", "inclusivity" vs "intolerance" and "bullying" gained a central position in the public debate. However, at other times, the LGBTQ+ debate was connected with the concept of "traditional family" vs "diverse families".

Given that the opposition between mainstream and alternative media is co-extant with the birth of mass media, today's fragmented scenario of means of communication makes it difficult to decide whether there is one single media agenda and to determine how profound its influence is. Smaller cultures have always tried to set their specific agendas. Nonetheless, by definition, a mainstream agenda can still be identified and contribute to the definition of what is socially proper and acceptable either directly or by dint of opposition.

In Fig. 1(d), the rectangle with round corners represents the last layer of context. It is the situational context generated in a scientific research setting, such as a laboratory experiment, an interview, a focus group, or a questionnaire. It is at this level of concept building that participants in an experimental procedure conceptualise the events they are experiencing to satisfy researchers' expectations and behave accordingly. At the same level, participants answer the questions of a researcher in a way that they deem socially appropriate and desirable because this is how they want the researchers involved to consider them (cf. Ruame 2005: 72-73; Bailey 1994: 134f and 220).

The research setting can affect all other levels of contextual frames and be affected by them. In fact, the intersections of all squares in Fig. 1 point out that, as discussed above, they do not act independently; conversely, they interact to make areas of the conceptual frame at hand more prominent and significant than others. For example, researchers rarely unveil the specific goals of their study to avoid biased reactions by the participants to the procedure. Thus, informants will probably infer researchers' expectations referring to ideologies that belong to mainstream and larger cultures rather than alternative media and smaller cultures because they are more likely to be lined up with an academic venue.

Moreover, when researchers use a text as a stimulus in an experimental procedure, the inner dashed frame of the situation in which the text is produced and used becomes a virtual frame because the implicit request of the researcher is to "read" the text as if it were in the real world, meaning outside the experimental venue. However, the laboratory or the questionnaire are not the real world: all the performative aspects of the speech acts connected to the interpretation of a text and the reaction to it are deleted or better not realised and only actualised in Greimas' words about the generative trajectory of meaning (Greimas and Courtés 1979: s.v. *actualisation* and *génératif, parcours* –). Oversimplifying, when informants are asked to comment on the international signs indicating toilets for men, women and people living with disabilities, they must not perform an action that will make their decision process concrete and satisfactory for a physiological need. All this is brought to the informants' attention, but then the realisation, namely, the semiotic performance, will be about the meaning and significance of those signs.

4. Meta-frames and a survey

The articulated configuration of frames shown in Fig. 1 (d) has been applied to devise the pre-survey first and then to analyse the answers of the students who joined a seminar on queer studies at the University for Foreigners of Siena, Italy, in the academic year 2021-2022. The seminar comprised lectures within regular courses in all degree programs (bachelor and master). Professors of a diverse group of disciplines (comparative linguistics, English, Japanese, educational linguistics, semiotics and sociolinguistics) taught at least a two-hour lesson on topics pertaining to queer studies. The professors recruited students with a blurb that introduced the seminar with these words:

"Queer studies" is the name of a research area that started in the United States in the early 1990s. Since the 1920s, the word queer was used as a derogatory expression to address gays and lesbians. But towards the end of the 1980s, activists reclaimed the word to identify themselves and other individuals with non-binary attitudes towards sex, gender, sexual orientation, sexuality, and other "categories." Very soon, several American academics took on the word, these topics, and these perspectives in their scholarship.

The seminar will deal with this non-binary attitude. You are likely to leave this seminar with many more questions than answers, which is precisely what queer studies do, that is, to observe the world from a different angle. However, we do hope that you can also take one or two ideas for your thesis work with you.

A group of professors (see the table below) will cover a few major framing issues in at least one lesson of their regular courses. This is why the seminar is called "distributed." You will be able to attend those specific lessons even though you are not registered for the entire course.

The other recommended practice was to exploit the logo (Fig. 2) to create a sensory-motor stimulus to instantiate the prompt "to observe the world from a different angle" by asking the students to stand up and lean their bodies and heads to the right so to re-frame the big Q in the middle of the graphics.

After collecting the names of people interested in the seminar with a Google Form, all students were invited to fill out a questionnaire to collect practical information and their comments on one audiovisual and three visual texts. Out of the 100 applicants for the seminar, 20 signed the informed consent to participate in the study. This section discusses students' comments on two visual items to support the theoretical hypothesis proposed above.

FIGURE 1. FRAME, SCENE AND CONTEXTUAL LAYERS

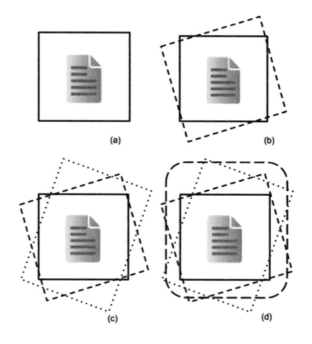

FIGURE 2. LOGO OF THE DISTRIBUTED SEMINAR

Like the blurb, the whole pre-survey was written both in Italian and in English because the seminar addressed all students of the undergraduate and master's degree programmes. The question for all four items was structured like the two analysed here, "Comment on these signs for public restrooms/this cartoon. Record your answer in an audio file and upload it clicking on the button below. Your answer should be no longer than 2 minutes". The signs are international icons for men, women and people living with disabilities. The cartoon is a meme circulating in social media at the time of the seminar and shows a firefighter standing on a pompier ladder trying to reach out for the body of a woman standing outside the window of a high building and wearing a two-piece bikini. Both characters can only be seen from the back, and the right hand of the firefighter touches the woman's buttock. The meme carries a sentence in Italian overwritten on two lines whose translation for the informants was, "once in a while a joy / for these heroes too". The other two stimuli were the movie trailer of Disney's new Cinderella and a US advertisement for a bathing cap printed in the 1960s.

Voice-recorded answers aimed to weaken the professor-student frame because they are not a typical modality to reply to a written question in the Italian educational system. They also increase spontaneous reactions because writing always interposes a filter between our ideas and their expression on paper. False starts, hesitations, re-castings and self-corrections in the recordings attest to looser monitoring of form and a more impromptu delivery, instead.

Before commenting on the most relevant results, the answers to the two stimuli were recorded with an average length of 54.2 seconds (range: 12-118 seconds) using an average number of words of 106.7 (range: 20-264 words) for Item1 (toilet signs); for Item2 (cartoon): average length 57.7 seconds (range: 18-120 seconds) and average number of words 107.9 (range: 22-267). For Item2, one participant uploaded the same file used to comment on another item in the survey. All students reside in Italy, but two students with international backgrounds and two Italian students decided to answer the questions in English. All participants posted their answers between October 12th and 18th, 2021. Finally, Tables 1 and 2 show the full array of access points to the frames activated in the answers. The values under column N are the number of participants who mentioned the access point reported in the row heading at least once in their answers. This means the same access point or its variants could also appear several times in the same recording, but for the sake of this discussion, neither the frequency of access to each frame nor the order is relevant knowledge.

4.1. Public restrooms signs

Undoubtedly, all participants recognised the signs and accessed the frame of PUBLIC TOILET as shared knowledge in the general cultural frame to the point that one participant used the scene for a simulation of reality answering that through the signs people know where to go. The division into genders and disability conditions was simply presupposed. Conversely, all other participants started a critical discussion from three possible anchor points in the frame: the genders identified with the icons of the stylised man and woman, the existence of non-binary gender, or in one case jumping directly to the conclusion that the signs are too simplistic and need a revision.

As mentioned above, at the time of the survey, Italian media allowed Zan's bill against homo-trans-phobia to earn some space in the public discussion which often touched on discrimination and bullying in schools and concrete problems for people living in their transition period. Moreover, even though just two participants used the specific concept of "gender dysphoria", other words were used to access this part of the frame that was also often covered by media.

The toilet signs were meant to make respondents tackle the issue of inclusiveness of non-binary people. However, the aim was also to elicit broader reflections. Among other possible topics, regardless of how many genders we consider, no participant asked why gender should divide toilets in the first place. The sign for restrooms equipped to host people living with disabilities, that is, the international stylized image of a person in a wheelchair was also included because we expected students to comment on at least two issues. First, the sign does not distinguish users according to gender/sex. Chances are that this is not pointing to gender inclusivity but rather to the fact that these restrooms usually host just one user at a time. Only two participants quickly pointed out that the sign for people with disabilities does not carry any gender distinction.

Second, the representation itself of disability through a wheelchair points to an exclusive vision of the type of disability that deserves a dedicated restroom, but as one participant remarked, other types of disability need differently equipped spaces. This reasoning could have provided access to the frame of the essentialist fallacy, discussed in queer studies.

TABLE I. FRAMES IN ANSWERS TO FIRST ITEM

Participant	01	02	03	04	05	06	07	08	09	10	11	12	13	14	15	16	17	18	19	20	N
Frames																					
Gender/category Male	I	I		I	I	I		I	I	I	I		I	I		I					**12**
Gender/category Female	I	I		I	I	I		I	I	I	I		I	I		I					**12**
Category Person with disability	I	I		I	I	I		I	I	I	I		I	I		I					**12**
Binary Vs Non-binary/ transgender/ transexual/ homosexual/ queer		I		I		I		I	I		I	I	I	I		I		I	I		**12**
Distinction/ (sub) division/ classification	I	I		I	I			I			I	I			I						**8**
Gender Dysphoria/ no gender/ do not identify		I	I	I					I	I	I					I		I			**8**
Inclusive vs disrespectful/ discriminatory/ non-inclusive/ humiliating		I			I				I		I	I	I					I	I		**8**
Transition (not completed)								I	I									I	I		**4**
complexity/ more sensitivity/ change VS simplification					I	I							I					I			**4**
Bullism/ abuse/ violence								I	I					I							**3**
"Where to go"			I																		**1**
Difference between bio sex and gender/ gender at birth									I				I								**2**
No gender difference for disabled people											I							I			**2**
Other disability (different from wheelchair)					I																**1**
coming-out/ outing								I													**1**

Finally, one participant stated that the answer provided was conceived based on the topics of the seminar that was about to start. This is evidence that the small cultures defined above can emerge around single occasions and can affect the interpretation of reality.

4.2. The joy for the hero cartoon

The cartoon was selected to tackle two issues frequently addressed in Italian media in 2021: (a) the issue of civil servants who are dubbed heroes when an emergency must be coped with but are soon forgotten when the contingency is over, and (b) a series of femicides that had entered the news very often. Therefore, Table 2 ranks the sexualisation, commodification and objectification of women's bodies in the top position, followed by a combination of access points that refer to the heroic nature of firefighting.

Then, there is a chain of nodes that shift the discussion on the nature of a cartoon used as a meme. In today's social media, memes are framed as humorous texts, but many participants remarked that this one is not, either because it is "simply sexist and chauvinist", or because it exploits and objectifies women's bodies, or it is the humour that can make adolescents or adults in their fifties and sixties laugh.

Seven participants entered the firefighting frame, which licensed six of them to explain the circumstances of the situation pictured in the picture, thus separating it from the meme. The seventh participant explained the situation to emphasise how derogatory the meme was.

The cartoon was also intended to elicit the assumptions of the pun: (a) the firefighter must be male and heterosexual, (b) the naked body must be a woman and heterosexual, (c) a-sexual people do not exist, everybody must have a sexual drive that makes sex a pleasure. Only two participants accessed the heteronormativity frame in assumption (a) above. One of the two also touched on assumptions (b) and (c) after the explicit statement of being a-sexual.

TABLE 2. FRAMES IN ANSWERS TO SECOND ITEM

Participant	01	02	03	04	05	06	07	08	09	10	11	12	13	14	15	16	17	18	19	20	N
Frames																					
Sexualised body/ exploited/ objectification/ commodification					I	I	I	I	I		I	I	I	I		I		I	I		12
Firefighter	I		I	I		I		I		I		I	I		I		I				10
Rescue/ help/ save			I		I		I			I			I		I	I	I	I			9
(not) make people laugh; (not) funny; satirical	I		I	I		I		I	I	I			I								8
Naked woman/ woman in underwear			I		I		I			I			I					I	I		7
Danger risk					I			I		I		I				I	I	I			7
Picture of situation				I				I		I		I			I			I	I		7
Sexist/ chauvinist	I					I			I		I	I						I			6
Joy inducing	I	I						I				I						I	I		6
Repulsive/ disgusting/ shameful/ annoying						I	I		I			I			I			I			6
Generation/ childish/ boomer	I		I					I	I				I								5
Embarrassed		I										I		I							3
Picture of meme		I										I				I					3
Hero							I		I						I						3
Gender roles/ male-white-cis/ patriarchal								I				I	I								3
Heterosexual (assumption)				I															I		2
Bad meme/ tweet														I					I		2
Harassment		I																			1
Judgemental					I																1
"This makes me laugh, even though..."																	I				1
A-sexual																			I		1

5. Closing remarks

The meta-analytical frames that the research setting activates suggest that in the experimental or survey design, researchers can choose to adopt or reject procedures and phrasing that are prototypical of settings that are more likely to trigger a response set. In the case of the pre-survey analysed above, for instance, the request to answer written questions with audio recordings was the anti-prototypical selection to counter the possible effects of the activation of the educational frame with professors and students or the judicial frame with judge and defendants. On the other hand, selecting examples that directly recall topics in the media and political agendas can help understand how ready participants are to "power on", to cite the logo of the seminar, and use their critical thinking about everyday events and scenes.

Therefore, analysing response sets with frames also helps better sketch informants' unaware biases because answering according to mainstream thinking is an implicit acknowledgement and licensing of the assumptions that warrant those ideas, regardless of participants' beliefs on the aspects brought to their attention. By contrast, a clear departure from mainstream conceptualisation shows that its assumptions have been considered at the very least, again, regardless of participants' actual beliefs.

One last word about the Schachter and Singer study on emotions might suggest other areas of application of the central hypothesis in this article. As Gergen and Gergen (1986: 98) contend, attempts at replicas of the experiment failed, and other scholars criticised some theoretical and procedural aspects. Nonetheless, my discussion of Schachter and Singer's study points to another dimension of frames that deserves further exploration. Whether emotions are a phenomenon based on two factors, namely physiological arousal and a cognitive component, or not, the labelling of the emotional state relies on frames. Therefore, the role frames play in triggering, building, and telling emotions is another level of analysis. Moreover, provided that any concept can grant access to an area of the network that readers can load with emotional value because of their personal history, discourse makers look for more or less explicit access nodes when they want to engender a certain rhetorical *pathos* in their discursive practices.

References

ATKINSON, DWIGHT, 2004, "Contrasting rhetorics/contrasting cultures: Why contrastive rhetoric needs a better conceptualization of culture", *Journal of English for Academic Purposes* 3 (4), pp. 277-289.

BAILEY, KENNETH D., 1994, *Methods of Social Research*, Free Press, NY.

BIRDSELL, BRIAN, 2014, "Fauconnier's theory of mental spaces and conceptual blending", in J. Littlemore and J.R. Taylor (eds), *The Bloomsbury companion to cognitive linguistics*, Bloomsbury, London, pp. 72-90.

CASAGRANDE, DAVID G., 2000, "Human taste and cognition in Tzeltal Maya medicinal plant use", *Journal of Ecological Anthropology* 4, pp. 57-69.

CASAGRANDE, DAVID G., 2002, *Ecology, cognition, and cultural transmission of Tzeltal Maya medicinal plant knowledge*, PhD dissertation, Department of Anthropology, University of Georgia, Athens.

CASAGRANDE, DAVID G., 2017, "Ethnoscientific implications of classification as a socio-cultural process", in H. Kopnina and E. Shoreman-Ouimet (eds), *Routledge handbook of environmental anthropology*. Routledge, London, pp. 55-68.

CROFT, WILLIAM and CRUSE, D. ALAN, 2004, *Cognitive linguistics*, C.U.P., Cambridge.

ECO, UMBERTO, [1975]1976, *A theory of semiotics*, Indiana U.P., Bloomington.

EVANS, VYVYAN and GREEN, MELANIE, 2006, *Cognitive Linguistics. An introduction*. Edinburgh U.P., Edinburgh.

FAUCONNIER, GILLES, 1994, *Mental spaces. Aspects of meaning construction in natural language*, Cambridge UP, Cambridge.

FILLMORE, CHARLES J., 1977, "Scenes-and-frames semantics", in A. Zampolli (ed), *Linguistic structures processing*, North-Holland, Amsterdam, pp. 55-81.

FILLMORE, CHARLES J., 1982, "Frame semantics", in Linguistic Society of Korea (ed.), *Linguistics in the morning calm*. Hanshin, Seoul, South Korea, pp. 111-138.

GERGEN, KENNETH, and GERGEN, MARY, 1986, *Social Psychology*, Springer, NY.

GOFFMAN, ERVING, 1981, *Forms of talk*, Pennsylvania U.P., Philadelphia.

GOFFMAN, ERVING, [1974]1986, *Frame analysis: An essay on the organization of experience*, Northeastern U.P., Boston.

GREIMAS, ALGIRDAS JULIEN and JOSEPH COURTÉS, 1979, *Sémiotique. Dictionnaire raisonné de la théorie du langage*, Hachette, Paris.

MANDLER, GEORGE, 1985, *Cognitive Psychology. An essay in cognitive science*, Lawrence Erlbaum, Hillsdale, NJ-London.

OAKLEY, TODD and HOUGAARD, ANDERS, 2008, *Mental Spaces in Discourse and Interaction*, John Benjamins, Amsterdam-Philadelphia.

ROSCH, ELEANOR, 1973, "Natural categories", *Cognitive Psychology* 4, pp. 328-350.

ROSCH, ELEANOR, 1975, "Cognitive representations of semantic categories", *Journal of experimental psychology: General* 104.3, pp. 192-233.

RUANE, JANET M., 2005, *Essentials of Research Methods. A Guide to Social Science Research*, Blackwell Publishing, Maiden (MA).

SCHACHTER, STANLEY and SINGER, JEROME, 1962, "Cognitive, social, and physiological determinants of emotional state", *Psychological review* 69.5, pp. 379-399.

SCHANK, ROGER C. and ABELSON ROBERT P., 1977, *Scripts, plans, goals and understanding*, Erlbaum, Hillsdale.

SWEETSER, EVE, 2000, "Blended spaces and performativity", *Cognitive Linguistics* 11-3/4, pp. 305-333.

TAYLOR, JOHN R., 1995, *Linguistic categorization,* Clarendon Press, Oxford.

How Political Deepfakes Shape Reality: A Visual Framing Analysis

Anna Mongibello

Abstract

The present study aims to critically analyse political deepfakes using visual framing analysis (Coleman 2010). As a form of framing analysis, visual framing analysis relies on the understanding of visual framing as the selection of one view, scene, or angle (i.e. a frame) in order to make some aspects of a perceived reality more salient and therefore promote a particular "problem definition, casual interpretation, moral evaluation, and/or treatment recommendation" (Entman 1993: 52). I claim that visual framing analysis can be useful for the investigation of political deepfakes as sophisticated means of textual and visual disinformation which construct frames that encode ideologies. In other words, the study aims to unveil the means used by political deepfakes to build (fake) realities. The study addresses the following research questions:

RQ1. What frames appear in political deepfakes?
RQ2. How do visual and textual material construct the frames?
RQ3. What are the social implications and political functions of these frames?

To answer such questions, a qualitative analysis is conducted on a sample of five verified political deepfakes in English circulated through social media. The ultimate aim of the study is to shed some light on the role that political deepfakes play in our society and the representational strategies employed in the larger landscape of disinformation.

Key-words: political deepfakes, visual framing analysis, disinformation, ideology.

1. Introduction

In March 2022 a fake and heavily manipulated video depicting Ukrainian president Volodymr Zelensky was circulated on social media. The video showed Zelensky announcing his surrender to Russia's invasion. Having quickly been identified as a deepfake, it was removed from Facebook and YouTube for violating

ISSN 1824-3967

misinformation policies. A few years earlier, in 2018, another fake video showing another president, Barack Obama, had gone viral on social media. In the video, Obama called president Trump "a total and complete dips**t" from what appeared to be the Oval Office. Both videos exemplify the threatening potential of "synthetic media" or "deepfakes" (Vaccari and Chadwick 2020), a new type of artificial media through which highly convincing videos of politicians, currently available online, contribute to the spread of video-based disinformation and deceptiveness by malicious actors.

Deepfakes originate from the misuse of deep learning technologies and digital manipulation through which images and videoclips are combined. Using these technologies, body, face and visual information about a real-life person can be replaced or superimposed into false settings to create fake videos that appear authentic (Westerlund 2019). The AI technology employed by deepfake creators is called Generative Adversarial Networks (Goodfellow et al. 2014) and relies on a series of training sets based on authentic video footage to generate synthetic audio and video content, including the replication of facial expressions and mimicking of human voice, in such a way that the fabricated videos look authentic and genuine. The more complex these technologies are, the easier it is to replicate voice and movements so that the videos and the people appearing on screen end up looking real. While access to sophisticated software programs used to be limited since it required advanced expertise and expensive digital tools, user-friendly, open-source apps, such as FakeApp, Deepfake Web and Zao have now become increasingly more popular. These applications allow the basic, homemade manipulation of footage through cutting, slowing, re-staging and re-contexualizing. In other words, virtually anyone with rudimentary knowledge of how video-editing works can produce so-called 'cheapfakes', i.e. videos manipulated in less sophisticated ways that still look authentic to the average person. However, only the most advanced technologies allow the production of videos that look authentic and credible. Nevertheless, despite some of the deepfakes circulating on social media are now created through user-friendly apps, their dissemination continues to be extensive due to the fact that unverified contents on social media can be easily shared and soon become viral. Their wide circulation raises concerns with regard to the challenges that deepfakes can pose, especially when it comes to politically related videos.

A co-hashtag analysis conducted within a wider study on how to map deepfakes showed that in 2017, when deepfakes first emerged as a new phenomenon, the technology was used for the production of non-consensual pornography (Winter and Salter 2019). The videos including faces of actresses such as Emma Watson and Megan Markle represent a particularly violent form of objectification and image-based, non-consensual digital sexual abuse, since they aim at humiliating their targets. Starting from 2018, as Chesney and Citron (2019) remark, a shift occurred from pornographic to politically and economically related content. By the end of 2019, audio-visual manipulations, also relying on face-swapping technologies of political speeches, started to enter the market of political disinformation as major issues concerning COVID-19 and US elections emerged. Before 2020, deepfake videos were still mainly pornographic (96%, as mentioned in Ajder, Patrini, Cavalli, Cullen 2019) but their number doubled compared to 2018 (14698 vs. 7964). These new kinds of synthetic but realistic videos of politicians making forged statements can be defined as political deepfakes. In 2019, a video showing Nancy Pelosi, the speaker of the US House of Representatives, appearing to slur drunkenly through a speech, was shared on social media and gained thousands of reposts and likes. The video was first uploaded to Twitter by a Trump superfan from New York with the caption "Pelosi stammers through news conference", then it was retweeted and reposted on other social media platforms, including Facebook. Although the video was later found to be false, it still went viral. Many other representatives of political elites worldwide have been targeted so far.

A study conducted in 2021 by Bakari et al. showed that political deepfakes are credible to up to 50% of a representative sample of 5,750 subjects, which implies that highly manipulated political videos featuring important representatives of world politics can concretely affect the electorate's ability to evaluate public officials and elect competent leaders (Jerit and Zhao 2020). The reason why political deepfakes seem to be perceived as more credible than other forms of misinformation lies in the fact that audiovisual information has been identified as the primary form of persuasive

communication enjoying high degrees of credibility (Dunn 2006).
Text-based disinformation can be easily dismissed due to lack of
visual proof. Conversely, deepfakes are perceived as more credible,
as they rely on visual communication. Moreover, on social media
people are more inclined to share videos and still images, rather
than text-based information (Goel, Anderson, Hofman, Watts 2015),
which makes deepfake videos particularly challenging to contain.
The multimodal nature of deepfakes is also the reason why they
are hard to fact-check. As a matter of fact, in June 2020, Facebook,
partnering with other industry leaders and academic researchers,
joined the Deepfake Detection Challenge to detect potentially
bogus photos and videos and improve the accuracy of its machine-
learning model in detecting disinformation. Despite this and other
efforts, there is to date a paucity of technological resources capable
of automatically detecting deepfakes and labelling them as forged
material before they go viral. As highlighted by Kalpokas and
Kalpokiene (2022: 69), "[w]ith the growing accessibility of deepfake
production tools, manual moderation becomes an impossibility due
to the sheer volume of content, not to mention its sophistication".
The automatic detection of deepfakes would involve speech
recognition, the verification of the speaker's personality based on
training data, the detection of specific patterns in voice and facial
features along with the examination of background inconsistencies,
pixel variations and other distortions.

While technological approaches are being studied, state
regulations are trying to discipline the production of deepfakes.
In California, for example, specific regulations have made
political deepfakes illegal in the leap up to elections (Cover,
Haw, Thompson, Daniel 2002). Other states and international
organizations have also raised their concerns over the misuse
of digitally manipulated media. The European Parliamentary
Research Service, for example, has recently published a report
(van Huijistee, Boheemen, Das 2021) focused on the assessment
of underlying technologies for deepfake videos, audio and text
synthesis, showing how these are becoming cheaper and more
accessible. The report also addresses the necessity of advancing
legislative frameworks within the already proposed EU Artificial
Intelligence framework, aimed at mitigating the risks of deepfakes.
Both private industries and governmental responses to the

production of deepfakes confirm how forged videos, featuring political content in particular, represent a threat to the circulation of information. In other words, as also pointed out by Westerlund (2019), deepfakes embody the quintessential quality of post-truth communication which is marked by false information, manipulation, undermined confidence in traditional media, and increasing difficulty in discerning what is real from what is fake. In this sense, deepfakes problematize our ability to access and recognize 'the truth'. As the other facet of the coin, the inability to tell what is fake and what is real also allows politicians to claim that authentic videos depicting them in real-life compromising situations are fake, which is another challenging aspect of the rise of deepfakes.

2. Previous studies on political deepfakes

The research on political deepfakes is relatively recent. Much of this research has concentrated on machine learning, deep learning and artificial intelligence, and on methods for detecting deepfakes (Yang, Li, Lyu 2019; Güera and Delp 2018). These studies examine deepfakes from a technological perspective. Several other studies deal with the legal regulation of deepfakes, thus taking into consideration issues regarding, for example, the infringement of rights and copyright regulations, the damaging of reputation, the humiliation that comes with pornographic deepfakes and other similar aspects (Citron and Chesney 2019, 2018). To date, relatively few studies have dealt with the investigation of the effects that deepfakes may have on people's perception of reality. A research study by Vaccari and Chadwick (2020) compared the responses of participants exposed to two deceptive deepfake videos and showed that political deepfakes may sow uncertainty while also reducing trust in news on social media. Similarly, a study by Dobber, Mtoui, Trilling, Helberger et al. (2020) analysed the effects of deepfakes on audiences through an online experiment. The researchers found that attitudes toward the depicted politician changed after seeing the deepfake, thus showing that people can easily be influenced by false information on social media. Overall, these studies have pointed out how political deepfakes seem to be part of wide-scale propaganda whose ultimate goal is to trash the information space so that audiences give up looking for any truth, thus generating a systemic state of uncertainty (Chadwick, Vaccari, O'Loughlin 2018). Broadly speaking, there is a general lack of studies that analyse visuals in relation to misinformation since such studies pose significant methodological challenges.

Although the interest in deepfakes as a social phenomenon is growing, not much attention has been devoted to the analysis of how deceptive communication is construed and how reality is shaped by and through deepfake videos from a discursive perspective. However, a few scholars have worked on so-called "deepfake discourse", which is the discourse surrounding deepfakes on social media and everyday discourse. For example, Brooks (2021) investigates how deepfakes are situated in public conversation through a qualitative analysis of news and magazine outlets, whereas Capistràn (2022) analyses the evolution of the semantic fields and discourses surrounding the term *deepfake* from its appearance in 2017 to 2021. Therefore, the present study aims at filling a gap in the current research by providing a first attempt to critically analyse deepfakes. In order to do so, we will be looking at a small selection of political deepfakes as multimodal narrative devices to unveil how, through the interplay between text and visual material, they manage to shape realistic scenarios and perform persuasive functions and disinformation.

3. Methodological approach and research questions

Given the above premise, it is clear that political deepfakes are complex multimodal material, forged for reasons that, in similar ways to how fake news works in the post-truth era, range from deceptiveness and disinformation to manipulation and amusement. As complex multimodal material, deepfakes can be looked at as layered media, i.e. "narrative comprised of – or fused between – moving image and sound, audio which includes dialogue, effects, incidental and narrative-related music" (Cover, Haw, Thompson 2002: 65). Individual components of deepfake videos cannot be analysed without taking into consideration the range of elements composing the final mash-up.

As an effect of the re-contexualization of already existing visual and textual material into realistic scenarios, new meanings are produced that serve different communicative and social functions, which is what makes deepfakes an interesting case to analyse from a discursive perspective. For example, deepfake technology has been used in order to produce false evidence of political leaders' incapability or inappropriateness through the forgery of embarrassing scenes, for demonization or reputation-damaging purposes. While this is not new if we think of how repressive regimes have often tried to discredit opponents through the manufacture of compromising material, however, given the realistic illusion that deepfakes create, the credibility effect that is triggered is increased. This is due to both the technologies being used and the easy circulation of digital material across social media platforms.

The present study employs visual framing analysis (VFA) in combination with Kress and van Leeuwen's theoretical framework for analysing visual communication (2006; 2001) as its primary methodology. VFA, as a form of framing analysis, revolves around the concept of frames that help people make sense of a situation by facilitating the organization of an experience and the perception of particular aspects of the information. As a methodology for analysing frames, VFA derives from Entman's theorization of visual framing as the "selection of one view, scene, or angle when making the image, cropping, editing or selecting it" (Coleman 2010: 237). Such a selection includes the foregrounding of one or more aspects of a perceived reality that are made more salient in the communication process, "in such a way as to promote a particular problem definition, causal interpretation, moral evaluation and/or treatment recommendation" (Entman 1993: 52). For instance, VFA has been used to investigate how television editing shapes audiences' perceptions of an event (Messaris and Abraham 2001). In this sense, messages can be strategically framed in a certain way, in order to give emphasis to what is relevant to the producer's agenda. Past studies considered news framing in particular, and pointed out how news frames guide the interpretation of the news through patterns of selection, emphasis and exclusion. Domke at al. (2002) have shown how the inclusion of a given image or varying head angles and gestures in visual communication shape judgments and impressions. Studies by Fahmy (2007) and Fahmy and Kim (2008) focus on the visual representation of the Iraq invasion in US and UK press and the analysis of the Saddam statue toppling through a cross-country comparison that foregrounds the power of visual images in driving public opinion. According to Shoemaker and Reese (1996), visual framing can be influenced by organizational and/or ideological variables, including advertising and/or governmental pressures. However, there is a significant gap in disinformation literature when it comes to the analysis of visuals. Studies employing visual framing are much less common than studies employing textual framing, because identifying visual frames is a challenging task.

Since VFA has traditionally focused on a wide range of news, and political and scientific content (Wessler, Wozniak, Hofer, Lück 2016; Grabe and Bucy 2009), we claim that it can be used to investigate political deepfakes as complex methods of textual and visual disinformation, because they employ frames that encode ideologies. As Coleman puts it, "visual framing is a prime site of ideological construction within news stories" (2010: 238). This is due to the fact that visuals are iconic, indexical (i.e. causally linked to the external world) and complement the syntactic explicitness of the verbal message. Therefore, they seem to be effective tools for articulating and framing ideological messages (Messaris and Abraham 2001: 220). At the same time, visual frames can create illusions and be misleading, which is the aspect we are interested in in this chapter. In fact, we claim that political deepfakes construct particular ideative patterns through which the realistic scenarios can be understood by audiences. This is to say that political deepfakes are performative in that they do not just represent but also constitute and coproduce (MacKenzie 2006) realities through visual symbols and other cues that can accentuate one aspect of the construed reality in order to advance a specific evaluation and understanding of that reality. In this sense, VFA helps to unveil the ideological constructs that are used to strategically frame specific topics, "like a picture frame that accentuates certain things, hides others, and borders off reality in a certain way" (Lindekilde 2014: 200). In other words, what we are interested in is unveiling how political deepfakes build (fake) realities, how these represented realities/scenarios are embedded in social practices (i.e. by means of what visual and textual/discursive strategies), and how they mediate authority and power. In fact, ideology is another focal issue in visual framing theory, especially in the investigation of media artefacts: to investigate frames in media "[..] is, at heart, an inquiry into the intent of their creators, and therefore, an ideological project" (Bock 2020).

Using the above mentioned methodological framework, the present study aims at addressing the following research questions:

RQ1. What frames appear in political deepfakes?

RQ2. How do visual and textual material construct the frames?

RQ3. What are the social implications and political functions of these frames?

Considering the scarce literature on VFA, this study mainly relies on the four level analysis of visual framing theorized by Rodriguez and Dimitrova (2011), which is a model that can be applied to any unit of analysis coming from any media material. At level 1, images are examined as denotative systems. Thus, frames are identified through the enumeration of objects and elements that are clearly shown. This is a descriptive level. Level 2 encompasses the editorial and design conventions as well as the stylistic conventions and technical transformations inherent in the visuals. At this level of analysis, the kinds of shots and angles are pointed out in light of their social meaning. For example, while "a close-up shot signifies intimacy, a medium shot signifies personal relationship, a full shot signifies social relationship and a long shot signifies context, scope and public distance" (Rodriguez and Dimitrova 2011: 55). Here social distance, modality and behaviour are examined. According to Hodge and Kress (1988: 124), modality "refers to the status, authority and reality of a message, or to its ontological status, or to its value as truth or fact." At level 3 of the analysis visuals are seen as connotative systems, which means that persons and objects in the visual are analysed as representing ideas and concepts attached to them. Frames are analysed through the identification of symbols which can be abstract, notably objects that embed symbolic values, or figurative common places, persons and things with symbolic value (Kress and van Leeuwen 2006). Level 4 of the analysis sees visuals as ideological representations and aims to unveil how images work as powerful instruments shaping realities and public consciousness.

4. Data collection

As for data collection, the analysis was conducted on a small sample of five verified political deepfakes in English. The videos were selected starting from the annotated media list of the "Just Joking" report (2021)[1] that analyses seventy cases of wide range deepfakes. The initial selection included a wider sample of political deepfakes featuring real-life politicians. However, since the videos circulated through major social media platforms, most of them were either flagged or removed. For this reason, retrieving the final sample was particularly challenging, as most of the selected material had become inaccessible due to updated policies against deepfakes. After conducting an advanced search on Google Search for video content, five deepfakes from the original list of videos were identified and downloaded (Tab. 1).

TABLE 1. LIST OF SELECTED DEEPFAKES

Identification code	Video description	Year of circulation
1	Donald Trump announces AIDS cure	2019
2	Boris Johnson endorsing Jeremy Corbyn for Prime Minister	2019
3	Jeremy Corbyn endorsing Boris Johnson for Prime Minister	2019
4	Joe Biden endorsing Donald Trump for President	2020
5	Nancy Pelosi stammers	2020

All videos circulated between 2019 and 2020 and feature popular politicians. Despite being a small sample, the videos cover a range of different types of deepfakes, including cheapfakes (#1), misleading video editing (#4), slowing (#5), and synthesized personas (#2 and #3). Based on their core content, the five videos can be divided into subcategories according to their different communicative functions.

Deepfake #1 features a synthetic version of Donald Trump announcing at a fake press conference that AIDS is over because

---

[1] The report is accessible online at https://cocreationstudio.mit.edu/just-joking/

he "fixed it". The communicative function of this video is to misinform. Deepfakes #2 and #3 were developed by Future Advocacy as part of an independent project highlighting the dangers of deepfakes for democracy. In these videos, two popular UK political leaders, Boris Johnson and Jeremy Corbyn, endorse each other despite being political opponents. In the first part of the videos, the politicians address the audience in ways that look and sound convincing; however, by the end of the videos, they unveil their true nature as deepfakes and advise the audiences to be particularly careful with political content circulating online. These videos pertain to the subcategory of educational deepfakes in that they serve an educational purpose. Despite their intended purpose, the videos were fragmented and circulated online by malicious actors on social media as authentic; I am therefore considering them here in their shortened versions as deepfakes meant to disinform. Deepfakes #4 and #5 feature US politicians Joe Biden and Nancy Pelosi. In both videos, the political actors speak at public arenas and either sound drunk (as in the case of Pelosi) or speak nonsense (as in the case of Joe Biden publicly endorsing Donald Trump by saying "we cannot, we cannot but re-elect Donald Trump"). In both cases, the videos were doctored to forge embarrassing scenes, with the ultimate intent to ridicule and damage the politicians' reputation by framing Pelosi as a drunk and Biden as too old to be president.

5. The four level analysis of deepfakes

For the purposes of the investigation, the four level analysis of visual framing devised by Rodriguez and Dimitrova (2011) was employed. At level 1 of the analysis, each video was first examined at the descriptive level in order to identify the most evident characteristics at the visual level, subdivided into the following categories: actor and setting. At level 2, I examined each deepfake for shots and angles, as well as visual frames indicating distance, modality and behaviour. I then turned to level 3 to consider symbols. For space constraints, the first three levels of analysis are represented in Tab. 2. Lastly, in level 4, I focused on the ideological meaning of the visual frames.

TABLE 2. ANALYSIS OF THE DEEPFAKES UNDER INVESTIGATION DIVIDED INTO THREE LEVELS

Identification code	Level 1	Level 2	Level 3
1	*Actor*: Former US president *Setting*: press conference	*Angle*: medium close/ low frontal *Distance*: close social *Modality*: high modality (Trump), low modality (background) *Behaviour*: personal language, demand gaze	*Symbols*: US flags; news banner, camera flash;
2	*Actor:* Boris Johson *Setting:* national address press conference from office	*Angle:* medium close/ low frontal *Distance*: close social *Behaviour:* personal language, demand gaze *Modality*: high modality	*Symbols*: UK flag
3	*Actor:* Jeremy Corbyn *Setting*: national address from private room with a window and curtains	*Angle:* medium close/ low frontal *Distance*: close social *Behaviour*: social language; demand gaze *Modality*: high modality (Corbyn), low modality (background)	*Symbols*: window and curtains
4	*Actor*: Joe Biden *Setting*: presidential campaign event	*Angle*: medium close/ high frontal *Distance:* medium social *Behaviour*: public language; offer gaze *Modality*: low modality	*Symbols*: N/A
5	*Actor*: Nancy Pelosi *Setting:* public conference	*Angle:* medium close/ high frontal *Distance*: medium social *Behaviour*: public language; offer gaze *Modality*: low modality	*Symbols:* N/A

All the videos, except #3, feature popular political actors addressing the audience at public events like press conferences and national addresses (#1 and #2); public conferences (#5); and presidential campaign events (#4). The analysis shows that the same angle is chosen to frame the actors from their waist up. The angle is used to signify the relations between the actor on screen and the audiences. In Hallidayan terms, it both suggests and creates different relations between the participants and the viewers, thus serving an interpersonal function. This is particularly relevant when it comes to deepfakes, since the degree of reliability that the deepfakes can establish also relies on their ability to construe a relationship with the viewers that is convincing. The actors in the deepfakes analysed are shown frontally, with the shot framing them from a close or medium distance that may be defined as 'social', i.e. a distance for business or social interaction that tends to be more formal than personal. In #1, #2 and #3 synthetic Trump, Johnson and Corbyn stare directly at the camera in a demanding position, sitting behind a podium or a desk (#1 and #2). Therefore, the camera angle infuses an aura of authority and respect. The low frontal angle makes them look imposing and credible. Conversely, in #4 and #5 the distance is medium social, because the actors do not engage directly with the viewers but seem rather objectified as if being observed without realizing it. In this case, the angle is high and tends to depict the actors as smaller and insignificant. The chosen angle and distance serve ideological purposes: besides determining the realization of specific interpersonal relationships, they also frame the actors and the message from an authoritative (#1, #2 and #3) or delegitimizing (#4 and #5) perspective.

In #1, #2 and #3 the actors are shown in sharper focus with saturated and differentiated colours. The actors' skin texture is shown in sharp detail, with wrinkles and imperfections fully visible. The visuals are therefore given high modality and higher reality value. However, in #1 and #3 the background is out of focus; in this case, while colour saturation is a marker of higher modality, the absence of a detailed background lowers modality, which creates a certain degree of inconsistency. Deepfake #2 presents higher modality than #1 and #3 because the background is detailed. Conversely, the resolution, colour saturation and brightness of #4 and #5 is lower. Nonetheless, lower modality in this case does not decrease credibility, in that the visual rhetoric is delegitimizing and the low modality, along with the high angle and the offer gaze, may indicate that the videos were recorded by amateurs rather than professionals, who captured a fragment of a public speech that was not meant to be circulated officially.

One relevant aspect to be taken into consideration is the verbal communication, and in particular how the textual and visual dimensions interact. Although the textual dimension is often overlooked in research on deepfakes, it can provide useful insights into the way deepfake creators manage to construe realistic fakery. According to Messaris and Abraham (2001), text and image frame one another with text highlighting certain elements of the imagery, and imagery drawing attention to particular aspects of the text. In all videos, conversational forms of political discourse are opted for as opposed to more formal, high political oratory. The conversationalisation of public discourse equates to "a simulation of conversational interaction in, for instance, institutional interviews or the way in which politicians address public audiences" (Fairclough and Mauranen 1998: 91). Conversational elements are manifested at the linguistic level through personal addresses and informal greetings, as well as through colloquialisms. The linguistic choices are particularly interesting here because they are instrumental in the articulation of the forgery. In creating deepfakes, language is, in fact, a powerful tool for reaching ideological aims, starting with the manipulation of authenticity. In other words, the way fake political actors speak in doctored videos is crucial to foster credibility. In #2, for instance, a fake Boris Johnson addresses the audience with the opening sentence "Hi folks, I am here with a very special message". While the formality of the setting (Johnson's office) stands in contrast with the conversational style of the speech, colloquialisms echo Johnson's rhetorical style. The same applies to the fake Trump's speech announcing that he has defeated AIDS in #1 ("I have tremendous news. Today I eradicated AIDS. It's done. I took care of it. It's all done folks"). In both cases, language serves the purpose of persuading the viewers into believing that the videos are real, since they recall the way both Trump and Johnson would normally address the public. In fact, as pointed out by Berinsky (2017), people are more likely to accept that messages are true if they perceive them as familiar. Exaggerations, repetitions and simple phrases are salient features of real Trump rhetoric, all re-produced in #1, with the sentences uttered in persuasive tones, typical of Donald Trumps' speaking style (Björkenstam and Grigonytė 2020). As pointed out by Shugerman (2018), among others, Trump's speech style equates to the level of an 8-year-old. Short words, simple vocabulary and a simple syntax characterise artificial Trump as well. Suffice it to notice how the video relies on a chain of short sentences reproducing the typical patterns of real Trump's communication. The use of contractions ("it's all done") reinforce the colloquial style of the artificial speech.

In #3, fake Corbyn appeals to emotionality to boost trustworthiness. The speaker's initial sentence ("Once upon a time I called for a kinder and gentler politics") recalls his representation in the press as a "long-time peace activist" (*The Guardian*, 11/09/15), thus staging consistency between what the audience is seeing on screen and what they may already know about Corbyn. In #4 and #5, the original speeches are authentic but doctored (either slowed down or cut and pasted). In Nancy Pelosi's video, the speaker appears to be stammering as if she was drunk. The slow-down effect applies to both the visual and the audio level, thus making the speaker not only sound but also appear fuzzy. The video seems legitimate because it relies on previous hoaxes targeting Pelosi. Since 2019, several false claims about Pelosi being intoxicated have circulated, ranging from out-of-context photos to manipulated videos that make her look drunk. The goal is to diminish her credibility and spread misinformation. Since this video refers to similar hoaxes on Pelosi, it automatically gains credibility. Here familiarity triggering reliability is activated both through the authentic but slowed down version of her speech and through the modality and angle employed. These elements convey the perception that the video was 'stolen', as secret material that was supposed to be censored but nevertheless circulated online. Similarly, Joe Biden's doctored clip showing the politician stammering and ultimately endorsing his opponent Donald Trump relies on the same previous hoaxes that gained him the nickname "sleepy Joe".

Much of the credibility of the deepfakes under investigation comes from the physical appearance of the political actors, especially in #1, #2 and #3. The synthetic versions of Donald Trump, Boris Johnson and Jeremy Corbyn wear their usual suits and neckties. Fake Donald Trump wears a red necktie paired with a white shirt and a blue suit. In the background, a number of US flags are visible although they look blurred, while the flashes of cameras contribute to building the realistic scenario of a real press conference. A UK flag is also visible in the background of Johnson's video.

TABLE 3. DESCRIPTIONS OF THE DEEPFAKES UNDER INVESTIGATION

Identification code	Video description
#1	Donald Trump stares directly at the camera in a commanding position, sitting behind a podium. He is wearing a red necktie paired with a white shirt and a blue suit. In the background, a number of US flags. A breaking news banner overlay is visible at the bottom of the screen announcing that "AIDS is over".
#2	Boris Johnson stares directly at the camera in a commanding position, sitting behind his desk. He is wearing a black suit and a red necktie. The Union flag is visible in the background, on the left.
#3	Jeremy Corbyn stares directly at the camera in a commanding position, speaking from what appears to be a private household, with a window and curtains visible in the background. He is wearing a blue suit and a red necktie.
#4	Joe Biden addresses a crowded audience. He is visible while speaking from a podium at a public event, probably during his presidential campaign. He is wearing a blue jacket and a light blue shirt. The quality of the clip is low as if it was recorded using a phone or an amateur camera.
#5	Nancy Pelosi is speaking at a public event. She is holding a microphone while sitting on a chair or a sofa. She is wearing a blue dress. The background is plain.

The flags can be read as a visual metaphor representing governmental authority, and convey an official aura to the video. Visual symbols are able to communicate social meaning and therefore are granted a high degree of saliency. Even when blurred in the background, the flags are easily recognizable. In both #1 and #2, red is the dominant colour and is given a relevant place by lighting and contrast. The flags in the background seem to frame the subject and direct the viewers towards an interpretation of the videos as conveying an official message, since flags metonymically represent the government, a sense of unity, responsibility and patriotic symbolism. Overall, the flags in #1 and #2 reinforce the construction of an authoritative frame. In #1, the presence of other symbols like the breaking news banner and the flash of the reporters taking photos of Donald Trump convey an idea of celebrity along with a sense of prominence and timeliness that add more complexity to the visual frames herein employed. In #3, the actor is framed as speaking from what appears to be a private household, with a window and curtains visible in the background. The curtains frame Corbyn by placing him at the centre as if he were on stage, thus conveying prominence to the speaker and directing the attention towards him. Prominence is also boosted by the demanding gaze and the low angle. The simple background conveys an idea of intimacy and authenticity, which frames fake Corbyn as real and honest. This is consistent with Corbyn's representation as an 'authentic' leader in the British Press during the 2017 UK general election campaign, when his claimed authenticity stood in contrast with Theresa May's alleged machine-like inauthenticity (Crace 2017). Therefore, #3 relies on previous representational material and shared perception of Corbyn in order to boost its own credibility. While in #1, #2 and #3 the setting is staged, in #4 and #5 the clip is taken from authentic footage, therefore the analysis of background and/or symbolic elements is not relevant to the identification of forged discursive frames.

At level 4 of the analysis, we try to point out the ideological standpoint underpinning the deepfakes under investigation in light of the elements that emerged from level 1, 2 and 3. In #1 and #2 the authoritative frame feeds an interpretation of the message as reliable, and a perception of the deepfake as credible because of its official aura. In #3 the authenticity frame is chosen strategically in order to foster trustworthiness. The linguistic and symbolic devices employed here (i.e. the language and visual symbols) serve a persuasive function that is manipulative. The recourse to colloquialisms emulating the language of the real-life politicians (#1 and #2), the presence of visual metaphors (#1, #2 and #3) as well as the choice of angle, modality and distance, lead the audience to draw misplaced conclusions about the credibility of the clip, and ultimately shape an interpretive texture that pushes the viewers towards accepting the reality they are seeing on screen. In #4 and #5, the frame is delegitimizing in that the actors are seen from a higher angle that ultimately diminishes their real-life role, flattening them morally and reducing them to ground level (Martin 1968). Consequently, given the chosen perspective, the viewer is given more power over the actors. In the last two cases, the ideological standpoint emerging from the adopted frame is one that pushes the viewers towards a perception of both Nancy Pelosi and Joe Biden as unfit for leadership, thus backing up the doctored manipulation of the audio. Overall, their institutional role is diminished because both apparently make inappropriate statements. Therefore, the delegitimizing frame reinforces the idea that the deepfake is credible. While all the analysed political deepfakes pursue credibility because they enforce truthfulness, the way the politicians are represented is different: in #1, #2 and #3 the actors are presented as authoritative or authentic; in #4 and #5, they are framed as unfit to govern. In all cases, they spread misinformation and construe realistic scenarios.

6. Conclusions

The present study focused on the analysis of a small sample of five political deepfakes, i.e. new kinds of synthetic realistic videos of politicians making forged or altered statements. Research on political deepfakes is recent and is still lacking studies that consider both how realistic scenarios are construed and the effects of deepfakes in the construction of reality. The study presented in this article was a first attempt to analyse political deepfakes through a discourse-analytical lens. A methodology combining VFA with Kress and van Leeuwen's theoretical framework for analysing visual communication (2006; 2001) was chosen for the purpose of the analysis, which aimed at unveiling how visual and textual material construct discursive frames along with the social implications and political functions of such frames.

The analysis confirmed that the deepfakes under investigation are intrinsically problematic because they feed disinformation with the ultimate intent of deceiving audiences and persuading viewers into believing that what they see is real. All the analysed deepfakes are based on likelihood both from a visual as well as a textual and, therefore, rhetorical level. The synthetic versions of Trump, Johnson and Corbyn, despite being forged, look realistic because of the rhetoric they use and because of their credible appearance. The doctored videos of Pelosi and Biden rely on previous hoaxes and disinformation circulating on the two politicians. The adopted frames of authority, authenticity and delegitimation show the political actors as either authoritative or authentic and therefore credible, or depict them as unable to govern because drunk or too old. In all cases, they serve the same social and political functions: persuading the audience into believing that what they are seeing is true. The ultimate aim is to disinform by circulating misleading information about the politicians, their reliability and political agendas. In this sense, the deepfakes under investigation do not simply represent reality. Instead, they construct and produce credible scenarios precisely because of their increasing ability to replicate typical linguistic and rhetorical features which, as a result, makes them more believable. In the wider landscape of visual disinformation political deepfakes risk to sow uncertainty and undermine confidence in leaderships and parties, with serious implications on public opinion.

References

AJDER, HENRY, PATRINI, GIORGIO, CAVALLI, FRANCESCO, CULLEN, LAURENCE, 2019, *The State of Deepfakes: Landscape, Threats, and Impact*, Deeptrace, Amsterdam.

BERINSKY, ADAM, 2017, "Rumors and Health Care Reform: Experiments in Political Misinformation", *British Journal of Political Science* 47 (2), pp. 241-262.

BJÖRKENSTAM, KRISTINA NILSSON, GRIGONYTĖ, GINTARĖ, 2020, "I Know Words, I Have the Best Words: Repetitions, Parallelisms, and Matters of (In)Coherence", in U. Schneider, M. Eitelmann (eds), *Linguistic Inquiries into Donald Trump's Language: From 'Fake News' to 'Tremendous Success'*, Bloomsbury Academic, London, pp. 41-61.

BOCK, MARY ANGELA, 2020, "Theorising Visual Framing: Contingency, Materiality and Ideology, *Visual Studies*, online at https://doi.org/10.10 80/1472586X.2020.1715244.

BROOKS, CATHERINE FRANCIS, 2021, "Popular Discourse Around Deepfakes and the Interdisciplinary Challenge of Fake Video Distribution", *Cyberpsychol Behav Soc Netw* 24 (3), pp. 159-163.

CAPISTRÁN JACOB BAÑUELOS, 2022, "Deepfake Evolution: Semantic Fields and Discursive Genres (2017-2021)", *ICONO 14, Revista de comunicación y tecnologías emergentes* 20 (1), online at https://icono14. net/files/articles/1773-EN/index.html.

CHADWICK, ANDREW, VACCARI, CRISTIAN, O'LOUGHLIN, BEN, 2018, "Do Tabloids Poison the Well of Social Media? Explaining Democratically Dysfunctional News Sharing", *New Media & Society* 20 (11), pp. 4255-4274.

CHESNEY, ROBERT, CITRON, DANIELLE KEATS, 2019, "Deep Fakes: A Looming Challenge for Privacy, Democracy, and National Security". *California Law Review* 107 (6), pp. 1753-1820.

CITRON, DANIELLE K., CHESNEY, ROBERT, 2019, "21st Century-style Truth Decay: Deepfakes and the Challenge for Privacy, Free Expression, and National Security", *Maryland Law Review* 78 (4), pp. 882-891.

COLEMAN, RENITA, 2010, "Framing the Pictures in Our Heads", in P. D'Angelo and J. A. Kuypers (eds), *Doing News Framing Analysis: Empirical and Theoretical Perspectives*, Routledge, New York, pp. 233-61.

COVER, ROB, HAW, ASHLEIGH, THOMPSON, JAY DANIEL, 2002, *Fake News in Digital Cultures: Technology, Populism and Digital Misinformation*, Emerald Publishing, Bingley.

CRACE, JOHN, 2017, *I, Maybot: The Rise and Fall*, Guardian Faber Publishing, London.

DOBBER, TOM, METOUI, NADIA, TRILLING, DAMIAN, HELBERGER, NATALI, DE VREESE, CLAES, 2020, "Do (Microtargeted) Deepfakes Have Real Effects on Political Attitudes?", *The International Journal of Press/Politics* 26 (1), pp. 69-91.

DOMKE, DAVID, PERLMUTTER, DAVID, SPRATT, MEG, 2002, 'The Primes of Our Times? An Examination of the "Power" of Visual Images', *Journalism* 3 (2), pp. 131-59.

DUNN, ANNE, 2006, "The Genres of Television", in H. Fulton, J. Murphet, R. Huisman, A. Dunn (eds), *Narrative and Media*, CUP, New York, pp. 125-139.

ENTMAN, ROBERT M., 1993, "Framing: Toward Clarification of a Fractured Paradigm." *Journal of Communication* 43 (4), pp. 51-58.

FAHMY, SHAHIRA, 2007, '"They Took It Down": Exploring Determinants of Visual Reporting in the Toppling of the Saddam Statue in National and International Newspapers', *Mass Communication & Society* 10 (2), pp. 143-170.

FAHMY, SHAHIRA, DAEKYUNG, KIM, 2008, "Picturing the Iraq War: Constructing the Image of War in the British and U.S. Press", *Gazette: International Communication Gazette*, 70 (6), pp. 443-462.

FAIRCLOUGH, NORMAN, MAURANEN, ANNA, 1998, "The Conversationalisation of Political Discourse. A Comparative View", *Belgian Journal of Linguistics* 11, pp. 89-119.

GOEL, SHARAD, ANDERSON, ASHTON, HOFMAN, JAKE, WATTS, DUNCAN J., 2015, "The Structural Virality of Online Diffusion", *Management Science* 62 (1), pp. 180-196.

GOODFELLOW, IAN, POUGET-ABADIE, JEAN, MIRZA, MEHDI, XU, BING, WARDE-FARLEY, DAVID, OZAIR, SHERJIL, COURVILLE, AARON, BENJIO, YOSHUA, 2014, "Generative Adversarial Nets", *Advances in Neural Information Processing Systems* 3, pp. 2672-2680.

GRABE MARIA, BUCY, ERIC, 2009, *Image Bite Politics: News and the Visual Framing of Elections*. OUP, Oxford.

GÜERA, DAVID, DELP, EDWARD J., 2018, "Deepfake Video Detection Using Recurrent Neural Networks", *IEEE 15th International Conference on Advanced Video and Signal Based Surveillance*.

HODGE, ROBERT, KRESS, GUNTHER, 1988, *Social Semiotics*, Polity Press, Cambridge.

JERIT, JENNIFER, YANGZI, ZHAO, 2020, "Political Misinformation", *Annual Review of Political Science* 23, pp. 77-94.

KALPOKAS, IGNAS, KALPOKIENE, JULIJA, 2022, *Deepfakes A Realistic Assessment of Potentials, Risks, and Policy Regulation*, Spinger, Cham.

KRESS, GUNTHER, VAN LEEUWEN, TEUN, 2001, *Multimodal Discourse: The Modes and Media of Contemporary Communication*, Arnold Publishers, London.

KRESS, GUNTHER, VAN LEEUWEN, TEUN, 2006, *Reading Images: The Grammar of Visual Design,* Routledge, London-New York.

LINDEKILDE, LASSE, 2014, "Discourse and Frame Analysis", in D. Della Porta (ed.), *Methodological Practices in Social Movement Research*, OUP, Oxford, pp. 195-227.

MACKENZIE, DONALD, 2006, *An Engine, not a Camera: How Financial Models Shape Markets*, MIT Press, Cambridge.

MARTIN, MARCEL, 1968, *Le Langage Cinématographique*, Editions du Cerf, Paris.

MESSARIS, PAUL, ABRAHAM, LINUS, 2001, "The Role of Images in Framing News Stories", in S. D. Reese, J. Gandy, A. E. Grant (eds), *Framing Public Life: Perspectives on Media and Our Understanding of the Social World*, Lawrence Erlbaum, Mahwah, pp. 215-26.

RODRIGUEZ, LULU, DIMITROVA, DANIELE V., 2011, "The Levels of Visual Framing", *Journal of Visual Literacy* 30 (1), pp. 48-65.

SHOEMAKER, PAMELA J., REESE, STEPHEN, 1996, *Mediating the Message: Theories of Influences on Mass Media Content*, New York, Longman.

SHUGERMAN, EMILY, 2018, "Trump Speaks at Level of 8-year-old, New Analysis Finds," *Independent*, January 9. Available online: https://www.independent.co.uk/news/world/americas/us-politics/trump-language-level-speaking-skills-age-eight-year-old-vocabulary-analysis-a8149926.html.

VACCARI, CRISTIAN, CHADWICK ANDREW, 2020, "Deepfakes and Disinformation: Exploring the Impact of Synthetic Political Video on Deception, Uncertainty, and Trust in News", *Media and Society*, pp. 1-13.

VAN HUIJSTEE, MARIËTTE, VAN BOHEEMEN, PIETER, DAS, DJURRE, 2021, "Tackling Deepfakes in European Policy" online at https://www.europarl.europa.eu/RegData/etudes/STUD/2021/690039/EPRS_STU(2021)690039_EN.pdf

WESSLER, HARMUT, WOZNIAK, ANTAL, HOFER, LUTZ, LÜCK, JULIA, 2016, "Global Multimodal News Frames on Climate Change: A Comparison of Five Democracies around the World", *The International Journal of Press/Politics* 21 (4), pp. 423-45.

WESTERLUND, MIKA, 2019, "The Emergence of Deepfake Technology: A Review", *Technology Innovation Management Review* 9 (11), pp. 39-52.

WINTER, RACHEL, SALTER, ANASTASIA, 2020, "DeepFakes: Uncovering Hardcore Open Source on GitHub", *Porn Studies* 7 (4), pp. 382-397.

YANG, XIN, LI, YUEZUN, LYU, SIWEI, 2019, "Exposing Deepfakes Using Inconsistent Head Poses", *IEEE International Conference on Acoustics, Speech and Signal Processing*, pp. 8261-8265.

Discursive Duelling
in International Criminal Justice:
Dialogical Framing in Opening
and Closing Statements
at the International Criminal Court

Jekaterina Nikitina

Abstract
The study explores dialogical framing as a story-telling device in two genres that stand on the margins of proceedings at the International Criminal Court: opening and closing statements. As these two genres are still relatively under-researched in linguistic literature, the study contributes to research in this area by outlining their generic features. By using Corpus-Assisted (Critical) Discourse Analysis, the study provides both qualitative and quantitative overview of the most prominent frames and interpretation suggestions across the two genres and across the main participants involved: the Prosecution, the Defence and the Legal Representatives of Victims. The findings identify a paradoxical combination of humanising and dehumanising (stereotypical) frames by the parties when depicting the Defendants or rebutting each other's story. The opening statements are characterised predominantly by event – and character-building frames, whereas the closing statements shift attention to the trial, dialogically delegitimising the opponents. The evidence suggests that instead of a tripartite model, the framing choices are indicative of an oppositional model: Defence vs. Prosecution and Victims' Representatives.

Key-words: dialogical framing, International Criminal Court, opening statements, closing statements, corpus-assisted discourse analysis.

1. Introduction

Dramatised television or cinema cases often depict opening and, especially, closing statements as the decisive moment for the trial, when the main character sways the jury through emotionally charged rhetoric. While real-life domestic proceedings predictably fall short of their on-screen portrayal, there is a grain of truth in this description if the criminal case is tried by an international court. The International Criminal Court (ICC), established in 2002 in

ISSN 1824-3967
© Carocci Editore S.p.A.
Textus 1-2023, pp. 113-134

The Hague, investigates and puts on trial individuals who allegedly committed "the gravest crimes of concern to the international community: genocide, war crimes, crimes against humanity and the crime of aggression" (ICC, https://www.icc-cpi.int/about/the-court[1]). The gravity of the crimes and the individual responsibility of the defendants creates the so-called "paradox of the inhuman human" (Stolk 2018: 696) perpetrator. In order to bear individual responsibility, defendants have to be portrayed as men. At the same time, detailed accounts of crimes – both by the Prosecution and the victims – amount to "a captivating tale of horror" (Stolk 2021: 3) that frequently frames the person allegedly responsible for such horrors as somewhat inhuman. The defendants are guaranteed procedural fairness and a voice in proceedings, transforming the trial into "a universe constructed in language" (Tallgren 2015: 138).

This study investigates the duelling construction of reality in the portrayal of defendants at the ICC in two genres that stand on the margins of the proceedings, yet take on a very important role in providing interpretation and making sense of the trial: opening and closing statements (see Section 2). Despite their importance in framing and re-framing the case, including their impact on providing interpretation to historically relevant events (Hassellind 2021), these genres have been largely neglected in the linguistic literature. To the best of my knowledge, no linguistic study so far has addressed the opening and closing statements at the ICC from a dialogical framing standpoint, and this study intends to fill the existing gap.

The research is informed by Entman's (1993) and Goffman's (1974) notion of framing understood here as the selection and foregrounding of certain aspects of reality to promote a particular view of the situation, its interpretation or evaluation. Specifically, the study relies on framing as communication in a heteroglossic context (Bakhtin 1981) (see Section 3) of duelling narratives in a corpus of opening and closing statements before the ICC, applying a combined methodological framework of Corpus Linguistics and (Critical) Discourse Analysis (Section 4). The findings are presented in Section 5 followed by concluding remarks in Section 6.

---

[1] Unless otherwise specified, all websites were last accessed on July 27, 2022.

2. Opening and closing statements

The ICC procedure is characterised by a "unique compromise" between civil and common law mechanisms (Schmitt 2021: 485). Similarly to common law criminal trials, the trial stage starts with opening statements and ends with closing statements. However, differently from the domestic settings, the trier of fact is a Chamber composed of professional judges and not jurors. Similarly to common law adversarial proceedings (see Chaemsaithong 2014, 2018 on the US context) and in contrast to civil law inquisitorial proceedings (see Du 2021 on China), all parties in the proceedings at the ICC are given an opportunity to address the Court in their opening and closing statements. The peculiarity of the ICC procedure is that besides the classical duelling parties – the Prosecution and the Defence – a third participant[2] is added: the Victims, acting through the so-called Legal Representatives of Victims[3]. Victims may choose their legal representatives in addition to the Office of Public Counsel for Victims (OPCV) at the ICC. The defendants, too, have the right to address the Court (Article 67(1)(h) of the Rome Statute)[4] during the opening and closing statements. As a consequence of multiple participants, the linguistic practice of opening and closing statements is frequently a duel or even a "truel"[5] of narratives.

Despite the obvious importance of these oral courtroom genres, there is still little linguistic research on this topic in international criminal trials, probably because they represent "a taken-for-granted practice, which is both overexposed and underexplored" (Stolk 2021: 3). *Closing statements*, also known as *closing arguments* (Hobbs 2003) or *closing speeches* (Schmid and Fiedler 1996) in national proceedings were previously analysed from a variety of standpoints: the heteroglossia and reported speech (Chaemsaithong 2014, 2017; Sneijder 2014; Chaemsaithong and Kim 2018), interpreter-mediation (Du 2021), representation, framing and genre (Felton

---

[2] Victims are recognised as participants but not as parties (Rome Statute, Article 68(3)).
[3] See Wheeler 2016 on the impact of victim participation.
[4] See also D'Hondt 2021 on the integration of the defendant's apologies.
[5] The neologism "truel" stands for a three-way duel and has been taken from game theory (Kilgour and Brams 1997).

Rosulek 2015), and use of rhetoric for persuasion purposes (Hobbs 2003). As concerns studies on closing statements in international trials, Schmid and Fiedler (1996) should be mentioned for attributions in the Nuremberg trial. In this study, the term "closing statement" is preferred to "closing argument" to reflect the ICC terminology. There is less research on *opening statements*. To the best of my knowledge the only studies on opening statements at the ICC belong to Stolk (2017, 2018, 2021). Other, limited, research analyses opening statements in domestic settings: Chaemsaithong (2018) on the opening statements in Michael Jackson's 2005 trial, Chaemsaithong and Kim (2018) on the same trial comparing the use of reported speech in opening and closing statements. When addressed, opening statements are typically analysed from a legal perspective in terms of what effect they might have on the jurors (Spiecker and Worthington 2003) and for their pedagogical potential / story-telling training (Powell 2001).

The two genres are rather similar in that both are "extended monologues that bracket" (Hobbs 2003: 273) the presentation of testimonial evidence, and the speakers have complete control over their discursive construction. Both are intertextual, and both reanimate multiple voices (Bakhtin 1981; see Section 3), frequently through segments of speech of other authors. Both are specifically directed at the Chambers (or jurors in a domestic context), in contrast to the so-called "display talk" (Goffman 1981) of witness examinations, where counsel, despite addressing witnesses, plan their conversations to be overheard by the trier of fact. Opening and closing statements exhibit "generic homogeneity" (van Leeuwen 2008: 4) in terms of form, structure, and linguistic patterns, also because the regulations on "what is relevant and possible are formally policed and externally controlled. Non-compliance can have significant real-world consequences" (Felton Rosulek 2015: 38). However, their communicative purpose differs. Opening statements outline the facts and are intended to be informative, rather than argumentative (Chaemsaithong 2017: 2), allowing the parties to describe "the personality of the defendant rather than merely focusing on his deeds" (Stolk 2018: 677). In contrast, closing statements or arguments, as the name suggests, can be argumentative. They may vary in structure because lawyers may construct their arguments differently (Felton Rosulek 2015: 4). Courtroom advocacy manuals and trainings typically list several moves for opening and closing statements that are summarised in Table 1 (based on Hobbs 2003; Mauet 2009; American Bar Association 2015, 2017[6]; Stolk 2018).

TABLE 1. GENERIC STRUCTURE OF OPENING AND CLOSING STATEMENTS

Opening statements	Closing statements
Importance of trial and tribunal	Importance of trial and tribunal
Introduce the characters and personality	Describe the characters
Introduce a plot summary (story-telling, theme foregrounding; "crime story" (Heffer 2005))	Weave evidentiary inferences into your plot summary (story-telling, theme foregrounding; "trial story" (Heffer 2005))
Preview of what the evidence will show (no inferences allowed)	Comment on the credibility of evidence/ witnesses (contradict the opponent)
State the expected (desirable) outcome	Argue why the trier of fact should decide in your favour

As emerges, the generic structure of these two oral genres is mirror-like and the main difference concerns the balance between persuasion and argumentation. Trial manuals advise counsel to focus on a number of themes or claims to develop, using story-telling and figurative language, which can be successfully addressed through framing (Section 3). The American Bar Association (2015) recommends lawyers to "assemble facts persuasively" in opening statements, leaving to the lawyer's discretion whether to introduce "bad facts" or not, whereas for closing arguments the recommendation is to "tackle any unfavorable facts head-on" (ABA 2017). According to Heffer (2005), the story told in opening statements is a "crime story" referring to the events discussed, but it transforms into a "trial story" in closing statements, combining the event narratives with trial-based developments and projections (Felton Rosulek 2015: 6). In an international arena, both genres are supplemented by the first move: highlighting the importance /

---

[6] These sources refer to adversarial context; however as the ICC Judge Schmitt notes (2021: 490), most trial lawyers in the ICC were trained in the common law tradition, so it is reasonable to expect that they transfer knowledge structures typical of their original community of practice.

legitimacy of the trial and the court, which is particularly relevant for the ICC as a relatively young court[7]. Opinions on such topics as credibility, guilt/innocence, or the magnitude/importance of the evidence are considered ethically dubious (Felton Rosulek 2015: 5; cf. Bacigal 2014), yet these are highly recurrent in closing statements.

3. Dialogical framing

In opening and closing statements, discourse and reality are interactively shaped, negotiated and co-constructed (Chaemsaithong 2018) by different participants to create meaning (Felton Rosulek 2015: 39). The transformation of reality into discourse occurs through an inevitable set of interpretative *frames* allowing the participants to "locate, perceive, identify, and label" (Goffman 1974: 21) elements of reality that are reflected in discourse. This study relies on Entman's re-elaboration of Goffman's (1974) idea of framing that aims to "select some aspects of a perceived reality and make them more salient in a communicating text, in such a way as to promote a particular problem definition, causal interpretation, moral evaluation, and/or treatment recommendation" (Entman 1993: 52). In a trial, by selecting or excluding, emphasising or de-emphasising some elements in discourse (see, e.g. the mention of "bad facts" discussed in Section 2), participants create "a representation but not a perfect re-creation of the original" (Felton Rosulek 2015: 40) that fits best into their story. To wit, this study uses the paradigm of framing as communication and story-telling by different participants in the context of international criminal trials.

There is no dearth of research highlighting the narrative quality of courtroom discourse (Powell 2001; Felton Rosulek 2015; Chaemsaithong 2018; Stolk 2021) and its plurality of voices (Garzone and Degano 2012; Chaemsaithong 2014, 2018; Felton Rosulek 2015; Garzone 2016; Etxabe 2022), which lead to different framing options, or "themes" in lawyers' terms (see Section 2). Multiple voices incorporated in monologues are conceptualised here following Bakhtinian notions. For Bakhtin *raznorečie*, or *heteroglossia* reflects the non-unitary nature of language comprising a plurality of views, ideas, generations, professions, etc. (Bakhtin 1981: 288).

---

[7] See Stolk 2018: 680 on opening statements; this corpus for closing statements.

In Bakhtinian dialogism "every word is directed toward an answer and cannot escape the profound influence of the answering word that it anticipates" (Bakhtin 1981: 280), which becomes particularly relevant for an exchange of opening / closing statements and a potential evolution of framing between the opening and the closing statement stage, which takes account of the story transformation from a "crime story" into a "trial story" (Heffer 2005), as the findings will demonstrate.

4. Materials

This study examines a corpus of opening and closing statements in the ICC featuring three defendants: Thomas Lubanga Dyilo (ICC-01/04-01/06), Germain Katanga (ICC-01/04-01/07) and Mathieu Ngudjolo Chui (ICC-01/04-02/12). The cases were chosen on the basis of their closed status[8] and in relation to the verdict: one defendant was acquitted (Ngudjolo Chui) and two were convicted (Katanga and Lubanga). Katanga's and Ngudjolo Chui's cases were joined, so where possible I separated the statements by the defendant involved (e.g. the defence statements) but in some cases the same statement refers to both defendants (in italics in Table 2). There are fourteen texts altogether, totalling 146,066 tokens.

Before proceeding with the analysis, a brief description of the cases is needed. The cases refer to internal and international conflicts involving the Democratic Republic of Congo, where the defendants were (alleged) leaders of local militias (Lubanga: *Union des Patriotes Congolais/Forces Patriotiques pour la Libération du Congo* (UPC/FPLC) composed of the Hema ethnicity; Katanga: *Force de résistance patriotique en Ituri (FRPI)* composed of the Ngiti; Ngudjolo Chui: *Front des Nationalistes et Intégrationnistes* (FNI), Lendu tribes) engaged in fight against or along with each other. They were tried for war crimes and crimes against humanity in the context of "a massive international conflict in which nine states were involved and resulted in the deaths of approximately four million people between 1998 and 2004" (International Justice Monitor 2011, https://www.ijmonitor.org/2011/03/prosecution-

---

[8] Cases that are not closed are frequently heavily redacted, which makes linguistic analysis challenging.

opening-statement/). Even though all events on trial happened on the
territory of Congo, different parties offered divergent classification
of conflict – international vs. national – as these categories envisage
different legal consequences. Lubanga was convicted for "war crimes of
enlisting and conscripting children under the age of 15 years and using
them to participate actively in hostilities" described above (ICC, https://
www.icc-cpi.int/drc/lubanga). Katanga was convicted "as an accessory,
of one count of crime against humanity: murder; and four counts of war
crimes: murder, attacking a civilian population, destruction of property
and pillaging, committed on 24 February 2003 during the attack on
the village of Bogoro, in the Ituri district of the DRC" (ICC, https://
www.icc-cpi.int/drc/katanga). Ngudjolo Chui (acquitted) was initially
charged with "three crimes against humanity and seven war crimes
allegedly committed on 24 February 2003 during an attack against the
Bogoro village in the Ituri district of the DRC" (the same attack as
Katanga) (ICC, https://www.icc-cpi.int/drc/ngudjolo).

TABLE 2. CORPUS COMPOSITION

Defendant	Opening statements	Closing statements
Lubanga Prosecution	7,401	11,565
Lubanga Defence	7,995	11,913
Lubanga Legal Representatives of Victims	8,477	8,887
Katanga and Ngudjolo Prosecution	*5,173*	*20,768*
Katanga Defence	2,044	22,679
Ngudjolo Defence	5,172	18,504
Katanga and Ngudjolo Legal Representatives of Victims	*2,869*	*12,619*
Total	39,131	106,935

The statements were downloaded from the ICC website
(Transcripts), using the English version of the transcript, and
converted into a .txt format. Any bracketing text (e.g. Court usher's
introduction, Judges' address, line numbering, case number, etc)
was eliminated, leaving only the statement. The analysis began with
a first "unassisted" reading, combined with the time-consuming
text preparation described above. Critical Discourse Analysis

(van Leeuwen 2008) zooms into power relations inherent in discourse, and courtroom interactions represent a privileged arena to study such a power battle, which frequently transforms into a story-telling tug of war (Heffer 2005). At the ICC internationally significant events are reconstructed in discourse, bringing to life various characters and events through their linguistic description in a frequently "hyperbolic, self-legitimising narrative" (Stolk 2018: 681) of the international criminal law, which makes it particularly suitable for the analysis using critical discourse and framing toolkit.

The initial critical reading allowed me to identify macro-frames. This stage was followed by corpus-assisted discourse analytical procedures (Baker et al. 2008; Partington et al. 2004), exploiting the synergy between critical discourse analysis and corpus linguistics software #LancsBox 6.0 (Brezina et al. 2020). The software was used to verify and quantify relevant lexicogrammatical items that function as frames across the two genres (opening vs. closing statements) and as used by different actors (defence vs prosecution vs victims' representatives). Table 2 shows that opening statements (OS) were on average 3.9 times shorter than closing statements (CS), with two exceptions: in Lubanga's case victims' OS and CS were almost the same length, whereas Katanga's defence OS were 11 times shorter. As the number of tokens differed across texts, a normalization base of 10,000 tokens was introduced to render all quantitative data comparable.

5. Findings

Not every text has sections that straightforwardly describe the personality of the defendant. It would be naïve to expect ready-to-use portrayals, and this is not the aim of the study. The analysis of the defendants' personality framing includes both explicit characterisations and implicit background description of events and other participants that by extension also frame the defendants. Given the complexity of materials, the findings are organised by the framing party around two macro-frames – humanity and inhumanity, which are not always placed in an oppositional relationship but at times coexist in the same genre by the same actor. The quantitative data – which are not reproduced in their entirety for reasons of space limitations – include lexical items that function as frames (e.g.

"control*"[9], "leader", "military") and lexicogrammatical features that perform framing (e.g. mood adjuncts "merely", "clearly", "oddly enough", "in reality", antithetical, negative and concessive syntactic structures, etc), and are categorised, grouped and calculated using MS Excel spreadsheets. All lexical and lexicogrammatical items were checked in the context using the concordances to avoid reporting words but not meanings.

5.1. Prosecution's statements

As Stolk (2018: 696) observes, criminal trials "are designed to hold a human being to account and aspire to influence future human behaviour" and hence foregrounding human framing of the defendant becomes a matter of accountability. The Prosecutors expectedly emphasised elements of the defendants' humanity (negative character sketches such as a deceitful or power-hungry nature, intelligence and violence, etc), as well as provided implied characterisation through the defendant's actions. Character sketching with explicit description of character traits was more prominent in the opening than in the closing statements (Table 3), which shows how opening statements prepare the audience for the coming trial by providing an interpretation key.

TABLE 3. MAIN HUMANISING FRAMES IN THE PROSECUTION STATEMENTS

Defendant / Frame	Opening statements (NF)	Closing statements (NF)
Lubanga Prosecution		
Military leader in control	339	397
Power lust and ambition	85	–
Educated and knowledgeable	31	42 (knowledge)
Deceitful and unscrupulous	32	27 (cover up)
Opportunist	23	–
Katanga and Ngudjolo Prosecution		
Military leaders in control	383	291
Common plan	95	54
Courageous (Katanga)	–	4
Total humanising frames	988	815

[9] The asterisk allows retrieval of all word forms of "control", such as "controlling", "controlled", etc, as it replaces any letter combination.

For instance, in Lubanga's case, the Prosecutor framed the defendant as an educated (1), power-hungry (2), double-faced ((3), note the parallel antithetical structure) opportunist (2).

(1) Lubanga is *an educated man*; in 1985 he *graduated in psychology* from the University of Kisangani [Lubanga Prosecution OS]

(2) Lubanga, *an educated Hema leader*, at that time a minor member of the Ituri Assembly, *saw his chance*. [...] He *impressed* Ugandan officials and *started to develop the idea to create a political party*. [...] Lubanga *took advantage of the situation*. [...] In sum, *Lubanga used the opportunity* of the Hema mutiny *to establish a political alliance* with Ugandan officials and to build within the Rassemblement Congolais *an army loyal to him only*. [Lubanga Prosecution OS]

(3) He announced programs of pacification *and he* was sending his troops to kill all the Lendus *at the same time*. He promised to demobilise the child soldiers *and he* was recruiting them *at the same time*. [Lubanga Prosecution OS]

(4) The execution of the attack showed the *common plan*. The weapons *previously distributed* were used, the combatant's movements were *coordinated* and the village was *surrounded*. There was *perfect synchronization*. [Katanga and Ngudjolo Prosecution OS]

By highlighting the defendant's education in psychology, the Prosecutor emphasises that the choice to enlist child soldiers was a conscious choice of a despicable man who knew that children are "fearless", "loyal" and "easier and more convenient to use" (Lubanga Prosecution CS). Not only is Lubanga charged with specific crimes, but he is also framed as a manipulative person who systematically lies and betrays even his own kind exploiting his intelligence to pursue power by any means. In Katanga and Ngudjolo's case the main humanising frame was that of military leaders who planned the attack (4); however, in contrast to Lubanga's case, humanising character sketching was quite scant giving more space to dehumanising frames (see Table 4). The system of discipline and punishment portrayed Katanga and Ngudjolo as effective heads of their militias. In addition, in closing statements, the prosecution added a characterisation of Katanga as courageous and active on the field as it served the purpose of explaining his fast promotion to the position of leader.

In Lubanga's case the character-building frames disappeared in closing statements or evolved. The "educated man" frame evolved into a "knowledge and intention" frame and the double-facedness transformed into a specific and more legally oriented framing of child soldier demobilisation decrees as fake, sham or cover-up (5). In other words, the characterising frame was transformed into a legally-oriented argument in the closing statements.

> (5) We submit that these demobilisation decrees *were used as a cover-up* for the crimes that were being committed […]. […] an NGO worker, in describing the demobilisation attempts at that period said that the UPC/FPLC were *simply pretending* to demobilise. They were, as he said, *a sham* [Lubanga Prosecution CS].
>
> (6) The following documents […] show that there was *continuity in Katanga's work, in Katanga's position*. Letter […] *to the president of the FRPI* in Bolo is written to *Katanga* pointing out issues relating to taxes on the purchase of gold. Any such letter to such *a president* was confirmation that he was indeed *president* […].
>
> (7) The Defence claims that Mathieu Ngudjolo must be acquitted because the Prosecution failed to prove that his group was called the FNI. […] The Prosecution has proven that the group of which Mathieu Ngudjolo *was a commander, or the commander*, did indeed participate in the Bogoro attack. Beyond the name, we are dealing here with *the same people, the same group, the same troops*, whether it was the FNI or not. It was *Ngudjolo's combatants* who were in Bogoro on 24 February 2003 and this issue of name alone cannot bring about the acquittal of the accused.

In Katanga and Ngudjolo's case the main humanising frames deployed by the Prosecution remained the same in the opening and closing statements, i.e. the defendants as military leaders who planned the attack, who can interrupt other commanders, whose orders are executed automatically, who are respected by their organised and well-structured troops. Examples (6) and (7) show how the Prosecution answers to the Defence teams' submissions contesting the role of leaders, based on the terminology employed: commander and president. They provide arguments that help them reframe the defendants as effective leaders of the militia, which in practical terms translates into an issue of accountability.

The emphasis on a highly effective and obedient military structure points out the inhumanity of the Defendants as people who ordered child soldier enlistment, allowed sexual slavery or planned the attack which led to "unspeakable" atrocities, looting, pillaging, killings, rapes. In other words, it was their will that the crimes were committed. Table 4 gathers the main dehumanising frames in the Prosecution's statements. While dehumanising frames were numerically inferior (OS = 707; CS = 354; total = 1,061) than humanising frames (OS = 988; CS = 815; total = 1,803) they served an important communicative purpose.

TABLE 4. MAIN DEHUMANISING FRAMES IN THE PROSECUTION STATEMENTS

Defendant / Frame	Opening statements (NF)	Closing statements (NF)
Lubanga Prosecution		
Stolen childhood	–	86
Training as abuse	136	59
Sexual violence on girls	70	24
Militia as a forced replacement for family	76	–
Katanga and Ngudjolo Prosecution		
Cold-hearted	6	12
Vengeance and hatred	4	15
Extermination	159	45
Brutality and hunting	135	26
Sexual violence	79	78
Looting and pillaging	39	9
Total dehumanising frames	704	354

Katanga and Ngudjolo were portrayed as cold-hearted and ruthless people who not only ignored, but celebrated intentional killing (8; 9), giving their soldiers "carte blanche" to "raze down" or "wipe out" Bogoro. Whereas the opening statement focussed on the frames of extermination, brutal animal-like killings and sexual violence, the closing statements added the frame of ethnic hatred and vengeance to the mix as motives that could be interpreted as both humanising and dehumanising, again activating the argumentation inherent in the closing statements.

(8) [...] Once the objective of *wiping out* Bogoro was successful, Ngudjolo and Katanga met up with *other commanders* of the FNI and the FRPI at the village centre. It was possible to *see dead bodies of civilians*. The commanders and fighters of the FNI and FRPI

celebrated victory in the shadows – *in the shade of the mango trees while the massacres and pillaging continued.* This attack *wiped out* Bogoro from the map. [Katanga and Ngudjolo Prosecution OS]

(9) Ngudjolo and Katanga *seated under mango trees* at the intersection next to the Bogoro institute to receive reports about the fighting, *to jubilate and relax.* [...] Ngudjolo *ordered the burial of the bodies for hygienic reasons*, and this is highly indicative of the truth. Ngudjolo with his *training as a nurse* in Bunia *wanted to avoid an epidemic.* This is not a detail that can simply be made up. [Katanga and Ngudjolo Prosecution CS]

(10) They described how *civilians were systematically targeted and brutally killed*; some *burnt alive* as their houses were *set on fire*; how *babies were thrown against the wall*; how *women were raped*; how the *village was wiped out and destroyed.* [Katanga and Ngudjolo Prosecution CS]

The cold-hearted frame emerges particularly in the closing statements in contrast to the inhuman cruelty of the plan to "wipe out" the entire village and exterminate everyone and everything (10). Example (9) dialogically reframes the main humanising trait used by Ngudjolo's defence (see 5.2), i.e. that Ngudjolo was a nurse, incorporating it into an argument based on his cold-hearted character: his training as a nurse helped him dispose of corpses in an efficient manner.

5.2. Defence statements

The Defence, understandably, counteracted the negative framing by systematically silencing the military leader frame and foregrounding their main humanising positive traits (Table 5) that were dialogically incompatible with the framing of the prosecution, e.g. the defendant's age (Katanga was only 24) or profession (Ngudjolo was a nurse; Lubanga was a political leader), see (13). A common scapegoating frame emerged in all three cases, along with accusations of bad prosecution and lying witnesses activated in the "trial story" (Heffer 2005) of the closing statements (marked by * in Table 5, 60% of frames in CS). Stereotypical framing based on a logical juxtaposition INEXPERIENCED NON-MILITARY PERSON vs. WAR CONTEXT was a common defence strategy in all three cases, besides paradoxically replacing the INTERETHNIC HATRED frame with WAR.

TABLE 5. MAIN HUMANISING FRAMES IN THE DEFENCE STATEMENTS

Defendant / Frame	Opening statements (NF)	Closing statements (NF)
Lubanga Defence		
Victims as second prosecutor*	24	–
Bad Prosecution*	56	24
Non-transparent trial*	63	8
Political leader	9	34
Scapegoating	36	32
Lying victims*	–	76
Negligent Prosecution*	–	61
Katanga Defence		
Inexperienced young man	64	17 (no military)
Conflict as excesses	29	12 (war not ethnic)
Untrained local resistance (Ngiti = good people)	34	17
Other powerful aggressors	44	43
Sophisticated operation / camp as a fortress	64	16
Lying witnesses / credibility*	–	82
Bad prosecution*	–	33
Ngudjolo Defence		
Not involved/ scapegoat	17	9
Nurse	-	14
Untrained local resistance (against Lendu genocide)	62	–
Other powerful aggressors	166	64
War, not interethnic conflict		32
Lying witnesses / credibility*	–	51
Bad prosecution*	14	84
Victims as second prosecutor*		9
Total dehumanising frames	62	–
Total humanising frames	432	718
Total "crime story" frames	337 (68%)	290 (40%)
Total "trial story" frames	157 (32%)	428 (60%)

(11) Why has *the Prosecutor targeted* Thomas Lubanga for this first trial? There is *no lack of suspects* of war crimes and crimes against humanity between Kinshasa and Kampala. Madam Prosecutor, *you know better* than anyone. [...] Those who have sowed chaos and

have manipulated hate, armed militias, organised massacres, and *turned to their benefit all of it.* [Lubanga Defence, OS]

(12) In 2003, *at age 24,* was Germain Katanga *so gifted in the arts of war* as to be able to plan a successful attack on an entrenched and trained military position such as existed at Bogoro? *Rather surprising, if that was the case.* So who did do the planning? There are stones here that the Prosecutor – whose duty it is, of course, to search out exculpatory material, *stones that have not been turned.* [Katanga Defence OS]

(13) This was not either a plan that had been hatched by *a 24-year-old young man still at school,* Germain Katanga, with *some skills in hunting,* and Mathieu Ngudjolo who was essentially, whatever else, *a maternity nurse.* [Katanga Defence CS]

(14) [...] the Prosecutor left us all in *utter darkness, darkness, concealing* his utter inability to make his case beyond all reasonable doubt. [...] the Prosecutor's investigation is *nothing more than a cocktail of bad choices.* [Ngudjolo Defence CS]

Lubanga's Defence accused the Prosecution of misconduct and framed the trial as lacking transparency, a "smokescreen", "secretive", "carefully redacted", with many "anonymous" sources, thus challenging the legitimacy of proceedings. Similarly, Ngudjolo's defence framed the Prosecution's work through metaphors of darkness, opacity, silence, "harassment", "glaring absence" and "a cocktail of bad choices" (14). In addition to an open confrontation between the Defence and the Prosecution, Victims' Representatives were framed as a second prosecutor undermining the fairness of proceedings, and victims were portrayed as unreliable and lying. As emerges, most rebuttal frames are based on procedural matters, confirming the difference between the "crime story" of the opening statements (68% of frames) and the "trial story" of the closing statements (60% of frames) that shifted attention to the reality of proceedings.

Whereas most Defences' frames were humanising, they still engaged in producing "conflated, stereotypical depictions" (Stolk 2018: 680) of the dehumanised Other, especially when shifting the blame to a stereotypical evil (11; 15), be it "rapacious" and "ferocious" Uganda and Rwanda or the Kinshasa government and unnamed western power players, which was recurrent in Ngudjolo's Defence OS (NF = 62).

(15)   The Lendu were *systematically massacred* by the Hema and the Ugandans. Everything seems to point towards a true desire to commit *genocide.*[...] What were the Lendu to do while this happened, stand by and do nothing as they were being *killed, exterminated?* Allow their tribe and their people to be *slaughtered?* [Ngudjolo Defence OS]

(16)   The attack on 24 February, therefore, was *not the picture painted by the Prosecution of a powerful warlord*, Germain Katanga, falling on the village of Bogoro *like the wolf on the fold to slake his thirst for ethnic revenge*. There were far more *powerful interests* being served and at work and essentially in control than he. [Katanga Defence CS]

Alternatively, dehumanising frames used by the Prosecution (see, e.g. animal-like portrayal in (16)) were rejected. While explicitly attributing the frame to the opponent, who was also previously subtly discredited, the Defence counsel re-contextualised and delegitimised such frames, placing them next to a favourable to their case frame.

5.3. Victims' statements

The Victims' representatives narrated of unspeakable events marked by victims' suffering, incorporating a multitude of voices and focussing on the crime story (OS = 99%; CS = 97%). By ascribing the responsibility for atrocities to the men on trial ("man who is responsible"), the latter were dehumanised as transcendental evil capable of such crimes. In the closing statements, either a more detailed legal classification emerged (e.g. framing of the conflict as both international with foreign powers, and interethnic fuelled by hatred in Katanga and Ngudjolo's case) or a characterisation of the defendant emerged (in Lubanga's case), see Table 6, which differentiated Victims' statements from those of the Prosecution and the Defence that tended to sketch the Defendant's personality in the opening statements.

In general, dehumanising frames (NF = 1452) prevailed over humanising depictions (NF = 232), with a slight tendency to increase the number of humanising frames in the closing statements, probably, to reinforce the perception of accountability.

TABLE 6. MAIN FRAMES IN THE VICTIMS' STATEMENTS

Defendant / Frame	Opening statements (NF)	Closing statements (NF)
Lubanga Victims' Representatives		
Stolen childhood	100	115
Suffering and fear	121	56
Sexual violence on girls	115	34
Weaponising children	134	170
Broken life / time bomb	50	12
Lubanga as a demi-god	-	17
Lubanga as a powerful military leader	-	*16*
Katanga and Ngudjolo Victims' Representatives		
Stolen childhood	115	49
Suffering and losses	139	7
Extermination and atrocities	70	(interethnic conflict)
Weaponising children	35	–
Warlords and other powerful aggressors	*56*	*(international and interethnic)*
*Not a second prosecutor, Trial as a truth-finding process**	*10*	*22*
Military structures	–	*101*
External powerful aggressors (international conflict)		*37*
Interethnic internal conflict		113
Total dehumanising frames	879	573
Total humanising frames	66	176
Total "crime story" frames	935 (99%)	727 (97%)
Total "trial story" frames	10 (1%)	22 (3%)

(17) For the Defence he was first and foremost someone who took up arms, I quote, "to resist oppression". Our clients have *never known Thomas Lubanga as a human rights activist*. [Lubanga Victims CS]

(18) *Papa Lubanga*, as they referred to him, was some *sort of a semi-god whose praise was chanted* during training [...].

Remarkably, in Lubanga's case both humanising (17) and dehumanising (18) character-building frames were added in the closing statements. By using sarcasm, the Representative dialogically rebutted the Defence's portrayal of Lubanga as "a human rights activist" foregrounding his deceitful and power-hungry nature instead. To counteract accusations of witness unreliability, the Representative activated the mystical frame depicting "Papa Lubanga" as an influential and charismatic being, "a semi-god", whose very physical presence affected the witnesses.

6. Final remarks

The context of international criminal trials proved to be a fertile ground for the promotion of stereotypical frames, which – to the extent of my limited corpus – seemed to be quite transversal. The Prosecutors and the Victims brought to life a picture of an "ideal perpetrator" (Stolk 2018: 678) through a paradoxical combination of humanising (despicable, deceitful, power-hungry, opportunist) and dehumanising frames (animal brutality, extermination, mystical influence, etc), recreating the real person present in the courtroom through discourse in an ideologically skewed way, which legitimised the very existence of the ICC. The Defence teams vehemently opposed such framing and foregrounded non-military humanising frames, and offered even more stereotypical framing (young as inexperienced, a nurse as unable to plan an attack, any inconsistency as a lie). Humanising frames were the most prominent in the Prosecutions statements (NF = 1,803) and the least frequent in the Victims' statements (NF = 242); expectedly, dehumanising frames peaked in the Victims' statements (NF = 1,452). The frames evolved dialogically with the unravelling of proceedings even within statements by the same party who often chose to emphasise the frames that best fit their final argument, using framing as a key semiotic resource for discursive reconstruction and negotiation of reality.

The study contributed to the description of opening and closing statements in international criminal trials in a comparative perspective adopting the frame paradigm. The opening statements are characterised by narrative event – and character-oriented frames, painting a broad-brush sketch of what Heffer (2005) called the "crime story". The framing choices mutate towards the closing statements to trigger legal argument schemata and become increasingly opponent-discrediting, shifting to the "trial story" (Heffer 2005) rhetoric that peaked especially in the Defence closing statements (22% of frames). The evidence suggests that the Defence teams perceive the Legal Representatives of

Victims as their opponents, similarly to the Prosecution, as the amount of delegitimising frames referred to them is comparable, making the reality construction a duel, rather than a truel. As the trials analysed were among the first at the ICC when the system with victims' participation was an absolute novelty in international criminal justice, it would be interesting to analyse the development of this tripartite system from a diachronic perspective. Finally, as the cases heard by the ICC are high-profile and subject to reverberations in mass media, future research could develop in a cross-generic direction exploring if and how framing choices adopted by different participants are echoed, changed or silenced in news discourse.

References

AMERICAN BAR ASSOCIATION (ABA), 2015, "5 tips for engaging opening statements". Available at https://www.americanbar.org/groups/ litigation/committees/trial-practice/practice/2015/5-tips-for-engaging-opening-statements/, last accessed July 27, 2022.

AMERICAN BAR ASSOCIATION (ABA), 2017, "10 tips for effective opening and closing arguments". Available at HTTPS://WWW.AMERICANBAR. ORG/NEWS/ABANEWS/PUBLICATIONS/YOURABA/2017/JULY-2017/10-TIPS-FOR-EFFECTIVE-OPENING-AND-CLOSING-ARGUMENTS/, last accessed July 27, 2022.

BACIGAL, RONALD, 2014, *Criminal Law and Procedure: An Overview* (4th ed.), Delmar Cengage Learning Clifton Park, NY.

BAKER, PAUL, GABRIELATOS, COSTAS, KHOSRAVINIK, MAJID, KRZYŻANOWSKI, MICHAŁ, MCENERY, TONY, WODAK, RUTH, 2008, "A useful methodological synergy? Combining critical discourse analysis and corpus linguistics to examine discourses of refugees and asylum seekers in the UK press", *Discourse and Society* 19 (3), pp. 273-306.

BAKHTIN, MIKHAIL M, 1981, "Discourse in the Novel", in M. Holquist (ed.) *The Dialogic Imagination*, University of Texas Press, Austin.

BREZINA, VACLAV, WEILL-TESSIER, P., MCENERY, TONY, 2020, #LancsBox 6.0 [software]. Available at: http://corpora.lancs.ac.uk/lancsbox.

CHAEMSAITHONG, KRISDA, 2014, "Interactive patterns of the opening statement in criminal trials: a historical perspective", *Discourse Studies* 16 (3), pp. 347-64.

CHAEMSAITHONG, KRISDA, 2017, "Speech reporting in courtroom opening statements", *Journal of Pragmatics* 119, pp. 1-14.

CHAEMSAITHONG, KRISDA, 2018, "Use of voices in legal opening statements", *Social Semiotics* 28 (1), pp. 90-107.

CHAEMSAITHONG, KRISDA, and KIM, YOONJEONG, 2018, "From narration to argumentation: intertextuality in two courtroom genres", *Lingua* 203, pp. 36-50.

D'HONDT, SIGURD, 2021, "One confession, multiple chronotopes: the interdiscursive authentication of an apology in an international criminal trial", *Journal of sociolinguistics* 25 (1), pp. 62-80.

DU, BIYU JADE, 2021, "The mediated voice: a discursive study of interpreter-mediated closing statements in Chinese criminal trials", *Target: international journal of translation studies* 33 (2), pp. 341-67.

ENTMAN, ROBERT, 1993, "Framing: towards clarification of a fractured paradigm", *Journal of Communication* 43 (4), pp. 51-8.

ETXABE, JULEN, 2022, "The Dialogical Language of Law", *Osgoode Hall Law Journal* 59 (2), pp. 429-515.

FELTON ROSULEK, LAURA, 2015, *Dueling Discourses: The Construction of Reality in Closing Arguments*, O.U.P., Oxford.

GARZONE, GIULIANA, 2016, "Polyphony and dialogism in legal discourse: focus on syntactic negation", in G. Tessuto, V. Bhatia, G. Garzone, R. Salvi, and C. Williams (eds) *Constructing Legal Discourses and Social Practices: Issues and Perspectives*, Cambridge Scholars Publishing, Newcastle upon Tyne, pp. 2-27.

GARZONE, GIULIANA, and DEGANO, CHIARA, 2012, "Voices in arbitration awards: polyphony and language reports", in V. Bhatia, C. Candlin, and M. Gotti (eds) *Discourse and Practice in International Commercial Arbitration: Issues, Challenges and Prospects*, Ashgate, Surrey, pp. 179-208.

GOFFMAN, ERVING, 1974, *Frame Analysis. An Essay on the Organization of Experience*, Harper and Row, New York.

GOFFMAN, ERVING, 1981, *Forms of talk*, Blackwell, Oxford.

HASSELLIND, FILIP STRANDBERG, 2021, "The international criminal trial as a site for contesting historical and political narratives: the case of Dominic Ongwen", *Social and Legal Studies* 30 (5), pp. 790-809.

HEFFER, CHRIS, 2005, *The Language of Jury Trial: A Corpus-Aided Analysis of Legal-Lay Discourse*, Palgrave, Houndmills, UK.

HOBBS, PAMELA, 2003, "'Is That What We're Here About?': a Lawyer's Use of Impression Management in a Closing Argument at Trial." *Discourse and Society* 14 (3), pp. 273-90.

International Justice Monitor, 2010, "And here's what the prosecutor's opening statement said", *Lubanga's case*, available at https://www.ijmonitor.org/2010/01/and-heres-what-the-prosecutors-opening-statement-said/, last accessed July 27, 2022.

KILGOUR, MARC, and BRAMS, STEPHEN, 1997, "The Truel", *Mathematics Magazine*, 70 (5), pp. 315-26.

MAUET, THOMAS, 2009, *Trials: Strategy, Skills, and the New Powers of Persuasion* (2nd ed.), Aspen Publishers, New York.

PARTINGTON, ALAN, 2004, "Introduction: corpora and discourse, a most congruous beast", in A. Partington, J. Morley and L. Haarman (eds), *Corpora and Discourse*, Peter Lang, Frankfurt am Main, pp. 11-20.

POWELL, GERALD READING, 2001, "Opening statements: the art of storytelling", *Stetson Law Review* 31 (1), pp. 89-104.

Rome Statute of the International Criminal Court (last amended 2010), adopted on 17 July 1998 by the United Nations Diplomatic Conference of Plenipotentiaries on the Establishment of an International Criminal Court, entered into force on 1 July 2002. Available at https://www.icc-cpi.int/sites/default/files/RS-Eng.pdf (accessed on 30 June 2022).

SCHMID, JEANNETTE, and FIEDLER, KLAUS, 1996, "Language and Implicit Attributions in the Nuremberg Trials: Analyzing Prosecutors' and Defense Attorneys' Closing Speeches", *Human Communication Research* 22 (3), pp. 371-98.

SCHMITT, BERTRAM, 2021, "Legal diversity at the International Criminal Court", *Journal of International Criminal Justice* 19 (3), pp. 485-510.

SNEIJDER, PETRA, 2014, "The embedding of reported speech in a rhetorical structure by prosecutors and defense lawyers in Dutch trials." *Text and Talk* 34 (4), pp. 467-90.

SPIECKER, SHELLEY, and WORTHINGTON, DEBRA, 2003, "The influence of opening statement/closing argument organizational strategy on juror verdict and damage awards", *Law and Human Behavior* 27 (4), pp. 437-56.

STOLK, SOFIA, 2017, "Imagining scenes of mass atrocity from afar: maps and landscapes at the International Criminal Court", *London Review of International Law* 5 (3), pp. 425-51.

STOLK, SOFIA, 2018, "A sophisticated beast? on the construction of an 'ideal' perpetrator in the opening statements of international criminal trials", *European Journal of International Law* 29 (3), pp. 677-701.

STOLK, SOFIA, 2021, *The Opening Statement of the Prosecution in International Criminal Trials: A Solemn Tale of Horror*, London, Routledge.

TALLGREN, IMRI, 2015. "The voice of the international: who is speaking?", *Journal of International Criminal Justice* 13 (1), pp. 135-55.

The International Criminal Court, website, online. Available at https://www.icc-cpi.int/about, last accessed on July 27, 2022.

VAN LEEUWEN, THEO, 2008, *Discourse and Practice: New Tools for Critical Discourse Analysis*, O.U.P., Oxford.

WHEELER, CALEB H, 2016, "No longer just a victim: the impact of victim participation on trial proceedings at the International Criminal Court", *International Criminal Law Review* 16 (3), pp. 525-46.

Feminine and Masculine Wines: A Corpus-assisted Critical Specialised Discourse Analysis of Gender Framing in Promotional Tasting-Notes

Francesco Nacchia

Abstract

Winespeak comes as largely unintelligible to people lacking wine education due to the robust presence of loosely defined descriptors ascribable, among others, to the long-standing tradition of describing wines through the organicist-animist metaphor WINES ARE PEOPLE; this, in turn, encompasses using gender as a framing device aligned with traditional social constructs of *feminine* and *masculine* which has earned wine writers accusations of sexism and contribution to the ritualisation of gender and perpetuation of stereotypically gendered traits.

On the basis of these premises and considering gender framing as a way of "symbolically evok[ing] people's ideas about gender" (Winter 2005: 454) and disseminating gendered meaning, including pre-assumptions concerning inequality embedded in gendered meaning, this paper aims to (i) quantify instances of framing wines by gender and (ii) assess the correlation between a wine's organoleptic characteristics and its designation as *masculine* or *feminine* in promotional tasting-notes; subsequently, the study undertakes a critical examination of the results to assess the extent to which recurrent co-occurring descriptors from the domain PEOPLE contribute to the promotion of gender stereotypes (iii). The study demonstrates that although gender framing in British wine promotional communication is not common, when it does happen, it still relies on outdated notions of *masculinity* and *femininity* associated with certain human traits and organoleptic characteristics. The study places itself within the field of Corpus-assisted Critical Specialised Discourse Studies, by embracing a cross-disciplinary approach combining Critical Discourse Studies and Corpus Linguistics methods as applied to Languages for Specific Purposes.

Key-words: winespeak, gender framing, corpus-assisted critical specialised discourse analysis, personification, LSP.

1. Introduction

In recent decades, the critical analysis of male-dominated spheres of society has been the research topic of scholars in multiple scientific

ISSN 1824-3967
© Carocci Editore S.p.A.

fields, including Linguistics. Here, unequal power dynamics that have long been taken for granted have been unearthed with the aim of promoting equality and dismantling the traditional gender binary perpetuating gender inequalities and excluding individuals who identify as members of the LGBTQ+ community (see Lazar 2007, Litosseliti and Sunderland 2002). Although the existence and impact of heteronormativity and hegemonic *masculinity* in the wine industry has long been known, never before had this been addressed with such vigour by wine professionals. Among others, wine critic Mobley has brought the linguistic issue to the fore by noting that it is "commonplace to describe wines as 'masculine'[1] or 'feminine'" (2020: online) drawing on traditional notions of *masculinity* and *femininity*[2]; these – understood as "relatively enduring characteristics encompassing traits, appearances, interests, and behaviours that have traditionally been considered relatively more typical of women and men, respectively" (Kachel, Steffens, Niedlich 2016: 2) – lead wine writers to describe, for example, "a masculine wine [as] aggressive and muscular; [and] a feminine one [as] delicate and floral" (Mobley 2020: online). In this discursive context, at least three interrelated consequences of using a language endowed with a heterosexual male perspective can be identified: first, the fuelling of dangerous and outdated stereotypes of men as bigger and stronger, and women as fine and delicate, which do not conform to reality (Danitza 2020: online); secondly – and consequently –, the exclusion of "the women who do not necessarily identify with the common associations with [the] term [feminine]" (Areni Global 2021: online) – and vice versa – which poses a not inconsiderable risk to winemakers selling their wines in a market characterised by a high proportion of non-male buyers; finally, such words are not only seen as sexist but, when used as wine descriptors, denote "empty categories" (Whalen in Pariseau 2021: online) and are considered "vague and unhelpful" (Mobley 2020: online) to the same extent as non-standard, out-of-domain words that contribute to wine being perceived as inaccessible to non-experts.

Based on these premises, a corpus-assisted critical discourse analysis of present-day promotional wine-tasting notes (henceforth

---

[1] Terms and expressions are in single inverted commas.
[2] Concepts are in italics.

TNs) from UK-based multi-brand wine stores is conducted with the purpose of: (i) verifying and quantifying instances of framing wines by gender binary *feminine* and *masculine* and (ii) assessing the correlation between existing gender stereotypes in wine discourse and wine organoleptic characteristics; subsequently, the study undertakes a critical examination of the results to assess the extent to which recurrent co-occurring wine descriptors from the domain PEOPLE contribute to the promotion of gender stereotypes (iii).

To this end, section 2 sets the scene by introducing the language of wine with a focus on descriptors and gendered ones specifically; section 3 explains the theoretical underpinnings of the study; section 4 describes the corpus and methods for the subsequent qualitative and quantitative analysis, which is discussed in section 5. Finally, the results obtained are summarised in section 6.

2. Winespeak: the wine-tasting language

By resorting to Brochet and Dubourdieu's teachings, wine language is used "to exchange sensory data" (2001: 187) about wine in informal contexts as well as professional wine-tasting sessions. This professional practice is generally defined as an organoleptic assessment – i.e. involving sense organs – of wine according to some predefined steps: the visual analysis, followed by the olfactory, taste, tactile, and aftertaste inspections; it is at this point that wine-tasters are supposed to turn their perceptions into language and draw a TN that summarises the whole experience. However, since "the relationship between sensation and expression, between the word and the quality it describes, is not as straightforward as it is elsewhere" (Peynaud 1987: 161), it is difficult to describe a wine in such a way that it is interpreted consistently from individual to individual. This need to give a verbal form to hazy sensory perceptions is the reason why "tasters are led to juggle with words" (Peynaud 1987: 180) and enrich their writing with subjective and ambiguous words. Peynaud (1987) concluded that the specialised language of wine comprises a terminological dimension with precise terms for concrete sensations and a creative one for more subtle sensations conveyed by imprecise terms. Whereas in the former case words have intelligible and sometimes standardised meanings, in the latter one, words are drawn from general language or other domains and assigned a meaning whose interpretation might well change from receiver to receiver, denying non-experts access to the discourse community. Indeed, although these latter terms are not specialised in the strict sense, wine writers most frequently draw words from certain semantic domains (see Caballero, Suárez-Toste, and Paradis 2019) and are facilitated in their mutual understanding unlike those who are not actively involved in conversations about wine. In this respect, Silverstein (2006) underlined how "[m]astery of a register, a characteristic way of talking about some area of experience, indexes one's membership in the social group that characteristically does so" (491). In light of this, a sense of internal homogeneity is created and is perceived by others as having scientific value which, in turn, makes them feel excluded and unqualified to participate in the discourse. This deep-rooted lack of transparency and inclusiveness resulted in the emergence of negative labels with which the language of wine-tasting is commonly referred to, such as 'vinobabble' (Lehrer 2010: 49) and 'idiot-speak' (Gluck 2003: 107). The practice that is now known as "wine writing" has begun to form inside our current social milieu; specifically, the foundations of the magazines *Decanter* in the UK (1975) and the *Wine Spectator* (1976) in the US, allegedly coincide with the emergence of wine writing, much of which would be shaped by the rising politicisation of wine.

2.1. Wine and Gender

Shesgreen (2003), who identified four main domains – the language of social class; the language of gender; the pastoral language of fruit and vegetables; the culinary language – from which wine language has drawn new vocabulary, traces the roots of the language of gender in wine discourse to Victorian literary critic Saintsbury, who described a Hermitage as "the manliest French wine [he] ever drank" (Saintsbury 1886: 7) and a White Port as having "not the almost feminine grace and charm of Claret" (p. 44ff). While some assume the main reason for the emergence of this trend as being purely linguistic since wine was first produced by countries that speak "romance languages using gendered language" (Lambright in Pariseau 2021: online), others claim wine is to blame, being traditionally produced and drunk by men (see Cawley 2018). Indeed, male-dominance can be traced back to wine-making long before wine writing emerged (see Varriano 2010). In ancient Egypt, men were the only ones who participated in the production and sale of wine, whereas in Greece and Rome, wine vases and drinking cups portrayed male sexual supremacy. Then, wine writing surely fuelled male-centric views in the wine industry, with "most of the content from the years 1975 – 1995 in Decanter and similar publications [being] written by men" (Cawley 2018: 10) and the majority of the magazine's readership made up of successful men from the middle to upper classes – and they still are (Maguire 2016).

By virtue of this, and considering the alluring potential of sex in advertising, sexism has often stood out as a distinguishing trait of wine communication, where "[j]okes about bums, boobs and bonking were the norm [and] [w]omen were often depicted as adjuncts to men's important enjoyment of wine" (Cawley 2018: 10). Nowadays, although "prominent wine writing, journalism and social media have created new voices and mutable language" (Cawley 2018: 17), factors that maintain male-dominance in the wine industry are found in a variety of contexts, from training to consumption and verbal description; they can be summarised as follows: (i) "the pervasively patriarchal structure of the court of sommeliers" (Wylde in Pariseau 2021: online); (ii) the binary distinction that always resonates in wine training (Cord in Pariseau 2021: online); (iii) order-taking prioritizing women (Lambright in Paiseau 2021: online); and (iv) verbal descriptions that rely heavily on the organicist-animist metaphor WINES ARE PEOPLE (Negro 2012; Ţenescu 2014) which also entails the assignation of binary gender to wine. Indeed, Vedel (Vedel et al. 1972) standardised the terms 'feminine' and 'masculine' as wine descriptors in his *Triangle de Vedel*. The latter term was assigned to wines placing themselves towards the vertex of Astringency, whereas the former was intended for wines characterised by Softness/Sweetness. In general, which descriptors are regarded as *feminine* or *masculine* is generally the result of the interaction between chemical compounds – e.g. "the character of the tannins" (Gargantuan Wine 2017: online) – and traditional symbols associated with men and women – e.g. tobacco for men because of male-exclusive Victorian smoking rooms (Gargantuan Wine 2017: online) and flowers for women as a metaphor for the Virgin Mary, virginity, and cleanliness (Gargantuan Wine 2016: online). This intertwining has led to the adoption of sets of gender-biased metaphorical expressions based on the conceptual metaphor WINES ARE PEOPLE, such as "delicate and elegant" for *feminine* wines and "full-bodied, round, muscular and structured" for *masculine* ones (Danitza 2020: online).

3. Theoretical foundations

By relying on the assumption that "post-structuralism favours a more eclectic approach to research, whereby different methodologies can be combined together, acting as reinforcers of each other" (Baker 2006: 16), and given the aims of the study, its theoretical roots are necessarily cross-disciplinary. The major disciplines involved are: Frame Analysis and Corpus-assisted Critical Specialised Discourse Studies stemming from the convergence of Corpus Linguistics and Critical Discourse Studies as applied to Languages for Specific Purposes.

The origins of Frame Analysis – which stems from Pragmatics – are traced back to sociologist Goffman (1974) who thought of it as a way for helping deconstruct individuals' "organisation of experience" (p. 11) by identifying the principles governing events. As the expression suggests, the analysis concerns frames, generally defined as the group of primary elements through which "the acts of daily living are understandable" (Goffman 1974: 24) and "data-structure[s] for representing [...] stereotyped situation[s]" (Minsky 1974: 1). The type of framing considered for the study is gender framing, which is defined as a way of framing events by "symbolically evok[ing] people's ideas about gender" (Winter 2005: 454) and disseminating gendered meaning, including pre-assumptions concerning inequality embedded in it (Ridgeway 2011). Frame Analysis pioneer Goffman in his *Gender Advertisements* (1976) identified six categories of ritualised gender in advertising: relative size; the feminine touch; function ranking; ritualisation of subordination; licensed withdrawal; and the family. With the purpose of exploring gender framing in wine discourse, however, Țenescu's (2014) conceptual metaphor schema WINES ARE PEOPLE and its sub-categories – age within human lifecycle, physical traits/anatomy, personality and temperament features, economic status, general appearance (Țenescu 2014: 66) – was adopted as considered more relevant to the research. Frame Analysis shares many of the founding principles of Critical Discourse

Studies. The adoption of a critical approach is deemed necessary for drawing insights into the unequal relationship between *masculinity* and *femininity* in wine discourse.

The research intends to pave the way for Corpus-assisted Critical Specialised Discourse Studies, which concern the application of approaches typical of this field to Languages for Specific Purposes. Corpus-assisted Critical Discourse Studies originate out of the mixing of Critical Discourse Studies and Corpus Linguistics[3] (see Baker et al. 2008) and distinguish themselves from Corpus-assisted Discourse Studies (Partington 2004) because these latter ones have "no overarching political agenda" (Partington, Duguid, Taylor 2013: 10). As the present study suggests, the emphasis on specialised languages and the discourses they produce both inside and outside of a community of specialists in discourse is what makes Corpus-assisted Critical Specialised Discourse Studies unique. This means that the distinctive traits – lexical, syntactic, and textual – are to be viewed as the point of departure from which the researcher starts out to derive meaningful insights. Yet, this only means that the specialised nature of the discourse is acknowledged, not necessarily that those distinguishing traits are taken into account as units of analysis. For instance, the current study examines non-specialist elements (creative and conventional gendered metaphors) in a specialised discourse (wine-tasting discourse), whose lexical distinctive features (terminological metaphors) are acknowledged for the analysis. If this criterion were not followed, the data would be viewed from a non-specialised viewpoint.

4. Corpus and methodology

This section is devoted to the description of the corpus building criteria and the presentation of the methodological approach.

4.1. Corpus building

For the purpose of the study, an ad-hoc, domain-specific corpus of TNs extracted from promotional catalogues and brochures of

---

[3] "[…] the study of language based on examples of real life language use" (McEnery and Wilson 1996: 1).

UK-based online multi-brand wine stores was built[4]. The TNs selected for the research were either written by wine-tasters working on behalf of a winery or taken from external sources (e.g. wine-dedicated magazines, blogs etc.) and featured by wine stores in the selected wine-lists. The TNs used here are referred to as promotional TNs because they function "to advertise a wine and ha[ve] the unrestricted communicative goal of making consumers buy the targeted product" (Hommerberg 2011: 34). Unlike TNs published in dedicated resources (e.g. magazines, blogs, etc.), in which a wine may appear as more or less appealing to readers depending on the taster tastes, in the context of promotion the point is to increase the appeal of particular wines as much as possible and ultimately to convince consumers.

The overarching selection criteria of reliability (the author is an expert), representativeness (the texts exhibit most of the distinctive conventions of the textual genre), relevance (the texts are useful for the objectives of the study), and accessibility (the texts are freely available), were coupled with study-specific selection criteria that could help minimise bias in the actual selection phase. The author took into account:
– the first 10 results of a Google search including the expressions wine list, UK, and pdf;
– multi-brand stores selling wines from national and international wine-houses – individual wine-houses, menus of cafés, restaurants, and the like were excluded;
– the time-span 2012-2022 – so as to provide a portrayal of the synchronous state-of-art of the linguistic usages in the domain.

The extraction itself concerned the name of the wine and the TN; all data not included in the piece of prose were excluded (e.g. the amount of wine in the bottle was included only when part of the text, if it appeared as a distinct element – e.g. in a chart –, it was not included in the corpus). As reported in table 1 below, the final UKWINE2019[5] corpus comprises 10 sub-corpora including 5,305 TNs with a total of 178,928 tokens.

---

[4] Corpus building phase: June 2022.
[5] 2019 is the mid-date between 2016 (oldest wine-list) and 2022 (newest wine-list).

TABLE 1. CORPUS

	Catalogue	TNs	Tokens
1	Cambridge Wine Merchants 2021	367	13,523
2	Symmons & Allen Vintners 2016	372	8,712
3	The Vinorium 2016	286	17,746
4	Matthew Clarke 2021/22	1,158	44,376
5	James Pettit & Company 2018	471	8,189
6	Staustell Wines 2019	411	11,287
7	Laithwaite's Wine 2018	120	6,031
8	LWC 2020/21	763	16,658
9	Strictly Wine 2022	1,208	44,543
10	Buckingham Schenk 2022	149	7,863
		5,305	*178,928*

4.2. Corpus tool

The analysis of the corpus was carried out through corpus-query software *AntConc* (Anthony 2014) which offers a range of functions of which KWIC (Key Word In Context) and Collocate are relevant to the aims of the study. The former function helps identify regularities that constitute meaningful patterns in the corpus; the second function facilitates the identification of co-occurring words that might trigger associations and connotations (Baker 2006). However useful automated analysis may be for streamlining the identification phase, human intervention in the interpretation of data in a broader perspective is deemed necessary for the success of the critical investigation.

4.3. Method

In order to pursue the first aim of the study – namely the quantification of instances of framing wines by gender – and avoid misleading results that would invalidate the aim of the research, the range of words to be searched in the corpus was limited to the adjectives 'feminine' and 'masculine', which denote the conventionalised gender-binary-related concepts under investigation; the 10 sub-corpora were uploaded individually to *Antconc* and the frequency analysis was performed.

Then, a manual analysis of the concordance lines and complete TNs featuring the terms of interest for investigating the correlation between existing gender stereotypes in wine discourse and wine organoleptic characteristics was carried out. This research step considered the tasting event as envisaged by Hartung (1999), who classified the steps involved in the tasting in the 6 Ss of judging: *see* (visual inspection) *swirl* and *sniff* (olfactory inspection) *sip* and *savor* (taste and tactile inspection) and s*pit* (aftertaste inspection). Also, categories for aroma descriptors useful to classify organoleptic characteristics according to domain-specific standards were taken from Noble's (1990) *Aroma Wheel*[6].

Finally, an investigation into the role of recurrent co-occurring wine descriptors contributing to the perpetuation of conventional gender stereotypes was performed. These were categorised according to Țenescu's (2014) framework (see section 3) and analysed in a critical discursive perspective.

5. Findings

This section presents the results of the analysis aiming at providing answers to the three research questions; these are reported according to the methods described above and by following the alphabetic order ('feminine' first, then 'masculine').

First, the quantitative scrutiny revealed the limited use of the descriptors implementing gender framing; overall, 'feminine' is found in 5 TNs from 3 stores (Symmons & Allen Vintners 2016, The Vinorium 2016 – 2 occurrences –, and Matthew Clarke 2021/22 – 2 occurrences) and 'masculine' is reported in 6 TNs from 3 stores (The Vinorium 2016 – 4 occurrences –, Matthew Clark 2021/22, and LWC 2020/21). From a simple quantitative assessment, the size of the phenomenon within the textual genre can be said to be limited. The terms of interest occur in 11 out of 5,305 TNs, accounting for 0,21% of the total corpus. This is a preliminary finding that provides us with a snapshot of the size of the phenomenon. Clearly, the fact that the trend might be said to be waning is promising and shows that it only concerns a tiny proportion of people; at the same time, although the practice may not be extremely widespread in quantitative terms,

---

[6] Available at: https://www.winearomawheel.com/.

only data from qualitative examination can reveal evidence for or against gender stereotyping.

Then, the manual scrutiny of the 11 TNs in the corpus led to the identification of common sensory descriptors associated with either terms (see Table 2) and descriptors belonging to the domain PEOPLE (see Table 3) in line with the second and third research question. Two TNs that include the words of interest are displayed below to show the type of manual analysis performed. The sensory descriptors have been italicised and terms drawn from the domain PEOPLE have been underlined:

Volnay, Louis Jadot, 2012
Traditionally the most **feminine** and elegant of the Côte d'Or red wines; Volnay lies between the villages of Pommard and Meursault. The wine combines distinction, nobility, finesse and femininity and offers a complex bouquet of *red berries*, *violets* and *vanilla*. (Matthew Clark 2021/22)

Torbreck The Pict 2006
The 2006 The Pict is 100% Mataro (Mourvedre) aged in 100% new French oak for 24 months. The fruit was sourced from one section of a vineyard planted in 1927. *Purple*-colored, it offers up an aromatic array of *smoky oak*, *forest floor*, *black truffle*, *blueberry*, and *blackberry jam*. On the palate it reveals a brawny, **masculine** personality with some austerity that should round out with a few years of additional bottle age. It should offer prime drinking from 2013 to 2026. (The Vinorium 2016)

Considering all the 11 TNs, descriptors employed for describing *feminine* wines from a visual point of view are 'bright red color' and 'violet glints'. Both descriptors concur to the characterisation of the same wine; the other tasting notes displaying the term 'feminine' do not introduce the wine from a visual point of view. More conspicuous is the number of terms for aromas perceived by the nose; these are discernible in the *fruity* and *floral* category: 'blackcurrant', 'boysenberry', 'dark cherries', 'lime cordial', 'raspberry', and 'red berries' for the former group; '(light) floral', 'iris', 'rose', 'rosehip', 'vanilla', and 'violets' for the latter. Finally, 'complex bouquet' and 'detailed bouquet' express a general sense of positive qualities, and a reference to 'minerality' is reported. Terms attributable to the taste and tactile inspection are: 'citrus-fresh', 'fresh', 'fresh apricot', 'white peach', 'with a core of minerality'. One reference only to tannins is reported where they are described as 'filigree tannins' where 'filigree' refers to "delicate patterns made from thin gold or silver wire, used as decoration"[7] and fuels the popular imagination of women as 'delicate' as well as that concerning 'elegance'. 'Supple (palate)' was already noted by Bruce (1999), who reported the conventional usage of terms like "harsh, thick, rough and robust" for *masculine* wines as opposed to "fleshy, unctuous, honeyed, soft, supple and cloying" (p. 158) for *feminine* ones. Finally, 'cassis' and 'dark cherry fruit' are the two descriptors used in the aftertaste section of one TN.

Visually, *masculine* wines are 'opaque purple', 'purple-colored', 'bright purple (hues)', 'thick-looking' and present an 'intense depth of colour'. Compared to *feminine* wines, much wider is the range of semantic areas for *masculine* aromas:
– *fruity*: 'blackberry' (2), 'blackberry jam', 'blueberry', 'cassis', 'cranberry', 'redcurrant', 'ripe black fruits';
– *woody*: 'cedar', 'graphite' (2), 'mocha', 'pain grillé', 'pencil lead', 'smoky oak', 'vanillin smoky oak';
– *chemical*: 'tar';
– *caramel*: 'rich dark chocolate';
– *spicy*: 'liquorice' (2);
– *herbaceous or vegetative*: 'forest floor', 'underbrush';
– *earthy*: 'black truffle', 'crushed rock', 'limestone'.

The only non-classifiable expression according to Noble's *Aroma Wheel* is 'meat' – *edible parts of animals* was created as a tentative label. As far as the taste and tactile inspection is concerned, tannins are referred to as 'fine-grained' and 'attractive'; in the latter case the typically female feature of attractiveness is associated with *masculinity*. *Fruity* tastes are 'explosive' and 'savoury'; 'chalky' as opposed to 'smooth' for *feminine* wines. Apart from a generic positive adjective like 'savoury', in one instance the term 'sous-bois' is used to describe the final part of the tasting event. Similarly to 'forest floor' and 'underbrush', the French expression refers to a taste of undergrowth but that is "more than just a pile of dried leaves; there's a vegetative, mushroomy quality as well" (Wine Spectator 2006: online). In this respect, the associability of mushroom smell and taste with *masculinity* is confirmed by the 'black truffle' aroma found in a different TN.

---

[7] Filigree, n.d., in Macmillan Dictionary. https://www.macmillandictionary.com/dictionary/british/filigree, last accessed April 4, 2022.

TABLE 2. ORGANOLEPTIC CHARACTERISTICS ASSOCIATED WITH FEMININE AND MASCULINE WINES

Feminine Wines	
Visual inspection	Bright red, violet glints.
Olfactory inspection	(Light) floral, blackcurrant, boysenberry, complex (bouquet), dark cherries, detailed (bouquet), iris, lime cordial, minerality, raspberry, red berries, rose, rosehip, vanilla, violets.
Taste and tactile inspection	Citrus-fresh, filigree tannins, fresh apricot, fresh, white peach, with a core of minerality.

Masculine Wines	
Visual inspection	Bright purple (hues), intense depth of colour, opaque purple, purple-colored, thick-looking.
Olfactory inspection	Black truffle, blackberry (2), blackberry jam, blueberry, cassis, cedar, cranberry, crushed rock, forest floor, graphite (2), limestone, liquorice (2), meat, mocha, pain grillé, pencil lead, redcurrant, rich dark chocolate, ripe black fruits, smoky oak, tar, underbrush, vanillin smoky oak.
Taste and tactile inspection	Attractive tannins, chalky, explosive savoury, fine-grained tannins.
Aftertaste inspection	Sous-bois.

At this point an investigation into the role of recurrent co-occurring descriptors drawn from the domain PEOPLE contributing to the perpetuation of conventional gender stereotypes is carried out. By examining the co-occurrence of certain terms, a more nuanced understanding of gender characterisation in the wine industry can be achieved. References to *general appearance* are conveyed through conventional descriptors 'delicate', 'finesse' (2), 'pretty', 'silky (elegance)', and 'graceful' conveying softness and smoothness typically associated with females. A sense of elegance is retrievable in 'elegant' (5), 'distinction', and 'nobility' which also features (socio-)economic status-related feelings. The expression 'weightless elegance' testifies to the tendency of mapping the human concepts of physical musculature and

mass onto the domain of wine through the concepts of structure
– defined by the tannins – and alcohol content in a way that
lighter-bodied wines are typically considered *feminine* whereas
medium and full-bodied are *masculine*. Finally, the occurrence of
'English Rose', which traditionally denotes "an attractive English
woman with an appearance traditionally thought to be typical
of English women"[8] deserves special attention. The epithet
encapsulates both stereotypes of women associated with flowers
and attractiveness; also, the term is a literary and musical allusion
creating intertextual references with Basil Hood's *Merrie England*
(1902), a comic opera where the expression first appeared and
Elton John's 1997 version of his 1974 hit *Candle in the Wind* where
the singer bids farewell to Princess Diana through the adapted
lyrics reading "Goodbye England's Rose".

Instead, *masculine* wines are presented as 'brawny', 'burly'
'medium-bodied' (2), and 'full-bodied' (3) by virtue of the
stereotypical assumption of males as bigger and more muscular
than women; these terms are categorised under the *physical traits/
anatomy* sub-schema. Conventional ideas of males as stronger than
females are further conveyed through the descriptors 'powerful',
'immense power' (2), 'firm (structure)', 'tremendous (grip)', 'grippy
(finish)'; these partly fit the category *physical traits/anatomy* which
is extended to *physical traits/anatomy/skills*. At the same time, two
descriptors typically associated with females are spotted; these are
'elegance' – although it is preceded by the specification 'masculine'
–, and 'grace' which are categorised under the label *(socio-)
economic status* and *general appearance* respectively. 'Terse (finish)'
and 'austerity' are both classifiable under the label *personality
and temperament features* and also convey feelings of stereotyped
masculinity. Finally, although not creating a straightforward link with
the conceptual metaphor WINES ARE PEOPLE and its subcategories,
some descriptors might be claimed to still account for the bodily
properties of *masculine* wines: '(impressively) concentrated', 'pure',
'intense', and 'rich'.

---

[8] English Rose, n.d., in Macmillan Dictionary. https://www.macmillandictionary.
com/dictionary/british/english-rose, last accessed July 3, 2022.

TABLE 3. WORDS FROM THE DOMAIN PEOPLE ASSOCIATED WITH FEMININE AND MASCULINE WINES

Feminine Wines

General appearance	Delicate, finesse (2), graceful, pretty, silky (elegance).
(Socio-)economic status	Distinction, elegant (5), nobility, (weightless, silky) elegance.

Masculine Wines

Physical traits/anatomy/skills	Brawny, burly, firm (structure), full-bodied (3), grippy (finish), immense power (2), medium-bodied (2), powerful, tremendous (grip).
(Socio-)economic status	(Masculine) elegance.
General appearance	Grace.
Personality and temperament features	Austerity, terse (finish).

From a commercial perspective, assigning a certain gender can influence one's buying decisions and shape their views of what is considered acceptable for each gender. Consumers are more likely to purchase things to which they feel a connection or identification than those from which they feel alienated. A buyer might infer the wine whose gender corresponds to their perceived one is more likely to suit their taste, and this can lead to buyers making purchasing decisions based on preconceived notions about what is appropriate for them as individuals. At the same time, one who self-identifies as female or male may find the features mentioned about the wines inappropriate and hesitate to purchase the wine. Additionally, and maybe more importantly, a person who does not identify with either gender might feel left out, which could result in a reluctance to buy. When marketing products, it is critical to be mindful of the potential of language for alienation. Language that presumes a gender binary can exclude customers who do not identify within it. Additionally, gendering wines may cause people to make assumptions about the purchaser's identity that may or may not be accurate. Some might consider it important to assess the impact that these purchases may have on their self-image and how others perceive them. For a man, buying a masculine wine could be seen as a sign of strength, power and success, but it can also be seen as an attempt to conform to societal norms or even a sign of insecurity. In this respect, a key example concerns the birth of the term 'brosé' – resulting from the blending of 'brother' and 'rosé' – to counter the widespread perception of rosé wine as a girly drink – due to its "typically" feminine organoleptic characteristics – and encourage even the most *masculine* individuals to drink it without feeling emasculated (see Wilson 2015: online).

Overall, although nothing inherently sexist about framing wines by gender can be assumed – also in light of the ubiquity of the personification schema in wine discourse –, the problem arises when certain descriptors are exclusively associated with a certain gender and denied to the other. By assuming that it may be more acceptable for a man to be described as 'strong' than it is for a woman, stereotypes and gender inequality are reinforced. The results might lead to the assumption that promotional TNs are to some extent exempt from exploiting gender framing, possibly due to the risk of being labelled as sexist. On the other hand, one could still argue that the use of these gendered descriptors, even if limited, still exudes discrimination and testifies to the persistence of sexism in wine discourse.

6. Final Observations and Remarks

In this study dealing with the understanding of discursive aspects in specialised communication (Garzone, Catenaccio, Grego, Doerr 2017), the author set out to measure the impact of gender framing in promotional wine discourse in the UK by embracing a cross-disciplinary approach combining both quantitative and qualitative approaches.

With reference to the first research question, Mobley (2020) made the claim that "overtly gendered language has been falling out of favor in recent years" (online) by referring to derogatory labels men have been historically used to explicitly insult and harass women and that has intruded in the language of wine. Based on the results of this study, it might be argued that the process has affected internalised conventional stereotypes of *masculinity* and *femininity* as well, at least in terms of frequency of use with 5 and 6 occurrences of 'feminine' and 'masculine' respectively (0,21% of the corpus).

Then, the correlation between traditional stereotypes of *masculinity* and *femininity* and organoleptic features was examined. Based on the analysis of the 11 TNs containing the terms of interest, wines can be categorised as *masculine* or *feminine* on the basis of their organoleptic characteristics evoking gender-related symbols. Overall, feminine wines have brighter colours, aromas mostly limited to the *fruity* and *floral* category, and 'delicate' taste and tactile features. Contrarily, *masculine* wines have darker colours, cover a wider range of aromas, and tastes of earthy nature are perceived.

Thirdly, the second part of the manual analysis enabled the identification of typically co-occurring descriptors to assess their role in maintaining gender stereotypes. The results showed that on the rare occasions a wine is framed as either *feminine* or *masculine*, this beverage is said to possess human features traditionally associated with this or that gender. The consequences for consumers whose purchasing decisions might be affected by gender mismatches came under scrutiny and some commercial and identity-related issues were discussed.

Although not directly related to a specific research question, in this phase of the study the sub-categories of the conceptual framework as envisaged by Țenescu (2014) were found to only partly cover the wine descriptors used in the corpus. For this reason, the subcategories *economic status* and *physical traits/anatomy* were extended to *(socio-)economic status* and *physical traits/anatomy/ skills*.

In conclusion, since the meaning of such expressions is obviously founded on subjective preconceptions about *masculinity* and *femininity* and considering that they directly target people's identities in contrast to other blatantly subjective wine descriptors, the avoidance of gender framing is highly desirable. As wine expert Goeyvaerts suggests, wine writers are urged to adopt neutral terms and find "equivalents that will no longer be linked to a gender, but which are more universal, and also more understandable by all [...]" (ARENI Global 2021). In order to pursue the aim, a notion of deframing and concurrent adoption of a multi-frame perspective which implies the "need for an ability to step back from a reliance on the particular frames we currently rely on" (Dunbar, Garud, Raghuram 1996: 8) should be promoted. As the vast majority of TNs show, wine can be personified and given human features without determining its gender so consumers are left the choice as to whether assign it to the wine or not based on their subjectivity.

These results should be considered exclusive to the contemporary promotional wine discourse in the UK and research into TNs from other periods in the same genre is needed. Indeed, a study that adopts a diachronic perspective could verify the historical evolution of gender framing in wine discourse. Future research could also verify this tendency in promotional tasting notes in other countries as well as assessing the reliance on gender stereotypes in non-promotional tasting notes and spoken descriptions.

References

ARENI GLOBAL, 2021, "Deconstructing the Language of Wine to Attract New Consumers – In Conversation with Sandrine Goeyvaerts", *Areni Global*. https://areni.global/deconstructing-the-language-of-wine-to-attract-new-consumers-in-conversation-with-sandrine-goeyvaerts/, last accessed July 3, 2022.

ANTHONY, LAURENCE, 2014, *AntConc (Version 3.4. 3)[Computer Software]*, Waseda University, Tokyo.

BAKER, PAUL, 2006, *Using Corpora in Discourse Analysis*, Continuum, London.

BAKER, PAUL, GABRIELATOS, COSTAS, KHOSRAVINIK, MAJID, KRZYŻANOWSKI, MICHAL, MCENERY, TONY, WODAK, RUTH, 2008, "A Useful Methodological Synergy? Combining Critical Discourse Analysis and Corpus linguistics to Examine Discourses of Refugees and Asylum Seekers in the UK press" *Discourse and Society*, 19 (3), pp. 273-306.

BROCHET, FRÉDÉRIC and DUBOURDIEU, DENIS, 2001, "Wine Descriptive Language Supports Cognitive Specificity of Chemical Senses", *Brain and Language* 77 (2), pp. 187-196.

BRUCE, NIGEL, 1999, "Classification and Hierarchy in the Discourse of Wine: Émile Peynaud's The Taste of Wine", *Asp*. 23-26, pp. 149-164.

CABALLERO, ROSARIO, SUÁREZ-TOSTE, ERNESTO, PARADIS, CARITA, 2019, *"Representing Wine – Sensory Perceptions"*, John Benjamins Publishing Company, Amsterdam.

CAWLEY, DIARMUID, 2018 "The Power of Wine Language – Critics, Labels and Sexism", *Dublin Gastronomy Symposium 2018 (Food and Power)*, Conference Paper. doi: 10.21427/G5A7-X024.

DANITZA, VINKA, 2020, "Women, Wine and the Uncomfortable Conversation we Need to Have", *Bottled Bliss*. https://bottledbliss.wordpress.com/2020/09/10/women-wine-and-the-uncomfortable-conversation-we-need-to-have/, last accessed July 3, 2022.

DUNBAR, ROGER L. M., GARUD, RAGHU, RAGHURAM, SUMITA, 1996, "A Frame for Deframing in Strategic Analysis", *Journal of Management Inquiry* 5 (1), pp. 23-34.

GARGANTUAN WINE, 2016, "On Wine and Gender: Chambolle = Feminine. But Why?", *Gargantuan Wine*. https://gargantuanwine.com/2016/12/wine-and-gender-pt1/, last accessed July 3, 2022.

GARGANTUAN WINE, 2017, "On Wine and Gender: Chambertin = Masculine. But Why?", *Gargantuan Wine*. https://gargantuanwine.com/2017/01/on-wine-and-gender-chambertin-masculine-but-why/, last accessed July 3, 2022.

GARZONE, GIULIANA, CATENACCIO, PAOLA, GREGO, KIM, DOERR, ROXANNE (eds), 2017, *Specialised and Professional Discourse across Media and Genres*, Ledizioni, Milano.

GLUCK, MALCOLM, 2003, "Wine Language: Useful Idiom or Idiot Speak?", in J. Aitchison and D. M. Lewis (eds), *New Media Language*, Routledge, London, pp. 107-115.

GOFFMAN, ERVING, 1974, *Frame Analysis: An Essay on the Organisation of Experience*, Harper and Row, New York.

GOFFMAN, ERVING, 1976, *Gender Advertising, Studies in Visual Communication* 3 (2).

HARTUNG, ALEXIS, 1999, "Factors Considered in Wine Evaluation", *AWS Journal*, 31 (4), pp. 1-10.

HOMMERBERG, CHARLOTTE, 2011, *Persuasiveness in the Discourse of Wine: the Rhetoric of Robert Parker*, Intellecta Infolog, Gothenburg.

KACHEL, SVEN, STEFFENS, MELANIE C., NIEDLICH, CLAUDIA, 2016, "Traditional Masculinity and Femininity: Validation of a New Scale Assessing Gender Roles", *Frontiers in Psychology* 7, pp. 1-19.

LAZAR, MICHELLE M., 2007, *Feminist Critical Discourse Analysis*, Palgrave Macmillan, Basingstoke.

LEHRER, ADRIENNE, 2010, "What's New in Wine Language", in R. M. Goded and L. A. Poves (eds), *Proceedings of the First International Workshop on Linguistic Approaches to Food and Wine Description*, UNED, Madrid, pp. 37-56.

LITOSSELITI, LIA, SUNDERLAND, JANE (eds), 2002, *Gender Identity and Discourse Analysis*, John Benjamins Publishing Company, Amsterdam.

MAGUIRE, SMITH J., 2016, "A Taste of the Particular: A Logic of Discernment in an Age of Omnivorousness", *Journal of Consumer Culture,* Vol. 0(0) pp. 1-18.

McENERY, TONY, and WILSON, ANDREW, 1996, *Corpus Linguistics*, Edinburgh U.P., Edinburgh.

MINSKY, MARVIN, 1974, "A Framework for Representing Knowledge", Massachussets Institute of Technology, A.I. Laboratory, *Memo No.*

36.   https://dspace.mit.edu/bitstream/handle/1721.1/6089/AIM-306.
pdf?sequence=2&isAllowed=y, last accessed July 3, 2022.

MOBLEY, ESTHER, 2020, "Wine's Diversity Issue Starts With the Way we
Talk about the Taste of Wine", *San Francisco Chronicle,* September
4, 2021. https://www.sfchronicle.com/wine/article/Wine-s-diversity-
issue-starts-with-the-way-we-15544232.php, last accessed July 3, 2022.

NEGRO, ISABEL, 2012, "Wine Discourse in the French Language", *Revista
Electrónica de Lingüística Aplicada* 11, pp. 1-12.

NOBLE ANN C., 1990, The Wine Aroma Wheel, Davis, CA.

PARISEAU, LESLIE, 2021, "The End of Gendering Wine", *Punch* November
15, 2021. https://punchdrink.com/articles/end-gendering-feminine-
masculine-wine-language/#:~:text=In%20traditional%20wine%20
writing%2C%20education,Proven%C3%A7al%20ros%C3%A9%20
is%20for%20her, last accessed July 3, 2022.

PARTINGTON, ALAN, 2004, "Corpora and Discourse, a Most Congruous
Beast", in A. Partington, J. Morley, L. Haarman (eds), *Corpora and
Discourse*, Peter Lang, Frankfurt, pp. 9-18.

PARTINGTON, ALAN, DUGUID, ALISON, TAYLOR, CHARLOTTE, 2013, *Patterns
and Meanings in Discourse: Theory and Practice in Corpus-assisted
Discourse Studies (CADS)*, John Benjamins, Amsterdam.

PEYNAUD, ÉMILE, *Le Goût du Vin*, 1987, English trans. *The Taste of Wine: the
Art and Science of Wine Appreciation*, by Michael Schuster, Macdonald
Orbis, London 1989.

RIDGEWAY, CECILIA L., 2011, *Framed by Gender: How Gender Inequality
Persists in the Modern World*, O.U.P., New York.

SAINTSBURY, GEORGE, 1886, *Notes on a Cellar-Book.* https://archive.org/
stream/notesoncellarboooosain/notesoncellarboooosain_djvu.txt, last
accessed July 3, 2022.

SHAPIN, STEVEN, 2012, "Tastes of Wine: Towards a Cultural History",
Rivista di estetica 51 (3/2012), pp. 49-94.

SHESGREEN, SEAN, 2003, "Wet Dogs and Gushing Oranges: Winespeak for
a New Millennium", *The Chronicle of Higher Education* 49 (7), pp. 572-
575.

SILVERSTEIN, MICHAEL, 2006, "Old Wine, New Ethnographic Lexicography",
Annual Review of Anthropology (35) 1, pp. 481-496.

ȚENESCU, ALINA, 2014, "The Organicist Animist Metaphor in Italian Wine
Media Discourse", *Social Sciences and Education Research Review* 2,
pp. 62-72.

VARRIANO, JOHN, 2010, *Wine: A Cultural History*, Reaktion Books Ltd,
London.

VEDEL, ANDRÉ, CHARNAY, PIERRE, CHARLES, GASTON, TOURMEAU, JULES, 1972,
Essai sur la Dégustation des Vins, Société d'Édition et d'Informations
Viti-vinicoles, Macon.

WINE SPECTATOR, 2006, "What is 'sous bois'", *Wine Spectator*. https://www.winespectator.com/articles/what-is-sous-bois-5457, last accessed last accessed July 19, 2022.

WINTER, NICHOLAS J. G., 2005, "Framing Gender: Political Rhetoric, Gender Schemas, and Public Opinion on U.S. Health Care Reform", *Politics & Gender* 1 (3), pp. 453-480.

WILSON, JASON, 2015, "Brosé: Wine for the Angsty Bro who Blushes when he 'Drinks Pink'", *The Guardian*. https://www.theguardian.com/commentisfree/2015/jul/29/brose-wine-for-the-angsty-bro-who-blushes-when-he-drinks-pink, last accessed December 22, 2022.

Framing Disability and Sexuality:
An Analysis of Instagram Users' Comments

Maria Cristina Nisco

Abstract
In February 2022, Victoria's Secret announced the launch of the Love Cloud collection, which aimed to change the image of the brand. The collection was inspired by eighteen ordinary women, including a firefighter, a design consultant, and a woman with Down syndrome. Victoria's Secret described this as a groundbreaking campaign that celebrated and welcomed all women; however, the introduction of models with disabilities received mixed reactions from Instagram users. The paper examines Instagram users' responses to Victoria's Secret's campaign, focusing on the intersection of sexuality and disability. The concept of framing is used as an interpretative tool to analyze how the issue is framed and discussed in public discourse. A corpus of Instagram comments was collected to identify cognitive frames, linguistic patterns, and recurring features related to the debate. People with disabilities are often underrepresented, over-medicalized, infantilized, and desexualized in the media. Therefore, the contrasting images presented by Victoria's Secret made some viewers uncomfortable, as they felt the campaign either objectified or manipulated individuals with disabilities. The study reveals that ableist attitudes were camouflaged with patronizing concerns in the online responses, indicated by the language used by commenters. The campaign sparked a discussion about the representation of bodies with disabilities and highlighted the need for more inclusive and nuanced portrayals in the media.
Key-words: disability, sexuality, social media discourse, frames of understanding, ableist gaze.

In February 2022, the famous lingerie brand Victoria's Secret announced the debut of the Love Cloud collection of bras and panties centered around all-day comfort. The launch was considered as a milestone in the company's new vision, inspired as it was by eighteen dynamic and, above all, ordinary women. The explicit aim of this collection was to listen to the real needs of consumers for everyday comfort. In fact, in a press release, the company stated that their promotional campaign was a 'first of its kind campaign for

Textus 1-2023, pp. 157-178

ISSN 1824-3967

the brand, reinforcing Victoria's Secret's commitment to welcoming and celebrating all women'[1]. The collection was meant to be in line with the company's ongoing efforts to focus on comfort, diversity and inclusivity, and a major moment in its evolution. Interestingly, the company had also been recently reinventing its public image, moving away from the world-famous Angels, the supermodels who took part in the annual fashion shows organized until 2019[2], featuring, instead, women differing in age, race, and ability, coming from different walks of life, representing a wide range of backgrounds, body types and experiences – among them, soccer star and LGBTQ activist Megan Rapinoe, actress Priyanka Chopra, LGBTQ model and activist Valentina Sampaio, firefighter Celilo Miles, design consultant Gia Kelsey, production coordinator Yacine Ndaw, former graphic designer with disability Miriam Blanco, and Sofía Jirau, a Puerto Rican woman with Down syndrome. The group of models became a unique representative of the Love Cloud products, cutting ties with the past, just when the brand found itself under fire for objectifying and setting unrealistic expectations for women, while housing and reinforcing an abusive culture[3]. With the Love Cloud collection, the company made a bid to change its focus, regaining relevance with customers while showcasing unique stories within its campaign.

As Victoria's Secret continues its ongoing initiative to become more inclusive by giving prominence to a hard-to-find advertising representation especially of disability in the media, the images of Miriam Blanco and Sofía Jirau (probably the first models with

---

[1] https://www.victoriassecretandco.com/news-releases/news-release-details/victoriassecret-launches-love-cloud-collection-focusing-whole. Unless otherwise specified all websites were last accessed in July 2022.

[2] For nearly two decades (since 1995) the show and its models shaped pop culture, hitting the headlines and causing controversies. The Angels were an élite group of models, carefully selected to represent the brand; indeed, they were probably the most well-known part of the brand. Becoming an Angel was a proof, in itself, of supermodel status. The show was actually quietly halted in 2019 after a number of scandals were brought to public attention (including complaints about a lack of diversity, plunging show ratings, declining sales, and so forth).

[3] The marketing chief and brain behind the Angels' show also caused a backlash after he made controversial comments about plus-size and transgender models. See https://www.businessinsider.com/victorias-secret-why-ed-razek-didnt-resign-execs-say-2019-3?r=US&IR=T.

disability to be featured in a Victoria's Secret campaign) were welcomed with contrasting attitudes and opinions on social media platforms in general, and Instagram in particular. If, on the one hand, some commentators hailed the models' participation as a history-making achievement, others criticized it as objectifying and exploitative, arguing it is wrong to sexualize a person with disability and, above all, with Down syndrome. Instagram users' reactions to Victoria's Secret campaign are, therefore, taken into account to get insight into how the issue of sexuality at the intersection with disability is publicly framed and discursively elaborated. Indeed, the question of who is to count as a sexual subject is contested and uncertain. In this view, the Western discomfort with disability and sexuality is paradigmatic in that the very notion of sexual subjectivity excluding persons with disabilities (henceforth PWDs) is so sedimented that it is hardly ever challenged.

1. Disability and sexuality: some theoretical references

The topic under investigation appears extremely controversial and, at the same time, one of the most neglected areas in several fields of study (Shakespeare, Gillespie-Sells, Davies 1996; Garland-Tomson 2005; Esmail et al. 2010; Grue 2020). In 2008, the UN Convention on the Rights of Persons with Disabilities entered into force as the first binding international instrument enumerating a series of rights directly relating to the sexuality of PWDs and mandating awareness-raising strategies to combat stigma (UN 2011). While sexuality was recognized as a core component of human nature and a human right in itself (see also WHO 2010), encompassing sexual health as well as the complex interactions between biological sex, gender identity and roles, sexual orientation, intimacy and relationships, the sexuality-related rights in the Convention that was ratified were then far less explicit and affirmative than those included in the initial draft (Schaaf 2011). The sexuality of PWDs continued to be mostly discussed in terms of reproductive health, sexual abuse and exploitation, pregnancy prevention, and forced sterilization (UN 2003; UN 2011; Schaaf 2011; Lam et al. 2021). Surprisingly, it remained a peripheral topic also in disability studies until a few decades ago, while it is still under-addressed in social policies, politics and other contexts (Schaaf 2011). Indeed, disability theory itself – which is a rather young field of study – has historically only engaged with disabled women and children's need for special protection from sexual abuse since the latter are vulnerable subjects, while the former are commonly seen as sexually passive or asexual and dependent (Schaaf 2011).

Generally speaking, disability has often been associated with the fear of sexuality as a form of 'abnormality' to be subject to 'governmentality' (Foucault 1984: 338). As an attribute of the body intersecting with the control of the population, sexuality was a central topic in some theoretical contributions which elaborated what Foucault termed as "polymorphous techniques of power" producing effects of truth (Foucault 1984: 298). Power shapes paradigms and social rules through discourses that then frame the limits and boundaries of human behavior and realities. Interestingly, such discourses need not be explicit, as silences too hold power: "Silence itself – the things one declines to say or is forbidden to name [...] is less the absolute limit of discourse [...] than [...] an integral part of the strategies that underlie and permeate discourses" (Foucault 1984: 300). Therefore, the lack of recognition of disability in itself, and at the intersection with sexuality, is a way of regulating it.

Over the last two decades, this silence concerning disability has been partly undermined and tentatively broken (Shuttleworth and Mona 2000; Tepper 2000). In the wake of Foucault's bio-power critique, disability theorists have criticized existing paradigms: the so-called medical or individual model focused on the individual body and the limitations imposed by physical and/or mental impairment; the so-called social model (which was meant to replace the medical model) distinguished between impairment and disability: impairment as a physical or mental dysfunction, disability as a socially constructed assumption of incapacity stemming from an oppressive and discriminatory society (Shildrick 2009; Soder 2009). In this view, it is the social construction of disability that underlies the stigma affecting PWDs, not the impairments themselves. It is worth noting, however, that the social model was also challenged on the grounds that it is hidebound and dismissive of the importance of embodiment. Such critiques were precisely driven by the increasing attention to sexuality as much as by the contribution of feminist and queer theories, according to which the body should be brought back into the area of theoretical inquiry on disability (Shildrick 2009). In fact, dismissing the body at the expense of social analysis meant neglecting the relationship between the public and the private spheres (Shakespeare 1999; Soder 2009).

As a matter of fact, despite its centrality in human nature, the sexuality of PWDs is surrounded by societal stigma, with widespread misconceptions which tend to infantilize them, compromising their normalcy and expression, while causing such issues to be dismissed. A sort of polarity has always existed between sex and disability, which has reinforced the view according to which they are oppositional, and mutually excluding, spheres. The marginalization of disabled – or what were deemed 'atypical' – bodies dates back centuries. Indeed, the discourse of disabled sexual deviance is an extension of the historical legacy of the oppression suffered by PWDs in different contexts, from freak shows to Nazi Germany and present days[4]. Freak shows offered a contested space in which participants could use the "comic horror of monsters" to negotiate what it meant to be 'normal' (Durbach 2009: 4). Decades later, the practice of eugenics in Nazi Germany provided the most compelling example of how the so-called 'degeneracy' of PWDs was eliminated[5]. Moving to more recent times, current body ideals attributed to healthy sexual subjects tend to exclude the 'atypical' bodies of PWDs (De Boer 2014; Galvani 2019), and attractiveness is largely determined by hyper able-bodiedness: the further one deviates from hyper-ability the more their opportunities for sexual expression are compromised. Since sexual expression is believed to be reserved to able-bodied people, the "social attitudes toward disabled people perpetuate sexual exclusion" (De Boer 2014: 77). Therefore, the overt resistance to the sexuality of PWDs culminates

---

[4] Having a disabled body has long meant lacking righteousness and beauty. Determining the scale of humanity by beauty implied that anyone who deviated from the idealized norm could be 'justifiably' expunged. Whereas, in ancient times, PWDs featuring 'atypical' bodies were pushed to the periphery of society, they were embraced within carnivals and freak shows later on, in the 18th and 19th centuries. In such contexts they provided a repertoire for the collective rehearsal of the grotesque (Galvani 2019).

[5] Under the Nazi regime the sexuality of people with disabilities was reduced to their ability to genetically reproduce the fears surrounding the spread of their impure genetic makeup (Galvani 2019).

in its suppression, disability being completely segregated from the realm of sexuality. In this context, it is worth noting that "[r]epresentations of sexual 'correctness' tend to adhere to culturally palatable and societally acceptable standards of sexual normativity that disabled sexual subjects are perceived to not fully possess" (Galvani 2019: 20-21). In fact, mainstream portrayals usually adopt an able-bodied perspective – which has been termed 'ableist gaze' (Lindemann 2008: 110) – failing to challenge abled portrayals of disabled sexual expression. This ableist gaze usually frames PWDs as dependent on others because of a lack of (intellectual/ physical) competences, and invariably considers them permanently incapable of decision-making (Alphen et al. 2011). The concept of 'eternal children' also strengthens the view according to which they have no sexual desire, namely they are asexual (Di Giulio 2003), or they are perceived as non-sexual and less attractive, because they are not 'fit' enough compared to normative standards (Shakespeare, Gillespie-Sells, Davies 1996).

A number of studies have identified certain factors influencing attitudes towards sexuality and disability, among them the type of disability. For instance, while individuals with intellectual disabilities were considered neutral on physical attractiveness, other studies revealed an aversion to the naked body of women with physical disabilities or found women with physical disabilities sexually undesirable (Haring and Meyerson 1979; Chandani et al. 1989). Individuals with physical disabilities were seen as unable to perform sexually, asexual, or unable to provide sexual gratification (Esmail et al. 2010). Another study found that people with traditional gender role beliefs held more negative attitudes towards the sexuality of women with physical disabilities than they did towards the sexuality of men with disabilities (Hasson-Ohayon et al. 2014; Parsons et al. 2017). Variations in attitudes towards sexuality and disability are also related to the type of disability: this is the reason why people with intellectual disabilities are often seen as unable to consent or vulnerable to abuse, while people with physical disabilities are perceived to be asexual or not dateable/marriable (Esmail et al. 2010; Pebdani and Tashjian 2022).

The conjunction of disability and sexuality troubles the parameters of the social and legal policy that purports both to protect the rights and interests of individuals, while promoting the good of society and the socio-political order. The concern of the sociopolitical order is to encompass all bodies within a governmental frame, yet some forms of corporeality exceed the boundaries of what is deemed as 'normal' and, therefore, acceptable. When such 'anomaly' – which is nothing but otherness – relates to sexuality, the most acute overt and/or unspoken anxiety is evoked and mobilized. Such form of aversion to otherness classifies disabled bodies and sexuality as deviant (Galvani 2019). The more one's body deviates from the norm and is problematized the more deviant labels are ascribed to it: "how bodies get read, assessed, and interpellated [...] continues to inform, determine, regulate, and govern how bodies get treated in the world" (Garland-Thomson 2016: 10).

2. Conceptual and methodological framework and corpus design

Drawing on the previously mentioned conceptual constructs, this paper investigates Instagram users' reactions to the Victoria's Secret campaign, to get insight into how the issue of sexuality at the intersection with disability is publicly framed and discursively elaborated. For this purpose, a corpus of Instagram comments to the images posted on Victoria's Secret's official profile has been collected to examine the emerging cognitive frames on such a debated issue, by taking into account salient and recurrent linguistic features (lexical items), semantic properties (positive, negative, neutral connotation), emerging themes and frames, and the inherent tensions and personal stances.

Instagram, a photo and video sharing social networking service, was created in 2010 with the purpose to allow users to upload photographs and short videos that can be edited with filters and organised by hashtags, geotagging their content with the name of a location, adding shoppable features, etc. Users can browse other users' content, view trending content, follow other users to add their content to a personal feed. While social media, in general, are witnessing an exponential growth with more than 4 billion users, Instagram, in particular, has proved to have the potential to leave competitors behind: with its posts, stories, reels, it offers endless opportunities for brands, which is why it is widely preferred over other social media platforms[6]. According to social media statistics,

---

[6] https://www.socialpilot.co/blog/instagram-over-other-social-media-platform.

more than 1.15 billion people use Instagram every month, 90% of all users follow at least one business account, and almost 85% of users discover new products and services thanks to the platform[7]. Statistics also show that the majority of users become more interested in a brand when they see ads on Instagram and they get engaged in what they see more easily (indeed, Instagram has the highest engagement rates among social media platforms). This is the reason why the world's biggest brands choose it to promote their products and services: it has a greater scope of marketing success. It is also the fastest growing social platform around the globe, which certainly helps companies showcase their brand to the world[8].

For this study, users' comments were downloaded from Victoria's Secret's profile: at the time of corpus collection, the picture of Sofia Jirau featured 1.695 comments, while the image of Miriam Blanco featured 408 comments. Since viewers had also a preview of the campaign and of the models involved, comments to the brand's launching post of the Love Cloud collection were additionally retrieved (275 comments). The corpus thus collected was further refined by removing all metadata and comments consisting of emoticons which, despite being increasingly popular and common in social media discourse (where they display a pictorial representation of facial gestures) and despite being able to fully express people's feelings, mood and reactions, did not provide a textual component to be taken into account for analysis. Therefore, the total number of posts after refining data amounts to 1.537 comments.

The following research questions were then formulated:
1) What themes and frames do Instagram users mostly resort to as a reaction to Victoria's Secret's Love Cloud campaign in their online communication?
2) How do they negotiate discourses about disability and sexuality in response to the campaign?
3) To what extent is the sexual expression of people with disabilities still considered as a taboo?

A hybrid methodology integrating tools pertaining to quantitative analysis with frameworks for qualitative analysis was

---

[7] https://www.socialpilot.co/blog/social-media-statistics.
[8] https://www.forbes.com/sites/petersuciu/2019/12/26/is-instagram-the-social-media-service-for-business-in-2020/?sh=53024dd73bdf.

adopted (Baker 2006; Baker et al. 2008, 2013). Both approaches are intended to uncover relationships between language and social context, paying attention to the discursive strategies employed, as they are "systematic ways of using language [...] at different levels of linguistic organization and complexity to achieve a certain social, political, psychological or linguistic aim" (Reisigl and Wodak 2001: 386; see also Fairclough 1995). If all texts and discourses bear the mark of power, defining and maximising or minimising issues (Foucault 1980), in any society "there are manifold relations of power which permeate, characterise and constitute the social body, and these relations of power cannot themselves be established, consolidated or implemented without the production, accumulation, circulation and functioning of a discourse" (Foucault 1980: 93). Therefore, every instance of language use makes its contribution to reproducing and/ or transforming society and culture, doing ideological work while construing specific representations of events, realities, and identities. Within this frame of reference, the contribution of discourse analysis to disability theory is precisely aimed at identifying the exercise of power through language, providing room for the theorisation of the role language plays in the social construal of disability (Grue 2020). Discourse analysis can offer a theoretical procedure for investigation and a strategy for mapping different kinds and forms of knowledge concerning the issue which is taken into account. How is disability conceptualised? What kind of stories do we tell and read about disability? People's everyday lives are filled with (textual and visual) narratives, which then provide them with interpretative frames, forming the basis of their judgment (Grue 2020).

In this context, framing can be a key interpretative tool from a discourse analysis perspective (Tucker 1998; Scheufele 1999; Reese, Gandy and Grant 2001; Ziem 2014), which allows an examination of how discourse structures knowledge, representations and behaviours, providing the cognitive scaffolding to process empirical reality, to negotiate identities and codify phenomena into meanings. According to many views (Sniderman, Brody and Tetlock 1991; Kuypers 2009), frames have the tremendous power to shape the way in which we interpret certain issues and events, thus 'priming' values differentially: "[t]o frame is to select some aspects of a perceived reality and make them more salient in a communicating text, in such a way as to promote a particular problem definition, causal interpretation, moral evaluation, and/or treatment recommendation for the item described" (Entman 1993: 51). Frames can be, therefore, described as powerful rhetorical tools that induce us to filter our perceptions of the world in particular ways (Kuypers 2009). They appear as a rhetorical process whereby communicators construct a point of view that encourages specific interpretations of a given fact or event by other actors involved in communication (see Kuypers 2006).

Drawing on the concept of framing as an interpretative instrument, on disability theory along with discourse studies, this paper aims to explore the intersections between disability and sexuality in social media discourse, questioning how both sexuality and disability are (individually and collectively) understood and framed. Whereas PWDs are usually under-represented in the media, often over-medicalized, infantilized, and desexualized (Shildrick 2007; Loeser, Pini, Crowley 2017), this research investigates the extent to which the contrasting images proposed by Victoria's Secret were positively welcomed by Instagram users or made some viewers uncomfortable, camouflaging ableist attitudes with patronizing concerns, which is more or less overtly encoded in their online responses, signaled by the language they use.

3. Analysing the corpus

In an attempt to respond to the previously mentioned research questions, some linguistic and discursive features that may have been used – recurrent lexical items, labels, their connotative value, shedding light on how some themes are framed – will be specifically looked at, and some illustrative examples from the corpus will be provided with the aim of highlighting the way the Love Cloud campaign images of models with disabilities, namely Sofia Jirau and Miriam Blanco, are perceived and commented.

The first step of analysis was carried out adopting a quantitative approach. The *LoveCloud* corpus was uploaded to SketchEngine (Kilgarriff et al. 2004), which allowed the extraction of single words present in the corpus under investigation, sorted by frequency. The investigation initially considered lexical items in order to have an indication of the 'aboutness' of the corpus, to understand the main concepts, themes and attitudes emerging from the corpus (Phillips

1989). The absolute frequency values retrieved from SketchEngine through a wordlist pointed to a strong reference to 'beauty' (548), and how 'beautiful' (791) these 'models' (562) are, with their image of 'real' (483) women.[9] An analysis of the context of occurrence of the lexical items ranking in the first 50 positions (excluding grammar words) was then carried out through concordance analysis. Viewing the stretch of text where some specific terms appear can be extremely helpful in revealing common patterns and themes within the corpus, consequently, defining its overall focus. However, despite the substantial presence of lexical items which could be commonly said to hold a positive connotation (since they imply an affirmative, positive meaning, as the above-mentioned items which seemed to convey approval, favour and appreciation), an initial and random concordance analysis of such words revealed contrasting aspects. Indeed, in a consistent number of Instagram users' comments, some positively connoted lexical items were employed in a negative context, often ironically, thus taking on a negative connotation, instead, as they were used with a demeaning value to intentionally insult the models. Since automated, quantitative analysis cannot shed light on the connotative meaning of such linguistic forms (Rayson 2008), in order to have a comprehensive understanding of the collected data, an in-depth reading of all the concordances was carried out, to establish the use of the items in context (Baker 2006; Baker et al. 2008, 2013). Therefore, the accurate identification of particularly frequent linguistic forms was the starting point for a thorough and context-informed manual analysis.

Meticulous, close reading of the great majority of the Instagram posts comprised in the *LoveCloud* corpus, allowed their categorisation depending on the most recurrent themes persisting in the posts, which then led to an inductive discussion of how they were framed in discourse. Collectively the themes emerging from the posts can be briefly summarised as follows, and will be soon detailed:
– appreciation of the campaign for its inclusivity;

---

[9] Absolute frequency values are provided in brackets. Lexical items such as 'love' (967), 'cloud' (844), 'Victoria's Secrets' (593), 'women' (321), were not taken into account to identify the 'aboutness' of the corpus because, not surprisingly, they featured very high frequency values.

– appreciation of the models' physical appearance;
– criticism for the campaign;
– disdain and contempt for the models' physical appearance.

The majority of comments to the pictures of Sofia Jirau and Miriam Blanco certainly feature very positive feedback to the campaign. As the instances below show, several posts praise the company for their renewed inclusive approach which allows all women – in their wide-ranging body types – to feel comfortable and sexy at the same time. Most of all, Instagram users and (potential) Victoria's Secret's customers welcome the choice to normalize real women, whether they be curvy, disabled, and so forth, creating a healthy online and offline environment.

(1) Love your campaign VS…Very refreshing to see this in social media. My heart smiles. Beautiful women, beautiful souls[10]

(2) Finally some real female bodies. Some awesome women doing their best

(3) From a disabled woman, thank you!!

(4) Yay! It's about time Victoria Secret started normalizing REAL bodies!!! REAL people!!! Hallelujah!

(5) I love how they have so many body types, even skinny and small-chested like me. All these bodies are beautiful.

(6) Love this incorporate all body types as we are all beautiful and created differently

(7) Wait…is this Victoria's secret?? FINALLY real normal sized women

(8) Thank you for finally having disabled models!! As a disabled woman myself (blind and autistic), I find it very disheartening to see the lack of disability representation in fashion and the media. While I believe that disabled models should have been included long ago, just knowing that you're changing and including more diverse models is a step in the right direction. I'm thrilled to see a disabled model with mobility aids and a model with Downs Syndrome.

(9) I'm a wheel chair user in addition to other mobility aids – this brings me so much joy!

(10) Great to see more diversity and inclusive advertising for all walks of life…

---

[10] Please note that any inaccurate spelling/grammar forms or generally unconventional language features contained in the quoted posts are all authentic. The author has not modified the excerpts in any way.

Instagram users' posts tend to frame the debate highlighting the realness of the models included in the campaign, their beauty, their being grounded in real life, which moves away from the unattainable image of the famous Angels, who were increasingly viewed as out-of-touch and out-of-date. They acknowledge the company's repositioning, and their attempt to include most women rather than excluding them. Quantitative analysis has, indeed, revealed a significantly high presence of the lexical item 'real' (483) in the retrieved comments, which constitutes one of the major frames through which users have processed Victoria's Secret's images. The emerging frame, based on the idea of normalizing normal bodies, rides the wave of body positivity according to which everyone is beautiful and there is no ideal shape to be categorized in. It is no coincidence that another lexical item also featured a particularly high score: 'beautiful' (791). This adjective, bearing an extremely positive connotation, could be often found in relation to the models (as instances will later show) as much as in relation to the company's turnaround and initiative. Such initiative is further framed resorting to additional lexical items – among them 'love' (967), 'smiles' (211), 'joy' (175), 'great' (132), 'thrilled' (60), and so forth – that further stress and reinforce positive judgment and evaluations.

Generally speaking, Instagram users do endorse the concept of body positivity through their comments, fostering self-image and body acceptance regardless of shape, size, colour, gender, and ability. The images of the Love Cloud collection seem to challenge unrealistic beauty standards and ideals, speaking loudly against the practice of body shaming that is so widespread especially on social media and in online interactions. Indeed, body shaming and hate speech can be an everyday experience for some people, leaving terrible psycho-emotional scars (Sherry et al. 2020). The bodies now portrayed by Victoria's Secret have historically suffered from hatred, prejudice, and a lack of respect, they have often been perceived as different and, as such, directly or indirectly discriminated. Against this backdrop, the second emerging thread of comments – that appears linked, to some extent, to the previous one – is the appreciation of the models' physical appearance.

(11) She is GORGEOUS
(12) @miriamblanco Absolutely gorgeous!!!!!!!! Get it girl!!!!

(13) beautiful!!
(14) This is called giving ALL women the confidence they deserve and
    for them to embrace their unique beauty.
(15) I love seeing the unedited diversity of their bodies!
(16) I love to see @sofiajirau
(17) Amazing
(18) Look beautiful!!
(19) This is what we should be seeing more of!
(20) wow…absolutely Stunning!
(21) @victoriassecret thank you for choosing beautiful @sofiajirau !
    Now we will know that this will be opening doors to many girls like
    Sofia with the same dreams!
(22) Beautiful, a role model for all lil' girls with Down syndrome.
    Dreams do come true

Comments resorting to this frame of understanding make
extensive use of adjectives modifying nouns or pronouns. Whether
they be predicate adjectives (appearing in the predicate of a
sentence as a subject complement, as in [11] and [18]), participial
adjectives (based on participles, as in [17] and [20]), descriptive
adjectives (that describe the characteristics, traits or qualities of
a noun/pronoun, as in [13] and [22]), or attributive adjectives
(that are directly next to the noun/pronoun that they modify, as
in [12] and [21])[11], they invariably feature an extremely positive
connotation. Indeed, comments are linguistically structured so as
to convey appreciation and recognition not only of the brand's
dramatic shift to advocate for women's support, but also of
the models' beauty. Most Instagram users cognitively process
Victoria's Secret's images breaking down attitudinal barriers by
interpreting disability as human variation instead of inferiority.
They acknowledge diversity and the complexity of disability and
sexuality while, at the same time, reacting to those narratives by
normalising them.

In stark contrast with the previous themes, the third most
recurrent frame stems from explicit forms of criticism that emerge
from a substantial number of comments within the corpus. Such
instances could not be easily spotted through quantitative analysis
since they do not (necessarily) comprise overtly negative or

---

[11] https://www.merriam-webster.com/dictionary/adjective#note-1.

derogatory terms; therefore, a close (qualitative) reading of all the texts allowed the identification of this attitude.

> (23) Do you really believe in this values, or is it just a washing strategy?
> (24) What for? Does no one really want beauty, an ideal? Yes, it is necessary to support people in difficult situations, but what does it have to do with advertising underwear, which has always been worn by beautiful women with perfect figures. It was an incentive to be better
> (25) This is not VS's image. If people didn't shop there before, the average looking women in your marketing are not going to change that. Can your marketing people, stick with the angels, and sell better quality underwear at better price points.
> (26) Why don't you just make underwear and stop with all the political bullcrap.

The instances above show an emphasis on the belief that the choice of such models for the Love Cloud collection is nothing but a marketing move, or mere window dressing, rather than genuine advocacy efforts to help the cause of body positivity and acceptance. A certain number of posts explicitly asks for a reduced involvement in such political issues to stick, instead, to the production and advertising of underwear, as expected by a brand like Victoria's Secret.

As a matter of fact, an additional trait emerges from analysis of the comments included in the corpus: namely, a feeling of disdain and contempt for the models' physical appearance. Overall, a sadly unexpectedly high number of Instagram users expresses overt disapproval or even annoyance for the brand's changeover and the fact that the iconic Angels were abandoned, explicitly labelling the decision as a form of hypocrisy.

> (27) good old VS…where???
> (28) So is this the new Victoria secret models now??
> (29) I miss the old days with the REAL angels. Stop hypocrisy!
> (30) Oh come one guys, it is awful! It is not beautiful
> (31) Victoria secret needs to go back to their old way of doing things
> (32) you guys need to stop it
> (33) bring back the angels!! What's happening to this brand makes me so sad

Most of the comments are linguistically constructed through the opposition 'old vs. new' Victoria's Secret, which implies assigning a positive value to the company's old approach and a negative value to its new attitude, thus overturning the widespread appreciation for endorsing women's empowerment, diversity and inclusion. Indeed, in opposition to the second frame that was identified, in this case users' texts feature a linguistic prevalence of lexical items such as 'awful' (104), 'horrible' (97), 'wrong' (61), and so forth.

Most interestingly, a number of users which is anything but secondary go as far as to criticize the participation of Miriam Blanco and, above all, Sofia Jirau, on the ground that the campaign would objectify, exploit, and manipulate them.

> (34) So now we're sexualizing young ladies with Down syndrome? My sister has Down syndrome and I find this disgusting.
> (35) She's beautiful but feeling the need to show your body is sad to me. She's so much more than her body…all of these ladies are. The Down's Syndrome girl in her underwear is morally wrong. She has the mental development of a young teen. You should not sexualize vulnerable individuals. #boycottvictoriassecret
> (36) Poor people on display.
> (37) My cousin has Down syndrome and unless she's had a lot of plastic surgery – she doesn't look like she has downs
> (38) Why? Do disabled people need to feel sexy??? @victoriassecret
> (39) No people with downs should be promoting lingerie and underwear
> (40) So much wrong with this.

The main subject they raise in their comments concerns the sexualisation of Sofia Jirau, in particular, which they find utterly disturbing. They cannot cope with the – immoral – idea of a young lady with Down syndrome who becomes the model of an underwear promotional campaign. Linguistic analysis has revealed, indeed, the relatively frequent use of lexical items like '(morally) wrong' (61), 'disgusting' (47), 'sad' (38), 'shocking' (29). Therefore, the sexual lens offered by the Love Cloud campaign applied to PWDs solely frames the issue in terms of some form of deviance and moral abomination in a significant number of Instagram comments.

What can be inferred from the texts retrieved is that societal attitudes towards sexuality and disability still partly revolve around the concept of stigma. Stereotyping seems to remain a major factor when cognitively processing disability at the intersection with sexuality, which leads to a sociocultural conditioning culminating in the stigmatization of those who deviate from the 'norm' (see also Esmail et al. 2010). In fact, stigma appears as the public's attitude toward a person who possesses an attribute that fails to meet societal expectations and who is consequently perceived as "deeply discredited within a particular societal interaction" (Goffman 1963: 3). Any stigmatizing attitude stems from shared values, prejudices, and taboos, and is woven at the very deepest level of the fabric in society. Such attitude distinctly emerges from the Instagram comments to the Love Cloud campaign images of Miriam Blanco and Sofia Jirau.

4. Concluding remarks

This study has investigated the discursive construal of disability and sexuality within Western societies: while tremendous strides towards a formal integration of disabled people are made in terms of rights and living conditions, a counter-trend of segregation is equally at play. PWDs seem to continue to endure broad cultural discrimination and alienation, mostly because engagement with disability – even more so when intersecting with sexuality – elicits a deep-seated anxiety that devalues difference. Enquiring into the status of such issues has proved not only that such research is still a minor concern but also a dangerous ground for the resulting tension between the implicit fears that would simply silence or evade the topic and the optimistic hope for change. In fact, the 'instability' of disability seems to act to destabilize all categories of identity (including sexuality), disabled bodies transgressing the socio-cultural conventions of 'proper' bodily form. If – as Foucault (1984) suggests – power produces effects of truth which shape society through discourses that need not be explicit, as silences too hold power, and silence is an integral part of the strategies that permeate discourses, then the lack of images portraying women with disabilities through the lens of sexuality can be read as a form of 'visual silence'. Avoiding representation of the sexuality of PWDs equals avoiding acknowledgement of it, while still regulating it.

Gaining awareness of the role of power in informing the prevailing assumptions about disability and sexuality and the resulting representations can be a heuristic way of questioning certain values, by exposing the normative and socio-cultural context that originated and legitimated them. If frames shape the way in which we interpret issues and identities, 'priming' values differentially, a (rather excessive) number of (textual/visual) narratives of sexuality and disability appears to be construed through the ableist gaze which marks disabled bodies as different and, therefore, abnormal (Lindemann 2008: 110), abled perspectives tending to otherize disabled bodies.

In this case-study, investigation of the *Love Cloud* corpus aimed at examining how Instagram users classified and made sense of the images of Miriam Blanco and Sofia Jirau, thus processing visual information. Indeed, their bodies could be said to 'deviate' from the norm of accepted mainstream representations. Therefore, the underlying question guiding this study concerned how these bodies and subjectivities were read, interpellated, and treated in social media discourse, how they were semiotically construed and/or deconstrued. Maintaining that a frame is a central organizing idea that provides meaning (Gamson and Modigliani 1987), its signifying elements – lexical items and choices – functionally refer to some specific (and more or less shared) mental structures and perspectives collating ideas to form a coherent whole. Linguistic and discursive analysis of the *LoveCloud* corpus has revealed that the majority of users welcomed Victoria's Secret's models, responding to them through frames of appreciation both of the brand's decision and the models themselves. However, a significant number of users did criticize the company and show an aversion to the body of women with disabilities, probably deeply linked to an aversion for otherness, which possibly stems from framing the sexual expression of PWDs as a deviance and, thus, a taboo.

In the attempt to broaden existing perspectives, it seems worth noting that the ethical issue which is at stake when disability and sexuality are involved cannot be satisfied by an appeal to equality that is reliant on and, at the same time, hostile to difference. What should be uncovered are the universalized attitudes and taken-for-granted assumptions, the negative construal and values that lie behind mainstream representations and perceptions of disability and sexuality. By analyzing social media discourse – in the form of Instagram posts – this study has tried to shed light on the most common cognitive frames emerging from users' comments as a response to the circulating images, to question why meanings concerning disability and sexuality are construed as they are, to open up the parameters of sexuality for everyone, regardless of individual embodiment. Contributing to debates concerning such issues could gradually erode taboos, normalizing these portrayals, empowering PWDs, while providing greater opportunities to include disabled and all types of bodies in visual representations and discourses.

References

ALPHEN, LAURA M., DIJKER, AANTON J. M., BOS, ARJAN E. R., VAN DEN BORNE, BART H. W. AND CURFS, LEOPOLD M. G., 2011, "Explaining not-in-my-backyard responses to different social groups: the role of group characteristics and emotions", *Social Psychological and Personality Science* 2, pp. 245-52.

BAKER, PAUL, 2006, *Using Corpora in Discourse Analysis*, Continuum, London.

BAKER, PAUL, GABRIELATOS, COSTAS, KHOSRAVINIK, MAJID, KRZYŻANOWSKI, MICHAŁ, McENERY, TONY AND WODAK, RUTH, 2008, "A Useful Methodological Synergy? Combining Critical Discourse Analysis and Corpus Linguistics to Examine Discourses of Refugees and Asylum Seekers in the UK Press", *Discourse & Society* 19 (3), pp. 273-305.

BAKER, PAUL, GABRIELATOS, COSTAS AND McENERY, TONY, 2013, *Discourse Analysis and Media Attitudes: The Representation of Islam in the British Press*, Cambridge University Press, Cambridge.

CHANDANI, ASHOK, McKENNA, KRYSS T. AND MAAS, FREDERICK, 1989, "Attitudes of University Students towards the Sexuality of Physically Disabled People", *British Journal of Occupational Therapy* 52 (6), pp. 233-236.

DE BOER, TRACY, 2014, "Disability and Sexual Inclusion", *Hypatia* 30 (1), pp. 66-81.

DI GIULIO, GINA, 2003, "Sexuality and People Living with Physical or Developmental Disabilities: A Review of Key Issues", *Canadian Journal of Human Sexuality* 12 (1), pp. 53-68.

DURBACH, NADJA, 2009, *Spectacle of Deformity: Freak Shows and Modern British Culture*, available at http://ebookcentral.proquest.com/lib/sfu-ebooks/detail.action?docID=470936, last accessed July 3, 2022.

ENTMAN, ROBERT M., 1993, "Framing: Toward clarification of a fractured paradigm", *Journal of Communication* 43, pp. 51-58.

ESMAIL, SHANIFF, DARRY, KIM, WALTER, ASHLEA AND KNUPP, HEIDI, 2010,

"Attitudes and Perceptions towards Disability and Sexuality", *Disability and Rehabilitation* 32 (14), pp. 1148-1155.

FAIRCLOUGH, NORMAN, 1995, *Discourse and Social Change*, Wiley-Blackwell Publishing, Cambridge.

FOUCAULT, MICHEL, 1980, *Power/Knowledge: Selected Interviews and Other Writings 1972-1977*, Pantheon, New York.

FOUCAULT, MICHEL, 1984, *The Foucault Reader*, Pantheon Books, New York.

GALVANI, LUKE, 2019, *Challenging Discourses of Disabled Sexual Deviance: An Historic Overview and Critical Analysis* (MA dissertation), Simon Fraser University.

GAMSON, WILLIAM and MODIGLIANI, ANDRÉ, 1987, "The Changing Culture of Affirmative Action", *Research in Political Sociology* 3, 137-177.

GARLAND-THOMSON, ROSEMARIE, 2005, "Feminist Disability Studies", *Journal of Women in Culture and Society* 30 (2), 1557-87.

GARLAND-THOMSON, ROSEMARIE, 2016, "Becoming Disabled", *The New York Times*.

GOFFMAN, ERVING, 1963, *Stigma. Notes on the Management of Spoiled Identity*, Simon & Schuster, New York.

GRUE, JAN, 2020, *Disability and Discourse Analysis*, Routledge, London&New York.

HARING, MAX AND MEYERSON, LAURA, 1979, "Attitudes of College Students toward Sexual Behaviour of Disabled Persons", *Archives of Physical Medicine and Rehabilitation* 60 (6), pp. 257-260.

HASSON-OHAYON, ILANIT, HERTZ, IFAT, VILCHINSKY, NOA AND KRAVETZ, SHLOMO, 2014, "Attitudes toward the sexuality of Persons with Physical Versus Psychiatric Disabilities", *Rehabilitation Psychology* 59 (2), pp. 236-241.

KILGARRIFF, ADAM, RYCHLY, PAVEL, SMRZ, PAVEL AND TUGWELL, DAVID, 2004, "The Sketch Engine", in G. Williams and S. Vessier, (eds), *Proceedings of the 11th EURALEX International Congress: EURALEX 2004*, Université de Bretagne-Sud: Lorient, 105-116.

KUYPERS, JIM A., 2006, *Bush's War: Media Bias and Justification for War in a Terrorist Age*, Rowman & Littlefield Publishers, London.

KUYPERS, JIM A., 2009, "Framing Analysis. How to Conduct a Rhetorical Framing Study of the News", in J.A. Kuypers (ed.), *Rhetorical Criticism: Perspectives in Action*, Lexington Books, Lanham.

LAM, ANGUS, YAU, MATTHEW, FRANKLIN, RICHARD C. AND LEGGAT, PETER A., 2021, "Public Opinion on the Sexuality of People with Intellectual Disabilities: A Review of the Literature", *Sexuality and Disability* 39, pp. 395-419.

LINDEMANN, KURT, 2008, "'I can't be standing up out there': Communicative Performances of (Dis)Ability in Wheelchair Rugby", *Text and Performance Quarterly* 28 (1-2), pp. 98-115.

LOESER, CASSANDRA, PINI, BARBARA and CROWLEY VICKY, 2017, "Disability and Sexuality. Desires and Pleasures", *Sexualities* 21 (3), pp. 255-270.

PARSONS, ALEXANDRIA L., REICHL, ARLEIGH J., PEDERSEN CORY L., 2017, "Gendered Ableism: Media Representations and Gender Role Beliefs' Effect on Perceptions of Disability and Sexuality", *Sexuality and Disability* 35 (2), pp. 207-225.

PEBDANI, ROXANNA N. and TASHJIAN, AMANDA, 2022, "An Analysis of the Attitudes of the General Public towards the Sexuality of Individuals with Disabilities through a Systematic Literature Review", *Sexuality and Disability* 40, pp. 21-55.

PHILLIPS, MARTIN A., 1989, *Lexical Structure of Text* (Discourse Analysis Monograph no. 12, English Language Research), University of Birmingham.

RAYSON, PAUL, 2008, "From Key Words to Key Semantic Domains", International Journal of Corpus Linguistics 13 (4), pp. 519-49.

REESE, STEPHEN D., GANDY, OSCAR H., GRANT AUGUST E. (eds), 2001, *Framing Public Life: Perspectives on Media and Our Understanding of the Social World*, Routledge, London.

REISIGL, MARTIN and WODAK, RUTH, 2001, *Discourse and Discrimination: Rhetorics of Racism and Anti-Semitism*, Routledge, London.

SCHAAF, MARTA, 2011, "Negotiating Sexuality in the Convention on the Rights of Persons with Disabilities", *SUR International Journal on Human Rights* 14, pp. 113-131.

SCHEUFELE, DIETRAM A., 1999, "Framing as a Theory of Media Effects", *Journal of Communication* 49 (1), pp. 103-122.

SCIOR, KATRINA, 2012, "Public Awareness, Attitudes and Beliefs regarding Intellectual Disability", *Research in Developmental Disability* 32, pp. 2164-2182.

SHAKESPEARE, TOM, 1999, "The Sexual Politics of Disabled Masculinity", *Sexuality and Disability* 17 (1), pp. 53-64.

SHAKESPEARE, TOM, GILLESPIE-SELLS, KATH, DAVIES, DOMINIC, 1996, *The Sexual Politics of Disability: Untold Desires*, Cassell, London.

SHERRY, MARK, OLSEN, TERJE, VEDELER, JANNIKE S., ERIKSEN JOHN (eds), 2020, *Disability Hate Speech. Social, Cultural and Political Contexts*, Routledge, London-New York.

SHILDRICK, MARGRIT, 2007, "Contested Pleasures: The Sociopolitical Economy of Disability and Sexuality", *Sexuality Research & Social Policy* 4 (53), https://doi.org/10.1525/srsp.2007.4.1.53, last accessed July 6, 2022.

SHILDRICK, MARGRIT, 2009, *Dangerous Discourses of Disability, Subjectivity and Sexuality*, Palgrave Macmillan, New York.

SHUTTLEWORTH, RUSSELL, and MONA, LAURA R., 2000, "Introduction to the Special Issue", *Sexuality and Disability* 18 (4), pp. 229-231.

SNIDERMAN, PAUL M., BRODY, RICHARD A., TETLOCK, PHILIP E., 1991, *Reasoning and Choice: Explorations in Political Psychology*, CUP, England.

SODER, MARTEN, 2009, "Tensions, Perspectives and Themes in Disability Studies", *Scandinavian Journal of Disability Research* 11 (2), pp. 67-81.

TEPPER, MITCHELL S., 2000, "Sexuality and Disability: The Missing Discourse of Pleasure", *Sexuality and Disability* 18 (4), pp. 283-290.

TUCKER, LAUREN R., 1998, "The Framing of Calvin Klein. A Frame Analysis of Media Discourse about the August 1995 Calvin Klein Jeans Advertising Controversy", *Critical Studies in Mass Communication* 15, pp. 141-157.

UNITED NATIONS, 2003, *Standard Rules on the Equalization of Opportunities for Persons with Disabilities*, available at http://www.un.org/esa/socdev/enable/dissre00.htm, last accessed July 1, 2022.

UNITED NATIONS, 2011, *Convention on the Rights of Persons with Disabilities*, available at http://www.un.org/disabilities/default.asp?navid=13&pid=150, last accessed July 7, 2022.

WORLD HEALTH ORGANIZATION, 2010, *Developing Sexual Health Programmes. A Framework for Action*, available at https://apps.who.int/iris/handle/10665/70501, last accessed July 9, 2022.

ZIEM ALEXANDER, 2014, *Frames of Understanding in Text and Discourse*, Benjamins, Amsterdam.

(Re)framing Climate Change in a Climate Sceptic Online News Outlet

Jacqueline Aiello

Abstract
This paper centres on how climate change is framed in *The Daily Wire*, one of the most popular American right-wing alternative media outlets and one of the leading news sources of climate sceptical views in the US at the time of writing. Corpus-assisted discourse analysis methodologies and semantic analysis are applied to the study of the 376 articles published about climate change in *The Daily Wire* from 2018 to 2021. Specifically, it investigates the themes and concepts that the outlet made most salient and the ways in which framing devices (tags, titles, and visuals) and discursive strategies were used to articulate frames within these articles. The main topics and themes that emerge in the semantic analysis suggest that *The Daily Wire* provided a largely unbiased and objective account of climate change, but the analysis of comparative keywords and framing devices provides a contrasting view of how the issue and its advocates were presented. *The Daily Wire* equated environmentalism to religion, exploited frames identified as diminishing people's propensity to support climate action, and focused on the faults in the characters and experiences of leading (female) climate activists. The findings of this study can help glean insights into the discursive mechanisms that govern the advancement of climate scepticism and other antagonistic ideologies to conservative audiences.

Key-words: alternative media, climate scepticism, corpus-assisted discourse analysis, (de)legitimisation strategies, framing.

1. Introduction

Climate change is one of the most critical issues of our times. Notwithstanding the scientific consensus that climate change is happening, chiefly caused by humans, and a pressing threat, the issue remains fraught with conflict and division. In the American context, public opinion on climate change has become increasingly polarized. An overwhelming majority of Democrats believe in the

Textus 1-2023, pp. 179-197

ISSN 1824-3967
© Carocci Editore S.p.A.

climate science consensus, while supporters of the Republican Party are much more sceptical today than they were in the 1990s (Merkley and Stecula 2021). The intensification of environmental advocacy since 2018, ignited by global climate advocacy movements such as the youth-led Fridays For Future and the introduction into the US Congress of the Green New Deal (GND) resolution, the first policy proposal of its kind, has only exacerbated this tendency.

The present paper examines opinion polarization in the US on the climate science consensus by investigating how climate change is framed in *The Daily Wire,* one of the most popular right-wing alternative media outlets and one of the leading news sources of climate sceptical views in the US at the time of writing. Although audiences actively interpret news media content and are more eager to accept it if it adheres to their existing viewpoints (Bell 1994), news media do influence how audiences perceive issues. Considerations that are emphasized by trusted news sources can help shape or even determine attitudes and preferences on issues. For many American conservatives, a reliable source is *The Daily Wire.* From 2020 to 2021, stories published by *The Daily Wire* received significantly more user engagement (in terms of likes, shares, and comments on Facebook) than any other American news outlet, including both mainstream news sources like *The New York Times, The Washington Post, CNN* and *Fox News* and conservative alternative media sources such as *Breitbart News* and *The Western Journal* (Parks 2021). Therefore, the examination of the mechanisms that govern the framing of climate change in *The Daily Wire* can help glean insights into how climate scepticism and other antagonistic ideologies are advanced to conservative readers.

2. Frames and climate change

Framing is here defined, following Entman (1993: 52), as "selecting some aspects of a perceived reality and making them more salient in a communicating text, in such a way as to promote a particular problem definition, causal interpretation, moral evaluation, and/or treatment recommendation". Social actors invoke frames that emphasize some aspects of reality and make them more salient while de-emphasizing others as they strive to persuade their audiences to support their viewpoint. The masterly use of frames, which can be activated with just a single word, is crucial in the development of a cogent argument (Stecula and Merkley 2019). In addition to text, multimodal features including visual elements and online tools can act as framing devices that occasion 'framing effects', or "when (often small) changes in the presentation of an issue or an event produce (sometimes large) changes of opinion" (Chong and Druckman 2007: 104).

Effective framing has been identified as a pivotal mechanism for the success of social movements including within the effort to advance environmental policy. Nisbet (2009: 14) maintained that "reframing the relevance of climate change in ways that connect to a broader coalition of Americans […] can generate the level of public engagement required for policy action" and Lakoff (2010: 76) argued that, ideally, to make a convincing case for the environment "what needs to be done is to activate the progressive frames on the environment (and other issues) and inhibit the conservative frames" via "language (framing the truth effectively) and experience (e.g., providing experiences of the natural world)". Just as it has been embraced as a mechanism to cultivate environmental activism, so has framing been recognized as a powerful tool in maintaining the status quo. US Republican consultant Frank Luntz famously authored a memo in 2003 that laid the groundwork for contemporary conservative talk about climate change. He urged Republican Congressmembers to frame climate science as uncertain, and policy action as posing an economic burden unfairly borne by the US alone. Luntz also recommended that 'climate change' be used instead of 'global warming' to frame the issue in a less frightening way that de-emphasizes human causation (Lakoff 2010).

Scholars have followed in this vein with the examination of framing mechanisms and devices used in discourses about climate change and their effects. One area of research has zeroed in on the terminology used to name the issue, often revealing findings at odds with Luntz's recommendation. For instance, Schuldt, Konrath and Schwarz (2011: 124) found that 'global warming' was the preferred term by conservative thinktanks and that Republican survey respondents expressed more climate scepticism when the phenomenon was named 'global warming' instead of 'climate change'. The authors speculated that the focus on rising temperatures inherent in the name 'global warming' makes the issue vulnerable to contrasting argumentation (such as a cold spell), and it is therefore "a more appealing frame for those who favor the status quo in climate policy" (p. 122). Other studies such as Jaskulsky and Besel (2013), however, found no differences in perceptions of the significance of the phenomenon when 'global warming' or 'climate change' were used, and instead isolated 'climatic disruption' as the term that gave rise to the greatest response in terms of seriousness among survey respondents, even over 'climate crisis'. These studies suggest, albeit to varying degrees, that the terminology used to refer to environmental phenomena matters.

Another significant line of research has shed interesting interdisciplinary insights into the framing of climate change in its news coverage. Liu and Huang (2022) performed semantic analysis of *New York Times* articles in a 20-year period that contained the phrases 'global warming' or 'climate change' in their titles to determine the presence of three themes: environment, politics, and science. They also found differences in how the two terms were used, with a tendency for representations of 'climate change' to be framed as more politicized, contentious, and serious than 'global warming'. Of note, this is likely indicative of a general shift in how the newspaper framed the phenomenon due to the dramatic rise in the use of 'climate change' over 'global warming' in the *New York Times* since 2014. In another noteworthy study, political scientists Dominik Stecula and Eric Merkley (2019) examined diachronic changes in the use of three classes of frames identified as relevant to the societal debate on climate change – economic costs and benefits, ideologically conservative appeals, and uncertainty and risk in climate science – in articles about climate change in four prominent mainstream American news media outlets. Stecula and Merkley (2019) witnessed a decrease in frames found to lower support and engagement in climate action (i.e., economic costs of climate action and uncertainty of climate science), an increase in frames that highlight economic benefits and risks and dangers, and limited use of conservative ideological framing.

Although these two recent studies cast an important light on the prevalent frames used in the news coverage of climate change, their focus exemplifies the tendency for scholars of media representations of climate change to concentrate on mainstream print sources (Schäfer and Schlichting 2014). To address this gap, this study builds on previous research with an investigation into how *The Daily Wire,* an alternative yet influential partisan online news provider, frames climate change in its coverage of the issue. Specifically, it seeks to answer the following research questions: What themes and concepts does *The Daily Wire* make most salient in its coverage of climate change? In what ways are framing devices (tags, titles, and visuals) and discursive strategies used to articulate frames and to what effect?

3. Data and Methods

The data selected for this study were *The Daily Wire* articles about climate change posted on www.dailywire.com from 2018 to 2021. The search function of the website (www.dailywire.com/search/news) was used to identify articles that contained the tag 'Climate Change' in the four-year period of interest. This topic tag was deemed most appropriate because, as described previously, it is the term that is most frequently used by news providers and traditionally most favoured by conservatives. The search generated a list of 376 articles.

FIGURE I. MONTHLY FREQUENCY OF *THE DAILY WIRE* ARTICLES TAGGED CLIMATE CHANGE (2018-2021)

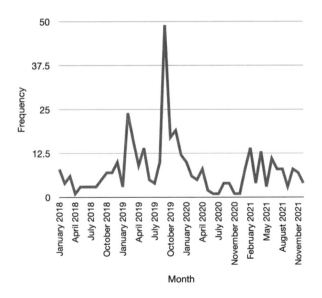

Figure 1 displays the monthly frequency of *The Daily Wire* articles about climate change in the designated period. Although 8 articles were posted per month on average, close to half (48%) were posted in 2019 alone, with two notable peaks in frequency. In the first peak (Feb-Mar), which corresponds with the presentation of the GND resolution to Congress, a combined 40 articles tagged 'Climate Change' were posted. During the second, more pronounced peak in September 2019, when the UN Climate Action Summit was held in NYC, 49 articles were posted on the topic.

The textual content of each of the selected articles, excluding author names and dates, constituted a 275,473-token corpus, named *The Daily Wire* Climate Change (DWCC) corpus. Other information about and within the articles, including the titles, visual elements, and other tags applied, was also collected.

To determine the most preferred themes, semantic analysis of the DWCC corpus was performed using the UCREL Semantic Analysis System within the corpus-analytic tool Wmatrix 3.0 (Rayson 2008), following the analytic procedure described in Liu and Huang (2022). A list of fifteen semantic categories was generated using this tool by comparing the DWCC corpus to the British National Corpus (BNC) Sampler written corpus in Wmatrix. The analysis of the tokens that constituted these categories led to the development of thematic areas. Next, keyness analysis was performed to extract keywords, or words that occur with unusual frequency that aid in "the understanding of the main concepts, topics or attitudes discussed in a text or corpus" (Gabrielatos 2018). This method involves comparing the frequency lists of a larger, more general reference corpus and a smaller, more specialized target corpus (in this case, the DWCC corpus). The reference corpus used for this study was English Web 2020 (enTenTen20; Jakubíček et al. 2013), which is readily available in Sketch Engine (www.sketchengine.eu), a corpus manager and text analysis software tool. enTenTen20, constituted by texts collected from the internet between 2019 and 2021, contains sub-corpora based on language varieties and – considering the context of *The Daily Wire* and the likely linguacultural background of the authors – the sub-corpora "US domain.us", with roughly 353 million words, was used as a reference corpus for the keyness analysis. A list of 15 keywords, which excluded proper names, was generated. This quantitative comparative keyword analysis was supported by the study of the keywords in context, first by using Sketch Engine's concordance tool and then by examining the discursive strategies delineated in the Discourse-Historical Approach (DHA), with a focus on nomination, predication, and perspectivization strategies (Reisigl and Wodak 2009) as well as (de)legitimization strategies (van Leeuwen 2007).

Subsequently, accompanying tags, selected titles, and selected visuals, which are herein viewed as framing devices, were analysed. First, the most frequent tags that appeared alongside 'Climate Change' were identified. Tags are keywords that are assigned to online resources for purposes of classification and indexing (Lee 2018). Although tagging may seem like a neutral categorization process, the analysis of tags can reveal the facets that a tagger wants to make most visible and salient as well as the use of (potentially) biased or value-laden terminology. The next analytical step focused on the titles of selected *The Daily Wire* articles on climate change, since titles are one of the first pieces of information that attract readers' attention and word selection within titles can influence readers' understandings of events and participants involved. Based on the findings of the tag analysis, two sets of five randomly selected article titles were generated by Sketch Engine from the list of all 376 titles and were analysed discursively, again drawing on the DHA. Although space constraints prohibited an in-depth look into visual elements, a cursory multimodal discourse analysis was performed of selected images depicting two social actors on which climate change coverage in *The Daily Wire* frequently focused.

4. Results

4.1. Semantic analysis and keywords: salient themes and concepts

Table 1 shows the top 15 key semantic categories (SMCs) in the DWCC corpus. Three themes emerge from the examination of the most frequent tokens in these key SMCs. The top key SMCs refer to the theme of 'environment', including the semantic tags 'weather' (e.g., climate – 2097 occurrences, weather – 95, wind – 47, storm(s) – 45), 'green issues' (e.g., environment(al) – 348, pollution – 53, nature – 38), and 'the universe' (e.g., world(s) – 620, planet(s) – 233, solar – 84, globe – 23). Another theme is 'politics', which included the semantic tags 'politics' (e.g., democratic – 175, political – 147, activist(s) – 174, socialist – 88), and 'government' (President – 349, government – 181, country – 144, presidential – 143). The third is 'science', in which there is the occurrence of the semantic tags 'substances and materials: gas' (gas and gases – 180, air – 89, carbon dioxide and CO_2 – 116), and 'science and technology in general' (science – 124, scientists – 68, nuclear – 50, scientific – 47).

TABLE 1. TOP 15 KEY SMCS IN *THE DAILY WIRE* CLIMATE CHANGE CORPUS

	Tag	LL	SMC
1	W4	5179.03	Weather
2	Z99	1684.85	Unmatched
3	W5	1270.79	Green issues
4	W1	1239.14	The universe
5	G1.2	952.93	Politics
6	S2	939.02	People
7	Q2.1	830.56	Speech: Communicative
8	A2.1+	825.85	Change
9	Q2.2	647.82	Speech acts
10	O1.3	597.51	Substances and materials: Gas
11	G1.1	518.47	Government
12	M5	366.23	Flying and aircraft
13	A13	358.61	Degree
14	A5.1---	358.19	Evaluation: Bad
15	Y1	336.07	Science and technology in general

Interestingly, these three themes are the same as those that transpired from Liu and Huang's (2022) analysis of the top key SMCs in *New York Times* articles with 'global warming' and 'climate change' in their titles. This suggests that the topics and themes of *The Daily Wire*'s climate change coverage are largely analogous to those selected by mainstream liberal-leaning news providers such as the *New York Times*.

To explore the DWCC corpus in more detail, keyness analysis was performed to generate the top fifteen keywords, included in Table 2. The keywords largely support the aforedescribed semantic analysis since all but four prominently featured keywords can be defined as closely related to environmental and scientific domains (i.e., 'net-zero', 'climate', 'extinction', 'environmentalism', 'anti-climate', 'environmentalist', 'fart' (in reference to bovine methane emissions), 'emission', 'fossil' fuels), and the political realm (i.e., 'far-left', 'congresswoman'), but the examination of these keywords in context paints a more nuanced picture.

TABLE 2. RESULTS OF THE COMPARATIVE KEYWORD ANALYSIS

	Item	Frequency (focus, case insensitive)	Score
1	far-left	57	105.57
2	net-zero	32	88.665
3	climate	2126	85.712
4	alarmist	56	69.202
5	extinction	110	54.253
6	congresswoman	45	53.046
7	environmentalism	30	50.148
8	anti-climate	13	47.448
9	environmentalist	63	46.913
10	existential	44	46.118
11	fart	27	44.911
12	emission	416	42.723
13	fossil	196	40.583
14	alarmism	15	39.688
15	activist	275	39.046

Taking the example of 'environmentalism', which encapsulates the way of thought central to climate advocacy and had 30 occurrences in the DWCC corpus, *The Daily Wire* uses the term in a neutral way (to describe a movement or issue) in only three instances. Other mentions of the term are accompanied by persuasive definitions and analogies that have the effect of delegitimizing and casting doubt on the stated intentions of the movement. One of the primary practices found in the corpus to this end defined the movement as a religion, a metaphor that is exploited by the outlet to frame the movement, its advocates, and followers in a negative light. As maintained by Jaspal et al. (2016: 811), in their study of climate scepticism in Australian newspaper articles, the "use of religious metaphors can serve to construct climate science as speculative and dogmatic, rather than empirically and scientifically grounded". In the DWCC corpus, in addition to explicitly qualifying the movement as the "religion of environmentalism", environmentalism is defined as "a doomsday cult" and "a religious cult", and it is described as "complete with saints, sacraments, and consequences for refusing to bow to their dogma" and as having "preachers of the apocalypse". One article explains that, "in environmentalism, the penitent environmentalist will not find salvation as long as the polluters pollute" and another article charges that "millions of kids are being indoctrinated into it". The use of (extremist) religious metaphors and labels such as 'cult', 'dogma', 'penitent', 'salvation' and 'indoctrinate' performs crucial rhetorical functions (Jaspal et al. 2016). Not only do these analogies define environmentalism not as science-based but as faith-based, but their extremist overtones also serve to delegitimize environmentalist efforts as rooted in fanaticism and propaganda, and to discursively characterize the leaders of the movement as zealous fanatics and its followers as gullible and brainwashed. This portrayal of radical environmentalists and credulous followers paves the way for *The Daily Wire* to claim that environmentalism is a "sham", it has "little to do with the environment", and it is enacted to satisfy the nefarious aims of its advocates (e.g., "[environmentalism] is an obvious power grab" and "[environmentalism] is more about money and power for politicians and self-aggrandizement for the activists blocking traffic in D.C.").

Relatedly, also of note are the uses of the keywords 'far-left' and 'alarmist', which are both used as attributes assigned to climate activists and their agenda. With respect to the former, which is used to discursively characterize activists like "far-left Rep. Alexandria Ocasio-Cortez" and "far-left activist Greta Thunberg", it explicitly politicizes climate change by situating it on a single pole of the political spectrum. Furthermore, along with 'socialist', which emerged within the aforementioned semantic tag 'politics', the recurrence of 'far-left' evokes the ideological threat of socialism and government interference and overreach, which is constructed, fallaciously, as analogous to climate actions and its advocates (Reisigl and Wodak 2009). With respect to the latter keyword, the negative predication 'alarmist' used with reference to climate activists and their message portrays the activists as catastrophists and fearmongers.

In sum, the topics and themes included in *The Daily Wire* coverage dedicated to climate change are on the surface comparable to the coverage of other news outlets, even the liberal-leaning *New York Times*. A closer look however reveals a concerted effort to delegitimize and cast doubt on the movement on the grounds that it is not an honest endeavour to safeguard the environment, but it is an extremist campaign orchestrated by Liberal politicians and advocates to secure power and influence.

4.2. Framing Devices: Tagging, Titles, and Visuals

Accompanying tags used alongside 'Climate Change' in the articles that constituted the DWCC corpus are displayed in Table 3.

TABLE 3. OTHER TOPIC TAGS APPLIED TO *THE DAILY WIRE* CLIMATE CHANGE ARTICLES

Topic Tag	Frequency	Topic Tag	Frequency
Global Warming	141	Leftism	16
Environmentalism	61	CNN	15
Alexandria Ocasio-Cortez	58	Green New Deal	14
Greta Thunberg	45	United Nations	13
Democratic Party	38	Al Gore	12
Donald Trump	35	Hollywood	12
Joe Biden	34	John Kerry	11
Bernie Sanders	17		

Based on traditional conservative discourse on the environment, one might expect the phrase 'global warming' to be altogether avoided in this media outlet. Yet, this was the most frequently recurring tag, applied to more than one third of articles. This co-occurrence may in part be suggestive of the tendency for the terms 'climate change' and 'global warming' to be increasingly used interchangeably in news media (Liu and Huang 2022), notwithstanding the fact that they are technically distinct phenomena that evoke different political meanings (See Luntz's memo). However, there is also evidence in the DWCC corpus that 'global warming' may be used by *The Daily Wire* contributors to undermine the climate science consensus. First, 'global warming' was often written when describing weather events characterized by atypically cold temperatures, as emblemized in the 05/01/2018 *The Daily Wire* article entitled "Bitterly Cold Global Warming Strikes East Coast", in which the juxtaposition of 'bitterly cold' with 'global warming' creates a paradoxical construction that can provoke a dismissive response by the reader. This usage displays how 'global warming' can be useful for climate sceptics interested in communicating the scientific uncertainty of climate change (Schuldt, Konrath, Schwarz 2011). Secondly, the co-occurrence of the two tags itself enacts the uncertainty frame. We can see how this is enacted in the body of the same 05/01/2018 article, where the author stated, "those same 'experts' are saying that global warming ... er, climate change ... means it can sometimes get a lot colder". Here, the two terms are occasioned to situate the phenomenon as doubtful, akin to climate experts whose expertise is dismissed with the use of scare quotes.

Just as the tags applied provide insight into how climate change coverage is framed in *The Daily Wire*, so do the tags that were never applied. For instance, 'Climate Crisis' was never used as a tag. Even in the corpus, where there were 120 instances of 'climate crisis', the phrase predominantly appears within direct quotations of climate advocates, within scare quotes (e.g., "'climate crisis' agenda") that serve as a perspectivization strategy that dissociates the author from the quoted content or preceded by the uncertainty markers "supposed" or "alleged". Unsurprisingly, 'Climatic Disruption', the term that was found by Jaskulsky and Besel (2013) to garner the most serious response to environmental issues, never appeared as a tag or within the DWCC corpus.

Most other tags suggest that the articles were about social actors from the realms of politics, environmental activism, media, and entertainment. The fact that one third of the top tags are Liberal politicians suggests that *The Daily Wire* strove to politicize the issue, an effort that is supported by the tags 'Democratic Party' and 'Leftism'. The politician whose name served as the most frequent tag was Alexandria Ocasio-Cortez, a Representative also known as AOC who was in her freshman term for most of the period under study. Although Ocasio-Cortez co-sponsored the GND policy package with Senator Ed Markey, who had served as an elected official since 1973, the latter appeared in only two tags. Ocasio-Cortez's name was used as a tag over three times more frequently in articles about climate change than Bernie Sanders, a US Presidential candidate who developed the GND into a fully-fledged policy (Galvin and Healy 2020). The GND resolution itself was a tag for only 14 articles. A focus on Representative Ocasio-Cortez over other environmentalist politicians and her proposed policy may be indicative of the attempt to undermine environmental advocacy by drawing on *ad hominem* attacks to personally discredit the Representative – an easier target as a political newcomer than other seasoned politicians – instead of presenting arguments against the GND.

A perusal of the titles of the articles in which Ocasio-Cortez was tagged provide insight into how contributors to *The Daily Wire* sought to delegitimize the politician and her environmentalist stance, and to frame climate change vis-a-vis the freshman politician. Sketch Engine was used to generate a list of five randomly selected titles that contained 'Ocasio-Cortez' or 'AOC', which follow in chronological order:

(a) "Ocasio-Cortez Can't Understand Ivanka's Problem With 'Green New Deal'" (27/02/2019)
(b) "Trump Savages AOC: 'Young Bartender' Has Dems 'Petrified'" (04/03/2019)
(c) "Ocasio-Cortez Appears To Change Mind Again On 'Climate Disaster' Deadline" (29/05/2019)
(d) "Ocasio-Cortez Gets Smacked By Meteorologist Over 'Climate Crisis' Claims" (09/07/2019)
(e) "Epidemiologist Ocasio-Cortez Warns That Melting Glaciers Could Release Ancient Diseases" (29/08/2019)

In these five titles, there are several strategies employed to delegitimize Representative Ocasio-Cortez. First, the titles use negative predications with reference to Ocasio-Cortez (Reisigl and Wodak 2009): she is dull-witted for her failure to comprehend a political adversary's critiques (a), she lacks (political) experience as a "young bartender" (b), and is inconsistent in her climate change beliefs (c). The portrayal of the politician as lacking the wits, expertise, and trustworthiness expected of elected officials has the effect of delegitimizing her institutional role, her anti-climate change policy proposal, and her environmentalist beliefs. The climate science consensus is also questioned with use of scare quotes (titles c and d) and with a satirical frame in title (e). In the latter, the inaccurate qualifier 'Epidemiologist' not only positions Ocasio-Cortez as a non-expert but also delegitimizes the claim that "melting glaciers could release ancient diseases", which has been sustained and supported by the scientific community (See Yarzábal, Salazar, Batista-García 2021). Lastly, sources that *The Daily Wire* deems as trusted are presented as successfully (and violently) quashing the Representative and her views ('Trump Savages AOC' in title b and 'Ocasio-Cortez Gets Smacked By Meteorologist' in d).

The images that frequently accompany articles that feature Representative Ocasio-Cortez reinforce this delegitimization by failing to portray her in a flattering manner. In these photographs, she is often not smiling, which promotes the view that she is not likeable (Paul and Perreault 2020), and not looking at the camera, suggesting that her attention is directed elsewhere. Moreover, she is frequently pictured with her mouth open, a facial expression that both makes it seem that she is shouting and evokes a sexualized image of the politician.

The second most frequently tagged actor was Greta Thunberg. Again, Sketch Engine was used to generate a list of five randomly selected *The Daily Wire* titles on climate change that contained the activist's name, reproduced below:

(a) "BACKLASH: Critics Lambast Melodramatic Greta Thunberg Speech As 'Child Abuse'" (24/09/2019)
(b) "WALSH: Asia Is Responsible For The Vast Majority Of Air And Water Pollution. Greta Thunberg Should Go Lecture Them" (25/09/2019)
(c) "Defeated Greta Whines Climate Strikes Have 'Achieved Nothing,' Claims People Are 'Dying Today'" (07/12/2019)
(d) "Greta Snaps Over Demands: 'We Want This Done Now – As In Right Now'" (12/01/2020)
(e) "Facebook Glitch Reveals Father, Activist Behind Greta Thunberg's Facebook Page. Greta Responds." (13/01/2020)

The titles of the articles present the activist as "melodramatic" (a) and "defeated" (c), and the actions attributed to her position her as abusive (her "speech" is characterized as "child abuse", a), immature (she "whines," an action often attributed to children, c), and unreasonable (she "snaps" and wants things "Done Now – As In Right Now" d). In title (e), it is claimed that her father is "behind" her Facebook page, which evokes the conspiratorial belief that "there is a secret master who pulls the strings behind the scene" of influential actors (Fuchs 2021: 118). By these means, Thunberg is delegitimized because she lacks the qualities associated with a leader: care, maturity, rationality, and agency. Notably, in title b) there is evidence of the conservative ideology often occasioned in climate sceptic discourse which affirms that other nations – namely India and China – cause a greater negative environmental impact than the United States.

Similarly to the pictorial representation of Representative Ocasio-Cortez, the stills selected to illustrate the activist in *The Daily Wire* articles tagged 'Greta Thunberg' largely portrayed her in an unflattering light. With facial expressions that depict the activist as showing disgust and disdain by grimacing, squinting, and scrunching her nose, she is visually situated as unfriendly and unlikeable.

5. Discussion and conclusions

This paper set out to investigate how climate change was covered in the popular online conservative news outlet *The Daily Wire*. The main topics and themes that emerged in the semantic analysis of this coverage were in line with those employed in the *New York Times* – or environment, politics, and science (Liu and Huang 2022). The use of these themes might suggest that *The Daily Wire* is purporting an image of its climate change coverage as unbiased and objective. However, comparative keyword analysis provided a contrasting view. *The Daily Wire* put forth a primary representation of environmentalism as religion. In fact, the discursive analysis of the keyword 'environmentalism' in context revealed that *The Daily Wire* contributors anchored the concept to an extremist, faith-based religious group using the metaphors such as 'doomsday cult' in relation to the movement, 'saints' and 'preachers of the apocalypse' in relation to the movement's leaders, and 'bow[ing]' and 'indoctrinat[ion]' in relation to the recruitment of followers. By using these metaphors, *The Daily Wire* transformed 'environmentalism' from a science-based social movement for the protection and wellbeing of the Earth to a speculative, superstitious, and radical campaign with nefarious (i.e., money, power, and self-aggrandizement) aims.

This narrative was reinforced with the use of predications, which emerged as keywords. The presence of the terms 'alarmist' and 'alarmism' suggests that the news outlet aimed to frame climate activists as untrustworthy, outrageous, and unreasonable, ultimately casting doubt on the scientific consensus on which they base their climate advocacy. The keyword 'far-left' (alongside the frequently used token 'socialist') evokes the ideological threat of climate activism, whereby opponents appeal to conservative values and connect climate action to 'big' government, compromised sovereignty, and impeding free market competition. This finding, which contradicts other studies that found an absence of conservative ideological frames, is significant because of the highly persuasive nature of this type of frame (Stecula and Merkley 2019).

The analysis of the concomitant tags used alongside 'Climate Change' further manifest the tendency for *The Daily Wire* to employ frames which scholars have identified as diminishing people's propensity to support climate action, including uncertainty in climate science and ideologically conservative appeals. With respect to the former, 'global warming' was used when referring to weather episodes characterized by extreme cold, and the terms 'climate change' and 'global warming' were jointly used with the effect of indexing the issue as uncertain and wavering. With respect to the latter, climate change was framed as a heavily politicized partisan issue promoted by the Left. Frequent reference to the political opposition and its members frames the issue as partisan, leaving little leeway for the conservative readers of this news outlet to support environmentalist endeavours. This effort is particularly poignant given that the aggressive communication of climate change to a conservative audience as intrinsically connected to the political opposition augments climate change scepticism (Merkley and Stecula 2021).

Indeed, this paper uncovered that much of the climate change coverage in *The Daily Wire* presented the issue in terms of its major proponents, who personified the effort, with a focus on the faults and shortcomings in their character and experience. Many of the 'Climate Change' articles homed in on freshman Representative Ocasio-Cortez to situate her as incapable and inexperienced, with the effect of discrediting and invalidating her environmentalist claims. The analysis of titles that contained Greta Thunberg depicted the activist as a whiny, irrational child who was maneuvered by others. The suggestion that she neglected to acknowledge the real culprits of global pollution advanced xenophobic and anti-China sentiments. The unflattering photographs selected to portray both Ocasio-Cortez and Thunberg presented images of the two public figures as unattractive, unlikeable, and unprofessional.

This paper only skimmed the surface of the many insights that the study of climate change coverage by *The Daily Wire* (and other similar sources) can impart. Future research should continue to delve into alternative sources that are information providers for a significant portion of the American and global population and are therefore deeply influential in our times. Only selected visuals used within the outlet were analysed but future research should delve into this dimension, such as by studying how visual synecdoches function to delegitimize the climate movement (O'Neill 2019). Since mid 2022, *The Daily Wire* has been incorporated into DailyWire+, an umbrella subscription platform that includes streamed content that is ripe with opportunities for multimodal investigations. Moreover, Merkley and Stecula (2021: 1444) posit that party cues – or *"explicit or implicit stance[s] on climate change science or related policy attributed to [political] elites"* – explain climate change polarization in the US, with cues coming from Democratic party elites accounting for most of the variance in Republican climate scepticism. The effects of climate change coverage on polarization by sceptical outlets such as *The Daily Wire* should be explored, particularly in light of its emphasis on young newcomers over veteran environmentalist politicians and activists.

Ultimately, as maintained by Stecula and Merkley (2019: 10), "frames play an essential role in distilling complex topics into more manageable components so that people can identify its relevance and form opinions". By means of focusing on specific themes, topics, and actors, the outlet enacted frames that delegitimized the climate change issue and aimed to (re)orient their audience's leanings about it (Chong and Druckman 2007). By boiling down the question of climate change to a partisan one, the incompetent nature of its advocates, and conservative ideologies that called to mind anti-China and anti-socialist sentiments, *The Daily Wire* framed the matter of climate change as a Leftist fixation and a moot point. *The Daily Wire*'s co-founder and former editor-in-chief Ben Shapiro wrote a book entitled *Facts Don't Care about Your Feelings.* Based on the findings of the initial analysis provided in this paper, *The Daily Wire*'s climate change coverage is all about feelings: feelings about the environmentalist movement, feelings towards the political opposition, and feelings towards leading (female) climate activists. These feelings effectively stifle and intentionally leave little room for the facts of climate science.

References

BELL, ALLAN, 1994, "Climate of opinion: Public and media discourse on the global environment", *Discourse & Society* 5 (1), pp. 33-64.

CHONG, DENNIS, and DRUCKMAN, JAMES N., 2007, "Framing Theory", *Annual Review of Political Science*, 10, pp. 103-126.

ENTMAN, ROBERT M., 1993, "Framing: Toward Clarification of a Fractured Paradigm", *Journal of Communication* 43 (4), pp. 51-58.

FUCHS, CHRISTIAN, 2021, *Communicating COVID-19*, Emerald Publishing, Bingley.

GABRIELATOS, COSTAS, 2018, "Keyness analysis: Nature, metrics and techniques", in C. Taylor and A. Marchi (eds), *Corpus Approaches to Discourse,* Routledge, London, pp. 225-258.

GALVIN, RAY and HEALY, NEL, 2020, "The Green New Deal in the United States: What it is and how to pay for it", *Energy Res. Soc. Sci.,* 67, pp. 1-9.

JAKUBÍČEK, MILOŠ, KILGARRIFF, ADAM, KOVÁ , VOJT CH, RYCHLÝ, PAVEL and SUCHOMEL, VÍT, 2013, "The TenTen Corpus Family", *7th International Corpus Linguistics Conference CL*, pp. 125-127.

JASKULSKY, LARISSA and BESEL, RICHARD, 2013, "Words That (Don't) Matter: An Exploratory Study of Four Climate Change Names in Environmental Discourse", *Appl. Environ. Educ. Commun.* 12 (1), pp. 38-45.

JASPAL, RUSI, NERLICH, BRIGITTE, and VAN VUUREN, KITTY, 2016, "Embracing and resisting climate identities in the Australian press: Sceptics, scientists and politics", *Public Understanding of Science,* 25 (7), pp. 807-824.

LAKOFF, GEORGE, 2010, "Why it Matters How We Frame the Environment", *Environmental Communication* 4 (1), pp. 70-81.

LEE, CARMEN, 2018, "Introduction: Discourse of Social Tagging", *Discourse, Context & Media* 22, pp. 1-3.

LIU, MING and HUANG, JINGYI, 2022, "'Climate change' vs. 'global warming': A corpus-assisted discourse analysis of two popular terms in The New York Times", *Journal of World Languages* 8 (1), pp. 34-55.

MERKLEY, ERIC and STECULA, DOMINICK A., 2021, "Party Cues in the News: Democratic Elites, Republican Backlash, and the Dynamics of Climate Skepticism", *British Journal of Political Science* 51, pp. 1439-1456.

NISBET, MATTHEW C., 2009, "Communicating Climate Change: Why Frames Matter for Public Engagement", *Environment: Science and Policy for Sustainable Development* 51 (2), pp. 12-23.

O'NEILL, SAFFRON, 2020, "More than meets the eye: a longitudinal analysis of climate change imagery in the print media", *Climatic Change* 163, pp. 9-26.

PARKS, MILES, 2021, "Outrage as a Business Model: How Ben Shapiro is Using Facebook to Build an Empire". *NPR – Special Series – Untangling Disinformation*, www.npr.org/2021/07/19/1013793067/ outrage-as-a-business-model-how-ben-shapiro-is-using-facebook-to-build-an-empire

PAUL, NEWLY and PERREAULT, GREGORY, 2020, "Picturing the President: Visual Analysis of the Donald Trump Presidency on US Magazine Covers between 2016 and 2018", *Journal of Magazine Media* 21 (1), pp. 51-81.

RAYSON, PAUL, 2008, "From key words to key semantic domains", *International Journal of Corpus Linguistics* 13 (4), pp. 519-549.

REISIGL, MARTIN and WODAK, RUTH, 2009, "The Discourse-Historical Approach (DHA)", in R. Wodak and M. Meyer (eds), *Methods for Critical Discourse Analysis*, SAGE, London, pp. 87-121.

SCHÄFER, MIKE S. and SCHLICHTING, INGA, 2014, "Media Representations of Climate Change", *Environmental Communication*, 8 (2), pp. 142-160

SCHULDT, JONATHON P., KONRATH, SARA H., and SCHWARZ, NORBERT, 2011, "'Global warming' or 'climate change'? Whether the planet is warming depends on question wording", *Public Opinion Quarterly*, 75 (1), p. 115-124

STECULA, DOMINICK A. and MERKLEY, ERIC, 2019, "Framing Climate Change: Economics, Ideology, and Uncertainty in American News Media Content From 1988 to 2014", *Frontiers in Communication* 4 (6), pp. 1-15.

YARZÁBAL, LUIS ANDRÉS, SALAZAR, LENYS M. BUELA and BATISTA-GARCÍA, RAMÓN A., 2021, "Climate change, melting cryosphere and frozen pathogens: Should we worry...?", *Environmental Sustainability* 4, pp. 489-501.

VAN LEEUWEN, THEO, 2007, "Legitimation in Discourse and Communication", *Discourse & Communication* 1 (1), pp. 91-112.

"Te Awa Tupua is a Legal Person": The Framing of Nature in the Whanganui River Deed of Settlement

Lorenzo Buonvivere

Abstract
The present article aims to address the framing of nature as a means to encourage positive attitudes towards the environment. Accordingly, it draws on ecolinguistics and Positive Discourse Analysis to examine Ruruku Whakatupua – the Whanganui River Deed of Settlement (2014), which represented the first step towards the recognition of legal personhood to Te Awa Tupua (the Whanganui River). The legal framing of the river promotes a favourable understanding of the environment, as it assigns nature an agentive role and allows the allocation of responsibility for harmful actions against it. Through a Systemic Functional Linguistics approach, the study suggests that relational clauses typical of legal discourse may stress identity and entanglement between humans and non-humans, which is further supported by the metaphor TE AWA TUPUA IS A PERSON activated by the framing. Ultimately, the conventional CONTAINER scheme conceptualising nature as an external object is displaced to uphold a vision of interconnection and respect.

Key-words: ecolinguistics, nature framing, Positive Discourse Analysis, Systemic Functional Linguistics.

1. Introduction

Understood by cognitive linguistics as mental structures which shape our visions of the world, frames play a significant role in the way environmental issues are viewed and accordingly tackled. For this reason, the framing of nature has been one privileged object of research within the field of ecolinguistics (Nerlich, Hamilton, Rowe 2002; Nerlich 2004; Boykoff 2008; Foust and Murphy 2009; Hulme 2009; Croney 2010; Hopke 2012; Freeman 2014; McNenny 2018), investigating for instance its conceptualisation as a resource, which has often justified attitudes of uncontrolled exploitation

Textus 1-2023, pp. 199-218

ISSN 1824-3967

(Stibbe 2021). While variously theorised across multiple disciplines (Goffman 1974; Minsky 1988; Tannen 1993), in their common conceptualisation as interpretive models of reality and social experience, frames are seen to "define problems" (Entman 1993: 52). Given that they are mainly unconscious, pointing out and critiquing this type of cognitive systematisations about the environment is paramount, since they prevent people from noticing the relevant facts on the state of our planet (Lakoff 2010). Nevertheless, and as claimed by Stibbe, exposing the problems is not enough "unless there are beneficial alternative forms of language available to move towards" (Stibbe 2018: 165).

The following analysis proposes Ruruku Whakatapua – the Whanganui River Deed of Settlement, which recognises legal identity to the geographical region of the Whanganui River in Aotearoa New Zealand – as an instance of framing that promotes a positive understanding of nature. Within the theoretical framework of ecolinguistics (Fill and Mühlhäusler 2001; Fill and Penz 2018; Stibbe 2021), Positive Discourse Analysis (PDA) (Martin 2004; Stibbe 2018) will be employed to single out linguistic features of the document that can be useful in construing new and beneficial discourses. In particular, attention will be devoted to relational clauses from the perspective of Systemic Functional Linguistics (Halliday and Matthiessen 2014) and to the metaphorical construction of the river Te Awa Tupua as a person implicit in the notion of legal personhood. Through these, nature is assigned the role of an agent and described as a single entity, while human and non-human beings – including all natural manifestations, i.e., animals, plants, and larger geographical bodies like rivers, forests, and mountains – are talked about as existing in a relationship of mutual respect and support.

2. Theoretical framework

Ecolinguistics is an umbrella term that is used to address two main strands of linguistics concerned with the relationship between language and ecology (Fill 2018). The first, and also earlier approach, can be summarised as 'the ecology of language'. It was initially proposed by Einar Haugen, who defined it as "the study of interactions between any given language and its environment" (Haugen 2001: 57). As such, ecolinguistics understands languages as part of an ecosystem, and thus is mainly interested in issues of language contact, major and minority languages, endangerment and revival. The second approach – the one adopted in this study – is described by the term 'ecological linguistics', and is about critiquing language uses which sustain destructive environmental behaviour and promoting forms of language that invite protection of the natural world.

Michael Halliday's talk given at the 1990 conference of the International Association of Applied Linguistics (AILA) in Thessaloniki is generally acknowledged as initiating the second perspective (Halliday 2001). Halliday was among the first to point out how grammar structures partake in the definition of modes of experiencing reality that are often unsustainable and anthropocentric. For instance, he shows that the English categorisation between countable and uncountable nouns presents natural resources as though they were unbounded and inexhaustible – e.g. "a reservoir of water" (p. 194). Moreover, at the syntactic level, human entities usually take up the most active position in clauses, fulfilling the function of Actor in material processes, whereas nature is either the inert object to be acted upon, or the subject of catastrophic events – e.g. "the earthquake destroyed the city" (p. 194).

These linguistic patterns are understood by ecolinguistics as relevant in the construction of "stories", which Arran Stibbe defines as "cognitive structures in the minds of individuals which influence how they think, talk, and act" (Stibbe 2021: 6). With reference to the natural world, they are mental models that structure our image of nature, and regulate the kind of interactions we maintain with it, starting with human/non-human relations. When these models become so pervasive that they spread across cultures and times, they can turn into "stories we live by".

Framing is indeed seen as one of the forms that stories can take (Stibbe 2021). In Stibbe's definition, which he adapts from Fillmore and Baker (2010), Darnton and Kirk (2011), and Lakoff and Wehling (2012a), a frame is "a package of knowledge about an area of life" (Stibbe 2021: 40). Frames are identified by three elements: a set of actors or participants; the relations that occur between them; and the typical actions that they perform. For instance, as exemplified by Lakoff (2010), a hospital frame will include actors such as Doctors and Patients, actions such as Operations, and relations such as

Doctors Operate on Patients, and so on. Framing occurs when a particular frame is used to conceptualise a different area of life, resulting in "the cognitive imposition of a package of knowledge from one area of life onto another area" (Stibbe 2021: 41). More specifically, framings involve the presence of a source frame and a target domain. The target domain is the area of life being talked about, whereas the source frame is the area of knowledge that is used to represent the target. Thus, framing consists in the mapping of a source frame onto a target domain[1].

The notion of framing has been dealt with variously within ecolinguistic analysis. Considerable attention has been devoted to the issue of climate change. For example, Boykoff (2008) focussed on its representation in UK tabloids, and found that news stories cover the subject developing four main frames: ecological/meteorological, political economic, culture and society, and scientific. Foust and Murphy (2009) pointed to the ubiquity of the apocalyptic frame to address the same concern in US elite and popular press, which usually emphasises a catastrophic ending to all forms of life. Further studies dealt with the very framing of climate change as a problem (Hulme 2009). Additional research on frames and environmental discourse has been concerned with, among others, animal rights and welfare (Croney 2010; Freeman 2014), food and mouth disease (Nerlich, Hamilton, Rowe 2002; Nerlich 2004), environmental justice and activism (Hopke 2012), and the Anthropocene (McNenny 2018).

However, most of these studies highlight how recurrent framings of nature result in destructive conceptualisations and behaviour. For example, Boykoff (2008) argued that the meteorological frame used in the press tends to overlook the alarming consequences of unusual heat waves, while it draws the attention to the pleasurable opportunities offered by the sunny weather, especially in the UK. Within the apocalyptic frame, instead, individual or collective agency in dealing with environmental issues is either entirely stifled, due to the representation of natural disasters as inevitable and

---

[1] This schematisation of framing closely resembles the one usually applied to metaphors, wherein a mapping occurs between a source domain and a target domain (Lakoff and Johnson 1980). Stibbe (2021) develops a single framework to analyse both framings and metaphors, according to which the latter can actually be seen as a specification of the former. This aspect will be discussed further on.

outside human control, or reduced. In the same vein, the problem frame is criticised because it entails that climate change can be solved, downplaying the need for adaptation.

This 'negative' approach is indeed prevalent in ecolinguistics, and it focusses the attention on language uses that affect our cognition of the environment and prevent us from perceiving the world ecologically (Stibbe 2018). This is in part a consequence of the adaptation of Critical Discourse Analysis (CDA) to ecolinguistic research. Although the adjective critical denotes an evaluative stance and does not necessarily imply a pejorative meaning, CDA generally aims to expose the discursive practices it investigates (Fairclough 1989; Van Dijk 1993), which are found to be conflicting with the analyst's ethical framework.

With this in mind, and in order to encourage social change through the promotion of virtuous examples, Stibbe (2018) proposes to complement CDA with Positive Discourse Analysis (PDA) in ecolinguistics. The concept of PDA was first developed by James Martin (2004), who identifies a gap between what he calls the "two faces of CDA", namely "CDA realis" and "CDA irrealis" (Martin 2004: p. 180). The former is understood as the deconstructive aim of CDA, which seeks to expose the connection between language and ideology and has been predominant in canonical discourse analysis. CDA irrealis instead refers to its constructive end, directed at identifying language uses that spur positive social action. Since this latter focus has been widely neglected, Martin suggests implementing PDA as a means to develop critical readings "which can energise social change" (p. 183). He exemplifies his claims by discussing the case of discourses around the reconciliation with indigenous people in Australia. Similarly, Tom Bartlett (2012) applies PDA to his work on discourse events in Guyana which testify to the appropriation of dominant discursive modes by local communities in order to oppose mainstream development schemes in post-colonial rule.

Because the general goal of PDA is to "renovate discourses that enact a better world" (Martin 2004: 197), it follows that it can apply also to discourses concerned with the state of the natural world. Accordingly, alongside critiques of discursive patterns that support the current industrialised society, ecolinguistics can perform PDA as a way to discover instances of language use promoting behaviour that "do not require over-consumption and treat the natural world with respect and care" (Stibbe 2018: 176). In particular, ecolinguistics can benefit from PDA as it may single out valuable discourses which are not pervasive yet, but could be promoted to become so.

Therefore, the present study is intended to offer a contribution in this sense, employing PDA through an ecolinguistic framework to examine how the legal framing of nature in the Whanganui River Deed of Settlement offers a case of positive discourse in terms of ecological responsibility.

3. Data and methodology

The object of the analysis is Ruruku Whakatupua, or the Whanganui River Deed of Settlement. The document is a treaty settlement signed on 5 August 2014 which was later passed into law on 20 March 2017 as Te Awa Tupua (Whanganui River Claims Settlement) Act 2017. It can be seen as one of the actions undertaken to seek reparations for the land and resources expropriated from Māori over the course of British colonisation, especially following the breach of the promises made in the Treaty of Waitangi (1840). This established New Zealand as a British colony, and it was signed between the Crown and Māori chiefs with the original aim of protecting indigenous rights (Henare 2007). The Whanganui River is Aotearoa New Zealand's longest navigable river, stretching for 290 kilometres from Mount Tongariro to the Tasman Sea. For centuries, Māori Whanganui Iwi (communities) have been sustained by the river and in turn have built a relationship of protection with it. Ruruku Whakatupua comprises two distinct documents: Te Mana o Te Awa Tupua – which recognises the *mana* or selfhood of Te Awa Tupua, the Whanganui River; and Te Mana o te iwi o Whanganui – which instead recognises the *mana* of the tribes of the Whanganui River.

The present study will specifically devote its attention to the first document, Ruruku Whakatupua – Te Mana o Te Awa Tupua[2],

---

[2] For the sake of convenience, in my discussion I will at times refer generally to "Ruruku Whakatupua", although by that I mean "Ruruku Whakatupua – Te Mana o Te Awa Tupua". A full version of the document is available on the

through which legal personhood is conferred to the Whanganui River. In particular, it will focus on the framing of the natural world which emerges from the document.

Ruruku Whakatupua is of particular interest because it translates into the legal context the Māori philosophy of kinship and entanglement between humans and non-humans. Māori worldview is based upon vitalism, and it recognises life as independent from form, that is to say, all things of the world, human and non-human, are animated by life (Henare 2001). As a result, Māori people do not understand themselves as separate from, or superior to, nature. In fact, their relationship with the natural world is one of reciprocity: they can "harvest the bounty" (p. 202) of Earth, whose resources however they do not own, and in turn they acknowledge and safeguard the vitality of Earth itself, in all its manifestations. This notion of responsibility over the environment is summarised by the principle of *kaitiakitanga* – "the ethic of guardianship of creation" (p. 214).

I suggest that the same belief system could be used as an ecosophy for PDA. The term "ecosophy" – a blend of 'ecology' and 'philosophy' – was coined by Naess (1975) with reference to ecological movements to indicate a "philosophy of ecological harmony or equilibrium" (p. 99) that is both descriptive and prescriptive. In ecolinguistic PDA, the ecosophy is the ethical framework against which discourses can be judged as positive (Stibbe 2018; 2021). Whereas in CDA concerned with issues such as gender and racism, ethical frameworks are usually self-evident, that is not always the case with ecolinguistic analysis, especially since there is no single 'correct' ecosophy. The latter will depend on the analyst's own value system, and thus it ought to be made explicit (Stibbe 2021).

Hence, for my analysis of Ruruku Whakatupua I will use an ecosophy inspired by the Māori principle of *kaitiakitanga*. In other words, I evaluate as positive those discourses which adhere to a worldview that addresses the agency of all natural manifestations and is based on the tenet of mutual stewardship between human and non-human subjects.

---

website of the government of Aotearoa New Zealand: https://www.govt.nz/assets/Documents/OTS/Whanganui-Iwi/Whanganui-River-Deed-of-Settlement-Ruruku-Whakatupua-Te-Mana-o-Te-Awa-Tupua-5-Aug-2014.pdf

4. Discussion

4.1. Framing and relational clauses in Ruruku Whakatupua

Ruruku Whakatupua is a deed of settlement, i.e., a legal document which regulates an agreement between the parties involved. In this case, the latter are the Crown and the Whanganui Iwi, the indigenous communities of the Whanganui River region.

As already mentioned, the first document composing the settlement – Te Mana o Te Awa Tupua – has the purpose of granting the status of legal person to the Whanganui River. This is achieved in clauses 2.2: "Te Awa Tupua is a legal person"; and 2.3: "Te Awa Tupua has the rights, powers, duties and liabilities of a legal person" (New Zealand Government 2014: 6).

The first step in the ecolinguistic analysis of framing is the identification of the source frame and the target domain. In the clauses, the adjective "legal", as well as the nouns "rights", "powers", "duties", and "liabilities" act as "trigger words" (Stibbe 2021: 41), and immediately bring forward a legal frame as a source frame to conceptualise the target domain of nature. Therefore, the document can be said to realise the framing NATURE IS A LEGAL ENTITY.

As a result of the suggested framing, nature, in the form of the Whanganui River, is identified as a participant together with the institutions and persons involved in the treaty settlement, who all take on the role of Legal Subjects. These include the Crown, or the government of Aotearoa New Zealand, as well as, according to clause 2.9, "any person exercising functions, duties or powers under a statute referred to in clause 2.10" (New Zealand Government 2014: 7). Among the statutes listed in clause 2.10 are the Biosecurity Act 1993, the Conservation Act 1987, the Queen Elizabeth the Second National Trust Act 1977, and the Wildlife Act 1953. These participants are therefore the terms of relationships of mutual Obligation, which are played out through actions such as Commitment, Recognition, and Provision. These are linguistically performed by means of features typical of legal discourse, comprising lexis, modality, and verb tense. For example: "The Crown confirms its commitment to Te Awa Tupua"; or "[...] any person [...] must: 2.9.1. recognise and provide for the status of Te Awa Tupua" (p. 7).

By specifying, and actually prescribing, the type of relationships occurring among the participants in the legal frame, the Whanganui River is indeed acknowledged the status of actor. In truth, the document provides a definition of Te Awa Tupua which presents it as a broad geographical entity, exceeding in scope the sole Whanganui River:

2.1. Te Awa Tupua is an indivisible and living whole comprising the Whanganui River from the mountains to the sea, incorporating its tributaries and all its physical and metaphysical elements. (New Zealand Government 2014: 6)

The previous example can be read as an instance of "definition rule" (Gunnarsson 1984; Bhatia 1993), whose content is primarily explanatory. With reference to Systemic Functional Linguistics (SFL), this function is performed by means of relational clauses. SFL identifies six main types of clauses defined by as many Processes: material, mental, relational, verbal, behavioural, and existential. Each is fulfilled by a verb and offers a specific representation of an aspect of reality (Halliday and Matthiessen 2014). Table 1 reports their occurrence in Ruruku Whakatupua, and the relational process type is in fact shown to range second in terms of frequency. Relational clauses "serve to characterize and to identify" (p. 259), and for this reason are consistently employed in the registers of science, administration, business and the law. They are described by the Process of being, and are used for "construing the abstract relationships of class-membership and identity in all domains of experience" (p. 262). There are three different types of relational clauses: intensive, possessive, and circumstantial, each of which can occur in two different modes, namely attributive and identifying. Clause 2.1 quoted above can be taken as a point for exemplification. It is found that it consists of three relational clauses: 1) "Te Awa Tupua is an indivisible and living whole"; 2) "[...] comprising the Whanganui River from the mountains to the sea"; 3) "[...] incorporating its tributaries and all its physical and metaphysical elements". All three take Te Awa Tupua as subject, but 1) is an intensive attributive clause of the type 'X is Y', defined by a neutral Process of being ("is"); whereas 2) and 3) are both possessive identifying clauses, characterised by a Process of "kind/part" (p.

269) ("comprising", "incorporating"), which sets up a relation of containment and involvement of the Whanganui River and its "physical and metaphysical elements" within Te Awa Tupua.

TABLE I. DISTRIBUTION OF PROCESSES IN RURUKU WHAKATUPUA

Type	Example of verbs	Occurrences	Frequency (%)
Material	work, protect	478	46
Mental	recognise, consider	36	3
Relational	is, have, comprise	467	45
Verbal	state, notify	42	4
Existential	is	13	1
Behavioural	/	0	0
Total		1036	100

What is relevant about relational clauses is that because they establish a link or connection, they always involve the presence of two participants, so that "a relationship of being is set up between two separate entities" (p. 261). For this reason, with reference to Ruruku Whakatupua, it can be said that relational clauses with natural elements as Participants in the document (Tables 2.1 and 2.2) linguistically reflect Māori's relational ontology, which understands humans and non-humans as equally belonging to a larger and cohesive unit of nature. This is best noticeable in instances such as the following:

Te Awa Tupua is a singular entity comprised of many elements and communities, working collaboratively to the common purpose of the health and wellbeing of Te Awa Tupua. (New Zealand Government 2014: 7)

First, "Te Awa Tupua is a singular entity" also consists of an intensive attributive clause, which ascribes the Attribute "entity" to the Carrier "Te Awa Tupua", with the result of recognising the Whanganui River an independent existence. Second, "Te Awa Tupua is [...] comprised of many elements and communities" again instantiates a possessive identifying clause construing class membership. The relationship between the class – "Te Awa Tupua" – and its members – "elements and communities" – is semantically achieved through hyponymy, which CDA understands as a form of "meaning inclusion" (Fairclough 2003: 101). With the nouns "elements" and "communities", the document refers both to the natural resources and the people inhabiting the Whanganui region, as specified in clause 2.7:

Te Awa Tupua is a spiritual and physical entity that supports and sustains both the life and natural resources within the Whanganui River and the health and wellbeing of the iwi, hapū and other communities of the River. (New Zealand Government 2014: 7).

In line with Māori philosophy, Te Awa Tupua is presented as a superordinate of both single natural elements, including the river itself, and humans, represented by Māori iwi and hapū.

TABLE 2.1. CLAUSES CONSTRUING A POSITIVE IMAGE OF NATURE

Type	Occurrences
Material	33
Mental	5
Relational	68

TABLE 2.2. EXAMPLES OF 'POSITIVE' CLAUSES FOR EACH PROCESS

Type	Example
Material	[...] *working* collaboratively to the common purpose of the health and wellbeing of Te Awa Tupua (p.7)
Mental	[...] any person [...] must [...] *recognise* and provide for the status of Te Awa Tupua (p. 7)
Relational	Te Awa Tupua *has* the rights, powers, duties and liabilities of a legal person (p. 6)

Hyponymy is also used to suggest how the complexity of Te Awa Tupua cannot be reduced to its minimum components. Section 6 of Ruruku Whakatupua defines the terms of "the vesting of the Crown-owned parts of the bed of the Whanganui River in Te Awa Tupua" in order to "address the actions of the past" (p. 29), which involved, among others, the extraction of minerals from the bed of the river (Whanganui District Council 2022). Clause 6.4 contains an intensive identifying clause that clarifies the meaning of *vesting* to precise that it "includes any pakohe, gravel, sand and shingle" (New Zealand Government 2014: 29), which are removed from the role of resources to be exploited and instead acknowledged as constitutive elements of the river.

Māori worldview concerned with the indivisibility of all things of natural reality is therefore supported by the grammar and lexis of the document. Firstly, the text makes explicit use of lexical items conveying a sense of inextricability and inclusion: nouns and modifiers, such as "ties" (e.g. "the intrinsic ties which bind the Whanganui River to the people and the people to the Whanganui River", p. 2), "whole" (p. 6), "indivisible" (p. 6), "all" (p. 6), "singular" (p. 7), "interconnection" (p. 7), "entwining" (p. 10); as well as verbs, like "link" (p. 1), "bind" (p. 2), "relate" (p. 5), "comprise" (p. 6), "incorporate" (p. 6), "reunite" (p. 29). Secondly, it is by means of relational clauses that Te Awa Tupua is consistently assigned the Attribute (Halliday and Matthiessen 2014) of "entity" or "whole".

Moreover, some of these structures stress the reciprocity of the Participants due to the fact that intensive identifying clauses have the property to be reversible (Halliday and Matthiessen 2014). Each section of Te Mana o Te Awa Tupua in the Ruruku Whakatupua settlement is introduced by some tribal proverbs both in Māori and English that outline the indigenous philosophy inspiring the deed. One is especially salient in the representation of human/non-human mutual dependence and exemplifies the point: "I am the River and the River is me" (p. 1), wherein both "I" and "River" in turn fulfil the two functions of Identified and Identifier. Their identity is co-construed: neither can be defined but with reference to the other.

Indeed, the language of the text appears to mirror the recognition of the reciprocal responsibilities between Te Awa Tupua and the people that the document seeks to address. Not only must the Crown and the parties involved "provide for" Te Awa Tupua – as prescribed in clause 2.7 reported above – but Te Awa Tupua in turn "supports and sustains" the life of its members. This confers nature an agency which is testified to, first, by the functional role of Actor attributed to Te Awa Tupua[3], and second, by assigning to it the

---

[3] Other types of clauses can be seen to contribute to the positive representation of nature in the document (see Tables 2.1 and 2.2). Here I am referring to the material

211 IS A LEGAL PERSON"

Attributes "duties" and "liabilities" through a possessive attributive clause: "Te Awa Tupua has the [...] duties and liabilities of a legal person".

4.2. The personification of Te Awa Tupua

As a consequence of the legal framing of Te Awa Tupua, the structures highlighted thus far also support the metaphorical representation of the Whanganui River region as a person. The notions of framing and metaphor can be seen as complementary, and Stibbe (2021) proposes to represent both as a mapping between a source frame and a target domain. Metaphors therefore constitute "a type of framing", however "one where the source frame is from a specific, concrete, and imaginable area of life" (p. 60). Whereas the framing of nature as a legal entity does assign the former an active role as the term of legal relations, the notion of entity is still a rather abstract one, and it resists a precise visualisation. Metaphors, by contrast, build up more concrete and vivid conceptualisations, since they draw from source frames which are usually "easy to imagine, see, hear, smell and taste, related to bodily action" (Semino 2008: 11). Hence the fundamental notion of embodiment, understood by cognitive linguistics as grounding many linguistic phenomena (Wen and Jiang 2021). This is indeed what happens with the special instance of metaphor recognisable as personification, implied in the very idea of legal person.

The metaphorical implications of the notion of legal personhood have been mainly analysed with reference to corporations (Koller 2009; Lakoff and Wehling 2012b; Stibbe 2013; 2021). The metaphor THE CORPORATION IS A PERSON is especially pervasive in the discourse of neoclassical economics, in which companies are described as people having goals and intentions that are essentially oriented at profit-maximisation (Stibbe 2021). In particular, this form of personification is deemed dangerous because by picturing

---

clause "Te Awa Tupua [...] supports and sustains both the life and natural resources within the Whanganui River and the health and wellbeing of the iwi, hapū and other communities of the River" (p. 7). However, the study focusses on relational clauses as they are deemed especially relevant in the linguistic construction of human/non-human co-dependence.

corporations as entities capable of self-decision, it becomes difficult to "locate responsibility for behaviour that damages people's wellbeing and the environment" (p. 73). Legal discourse contributes to this. Lakoff and Wehling (2012b) warn against the law being able to turn specific metaphorical constructions of reality into means to discriminate between licit or illicit actions. They refer to it as "the Metaphor Power of the Court", i.e., "the power to make metaphors legally binding" (Lakoff and Wehling 2012b).

However, this "malign personality" (Winter 2021: 120) associated to legal personhood may not apply to non-human nature. Like corporations, Te Awa Tupua is provided a human representative to act on its behalf. This is laid out in section 3 of the document: "The purpose of Te Pou Tupua is to be the human face and act in the name of Te Awa Tupua" (New Zealand Government 2014: 10). Te Pou Tupua is the name given to the role, which is "exercised jointly by two persons" (p. 11). More importantly, Te Pou Tupua is addressed in the text as "The human face of Te Awa Tupua", and again identified as "the face and voice of Te Awa Tupua" (p. 10). To claim that the Whanganui River system has a human face is to bring forward the metaphor TE AWA TUPUA IS A PERSON, reinforcing the metaphorical value already embedded in the notion of legal person. Nature is thus clearly attributed the ability to take on a human form, and indeed personifications have been praised in ecolinguistic research for their ability to blur the human/non-human boundary (Goatly 2017). In addition, this 'promiscuous' overlap of natural categories is further played out by the figure of Te Karewao, which clause 3.20 defines as "an advisory group established to advise and support Te Pou Tupua" (New Zealand Government 2014: 13), composed of three persons. In the Māori proverb that introduces the section, Te Karewao is compared to the "supplejack vine" used in the making of hīnaki (a trap used to catch eels):

The strong, pliable and readily available supplejack vine is utilised in the construction of hīnaki. Symbolising timely and robust support, Te Karewao is the advisory group that will provide advice to Te Pou Tupua. (p. 10)

Therefore, the image of "the entwining vine" evoked in the text contributes to the representation of human and non-human entities as being closely related. This connection is explicitly acknowledged by the document, and actually posed as a condition for Te Pou Tupua to perform its functions in clause 3.4.1:

[Te Pou Tupua] must, in recognising the inalienable interconnection between the iwi and the hapū of the Whanganui River and Te Awa Tupua, develop appropriate mechanisms for engaging with and reporting to those iwi and hapū on matters relating to Te Awa Tupua. (p. 11)

As a matter of fact, the superimposition of nature and humanhood by means of personification facilitates the recognition of Te Awa Tupua as an active subject entitled to legal representation. Nature is allowed to gain "a seat at the table" (Winter 2021: 116), while of course it becomes easier to allocate responsibility for harmful actions against it.

Furthermore, the definition of nature itself as an entity comprising all forms of being – "an indivisible and living whole" – can be deemed positive because it liberates it from its traditional conceptualisation as a static and enclosed space. Generally, people tend to describe their sense of connectedness to the natural world by claiming that nature is all around them or that they are immersed in it (Andrews 2018). From the perspective of cognitive linguistics, these wordings reveal the CONTAINER scheme according to which we interpret reality in terms of inward and outward movements with respect to a physical container (Tay 2021). This is found also in the very use of 'environment' as a synonym for nature, which construes the latter as a surrounding place (Goatly 2017: 49). However, the representation of nature as a container is not entirely coherent with an ecological framework. In fact, as a result of the conceptual metaphor IMPORTANT IS CENTRAL, the word 'environment' entails that "humans are central and thus more important than nature" (p. 49). Similarly, to picture nature as "the external nonhuman world" opens up to the possibility of drawing boundaries between humans and non-humans (Andrews 2018: 66).

By contrast, as it has been shown, the Whanganui River Deed of Settlement consistently opposes this kind of conceptualisation, while the image of the Whanganui River that emerges from the document is that of a complex entity encompassing both human and non-human beings.

5. Conclusions and directions for further research

Until recent years, ecolinguistics as a form of ecological linguistic analysis has devoted a great deal of its efforts to the identification of destructive discourses on nature (Stibbe 2021). However, because its aim is also to encourage the formation and circulation of alternative stories we live by, an interest in language use that supports ecological understandings of reality has been aroused. Through the use of PDA, whose deliberate goal is to point out the link between language and social change, this analysis has attempted to present Ruruku Whakatupua – the Whanganui River Deed of Settlement – as an example of beneficial discourse.

This article has argued that the document triggers the framing NATURE IS A LEGAL ENTITY, which results in describing the relationship between humans and non-humans in terms of an equal correspondence between legal subjects sharing obligations and responsibilities towards one another. Moreover, since one of the functions of the deed of settlement is to define the parties involved in the agreement, a Systemic Functional Linguistics approach has been adopted to show how this is achieved through the use of relational clauses. In the case of Ruruku Whakatupua, this type of clause establishes a relation of either identity or class membership between human and non-human participants, which ultimately describes Te Awa Tupua – the Whanganui River region – as a complex entity comprising a local and entangled system of flora, wildlife, and indigenous communities. This superimposition of natural categories is further supported by the personification of Te Awa Tupua entailed by the attribution of legal personhood to the Whanganui River and the area through which it flows. Finally, the conventional CONTAINER scheme regularly applied to conceptualise nature as a separate and discrete habitat is upturned. Instead, the legal framing of Te Mana o Te Awa Tupua brings forward a renewed picture of nature as a composite entity including all beings.

In conclusion, with reference to my ecosophy, the Whanganui River Deed of Settlement can be judged as positive discourse around nature, adhering to the Māori principle of *kaitiakitanga*.

Ruruku Whakatupua is part of a series of efforts undertaken by the government of Aotearoa New Zealand to address human responsibility towards natural features of the land that are important for Māori. Indeed, Te Awa Tupua is not the only geographical system in the country to have been recognised legal personhood. The Te Urewera Act 2014 grants legal identity to the region of Te Urewera in the North Island of the country, whereas a Record of Understanding was signed between the Crown and Taranaki Iwi in 2017 to state the intention to recognise legal status to Taranaki Maunga (formerly Mount Taranaki), as well. Ecolinguistic research could therefore benefit from extending its interest to these documents in order to understand whether language structures identified in Ruruku Whakatupua are replicated in similar texts and possibly assess their degree of pervasiveness.

Additionally, the recognition of personhood to geographical regions could be seen as a way to integrate Indigenous and Western epistemologies and ontologies (Winter 2021). As a further direction for linguistic research, it could be relevant to understand if and in which terms this combination of worldviews is reflected in a corresponding assimilation of discursive practices and genres. In fact, while it attempts to translate Māori's indigenous philosophy into law, Ruruku Whakatapua presents itself as a hybrid text, as the main body containing the legal clauses is accompanied by a set of traditional proverbs which would seem to belong to narrative or poetic texts. This may suggest that more positive representations of nature can emerge from the encounter of different types of discourses.

References

ANDREWS, NADINE, 2018, "How Cognitive Frames about Nature May Affect Felt Sense of Nature Connectedness", *Ecopsychology* 10 (1), pp. 61-71.

BARTLETT, TOM, 2012, *Hybrid Voices and Collaborative Change: Contextualising Positive Discourse Analysis*, Routledge, London-New York.

BHATIA, VIJAY K., 1993, *Analysing Genre: Language Use in Professional Settings*, Routledge, London-New York.

BOYKOFF, MAXWELL T., 2008, "The Cultural Politics of Climate Change Discourse in UK Tabloids", *Political Geography* 27, pp. 549-69.

CRONEY, CANDACE, 2010, "Words Matter: Implications of Semantics and Imagery in Framing Animal-Welfare Issues", *Journal of Veterinary Medical Education* 37 (1), pp. 101-6.

DARNTON, ANDREW and KIRK, MARTIN, 2011, "Finding Frames: New

Ways to Engage the UK Public in Global Poverty", *Bond*, http://findingframes.org/Finding%20Frames%20Bond%20Report%20 2011%20Executive%20Summary%20DRAFT.pdf, last accessed July 8, 2022.

ENTMAN, ROBERT M., 1993, "Framing: Toward Clarification of a Fractured Paradigm", *Journal of Communication* 43 (4), pp. 52-58.

FAIRCLOUGH, NORMAN, 1989, *Language and Power*, Longman, Harlow.

FAIRCLOUGH, NORMAN, 2003, *Analysing Discourse: Textual Analysis for Social Research*, Routledge, London-New York.

FILL, ALWIN F. and HERMINE PENZ (eds), 2018, *The Routledge Handbook of Ecolinguistics*, Routledge, London-New York.

FILL, ALWIN and PETER MÜHLHÄUSLER (eds), 2001, *The Ecolinguistics Reader: Language, Ecology and Environment*, Continuum, London-New York.

FILL, ALWIN F., 2018, "Introduction", in A.F. Fill and H. Penz (eds), *The Routledge Handbook of Ecolinguistics*, Routledge, London-New York, pp. 1-7.

FILLMORE, CHARLES J., and BAKER, COLLIN, 2010, "A Frames Approach to Semantic Analysis", in B. Heine and H. Narrog (eds), *The Oxford Handbook of Linguistic Analysis*, O.U.P., Oxford, pp. 313-40.

FOUST, CHRISTINA R., and O'SHANNON MURPHY, WILLIAM, 2009, "Revealing and Reframing Apocalyptic Tragedy in Global Warming Discourse", *Environmental Communication: A Journal of Nature and Culture* 3 (2), pp. 151-67.

FREEMAN, CARRIE P., 2014, *Framing Farming: Communication Strategies for Animal Rights*, Rodopi, Amsterdam.

GOATLY, ANDREW, 2017, "Metaphor and Grammar in the Poetic Representation of Nature", *Russian Journal of Linguistics* 21 (1), pp. 48-72.

GOFFMAN, ERVING, 1974, *Frame Analysis: An Essay on the Organization of Experience*, Harper and Row, London.

GUNNARSSON, BRITT-LOUISE, 1984, "Functional Comprehensibility of Legislative Texts: Experiments with a Swedish Act of Parliament", *Text – Interdisciplinary Journal for the Study of Discourse* 4 (1-3), pp. 71-105.

HALLIDAY, MICHAEL A.K., and MATTHIESSEN, CHRISTIAN M.I.M., [1985] 2014, *Halliday's Introduction to Functional Grammar*, Routledge, London-New York.

HALLIDAY, MICHAEL A.K., 2001, "New Ways of Meaning: The Challenge to Applied Linguistics", in A. Fill and P. Mühlhäusler (eds), *The Ecolinguistics Reader: Language, Ecology, and Environment*, Continuum, London, pp. 175-202.

HAUGEN, EINAR, 2001, "The Ecology of Language", in A. Fill and P. Mühlhäusler (eds), *The Ecolinguistics Reader: Language, Ecology and Environment*, Continuum, London-New York, pp. 57-66.

HENARE, MANUKA, 2001, "Tapu, Mana, Mauri, Hau, Wairua: A Mäori Philosophy of Vitalism and Cosmos", in J.A. Grim (ed.), *Indigenous Traditions and Ecology: The Interbeing of Cosmology and Community*, Harvard U.P., Cambridge (MA), pp. 197-221.

HENARE, AMIRIA, 2007, "Taonga Mäori: Encompassing Rights and Property In New Zealand", in A. Henare, M. Holbraad, S. Wastell (eds), *Thinking Through Things: Theorising Artifacts Ethnographically*, Routledge, London-New York, pp. 47-67.

HOPKE, JILL, 2012, "Water Gives Life: Framing an Environmental Justice Movement in the Mainstream and Alternative Salvadoran Press", *Environmental Communication* 6 (3), pp. 365-82.

HULME, MIKE, 2009, *Why We Disagree about Climate Change: Understanding Controversy, Inaction and Opportunity*, C.U.P., Cambridge.

KOLLER, VERONIKA, 2009, "Brand Images: Multimodal Metaphor in Corporate Branding Messages", in C.J. Forceville and E. Urios-Aparisi (eds), *Multimodal Metaphor*, Mouton de Gruyter, Berlin-New York, pp. 45-71.

LAKOFF, GEORGE, 2010, "Why It Matters How We Frame the Environment", *Environmental Communication* 4 (1), pp. 70-81.

LAKOFF, GEORGE, and JOHNSON, MARK, 1980, *Metaphors We Live By*, University of Chicago Press, Chicago-London.

LAKOFF, GEORGE, and WEHLING, ELISABETH, 2012a, *The Little Blue Book: The Essential Guide to Thinking and Talking Democratic*. Simon and Schuster, New York.

LAKOFF, GEORGE, and WEHLING, ELISABETH, 2012b, "Metaphor and Health Care: On The Power to Make Metaphor Into Law", *George Lakoff*, https://george-lakoff.com/2012/09/16/metaphor-and-health-care-on-the-power-to-make-metaphor-into-law/, last accessed July 8, 2022.

MARTIN, JAMES R., 2004, "Positive Discourse Analysis: Solidarity and Change", *Revista Canaria de Estudios Ingleses*, 49, pp. 179-200.

MCNENNY, GERRI, 2018, "Framing the Anthropocene: Educating for Sustainability", *Language & Ecology*, pp. 1-17.

MINSKY, MARVIN, 1988, "A Framework for Representing Knowledge", in A. Collins and E. Smith (eds), *Readings in Cognitive Science: A Perspective from Psychology and Artificial Intelligence*, Morgan Kauffman, San Mateo (CA), pp. 156-189.

NAESS, ARNE, 1975, "The Shallow and the Long Range, Deep Ecology Movement", in A. Drengson and Y. Inoue (eds), *The Deep Ecology Movement: An Introductory Anthology*, North Atlantic Books, Berkeley, pp. 3-10.

NERLICH, BRIGITTE, 2004, "War on Foot and Mouth Disease in the UK, 2001: Towards a Cultural Understanding of Agriculture", *Agriculture & Human Values* 21 (1), pp. 15-25.

NERLICH, BRIGITTE, HAMILTON, CRAIG, ROWE, VICTORIA, 2002, "Conceptualising Foot and Mouth Disease: The Socio-Cultural Role of Metaphors, Frames and Narratives", *Metaphorik.De* 2, pp. 90-108.

NEW ZEALAND GOVERNMENT, 2014, "Whanganui River Deed of Settlement – Ruruku Whakatupua – Te Mana o Te Awa Tupua", https://www.govt.nz/assets/Documents/OTS/Whanganui-Iwi/Whanganui-River-Deed-of-Settlement-Ruruku-Whakatupua-Te-Mana-o-Te-Awa-Tupua-5-Aug-2014.pdf, last accessed July 8, 2022.

SEMINO, ELENA, 2008, *Metaphor in Discourse*, C.U.P., Cambridge.

STIBBE, ARRAN, 2013, "The Corporation as Person and Psychopath: Multimodal Metaphor, Rhetoric and Resistance", *CADAAD* 6, pp. 114-36.

STIBBE, ARRAN, 2018 "Positive Discourse Analysis: Re-Thinking Human Ecological Relationships", in A.F. Fill and H. Penz (eds), *The Routledge Handbook of Ecolinguistics*, Routledge, London-New York, pp. 165-178.

STIBBE, ARRAN, [2015] 2021, *Ecolinguistics: Language, Ecology and the Stories We Live By*, Routledge, London-New York.

TAY, DENNIS, 2021, "Image Schemas", in X. Wen and J.R. Taylor (eds), *The Routledge Handbook of Cognitive Linguistics*, Routledge, London-New York, pp. 161-72.

TANNEN, DEBORAH (ed.), 1993, *Framing in Discourse*, Oxford, OUP.

VAN DIJK, TEUN A., 1993, *Elite Discourse and Racism*, Sage Publications, Newbury Park (CA).

WHANGANUI DISTRICT COUNCIL, "Te Awa Tupua – Whanganui River Settlement", https://www.whanganui.govt.nz/About-Whanganui/Our-District/Te-Awa-Tupua-Whanganui-River-Settlement, last accessed July 8, 2022.

WEN, XU and JIANG, CANZHONG, 2021, "Embodiment", in X. Wen and J.R. Taylor (eds), *The Routledge Handbook of Cognitive Linguistics*, Routledge, London-New York, pp. 145-60.

WINTER, CHRISTINE J., 2021, "A Seat At The Table: Te Awa Tupua, Te Urewera, Taranaki Maunga and Political Representation", *Borderlands* 20 (1), pp. 116-39.

The Metaphysical Reframing
of Sustainable and Inclusive Tourism
in the Post-pandemic Digital Era:
An ELF-mediated Approach

*Maria Grazia Guido, Pietro Luigi Iaia**

Abstract
The ongoing research introduced in this paper enquires into the reframing of the concept of 'sustainable tourism' prompted by the increasing digitalization of reality following the COVID-19 pandemic emergency which has recorded a growing number of participants in situations of intercultural communication interacting online (within the so-called 'metaverse') by using their variations of English as a lingua franca (ELF). Such virtual communicative situations are here assumed to strongly affect, modify, and even hybridise the intercultural participants' typologically different experiential frames for the perception and conceptualization of events. The purpose of the case study is to develop novel digital strategies of multimodal discourse which would offer participants an intense aesthetic experience by allowing the interpretation of typologically-hybrid cognitive and communicative framing processes emerging from these new ELF-mediated online interactions.

Key-words: Framing processes, English as a lingua franca, online intercultural communication, sustainable tourism, Metaphysical discourse, Vaporwave genre.

1. Research topic and objectives

This paper introduces an ongoing research enquiring into the reframing processes of the rapidly-evolving and highly-elusive concept of 'sustainable tourism' and its impact on environmental and social inclusion policies in an intercultural communication mediated by variations of English as a lingua franca (ELF)

---

* The authors have contributed equally to the overall drafting of this paper. Maria Grazia Guido is responsible for sections 1, 2 and 5; Pietro Luigi Iaia for sections 3 and 4.

Textus 1-2023, pp. 219-235

ISSN 1824-3967
© Carocci Editore S.p.A.

(Guido 2008; Guido, Iaia, Errico 2019). Following the COVID-19 emergency, which was marked by an increasing digitalisation of reality (cf. Hakovirta and Denuwara 2020), this paper will focus on the rapidly changing contexts of regional tourism (in the case-study in point, the seaside resorts in the southern-Italian area of Salento) principally triggered by the progressive 'dematerialisation', on the one hand, of the natural and urban environment (turned into a 'metaverse' – Narula 2022) – often used as a virtual landscape for the design of sustainable energy installations – and, on the other, of the bodies of people interacting online but physically inhabiting the same places – such as local residents and transient groups of international tourists and migrants – who regularly need to access municipal administration websites for information about tourist and social services. The aim is to investigate the extent to which:

a) the new pandemic-induced digitalisation of reality encompassing every dimension of the lives of people interacting in virtual environments is affecting and modifying the diverse socio-culturally established experiential frames for the perception and conceptualisation of events (in the case-study in point, characterised by a metaphysical time/space disruption, as well as by a merging of transitive/ergative logical conceptualisation of causation). The outcome is expected to have an impact precisely on the grammaticalisation processes that configure the different linguaculturally-marked ELF variations used by interacting participants in intercultural communication, to the point of blurring the typological specificities of the participants' native languages that normally come to be transferred into their respective ELF structures (Guido 2008; 2018);

b) this novel digitalised reality, therefore, questions the validity of established Frame Models for the conceptual and discoursal representation of reality in Cognitive Linguistics (Goffman 1974; Fillmore 1982) and in Construction Grammar (Croft 2001).

The study starts from the assumption that grammar structures of ELF variations are not independent from the cognitive frames that organise the logical perception and the experiential conceptualisation of events in reality within a speech community (cf. Sombre and Wermuth 2010). This is so because ELF grammar structures are precisely the result of users' unconscious transfer (Faerch and Kasper 1987) of their native typological-grammar structures (Greenberg 1973), underlying their experiential and linguacultural frames, into the grammar structures of the English language (cf. Guido 2008). And yet, in acknowledging the new virtual scenarios which have been developed in consideration of the need to interact online to contain the pandemic, and which are involving multicultural communities of participants in online interactions using their own ELF variations, this study specifically intends to question the existing monocultural frame models of Embodied Construction Grammar (cf. Johnson 1987; Lakoff and Johnson 1999). Such models have so far provided embodied frames for the linguacultural grammaticalisation of the transitive perception of events in Western languages, organising cognition into typologically predictable experiential relations affecting sentence structures (e.g., causation organised into transitive cause-effect logical patterns, or sensorimotor orientation in space and, metaphorically, in time – cf. Croft and Cruse 2004).

On such grounds, the theoretical objective of this research is to introduce an original model for the interpretation of typologically hybrid cognitive and communicative framing processes emerging from these novel modes of intercultural online interaction, to be employed for the advertising of ecologically sustainable and multiculturally inclusive resorts in Salento (Southern Italy). This model will be defined as "Cyber-Embodied Construction Grammar" in that the multicultural participants in ELF-mediated online interactions (in the form of 'chats' on websites dedicated to tourism) are expected to develop fresh 'embodied virtual frames' in response to visual and verbal stimuli produced in the context of advertisements devised for specific place marketing campaigns. Such advertisements are meant to adapt and mutually accommodate the participants' different native typological frames as they use their respective ELF variations in the contexts of intercultural digital interactions. The empirical objective of this paper is to illustrate the programmatic phases of this ongoing research enquiring into the extent to which such newly developing frames can affect the pragmatic forms of discourse so as to facilitate the unusual modes of digital intercultural communication in the contexts of regional policies for the sustainable conveyance of:

1) novel environmental and urban frames, often requiring the intrusive installation of clean energy devices spoiling natural and architectural landscapes and heritage/art sites – crucially threatening local economies, such as tourism (cf. Cock 2011; Torkington, Stanford, Guiver 2020). These clean energy installations are at the centre of a recent controversial political debate in Salento, focused, on the one hand, on the Italian Government's urge to strengthen clean energy sources to cope with the serious crisis of environmental pollution – and, at the time of writing this article, of the shortage of gas supplies – and, on the other, on the strenuous determination on the part of local residents and tourists to refuse such installations in order to preserve the original natural and urban landscapes of the place;

2) novel social frames for today's multicultural Western societies characterised by greater than ever waves of migrants and refugees coming to Europe (especially to Southern Italy) from the south and the east regions of the world, in need of socio-cultural integration. Such migration waves are perceived as actually threatening the cultural cohesion of local 'gated communities' and their economy based on tourism, often at risk for the presence in seaside resorts of migrants and refugees that impose upon tourists and local residents a reflection on such a serious humanitarian problem which requires social justice based on the rejection of every kind of exploitation of human beings and of the natural environment. This is indeed a reflection that would spoil the holiday atmosphere as well as the local economy deriving from it (cf. Lakoff and Ferguson 2006; Hart 2010; Lockie 2016).

This ethnographic research – to be carried out in the course of its application phases in collaboration with local cultural and governmental institutions – intends to propose the notion of a new 'mixed reality', halfway between an online-mediated virtual reality (where people are expected to interact within an unreal, digitalised 'metaverse'), and real life (where people physically interact within the actual environments). This entails creating promotional advertisements simulating the necessary sustainable changes in natural or urban landscapes to cope with the energy crisis. These advertisements are designed in such a way as to encompass history, natural settings and architecture, mixing together real environments and possible clean energy devices in order to turn a predictably unbearable experience of industrial architecture into an acceptable, if not even pleasant one, to residents, and also to tourists and migrants, who would feel welcomed in an eco-sustainable environment that, in addition, intends to offer them an unexpected and intense aesthetic and multicultural experience. The purpose, indeed, is to develop novel digital strategies of multimodal discourse which would foster a "commonality of experience and feeling" (Iaia 2016), in opposition to psychological distancing and rejection of the place.

FIGURE I. SALENTO – THE METAPHYSICAL METAVERSE WHERE ANCIENT AND MODERN GODS WELCOME YOU

More specifically, in the present study, a multimodal advertisement will be devised (henceforward referred to as Ad) so as to unexpectedly bring together contemporary industrial infrastructures – which will soon be installed on the unspoilt Salento coast – and

the natural and historical sites. The Ad, reported above, represents large contemporary wind turbines emerging off the coast of the eternal and unspoilt Mediterranean Sea, like giants of the ancient epic narrations of voyagers and refugees – such as Homer's Ulysses, or Virgil's Aeneas, who resemble contemporary travellers and migrants – reproducing novel artistic effects, similar to De Chirico's Metaphysical paintings of landscapes mixing old statues of gods and contemporary geometric urban buildings. The slogan is meant to contribute to the sense of immersion into such surprising 'mixed reality' scenarios – and, possibly, to the positive emotions that such an immersion would trigger in local and international viewers. The English language used in the slogan is conceived to encompass receivers' ELF variations grounded on their different native-language typologies that reflect different linguacultural conceptualisations of events.

The ultimate purpose is to enquire into the possibilities of employing ELF variations to persuade people who interact within 'mixed-reality' environments first to overcome their possible resistance to 'politically-correct' applications of environmental and social frames for sustainable and inclusive tourism and, then, to induce them to accept, or to adapt such frames to their own parallel linguaculturally-marked frames. This strategy is assumed to contribute to the enhancement of the local economy by means of place marketing based on socially-inclusive communities and on a multicultural turn in ecotourism.

2. Theoretical background and research rationale

The theoretical construct of Metaphysical discourse introduced in this study (meant as verbal, visual and, ultimately, multimodal discourse), envisages a disruption of the conventional semantic practices that habitually 'confine' imagination into socially-accepted patterns, so as to restore perception and expression to their original creativity within counterfactual possible-worlds environments (Guido 2005). Indeed, such a construct intends to challenge the Objectivist truth/non-truth polarity in that it questions current research on Possible Worlds which traditionally associates the conventional truth-conditional construct of Metaphysical thought – intrinsically entailing modality – with the abstract sense constructions identifying factual truth in reality typical of Logical Semantics (Hintikka 1989). Contrary to this view, this study fosters a fresh association between Cognitive-Experiential Linguistics (Johnson 1987) and Possible-Worlds Semantics in Modal Logic (Stalnaker 1994). This association is meant to represent not only the conventional domain of epistemic speculation in Metaphysical thought, but also the multiple linguacultural uses and multicultural non-linguistic forms that would revive the covert deontic dimension of Possible-Worlds Logic. This means that 'metaphysical constructions' (verbal, visual, or multimodal) by typically deviating from accepted 'factual' logic, are assumed to deontically trigger in receivers novel subjective emotional, behavioural, and even aesthetic responses.

As a consequence, receivers are crucially expected to activate in their minds two processes that will be defined as 'experiential pliability' (requiring an experiential adaptation to the paraconsistent logic of the possible worlds prompted by the visual structure of the Ad and its slogan) and 'cognitive suspension of disbelief' (requiring a distancing from the real-world logic so as to allow the activation of strategies of appropriation and embodiment of the counterfactual world suggested by the Metaphysical Ad) (Guido 2005). Such processes are assumed to be triggered by the typical performative nature of Metaphysical discourse that 'deontically' tries to induce receivers to believe that the counterfactual virtual environments that it 'epistemically' represents can be conceivable and, therefore, likely to be embodied – in the case in point – within the online contexts of the virtual metaverse.

Hence, two characteristics can be identified in a Metaphysical Ad structure:

a) its epistemic nature as a constative act built on propositional attitudes (e.g., to believe, assume, etc.), representing abstract speculations on possibilities, beliefs, and entailments;
b) its deontic nature as a performative act built on concrete images conveyed through abstract concepts exerting on receivers a sense of need – if not obligation – to accept such speculations.

The purpose of such concrete images is precisely to convey a particular illocutionary force aimed at persuasion by producing specific perlocutionary effects on receivers (cf. Bierwisch 1980). As such, they are assumed to be at the foundations of the discourse of advertising. In the case in point, with reference to the Ad, the intention is to offer receivers the aesthetic experience of being entirely immersed into a Metaphysical work of art where features of the ancient historical heritage of Salento (represented by the statue of Minerva – recently emerged from the archaeological excavations on the coasts of Castro – to which Virgil referred in the Aeneid when describing the landing of Aeneas in Italy) are brought together with contemporary colossal wind turbines in a still and estranging future landscape of the Salento coast. Obviously, the effects of such concrete images may be different on receivers with different culturally-marked world-views – or 'world schemata' (Rumelhart 1980) – through which they differently interpret real and possible events. Such world schemata are grammaticalized into the typological structures of the receivers' native languages, which are then transferred into their respective variations of English used as a 'lingua franca' in intercultural communication (Guido 2008). This means that the perception of a Metaphysical composition, such as the Ad, though making receivers realise that it is primarily concerned with mental projections of possible worlds that obviously exist only within an imaginary dimension (since this image 'semantically deviates' from entities and processes of the real world), does not, as expected, activate in all receivers with different linguacultural backgrounds the same 'visually-based system of transitivity'. In fact, the transitivity system based on a cause-effect perception of events is not a universal conceptualisation of reality, but it characterises only the typological SVO accusative structures of Western languages of Indo-European origin, where an animate agent in logical-subject position normally represents the cause of a process (Greenberg 1973). The counterfactual image in the Ad deviates from reality as, on the one hand, it represents the projection of the possible impact of a future national energy plan on the unspoilt Salento coast, and, on the other, it tries to induce in receivers the Metaphysical artistic effect of watching illogically distant images. The images in point that are brought together in the Ad are those of the contemporary wind turbines represented as anthropomorphic gods, and of the ancient Greek statue of the goddess Minerva, both represented as animate agents welcoming tourists and migrants to the Salento coast and helping them find their way by means of an old lighthouse –

as emphasised by the slogan: "Salento – the metaphysical metaverse where ancient and modern gods welcome you". Hence, receivers are required to activate in their minds processes of experiential pliability, as well as of suspension of disbelief that would allow them to bridge the logical inconsistencies in the Metaphysical image of the Ad and, thus, to access and enjoy the artistic experience as if it were true.

And yet, transitivity cannot be adapted to the typological OVS ergative structures of some non-Western languages of Afro-Asiatic origin (as some of the native languages of sub-Saharan Africa – from which many of the migrants present in Southern Italy come). Ergative clausal structures, differently from transitive ones, grammaticalize world schemata in such a way that different perceptions of causal dynamics may be due to inanimate objects that come to be perceived as animate agents in logical-subject position (Guido 2018). Applied to the Ad, modern wind turbines, the ancient Minerva goddess, and even the old lighthouse, may indeed be ergatively perceived as real forcedynamic entities (Guido 2018) welcoming migrants and tourists to a fair, eco-sustainable and multicultural utopian environment to be inhabited and experienced online within the counterfactual metaverse – as the slogan claims. This being so because the Ad is built on the following two world dimensions that are assumed to co-exist:

a) the indexical dimension of the actual world, where the conventional sense of a concept, or 'primary intension', determines the truth-conditions of the referent for the concept in the real world – which, however, are culture-bound, depending on the receivers' different world schemata;
b) the iconic dimension of the possible world, where the referent for a concept, or 'secondary intension', may deviate from its conventional sense in the real world insofar as truth-conditions are determined by the sense that a concept assumes within an alternative counterfactual world (Lewis 1973) – where even concepts considered illogical by Western receivers (like wind turbines seen as benevolent gods in the Ad) may be assumed to be true.

This entails that, at the level of the Ad production, receivers can recognise this two-dimensional process of meaning inference from the semantic patterns of the Metaphysical image and slogan. These patterns, by transcending conventional concepts of time, space, and causation, are expected to be perceived as incoherent with reference to real-world logic. Hence receivers, in order to inhabit the counterfactual possible world represented in the Ad, are expected to project its semantic patterns onto the alternative possible-world dimension of a paraconsistent logic capable of giving them a new and unconventional sense.

At the level of the Ad reception and interpretation, however, it is necessary to account for the interpretative strategies activated in the minds of the receivers to make sense of the Metaphysical Ad. Such strategies are grounded on their different world schemata; this entails that different receivers may relate to the features of the image and slogan different secondary, and even primary intensions. Yet, the ultimate aim is to make receivers with different world schemata develop a positive stance on the new epistemic conceptualisations conveyed by the images of the advertisement, whose pragmatic function is intrinsically deontic and performative, aimed at persuading receivers (local residents, tourists, and migrants) to share and accept sustainable choices that would drastically modify the natural environment and the social balance of local communities.

Indeed, the COVID-19 pandemic, by turning every relationship with the natural and social environment from real to virtual by means of digital communication, has forced participants in online interaction to live in the virtual Metaphysical dimension of the metaverse where truth-conditions in both actual and possible worlds come to coincide.

3. Multimodal application: vaporwave aesthetic

The Ad and a short video clip represent the multimodal output of this research. The Ad and the video are set in a virtual and undefined location, which is inhabited by objects, elements and participants that are associated with different resorts in the Salento area, and which belong to the schemata associated with unspoilt holiday destinations. The leitmotif of 'commonality of experience and feelings' is reflected by the visual and acoustic features of the 'metaphysical' and 'metatemporal' metaverse that is imagined. The result is a composition where objects and characters from the past and mythological accounts of sea journeys interact with modern technology – in particular, with those devices that remind viewers of sustainability and the search for renewable energy, such as wind turbines. All these features are presented as evocative hallmarks of the novel connotation of tourism.

The metatemporal and metaphysical qualities of the setting are conveyed by means of the visual art known as "vaporwave", the viral Internet aesthetic affecting music first and, then, other forms of entertainment (Born and Haworth 2018) since the early 2010s. This style is akin to memes – another Internet genre – for both are open to be re-edited, recycled and adapted, facilitating the direct involvement of receivers, who can author personal variations of the original versions (Shifman 2014). The core of vaporwave is the "evocative and ostentatious" blend of "nostalgia" and "irony" (Born and Haworth 2018) in multimodal compositions where imagery, pictures and sounds from different periods of human history, mainly 1980s and 1990s, are merged in a "neon-coloured" and "dehistoricized" world (Koc 2017). In the context of this research, its choice should help attract the potential recipients' interest, and its conventional traits are slightly modified to suit the positive combination of different epochs and audiovisual stimuli. Accordingly, the novel functional dimension of achieving the tourists' emotional involvement is pursued by guiding a multimodal reading wherefrom cultural connections with other works of art, in particular the ones by artist Giorgio De Chirico, are acknowledged or activated. The result is not a mere 'dehistoricized' collage, but a montage giving life to a metaphysical scenario where apparently undefined or unrelated symbols and figures interact with each other and with viewers, who end up being engaged in a poignant relationship with the Ad. 'Abstractness', 'suspension of defined time', 'suspension of disbelief' and also 'elements from factual reality' are properties of the same illustration, connecting this metaverse with the 'offline' experience. This is obtained by the inclusion of factual elements, from the sea to a sunny sky on a sultry day, to the statue of the goddess Minerva in the town of Castro, in the Salento area, as well as by the selection of a palette of colours discarding the neon tone of conventional vaporwave, opting for a sand- and mustard-coloured representation that is reminiscent of De Chirico's shade of yellow (Rogge, Dijkema, Rush 2020).

The hypothesis informing the multimodal composition (explored in the following section) is that viewers can be directed towards seeing the features of hospitality, art, respect for local territory and sustainability not only as traditional features of Salento, but also as the added value of their holiday destinations.

4. Multimodal analysis of the multimedia output

The examined multimedia will be available on a website where visitors can contemplate the Ad and click on it to play the video (link to the clip: https://drive.google.com/file/d/1-lvuTSV7UNLcz7xwgx67zOlf9uQGeM69/view?usp=sharing). The visual frame of the image can be divided into three parts, from left to right, following the suggested multimodal reading that serves the blend of "ancient" and "modern gods". In the first part, the elements from the past indicate the origins of the metaphysical flux that is presented to recipients. An "epic" goddess, Minerva, is shown, creating a connection between online and offline worlds. The statue torso evokes past memories to viewers – in particular, the mythical accounts of sea journeys – as well as a bond with Castro, where the ruins of a temple of Minerva were discovered. In the second section, the focus shifts on the metatemporal trait of the collage in the background, where past, present and future intermingle, whereas the position of wind turbines in the open sea has a complex semantic value. Their positioning is expected to link those modern devices with mythical creatures originating from water – and both water and wind are the natural and indomitable elements that are recurrent protagonists of epic narrations. At the same time, a temporal reference to the future is added, because of the controversy about the floating offshore wind farm project to be installed in the Adriatic Sea and the Salento area. Finally, the third section guides the viewers' gaze back towards the foreground of the frame, where another connection to offline world is created. The structure appearing on the right of the image is the Punta Palascìa lighthouse, which is located in Capo D'Otranto, Italy's easternmost point. In line with the vaporwave grounds, the counterfactual association between the torso, wind turbines and the lighthouse – which do not share the same location offline – allows for the development of a metaverse characterised by a commonality of positive qualities and feelings, inferring that the care for local territory, technological innovation and renewable energy do not belong to a town in particular, but to an entire area.

The integration between past, present and future, equivalent connections between ancient and modern gods, and a similar application of vaporwave are found in the short clip that will be played when clicking on the image appearing in the home page of the website. The video can be divided into three parts: "Introducing the metaverse" (00:00-00:12); "Salento and Ancient Gods" (00:13-00:41); "Salento and Modern Gods" (00:42-01:24). The first part hints at the implied receivers. In fact, the video addresses those viewers who are accustomed to consuming online texts and joining viral games, since the very first message that can be read is "#2022yearchallenge". It refers to the viral "#10yearchallenge" asking users to post and compare their past and recent pictures. This connection between ancient and modern times conditions the viewers' expectations, anticipating the metatemporal nature of the metaverse in the video. Written captions are also superimposed, reproducing the reactions to social-media posts by means of abbreviations (e.g., "OMG") and exclamation of surprise and appreciation (namely, "Awesome!).

TABLE 1. PART 1 OF THE VIDEO

Title of the part	Sound
#2022yearchallenge	Typing on a keyboard
Amazing! OMG! I like it!	Sound of an adventure film

Part two highlights the metaphysical and hybrid dimension of the setting, where online and offline realities are unified to enable that emotional response that was already triggered by the Ad. A storm, open sea and then the ancient god Triton is presented, alluding to the power of natural elements which can threaten voyagers' journeys and lives. This part aims to raise concerns in viewers, provoking in them apprehension and justifying their commitment to watching the whole video, thus accessing its entire message. The change in atmosphere is also conveyed by means of music, since the relaxing noises of wind and calm sea are replaced by a suspenseful soundtrack characterised by rapid increase in volume and sharp noises. The captions reproduce the ergative representations seeing gods as the cause of the actions of welcoming tourists and migrants and controlling wind and water.

TABLE 2. PART 2 OF THE VIDEO

Captions	Sound
The storm-blast comes?	Storm
Emoji of a scared face	Storm and thrilling soundtrack
An ancient god welcomes us	Thrilling soundtrack
He controls water and wind	

TABLE 3. PART 3 OF THE VIDEO

Captions	Sound
Emoji of puzzled faces	Thrilling soundtrack turning into a more relaxing score
Emoji of a scared face	Relaxing soundtrack
An ancient god welcomes us. He controls water and wind	Relaxing soundtrack
Ancient… and modern… gods… together	Water sound and relaxing soundtrack
I can see smooth sea	Water sound and relaxing soundtrack
Even an immortal being, in this place, might gaze and delight his soul	Relaxing soundtrack
Emojis of approval. SALENTO. The metaphysical metaverse where ancient and modern gods welcome you	Wind sound

In the third part, the video maintains the hybridisation of eras and images connoting the metatemporal and metaphysical view of tourism. A map of Europe is visible and the camera zooms in on Apulia, tagging the region as the object of promotion, while turbines emerge from the sea. The movement of the camera, from the bottom to the top of the screen, replicates the action of surfacing from water, whereas the devices should remind viewers of the ancient gods that can control natural forces – indeed, similar associations between modern technology and mythical deities are also present in the Ad. At the same time, the rhythm slows down and the atmosphere is again relaxing and pleasant, contributing to the development of a positive message, as is stressed by the acoustic score, substituting the thrilling soundtrack with the natural sound of water and calm sea, and by the scenes of a sunny day in Castro (the same town appearing in Figure 1's metaverse). The verbal elements reproduce the implied viewers' reactions, imagining that they are commenting on the different tone of the film, as if they were reacting to social-media posts. In order to replicate the hybrid texts that are exchanged in virtual communication, the caption "I can see smooth sea" is rendered by replacing the verb with the emoji depicting two eyes, or the 'thumbs-up' emoji is superimposed, entailing approval of the final scenes. Finally, cultural references to Odyssey and Aeneid are read. According to the captions, "the wind [travellers] longed for rises" (quoting Aeneas landing in Castro) and even an immortal being might "delight his soul" in those beautiful places worth exploring – just like the destinations being promoted – as happens to Hermes when visiting Calypso's cave. The connection between the picture and the video is reinforced at the end, when the same slogan, "Salento – the metaphysical metaverse where ancient and modern gods welcome you", expands in the middle of the screen.

5. Conclusions and research prospects

The ongoing research reported in this paper has accounted for the tenet that, in interpreting Metaphysical discourse employed for online advertisements in place marketing, the receiver's cognitive processes do not conform to a conventional truth-functional logic since a Metaphysical composition is essentially deviating from reality. This explains the receiver's exploration of the possibilities and necessities that lie unrealized in reality, but that can become real in the virtual contexts of the online metaverse. Hence the prospective receivers of the multimodal Metaphysical Ad analyzed in this paper, interacting online within the metaverse in search of useful information, have to transcend reality – with its conventional interpretations – and displace it into a modal logic that makes sense of the alternative possible worlds achieved from the semantic structure of the Ad. This is expected to grant receivers a novel experiential exploration of the logically-deviating Metaphysical environments represented in it – and this hypothesis is expected to be corroborated by the analysis of the data (collected in the course of fieldwork involving empirical receivers) that shall be soon available in further reports.

References

BIERWISCH, MANFRED, 1980, "Semantic Structure and Illocutionary Force", in J.R. Searle, F. Kiefer, and M. Blerwisch (eds.), *Speech Act Theory and Pragmatics*, Reidel, Dordrecht, pp. 1-35.

BORN, GEORGINA and HAWORTH, CHRISTOPHER, 2018, "From microsound to vaporwave: Internet-mediated musics, online methods, and genre", *Music & Letters* 98 (4), pp. 601-647.

COCK, JACKLYN, 2011, "Green capitalism or environmental justice: A critique of the sustainability discourse", *Focus* 63, pp. 45-51.

CROFT, WILLIAM A., 2001, *Radical Construction Grammar: Syntactic Theory in Typological Perspective*, Oxford University Press, Oxford.

CROFT, WILLIAM A. and CRUSE, ALAN D., 2004, *Cognitive Linguistics*, Cambridge University Press, Cambridge.

FAERCH, CLAUS and KASPER, GABRIELE, 1987, "Perspectives on language transfer", *Applied Linguistics* 8, pp. 111-136.

FILLMORE, CHARLES J., 1981, "Frame Semantics". In *Linguistics in the Morning Calm*, Hanshin, Seoul, pp. 111-138.

GREENBERG, JOSEPH H., 1973, "Some Universals of Grammar with Particular Reference to the Order of Meaningful Elements", in J.H. Greenberg (ed.), *Universals of Language*, The MIT Press, Cambridge, Mass., pp. 73-113.

GOFFMAN, ERVING, 1974, *Frame Analysis: An Essay on the Organization of Experience*, Harper and Row, London.

GOLDBERG, ADELE E., 1995, *Constructions: A Construction Grammar Approach to Argument Structure*, University of Chicago Press, Chicago.

GUIDO, M. GRAZIA, 2005, *The Imaging Reader: Visualization and Embodiment of Metaphysical Discourse*, Legas Publishing, New York-Ottawa-Toronto.

GUIDO, M. GRAZIA, 2008, *English as a Lingua Franca in Cross-cultural Immigration Domains*, Peter Lang, Bern.

GUIDO, M. GRAZIA, 2018, *English as a Lingua Franca in Migrants' Trauma Narratives*, Palgrave Macmillan, London.

GUIDO, M. GRAZIA, IAIA, PIETRO L. and ERRICO, LUCIA, 2019, "Promoting Responsible Tourism by Exploring Sea-voyage Migration Narratives through ELF: An Experiential-linguistic Approach to Multicultural Community Integration", *Eurasian Journal of Applied Linguistics* 5 (2), pp. 219-238.

HAKOVIRTA, MARKO and DENUWARA, NAVODYA, 2020, "How COVID-19 redefines the concept of sustainability", *Sustainability* 12 (9), p. 3727.

HART, CHRISTOPHER, 2010, *Critical Discourse Analysis and Cognitive Science: New Perspectives on Immigration Discourse*, Palgrave Macmillan, Basingstoke.

HINTIKKA, JAAKKO, 1989, "Exploring Possible Worlds", in S. Allen (ed.), *Possible Worlds in Humanities, Arts and Sciences: Proceedings of the Nobel Symposium 65*, de Gruyter, New York-Berlin, pp. 52-81.

IAIA, PIETRO L., 2016, *Analysing English as a Lingua Franca in Video Games. Linguistic Features, Experiential and Functional Dimensions of Online and Scripted Interactions*, Peter Lang, Bern.

JOHNSON, MARK, 1987, *The Body in the Mind: The Bodily Basis of Meaning, Imagination, and Reason*, The University of Chicago Press, Chicago.

KOC, ALICAN, 2017. "Do you want vaporwave, or do you want the truth?", *Capacious: Journal for Emerging Affect Inquiry* 1 (1), pp. 57-76.

LAKOFF, GEORGE and FERGUSON, SAM, 2006, *The Framing of Immigration*, University of California, Berkeley.

LAKOFF, GEORGE and JOHNSON, MARK, 1999, *Philosophy in the Flesh: The Embodied Mind and its Challenge to Western Thought*, Basic Books, New York.

LEWIS, DAVID K. 1973, *Counterfactuals,* Harvard University Press, Harvard.

LOCKIE, STEWART, 2016, "Beyond resilience and systems theory: reclaiming justice in sustainability discourse", *Environmental Sociology* 2 (2), pp. 115-117.

NARULA, HERMAN, 2022, *Virtual Society: The Metaverse and the New Frontiers of Human Experience*, Random House, New York.

ROGGE, CORINA E., DIJKEMA, DESIRAE and RUSH, KATRINA, 2020, "A discriminating yellow: The detection of anachronistic organic pigment in two backdated metaphysical paintings by Giorgio De Chirico", *Studi Online* VII (13), pp. 59-69.

RUMELHART, DAVID E., 1980, "Schemata: The Building Blocks of Cognition", in R.J. Spiro, B. Bruce, and W. Brewer (eds.), *Theoretical Issues in Reading Comprehension: Perspectives from Cognitive Psychology, Linguistics, Artificial Intelligence and Education*, Erlbaum, Hillsdale, N.J., pp. 33-58.

SHIFMAN, LIMOR, 2014, *Memes in Digital Culture*, MIT Press, Cambridge, MA.

SOMBRE, PAUL and WERMUTH, CORNELIA (eds.), 2010. *Framing. From grammar to application*, John Benjamins, Amsterdam-Philadelphia.

STALNAKER, ROBERT, 1994, "Modality and Possible Worlds", in K. Jaegwon and E. Sosa (eds.), *Blackwell Companion to Metaphysics*, Blackwell, Oxford, pp. 333-337.

TORKINGTON, KATE, STANFORD, DAVINA and GUIVER, JO, 2020, "Discourse(s) of growth and sustainability in national tourism policy documents", *Journal of Sustainable Tourism* 28 (7), pp. 1041-1062.

Layering in Frames, Frames in Layers: Dreaming of Naples*

Piergiorgio Trevisan, Eric Louis Russell

Abstract
In this article, we examine a travel documentary program focusing on Naples and the Amalfi Coast. Drawing upon Appraisal Theory and Multimedia Discourse Analysis, we examine three key components: one traditionally linguistic, one visuo-linguistic, and one meta-linguistic. We argue that the framing of Naples and Amalfi has as its ultimate *teleos* their neoliberal commodification. We trace how the authors of the episode call upon prior frames concerning Naples' danger and Amalfi's rurality, reshaping these into expressions of authenticity to be consumed by viewers. In this sense, framing involves layers that function not to complexify or provide depth to an object, but to further simplify it by inserting it into a globalised discursive order. This, we argue, is yet another manifestation of banal globalisation, a superficial recognition of difference that frames objects not as holistic linguacultural landscapes, but one that reduces these to products.
Key-words: appraisal theory, banal globalisation, media, prosody, visual semantics.

1. Introduction: framing and banal globalisation

How do language users reframe that which has been framed before, especially when the object of this frame is little more than a clichéd stereotype (Goffman 1974)? How does the act of framing give rise to internal tension with regard to this object? And how does framing intersect with preceding semiotic forces that shape both knowledge and knowability that stand in relation to this object (Foucault 1969)? These lines of inquiry ground the present work, facilitating a close

---

* Although this article represents a collaboration between the two authors, sections 3 and 6 were initiated by Russell, sections 4 and 5 by Trevisan, sections 1, 2 and 7 were co-written.

ISSN 1824-3967

description of how different framing mechanisms work to construct and re-construct the ideological substance of Italy, generally, and of a specific Italian region for a distal, allochthonous public.

Thurlow and Jaworski consider the ways in which various media, from television shows to targeted advertisement flyers, both reflect and reiterate "banal globalisation", a term that they use to describe the seemingly trivial, but often unnoticed ways in which meanings and material consequences of global forces are manifested in and through language, rendering a distal Other consumable for those having capital means to engage in such global movements (2011; see also Jaworski and Thurlow 2011; Garzone and Catenaccio 2009). The semiotic enactment of banal globalisation requires complex, iterative practices that can be understood as framing actions, i.e. as acts selecting some aspects of a perceived reality that are made more salient in a text in order to promote a particular problem definition, a causal interpretation, a moral evaluation, and/or a treatment recommendation for the item described (Entman 1993: 52). Certainly, examples of this manifested through discursive activity are not hard to come by in the case of Italy, including marketing campaigns (e.g. "Made in Italy") and regional tourism sloganeering (e.g. "SiAmo Friuli Venezia Giulia"). The case of Naples and its surrounding region presents a fascinating example that might appear rather simplistic at first blush but can be understood, upon closer examination, as far more complex and multifaceted. In the following pages, we provide a close examination of one example of banal globalisation that iterates pre-existing frames, also perpetuating the stereotyped content of these ideational schemata.

Among a wide variety of media sources cited by Thurlow and Jaworski, as well as many others, as sites of banal globalisation are mediatic portrayals of different socio-cultural objects, of which one of the most widely known is the travel documentary. Although the precise format of these programmes varies, all involve some sort of guide or host, typically ascribed expertise gained through experience, and interaction with different social strata in a defined linguacultural location, always directed at its proximation and consumption by a far-away imaginary public (i.e. the programmatic audience). Examination of the linguistic and meta-linguistic content of these media offers compelling insights into how various semiotic ingredients are deployed in order to frame a globalised object, involving not only words and sentences, but moving images and sounds, realised through interaction with persons, communities, and institutions.

Among the dozens of such programs produced for Anglophone (primarily North American) audiences is *Dream of Italy*, a series first aired in 2015 on the United States' (US) Public Broadcasting Service (PBS). Limited to two seasons, each of the series' thirteen episodes follows host Kathy McCabe, whose self-ascribed task already reveals much of how Italy and its various subregions are framed for the viewing public: she "reveals why Italy, with its mesmerizing landscapes, rich artistic treasures, deep ties to the past, and warm people, is a destination travelers [sic] dream of more than any other in the world" (IMDB.com). Following a tried-and-true pattern, *Dream of Italy* guides viewers through destinations ranging from *città d'arte* (e.g. Venice, Florence) to entire regions (e.g. Basilicata, Umbria). As with much media targeting North American Anglophone publics, the series is biased toward Northern Italy, with only five episodes given to destinations in the *Mezzogiorno*: the latter include one dedicated to the Campanese town of Castelvetere sul Calore, billed as the "ancestral village of [McCabe's] maternal great-grandfather" (IMDB.com). In each episode, McCabe first situates and then outlines the broad history of the city or region, introducing viewers to a handful of tropes involving cuisine, cultural practices, and commodities. Viewers are presented elderly cooks, traditional artisans, and multi-generational farmers; short interviews are interspersed with images of bucolic landscapes, bustling crowds, and any number of clichéd views. Particularly interesting is the presentation of language: some subject interviews are conducted in English, whereas others are done in Italian and regional dialects and languages, all variably accompanied by English subtitles, a matter taken up in more detail below.

Importantly, and as with all PBS programming, the series depends upon the financial backing of corporate sponsors: the booking service Viator, cruise operator AmaWaterways, and Perillo Tours. This alignment blurs the line between documentary programming, with its putative bias for factuality, and commercial marketing, with its overt capitalistic finalities. Equally important is the profile of PBS viewership and that of its sponsors: given published data pertaining to viewership, as well as information about the series' sponsors, it can be inferred that *Dream of Italy* targets relatively well-off US

Anglophones who, while eager for adventure, are more likely to travel in organised groups along well-trodden paths[1]. Summarily, this program serves as a vehicle through which the ideological object (Italy, different regions and cities) is framed as not only a political or geographic reality, but as an object with which the viewer can engage through travel and touristic consumption.

In the remaining parts of the paper, various framing resources used to represent Naples and Amalfi are introduced and discussed. Section 2 introduces the materials and methods used in the study; section 3 analyses the role of prosodic patterns and their ideological contexts; section 4 discusses how the resources of the Appraisal system of language (Martin and White 2005) are used to frame specific aspects of the cities, while backgrounding others; section 5 focuses on the resources selected by the authors to appraise and frame some specificities of the two cities from the visual point of view; section 6 analyses how framing is obtained through metalinguistic strategies during post-production editing techniques. A closing section briefly considers the broader implications of this type of analysis and hints at future directions of enquiry.

2. Methods and Data

For the purposes of this study, the authors chose one episode focusing on a southern Italian region, in part because this appeared to afford a heightened sense of the overall programme's aesthetic and approach, but also because it was subjectively judged to more clearly exemplify many of the themes central to **the present volume**. Originally aired in 2015, "Naples and the Amalfi Coast" presents the city and its surrounding region through a series of clips given to coffee culture, *la bella figura* (literally, 'a beautiful physique,' implicationally an individual's positive social persona). Vesuvius, limoncello making, fishing, and pasta. The episode is freely available through the program's YouTube channel and includes English subtitles and close captioning[2].

---

[1] See PBS documentation and US census data (https://www.census.gov/history/pdf/pbs-factsheet-82015.pdf, last consulted 31 May 2022).
[2] https://www.youtube.com/watch?v=yXUniFIbIXI&t=80s, first consulted 25 March 2022; last consulted 07 May 2022.

Following initial viewing, transcription of the entire episode (duration 24:58, including 1:10 of advertising) was done by the second author (a co-native speaker of English and near-native speaker of Italian). Subsequent verification of transcription and timing coordination relied upon close caption, auto-generated subtitles, as well as secondary viewing by the first author (a near-native speaker of English and native speaker of Italian). Linguistic transcription and all data tagging were done manually, labelling surface-level lexical and semantic forms (2846 words, including both English and Italian words). The vast majority of spoken data were generated by the host, herself, counting just under 2200 words: the remaining speech events concern ten interviewees (see Table 3). Additional tagged features included instances of prosodic emphasis, pauses, and hesitation. For such data, preliminary analysis was done manually by the first author and then blind verified by the second author, taking into consideration lexical and morphosyntactic components of the archive that received relative pitch, intensity, and length.

The study of prosodic features was complemented by the analysis of wider prosodic patterns realised at the level of discourse-semantics (Halliday and Mathiessen 2004: 106). After initial transcription of linguistic and meta-linguistic features, the text was tagged for its evaluative resources following Martin and White (2003)'s subdivision into the sub-systems of Affect, Judgement and Appreciation. Subsequently, description was extended to the visual domain, dominated by alternating images of Naples and the Amalfi region, e.g. crowded city streets, bucolic vineyards and pastures, and sweeping coastal terrain. For this, data evaluation proceeded again manually, with the second author first tagging the sequenced presentation of visual information (i.e. representation of people and objects, see Kress and van Leeuwen 2006; Machin 2016), subsequently verified by the first author: this involved the juxtapositional description of representations on the ideational plane and on the interpersonal one, mainly realised by waves of evaluative patterns used to trigger both positive and negative assessments.

Viewed holistically, the episode achieves a complex framing of Naples and the Amalfi coast. For the purposes of this paper, we consider three specific framing mechanisms, describing and interpreting sample data that offer a window into broader trends and suggest commonalities with other examples of banal globalisation, pertinent to Italy and many other mass tourism destinations. As an aside, it is important to note that our focal selection is already an interpretive act deriving from concerns of analytical economy as it has been done by perceptions of impactfulness: we do not pretend that the specific linguistic and metalinguistic mechanisms we highlight are the only ones at play in these data, but they are among the most clearly manifest and, because of this, perhaps the most important contribution to the meta-frame. The remainder of this article is the description and analysis of these, concluding with a general discussion.

3. Prosodic framing

The central task for this section is to describe and interpret the ways in which prosody is deployed to frame the two discursively constructed objects (i.e. Naples and Amalfi), as well as their ideological contents. The linguistic description below focuses entirely on the use of prosody by the narrator, a choice made due to her outsized role as the source of the vast majority of linguistic data in the episode.

Prior to description of episode data, a brief aside is warranted to better understand phonetic stress in North American English. Rather than corresponding to a singular articulatory factor, such moments of emphasis are phonetically realized through complex mechanisms of vowel amplitude or loudness, length, and tonal variability (Ladd 1980; 1996). While these can be quantified, it is not the raw phonetic output that is perceived as emphasis or focus, but the relation of this to surrounding phonetic material, necessitating the manual evaluation and tagging described above: stress is dynamic and fluid, rather than static or fixed, and relies as much, if not more upon impression as it does on empirical factors. Phonemic stress contributes in complex ways to the structuring of utterance information, being used to convey thematic focus, contextual prominence, or any number of emotional states, ranging from subtle disagreement to outright surprise (Pierrehumbert 1980; Selkirk 1995; Roettinger, Marht and Cole 2019). Such surface-level patterns contribute to the framing of an object through the foregrounding of particular qualities: lexico-semantic items given prosodic emphasis are, in essence, highlighted in the flow of information, focusing audience attention and framing their reception. In the case at hand, this involves a narrative establishment of that which is new or proclaimed and contrasting this to that which is old or known. Emphasis is given to assertions, as well as counter-assertions, constructing and hybridizing pre-existing frames.

Based on the data tagging following the methods described above, the episode included a total of 170 lexical items receiving prosodic emphasis on at least one syllable, representing just under six percent of the corpus (ignoring commercials). The distribution of these was not uniform across the three object-foci of the episode, Naples, Amalfi and Italy. Table 1 provides the relative frequency of prosodic emphasis, distinguishing between those concerning Naples, Amalfi, and Italy more generally, also providing frequency.

TABLE 1. COUNT AND FREQUENCY OF PROSODIC EMPHASIS

	Number	Frequency
Episode (all)	170	0.0597
Naples	84	0.0533
Amalfi	83	0.0726
Italy (general)	3	0.0566

Already from Table 1, it can be deduced that relatively more frequent emphasis was associated with Amalfi than Naples[3], a fact that clashes with the amount of lexical and temporal space dedicated to each. The former accounts for approximately 40% of the transcript and only just over nine of the twenty-four minutes of the examined episode, whereas the latter amounts to more than 55% of the transcript and over fifteen minutes of this program.

Beyond the qualitative concerns presented above, the content or semantic target of prosodic emphasis differs significantly across the Italian contexts. Naples and its immediate surroundings

---

[3] Patterns applying to Italy (in general) are very likely skewed by the relative paucity of data: less than 2% of the transcript and slightly more than this of overall time were given to the country at large.

are associated with superlative qualities, as in (1), canonically negative or overtly negated qualities, as in (2), those connoting tradition, as in (3), and verbs with clearly harmful or deleterious connotation, as in (4); in all examples, bold face indicates the lexical item in which one or more syllables received relative prosodic prominence.

(1) Its [Naples'] strategic location along a **magnificent** bay has beckoned waves of conquerors and rulers [min. 1:55]
(2) Today however this bustling city suffers from a **needlessly negative** reputation [min. 2:55]
(3) A **tradition** [artisanal carving] that is alive and well in this **ancient** city [min. 10:03]
(4) So why would people **continue to live** here? [...] What **draws** them to live beneath such a **deadly** force? [min. 11:52]

Other examples receiving prosodic emphasis include: *very best, most Neapolitan, very seriously,* and *perfect* (superlatives); *dangerous, densely populated, messy, frantic, fiendish,* and *wickedly* (negative qualities); *family run, deep roots, ancient,* and *old* (tradition); and *destroy, pile up, kill,* and *threaten* (verbal harm).

Showing both similarities to and distinction from Naples, Amalfi is instantiated through emphasis involving positive qualities, as in (5), alongside those that connote tradition, as in (6). As noted above, there are relatively fewer examples of this type of framing mechanism here, a by-product of unequal treatment of the two subjects.

(5) 30 miles south of Naples and Mt Vesuvius this coastline lures visitors with its **plunging** cliffs **gentle** climate and **jewel-like** villages [min. 15:27]
(6) And Rafael's father Gaetano leads a team of **friends and family** through a vineyard of the **local** grape called Bianca Lala [min. 17:26]

Additional examples are seen throughout the portion of the episode dedicated to this object: Amalfi is noted to be *unexpected, [have] good fortune, magnificent, beautiful, particular,* and *sun-drenched* (positive qualities), while at the same time it is asserted as *classic, small, true, tiny, [by] hand,* and *multi-generational* (tradition).

Beyond the surface forms targeted by prosodic emphasis, it is telling that only a few items are repeatedly manifest in this light. Again, the semantic qualities observed as cogent to each of the two foci stand in contrast: for Naples, *bella figura* and *danger* are repeatedly given prosodic emphasis, whereas for Amalfi this involves *true/truly*, *local*, and *homemade*. Such juxtaposition frames both destinations as steeped in history, albeit in contrasting ways. Naples is brought into contiguity with semantic fields of peril, whether from organized crime, the bustle of urban life, or a nearby volcano, whereas Amalfi's historicity is framed as a matter of bucolic nature and authenticity.

Summarily, the prosodic patterns of the episode can be interpreted as aligning with Appraisal Theory's understanding of intensification or amplification encoding, described as moments in which "the volume is turned up so that the prosody makes a bigger splash which reverberates through the surrounding discourse." (Martin and White 2003: 20-21). Such representations can be used to convey both positive and negative attitudes toward an object, often leading to a "fuzzification" or blurring of attitudinal lines (2005: 41). Importantly, amplification acts as a type of stand in for quantification, or the force and weight of a particular item (2005: 140). This is particularly interesting as it concerns Naples and the ambivalent goals of framing the metropolis as exciting, due in part to its intensity and hazards, but fundamentally approachable, due to its traditions and good nature. By repeatedly emphasizing the two ideational poles in alternation, a fuzzy boundary emerges, framing the city as a sort of exotic, dangerously un-dangerous locale, one that offers a taste of risk without much or any real threat – at least to the casual tourist.

4. Evaluative framing

In this section we show how Naples and Amalfi are framed by linguo-visual patterns that prime viewers' pre-existing mental schemata (Rumelhart 1980). Schemata are crucial cognitive models used to make sense of new experiences and situations by relating them to pre-existing mental representations of similar events, i.e. to schemata present in the mind of viewer-receivers. Following Eysenck and Keane, a schema is a "portion of background knowledge relating to a particular type of object, person, situation or event" (1990: 275). Each schema thus contains information about the elements of a particular domain, and the activation of a specific schema allows us to make particular predictions in the process of comprehension. Such mental models are themselves learned or inherited through anthropological experience (van Dijk 2006; Wodak 2006) and are expressed through linguistic form and structure (Sharifian 2011), such that meaning is constructed in the interaction between a text and the interpreter's background knowledge (Semino 1995: 4). According to Cook (1994), texts may either pose a challenge to the reader's existing schemata, destroying old ones (schema refreshment), or may project worlds perceived by an audience as conventional and familiar (schema reinforcement).

In addition to the ideational content of the video and the prosodic patterns discussed above, data pertinent to schema reinforcement phenomena and framing perpetuation rely heavily on the interpersonal resources underlying the semantic stratum of the whole episode. As suggested by Martin and White (2003: 19), this interpersonal dimension is rarely expressed in lexicogrammar or discourse semantics as configurations of discrete elements, tending instead to be spread throughout a text and being prosodic by nature (Halliday and Mathiessen 2004: 106). In the examined episode, waves of evaluative information were realised by the combination of verbal and visual resources that intensify specific features of the cities and of their social actors to the detriment of others, with 140 tokens observed. Evaluation is interpersonal by nature, as it is concerned with the speaker's ongoing intrusion into the speech situation. This may involve feeling (Affect), people (Judgement) and things (Appreciation), and can be significantly upscaled or downscaled by means of intensification and amplification resources. The distribution of tagged instances of various types of Evaluation are noted in Table 2.

As noted above, Appreciation dominates the evaluative resources of the episode, with very few instances of Affect. The latter are used almost exclusively by interviewed locals (e.g. minute 2:30: "Every Italian takes pride in their local brew"; 4:37: "people loves [sic] this very soft constructions"; 4:55: "We are relaxed because the Neapolitan attitude is very relaxed"), whereas McCabe resorts to Affect only at the episode conclusion, exhorting viewers to "Feel the soft breeze of the sea" and "Dream of Italy" (24:20). This unbalance may be explained by the producers' intention to perpetuate the stereotype of Italians as passionate, sentimental, and dreamy.

TABLE 2. EVALUATION: TOKEN COUNT AND FREQUENCY

	Token count	Token frequency
Affect	10	0.071
Judgement	26	0.186
Appreciation	104	0.743

Although a minority of occurrences, Judgement resources are more evenly distributed across episode data. Notably, locals are represented using these resources to evaluate that which viewers might understand as typically Neapolitan (e.g. 5:14: "It takes years for a tailor to learn the craft", implying that tailors are well trained; 6:47: "The students take their studies very seriously, implying that Neapolitan *pizzaioli* are trustworthy), while McCabe uses similar resources to assess the locals as authentic (e.g. 1:13: "In this series, we'll meet the authentic characters") and bound by family traditions (e.g. 2:37 "the owner of Naples' historic grand café Gambrinus"; 4:04 "the head of the family run Rubinacci tailoring business"). These patterns can be inferred to reflect producers' expectations vis-à-vis the programme audience. On the one hand, they may believe that North American customers are likely to appreciate a well-recognized institutional voice, reinforcing pre-existing schemata pertinent to authentic Neapolitans or Amalfitani; on the other hand, the very same audience might be intrigued and even reassured by expressions of self-confidence concerning tradition.

As noted above, Appreciation is the dominant evaluative resource observed in the episode, accounting for 74% of all instances. Both locals and McCabe use Appreciation extensively, but again, differently. The narrative voice tends to mainly use resources aimed to assess the value of traditional activities and products (e.g. 4:13: "A craft with deep roots in the city"; 10:03: "It is a true folk art" – both of them instances of [Appreciation: valuation]) or to convey a seeming objectivity (e.g. 5:01: "Rubinacci's taylors work hard to make this relaxed style), whereas locals are also represented using metaphors (e.g. 2:45: "The coffee in Naples has a big heart") or by using parallel constructions (e.g. 4:37: "We make the construction very soft, very natural. People loves [sic] this very soft constructions"). This distinction may be explained by a desire to frame different objects by a more institutional, authoritative voice that most viewers would recognise and trust, as it concerns McCabe, whereas viewers may recognise in the use of colourful expressions, unconventional, creative metaphors, and exaggerated repetitions a form of positively assessed authenticity, again reinforcing pre-existing mental schemata.

The different forms of evaluation observed are up-scaled or down-scaled by means of graduation resources. In Appraisal Theory, graduation operates across two axes of scalability: Focus, expressing the degree to which phenomena match supposed exemplary instances of a semantic category; and Force, concerning assessments about the intensity or amount of a phenomenon. Although both are widely used to emphasize assessments in the episode, what might be termed an evaluation signature is clearly identifiable. McCabe tends to resort to Focus, perhaps because she wishes to foreground how well Naples and Amalfi fit into the (putatively pre-existing) semantic field of authenticity. Importantly, this is noted in the first sentence of the episode (1:13: "In this series, we'll meet the authentic characters, uncover the hidden treasures and discover what makes Italy the most fascinating country in the world"), as well as in several other later instances, notably "The original bucket-list city" (1:45), "It is a true folk art" (10:03), "jewel-like villages" (15:27). Contrastively, locals almost exclusively deploy Force, allowing them to intensify specific aspects under discussion, for example, "A bespoke men's suit is made to fit only one man and to bring out the very best in him" (5:25) and "The Neapolitan attitude is very relaxed" (4:37). These patterns match above observations regarding the tendency to represent the institutional voice as more objectively involved and that of locals as more vividly involved.

Crucially, Force is also used both by host and locals to intensify negative aspects of Naples, reinforcing the dangerous-undangerous dichotomy already noted (e.g. 10:54 "The scientists they say that this is one of the most dangerous volcanoes in the world"; 11:20 "What makes Vesuvius so dangerous is that it sits in the middle of a densely populated region"; 12:48 "A sculpture of the Virgin

Mary was <u>nearly</u> destroyed"). This is promptly counterbalanced by the foregrounding of positive qualities, thus framing the city and its inhabitants as intriguingly risky, but never truly threatening (e.g. 12:23: "The area is <u>very</u> nice and the climate is <u>so</u> good"; 12:00: "Because this area is covered with an average of 300 feet of volcanic ashes. They are <u>very very</u> rich in minerals"; 12:16: "Vesuvius doesn't <u>just</u> destroy. She gives life as well").

5. Visuo-linguistic framing[4]

Visual choices made by producers of the episode reinforce those described above. Most images in the video function in parallel to accompanying verbal accounts: there are, however, several examples potentially triggering positive or negative assessment, even without a specific linguistic intervention on the part of the host, i.e. without an authorial flag. This is mainly realised by framing Naples and its inhabitants using the visual resources of Appreciation, (at minutes 1:38 and 2:10) and of Judgement (7:30 and 8:24).[5]

At minutes 1:38 and 2:10 the ideational content is realised by the representation of a bustling street and of a romantic sunset. These representations of specific aspects of the city on the ideational plane concurrently position the viewers interpersonally, what may be called an 'attitudinal positioning': negative and positive inferences are indeed likely to be produced by what is ideationally represented and by how it is represented. This follows Kress and Van Leeuwen's understanding, stating that:

We believe that visual design, like all semiotic modes, fulfils three major functions. To use Halliday's terms, every semiotic fulfils both an 'ideational' function, a function of representing 'the world around and inside us' and an 'interpersonal' function, a function of enacting social interactions as social relations. All message entities – texts – also attempt to present a coherent 'world of the text', what Halliday and Mathiessen call the 'textual' function (2004: 15).

---

[4] Here and throughout, we refer to specific points by time stamp: readers wishing to see these images are directed to the weblink for visual confirmation (See References).
[5] For a detailed account of how Appraisal Theory resources can be applied to the visual domain, see White 2014.

Interestingly, these images seem to simulate an objective representation of some aspects of the city: what is being shown on the ideational plane does not need an authorial flag to help viewers formulate inferences (attitudinal meanings) on the interpersonal plane (White 2014). Positive and negative assessments result from the ideational content: these tend to oscillate between negative ones regarding the well-known city excessive crowdedness, intensity and shabbiness (exemplified by Figure 1), and more positive ones triggered by reassuring, relaxing and alluring sceneries.

Similar patterns are reiterated in the representation of people, where images portraying participants on the ideational plane are likely to trigger negative inferences (Judgement). These subsets of images regularly alternate with positively portrayed representations of participants, flagging positive inferences on the interpersonal plane. At minute 7:30, for example, an instructor is scolding his apprentices: here, an apparently aggressive gaze and confrontational body posture provide explicit cues to his attitude, rendering the authorial voice unnecessary for the production of assessments in the viewers (Kress and van Leeuwen 2006: 114). The potentially negative inferences triggered by the instructor are, however, immediately mitigated by the more reassuring atmosphere depicted at minute 8:24, in which host McCabe herself becomes an apprentice *pizzaiola*: here, both gaze and physical position index a sort of paternal friendliness.

The content of these images functions attitudinally, much like the more canonically linguistic moments, where what is said suffices to trigger readers' inferences without any authorial intervention. At the same time, the video makes wide use of visual resources that clearly convey a specific authorial point of view. At minute 2:21, for example, the ideational plane shows a scooter which suddenly starts moving at a visibly unnaturally high speed. Here, the author's presence is evident thanks to the manipulation of what would be the "naturalistic representation" (Kress and van Leeuwen 2006: 26). Interpersonally, then, there is an authorial flag providing cues regarding the way in which the ideational content should be interpreted – in this instance, regarding possible speed-related dangers and a general atmosphere of chaos that dominates Naples' streetscape. The compositional choices made evident in this moment result in an intensified image, one that can be interpreted as the visual counterpart of Force patterns discussed above.

Throughout the episode, negative assessments actuated in the visual or visuo-linguistic domain are promptly counterbalanced by more positive representations, intensified by other means of speed manipulation, i.e. slowing down movement from scene to scene. At minute 4:40, for example, having represented the potential dangers of life in Naples' streets through unnatural manipulation of speed at minute 2:21, the camera moves inside the workshop of tailor Rubinacci, a markedly different atmosphere. Here again camera movements are manipulated: actions are portrayed as unnaturally slow, conveying a distinct authorial flag concerning the ways in which the ideational content should be interpreted: a sense of time that seems to stop thanks to the professional craftmanship, Old World charm, and concern for tradition that can only be achieved through a lack of speech and frenzy. This, in essence, serves to complement the chaotic cityscape outside. In the two examples, visual parallels to Force counterbalance each other, with juxtapositions between varying forms and manifestations of intensity.

6. Metalinguistic framing

A final mechanism used for the differential framing of objects concerns the framing of language itself, a metalinguistic act of inserting (or not inserting) various elements through post-production editing. Description here looks to the multimodal representations of speakers using different linguistic forms, including English, as well as the relative extent of Italian interference, Italian, and Italian dialects (e.g. Neapolitan), as well as the inclusion or exclusion of subtitles. These factors are summarized in Table 3, providing each interviewee in order of appearance, their stated profession, and pertinent language and subtitle information.

What is immediately of interest in these data is the non-uniform way that language is represented in the episode: some speakers appear using English and others Italian, despite their varying proficiency and use of dialectal forms and registers; some are subtitled, others are not; and background chatter is at times left untranslated at others glossed. This can hardly be considered an accident, leaving questions of why such editorial choices were made open for interpretation.

TABLE 3. LANGUAGE ALTERITY

M Rosati	Owner, Café Gambrinus, Naples	English, no subtitles
M Rubinacci	Tailor, Naples	English, thickly accented, no subtitles (when addressing camera) Italian (Neapolitan accented), no subtitles (when addressing clients)
E Coccia	Pizzaiolo, Naples	Italian (Neapolitan accented), subtitles (when addressing camera and host); interspersed with phrases in broken English Italian (Neapolitan), no subtitles (when addressing others)
R Addio	Geologist, Vesuvius	English, no subtitles
L Albano	Organiser, Naples	Italian (Neapolitan accented), subtitles Neapolitan in background, no subtitles
R Bove	Winemaker (daughter), Amalfi	English, subtitled
G Bove	Winemaker (father), Amalfi	Italian, subtitled
G Amatruda	Artisan papermaker, Amalfi	English, no subtitles
M Carbone	Amateur limoncello-maker, Amalfi	English, no subtitles
C Bob	Chef, Amalfi	English, German accented, no subtitles

With the exception of chef Christoph Bob[6], all interviewees in the episode are presumably native speakers of Italian. However, their command of English is variable, as are the forms of Italian that they use when addressing the host and her camera. Café owner Rosati and artisan Amatruda appear more fluent in English than do tailor Rubinacci or pizzaiolo Coccia, but only the very last one is subtitled. Even so, Coccia's use of English is limited to phatics and fixed expressions, e.g. "very good," invariably directed at the programme host. At the same time, winemaker R. Bove is subtitled,

---

[6] According to Gambero Rosso (https://www.gamberorosso.it/notizie/notizie-ristoranti/ristorazione-in-campania-bistrot-quartuccio-con-christoph-bob-e-le-altre-novita/, last consulted 31 May 2022), Bob is a German from Hamburg.

although her English is comparable to, if not less inflected, than other interviewees. Obviously, those who use little or no English are subtitled, including the father G. Bove and Albano, a local historian. However, even in such cases not all moments of linguistic activity are glossed. When Rubinacci addresses clients in Neapolitan-accented Italian, this is not translated, nor are the chanting of locals at the bonfire organized by Albano or the instructions from Coccia to his students. This is distinct from the non-instructional chatter between Coccia and students, as well as that directed at the host, which are accompanied by English subtitles.

Clearly, language is not being presented in these instances solely or even primarily as a vehicle of informational conveyance, but as a means of ideological conveyance (van Dijk 2006, see also Berger and Luckmann 1966). When, for example, Coccia uses Italian with students, the presentation of this (undoubtedly subject to editorial and production choices at many levels) actuates an ideological frame of authenticity: language is commodified in a way that closely resembles that of physical products, being rendered legible to an allochthonous audience. For this to happen, the supposed authenticity of an interviewee and their linguistic repertoire must be transliterated – and perhaps peppered with English, itself. The use of thickly accented English is another index of authenticity, but only when it emerges from persons that fit within this ideological frame. A gentlemanly tailor who makes frequent, if perhaps charming English errors, may not require subtitles, as the content of such linguistic signs (namely, information on style habits and their presumed importance) is less important than the performance itself. On the other hand, the content-specific information conveyed in highly-proficient English by a young, female winemaker – an image that hardly fits within the preconceived frame of authenticity – must be rendered for both form and content, and is thus provided in translation.

We interpret this differential projection of languages and shapes of language as itself another, layered framing act, working in concert with those noted above. This is in effect another example of the **Commodification of Otherness**, a common practice of banal globalisation that is also noted by Thurlow and colleagues. Italianness, in this case communicative and semiotic Italianness, is presented as flawed to the extent that it requires the occasional overlay of English, but even this is enregistered as charming and a symbolic representation of authenticity (Silverstein 2003; Agha 2003). Those who contribute to the ideological projection of Naples as approachably exciting and amiably impenetrable or Amalfi as a bucolic idyl are linguistically presented in this manner, thick accents and somewhat clumsy turns of phrase left *in situ*, whereas moments of informational importance are given subtitles, as are those moments when language use does not correspond to pre-existing schemata associated with positive aspects. In this way, language is represented in a manner similar to the visual semiotics discussed above, albeit within the auditory domain (see also Heller 2003).

These and other examples of metalinguistic patterns reinforce and interact with the frames presented above, while also rearticulating the tensions emergent from them. For example, the viewer understands a given speaker might have a thick accent or use halting English, but also understands that such errors, much like the chaos of Naples or the entrenched tradition of Amalfi, are something that they are to consume with pleasure, a part of what "makes Italy truly and authentically Italian," and, presumably, therefore something that a curious viewer-qua-future traveller might or should desire. They are also primed to understand the execution and consumption of this desire as possible, countering any hesitancy about inter-cultural understanding or cross-linguistic communication. In short, and much like the other mechanisms used to frame the city of Naples or the landscape of the Amalfi coast, the episode divorces language from its perlocutionary roots and rearticulates this as a commodity to be consumed, albeit from a distance. Language is no longer merely something that is shared between speakers and their audiences, a tool primarily used for the conveyance of information from locutor to interlocutor, but an objectified symbol, an object that is both consumable and deployed to further this consumption.

7. Discussion: globalising the local for distal consumption

Each of the above components contribute to ideological framing. By exploiting combined visuo-verbal resources that resort to the interpersonal category of evaluation, Naples is framed and reframed for the audience as an authentic, yet exotic city, slightly dangerous yet never too threatening for the potential consumer-travellers. By prosodically emphasizing Amalfi's tradition and beauty, this region is framed and reframed as a pastoral idyl, albeit one inhabited by persons who are oriented toward potential visitors. The resources of evaluation co-pattern to produce images of the city which are very likely to reinforce already existing viewer schemata, rather than producing new ones that may not work for the ultimate commercial purpose of the show and its producers. And by presenting language itself as a mark of authenticity, viewers are primed to consume this, albeit through the intermediary of translation and orientation toward the non-Italian-speaking world. The question remains as to how these framing acts should be understood in a broader symbolic and anthropological light: in other words, what the ideational facts of these frames, as well as their mechanisms of accomplishment, suggest about those who undertake this action and about their putative audiences. Here, it is helpful to take a step back and consider how the ideological world made manifest through these and similar linguistic and visuo-linguistic performances is integrated into the neoliberal, globalised world of tourism; also worthy of consideration is the positionality of North American Anglophone viewers, in this instance as the source of consumer-framers, and Italy, as that of the object-framed (Crouch et al. 2005; Springer 2016).

The Italian peninsula in general, and Naples and Amalfi, in particular, have long been commodified as exotic destinations, locales in which a mythological Other exists in tension with an equally mythological self who ventures toward them as an act of self-discovery and education. This is already noted in the *Grand Tours* of the seventeenth through early twentieth centuries, when destinations in the Mediterranean basin served to reinforce ideological notions of class and national superiority of those from the Anglo-Saxon, Atlantic north (Cohen 1992). Similar tendencies are seen today and are manifest in this episode. They are also increasingly noted in the globalised world of mass tourism, where the quest for authenticity and localism have displaced prior frames of inter-personal interaction and movement of the self beyond its cultural habitus, weaving travel and cross-cultural contacts into a neo-liberalized order of consumption and associated economic hierarchies (Jaworski and Thurlow 2011; Heller 2003). Globalising trends and corresponding semiotic frames are clearly noted in the examined episode, be this encoded through prosodic emphasis on danger or rurality, which situates corresponding objects within a frame of exotic or docile **allochthony**, respectively, or through the complex interplay of visuo-linguistic indices, which call upon pre-existing frames and their stereotyped contents. Specifically, the viewer is presented an object that is framed as a product that they can readily attain, be it for a day or a week, without having to fully engage with its content or inhabitants. The stereotypical frames of danger (Naples) or ruralness (Amalfi) are not disrupted, but rearticulated, rendering them consumable even by the most naïve viewer.

This examination and interpretation of **quotidian** semiotic material highlights an interesting factor, one that is hardly exclusive to Italy, Naples and the Amalfi, or any of the above data: that of intercultural contacts within the globalised order, in general, and within discourses of mass tourism, in particular. Thurlow and Jaworski note that language is increasingly an intrinsic component of the neo-liberalized tourist gaze toward the Other, specifically that "*local* languages often feature no less heavily than photos/images when it comes to tourists' search for authenticity and difference" (2011: 288, emphasis of the original; see also Thurlow and Jaworski 2012). They assert that the presentation of local languages and their insertion into a wider semiotic range, in which a way of speaking becomes a metonymic expression of place, contributes to a form of banal globalisation, one characterized by superficial contact under a veneer of mobility and authenticity (Heller et al. 2014; Urry 2005). What is striking about the data described and interpreted above is that this is presented without the need for direct contact between specific sociolinguistic and sociocultural landscapes and their inhabitants, on the one hand, and the distal tourist-consumer, on the other, as the latter presumably remains in their television viewing chair far from Naples and the Amalfi coast. In the examples cited by Thurlow and Jaworski – exaggerated and unidimensional as these may be – there is a commodification of difference that is accomplished through a complex interplay of linguistic and non-linguistic mechanisms. In the present example, the programme host acts as a stand-in or intermediary, bringing banal globalisation one step further, in that it can be accomplished without physical movement (Dunn 2005).

Moving beyond many of the examples examined in other literature cited above, this manifestation of banal globalisation and the framing mechanisms used to render its object legible – and therefore consumable – by a distant, imaginary audience shows how such acts permeate even the most superficially mundane spaces of mass media and their socio-economic power structures. Peeling back clichéd portrayals of other linguacultural landscapes, our description and interpretation offers a template for the deeper exploration of how different objects are rendered consumable within the broader dynamics of globalisation, asking how various modalities of semiotic production and consumption can be critiqued and their inner workings better understood. Indeed, the same approaches used here might well be used to unpack any number of other examples, involving Italy and things Italian, or any other linguistic, cultural, political and/or anthropological context.

The present analysis demonstrates that framing is never a singular semiotic activity. It also offers evidence for the ways that language and other semiotic signs, particularly those in the visual field, are themselves co-opted to reinforce and reiterate prior and newly established frames. In the case at hand, these work conspiratorially. Putatively extant frames that establish Naples as a city of crime and grime are not erased but are overlain with a veneer of consumer-oriented exoticism, whereas the Amalfi coast is framed as a rural idyl buttressed by a new form of modernity, one reframing tradition and authenticity for the benefit of the tourist gaze. Collectively, these framing acts can be understood as yet another emergent effect of banal globalisation, one that recentres the consumer-tourist-viewer and inverts the objectified, framed Other, be this a person or place, to a role of commodity.

Clearly, any number of possible paths lie open to future research pertinent to the framing – or perhaps dynamic and iterative reframing – of Italy within globalised orders and flows. These include a closer examination of how self-framing actions, perhaps best exemplified by the "Made in Italy" campaign of the first decades of the twentieth century, have rearticulated the country and the very notion of Italianness – and not only for **distal** consumers of products, services, and touristic moments, but also for Italians themselves. Other possible questions concern framing and reframing at the local, sub-national level, perhaps involving investigation into how different regions, cities, and communities frame and counter-frame themselves, activating and modifying ideological concepts such as locality, authenticity, and tradition, while also setting themselves in a complex tension vis-à-vis Italy and Europe. In any other pursuits, it will be increasingly important to consider, as we have done above, the complex interplay of not only language, as it is canonically understood, but of other, interleaved semiotic information, not only because various media that permeate the globalised forces and flows of inter- and intra-cultural discourse production are increasingly multimodal, but because these modalities are also shifting, expanding, and taking on new shapes.

References

AGHA, ASIF, 2003, "The Social Life of Cultural Value", *Language & Communication* 23, pp. 231-273.

BERGER, PETER L. and THOMAS, LUCKMAN, 1966, *The Social Construction of Reality: A Treatise in the Sociology of Knowledge*, Anchor Books, Garden City, NY.

COHEN, MICHÈLE, 1992, "The Grand Tour: constructing the English gentleman in eighteenth-century France", *History of education* 21, pp. 241-257.

COOK, GUY, 1994, *Discourse and Literature. The Interplay of Form and Mind*, O.U.P., Oxford.

"DREAM OF ITALY", 2015, https://dreamofitaly.com/tv-show/naplesamalfi-coast/, last accessed 12 May 2022.

"DREAM OF ITALY", 2015, https://www.imdb.com/title/tt7882810/, last accessed 12 May 2022.

CROUCH, DAVID, JACKSON, RHONA, THOMPSON, FELIX, 2005, *The Media and the Tourist Imagination*, Routledge, London.

DUNN, DAVID, 2005, "We are not here to make a film about Italy, we are here to make a film about me… British television holiday programmes' representations of the tourist destination", in D. Crouch, R. Jackson and R. Thompson (eds.), *The media and the tourist imagination: Converging cultures*, Routledge, London, pp. 154-169.

ENTMAN, ROBERT, 1993, "Framing: Toward clarification of a fractured paradigm", *Journal of Communication* 43 (4), pp. 51-58.

EYSENCK, MICHAEL W. and KEANE, MARK T., 1990, *Cognitive Psychology: A Student's Handbook*, Psychology Press, London.

FOUCAULT, MICHEL, 1969, *L'Archéologie du savoir*, Gallimard, Paris.

GARZONE, GIULIANA and CATENACCIO, PAOLA (eds.), 2009, *Identities Across Media and Modes: Discourse Perspectives*, Peter Lang, Bern.

GOFFMAN, ERVING, 1974, *Frame Analysis: An Essay on the Organization of Experience*, Harper and Row, London.

HALLIDAY, M.A.K and MATTHIESSEN, CHRISTIAN, 2004, *Introduction to Functional Grammar*, Routledge, London.

HELLER, MONICA, 2003, "Globalization, the new economy and the commodification of language and Identity", *Journal of Sociolinguistics* 7 (4), pp. 473-498.

HELLER, MONICA, PUJOLAR, JOAN, DUCHÊNE, ALEXANDRE, 2014, "Linguistic commodification in tourism", *Journal of Sociolinguistics* 18 (4), pp. 539-566.

JAWORSKI, ADAM and THURLOW, CRISPIN, 2011, *Making contact: Language, tourism and globalization*, Routledge, London.

KRESS, GUNTHER and VAN LEEUWEN, THEO, 2001, *Multimodal Discourse: The Modes and Media of Contemporary Communication*, Arnold, London.

KRESS, GUNTHER and VAN LEEUWEN, THEO, 2006, *Reading Images: The Grammar of Visual Design*, London, Routledge.

LADD, ROBERT, 1980, *The Structure of Intonational Meaning*, Indiana University Press, Bloomington.

LADD, ROBERT, 1996, *Intonational Phonology*, Cambridge University Press, Cambridge, UK.

MACHIN, DAVID, 2016, *Introduction to Multimodal Analysis*, Bloomsbury, London.

MARTIN, J.R. and WHITE, PETER R.R., 2003, *The Language of Evaluation: Appraisal in English*, Palgrave MacMillan, Basingstoke.

PIERREHUMBERT, JANET, 1980, *The phonology and phonetics of English intonation*, MIT Press, Cambridge, MA.

ROETTGER, TIMO B., MAHRT, TIM, COLE, JENNIFER, 2019, "Mapping prosody onto meaning – the case of information structure in American English", *Language, Cognition and Neuroscience* 34 (7), pp. 841-860.

RUMELHART, DAVID. E., 1980, "Schemata: The basic building blocks of cognition", in R. Spiro, B. Bruce and B. Brewer (eds.), *Theoretical Issues in Reading Comprehension*, Lawrence Earlbaum, Hillsdale, NJ, pp. 47-52.

SELKIRK, ELIZABETH, 1995, "Sentence prosody: Intonation, stress, and phrasing", in J. A. Goldsmith (ed.), *The handbook of phonological theory*, Blackwell, London, pp. 550-569.

SEMINO, ELENA, 1995, "Schema Theory and the Analysis of Text Worlds in Poetry", *Language and Literature* 4 (2), pp. 79-108.

SHARIFIAN, FARAZ, 2011, *Cultural Conceptualizations and Language: Theoretical framework and applications*, Benjamins, Amsterdam.

SILVERSTEIN, MICHAEL, 2003, "Indexical order and the dialectics of sociolinguistic life", *Language and Communication* 23 (3-4), pp. 193-229.

SPRINGER, SIMON, 2016, *The Discourse of Neoliberalism: Anatomy of a powerful idea*, Rowman Littlefield, London.

THURLOW, CRISPIN and JAWORSKI, ADAM, 2011, "Tourism Discourse: Languages and Banal Globalization", *Applied Linguistics Review* 2, pp. 285-312.

THURLOW, CRISPIN and JAWORSKI, ADAM, 2012, "Elite mobilities: The semiotic landscapes of luxury and privilege", *Social Semiotics* 22 (4), pp. 487-516.

URRY, JOHN, 2005, *The Tourist Gaze*, 2nd Edition, Sage, London.

VAN DIJK, TEUN A, 2006, "Discourse, context and cognition", *Discourse Studies* 8 (1), pp. 159-177.

WHITE, PETER R. R., 2014, "The attitudinal work of new journalism images: a search for visual and verbal analogues," *Quaderni del CeSLiC, Occasional Papers*, https://doi.org/10.6092/unibo/amsacata/4110.

WODAK, RUTH, 2006, "Mediation between discourse and society: assessing cognitive approaches CDA", *Discourse Studies* 8 (1), pp. 179-190.

Metaphor and Framing in Cognition and Discourse: 'War' and 'Journey' Metaphors for COVID-19

Elisa Mattiello

Abstract

This study investigates the notion of 'framing' as a function of metaphor from the interrelated cognitive and discourse-based perspectives. The study adopts a corpus-based approach to analyse 'war' and 'journey' metaphors used for COVID-19 in online newspapers and magazine articles about the pandemic, such as *the victory against the virus was won* or *the community saw light at the end of the tunnel*. The aim of the study is to show that the notion of framing can be applied at different levels of generality in metaphor analysis – from conceptual metaphors to linguistic metaphors – which should be taken into account when communicating about sensitive topics such as COVID-19. As a secondary goal, the study aims at showing the importance of a definition of framing which includes more specific scenarios and aspects such as agency and emotion.

Key-words: Metaphor, frames, framing, scenario, cognition, discourse.

1. Introduction

Metaphor is a pervasive linguistic phenomenon in different types of communication, from informal interaction through political speeches to scientific theorising. It plays a key role in communication and cognition because of its 'framing' function: i.e. it expresses and reflects different ways of making sense of particular aspects of our lives (Lakoff and Johnson 1980; Semino 2008; Ritchie 2013). The framing power of metaphor is particularly relevant in areas such as scientific communication and healthcare, where the choice of different descriptions of an illness and its treatment can have either positive or negative implications for the general well-being of vulnerable people such as ill patients (Sarangi 2004). For example, being ill with COVID-19 can be described as a 'war' or a 'journey',

ISSN 1824-3967

as in the two extracts in (1) and (2), both taken from the *Coronavirus Corpus*[1]:

> (1) Now in the fight against COVID-19, health care workers say they feel like they're the ones on the front line. (*Del Marva Now*, 10 May 2020)
>
> (2) Today we start the next crucial phase in our Covid-19 journey. In many ways, this may be the trickiest phase yet. (*The Spinoff*, 27 April 2020)

Different framings of the experience of being ill emerge from these two metaphors. In the 'war' metaphor, the disease is viewed as an enemy or aggressor against which we need to fight with the help and support of health care workers, who are regarded as soldiers on the front line (Mattiello 2022), while in the 'journey' metaphor it is described as a road along which to travel, with different routes and paths for travellers. The two framings imply different relationships between the patient and the disease, and may therefore suggest different ways of conceiving of the illness, with potential consequences on both individual and collective reactions to the disease.

The framing effects of metaphor can be considered from two interrelated perspectives concerned with the implications of the use of different metaphors. On the one hand, from a cognitive perspective, Lakoff and Johnson (1980) are primarily concerned with metaphors in thought and cognition, and investigate metaphorical expressions such as 'COVID-19 journey' in relation to conceptual processes. On the other hand, from a discourse perspective, Cameron et al. (2010) investigate the actual use of metaphors in discourse, taking into account the contexts where metaphorical expressions are employed and the potential effects produced on receivers such as patients. The notion of framing is relevant to both perspectives and can show how framing practically works in healthcare, and which linguistic metaphors should be preferred or banished in the context of communication about the COVID-19 pandemic.

---

[1] *Coronavirus Corpus* (2020-present, in July 2022 consisting of 1,481 million words, daily updated), available at https://www.english-corpora.org/corona/.

There is a current critical debate (Wicke and Bolognesi 2020, 2021; Garzone 2021) on the potential counterproductive effects of the use of military metaphors in communication about COVID-19, followed by proposals to replace the WAR frame with other conventional frames (e.g., FOOTBALL, STORM, TSUNAMI, MONSTER). However, as remarked by Garzone (2021: 175-176), 'war' metaphors can be avoided by political authorities in public speeches, but in popularisation discourse and spontaneous speech they are "so deeply ingrained" that their use cannot be controlled.

In this study, I examine the notion of 'framing' as a function of metaphor from the interrelated cognitive and discourse-based perspectives. The study adopts a corpus-based approach to analyse 'war' and 'journey' metaphors for COVID-19 in the *Coronavirus Corpus* (2020-present, currently about 1,500 million words), such as *in the fight against COVID-19, health care workers are the ones on the front line* or *we start the next crucial phase in our Covid-19 journey*. The aim of the study is to show that the notion of framing can be applied at different levels of generality in metaphor analysis – from conceptual metaphors to linguistic metaphors – which should be taken into account when communicating about sensitive topics such as COVID-19. As a secondary goal, the study aims at showing the importance of a definition of framing which, like for communication about cancer (Semino et al. 2018), includes aspects such as agency, empowerment, and emotion.

The study is organised as follows. Section 2 introduces the notions of 'frame' and 'framing', with a special focus on how the framing power of metaphor has been approached in the literature from the perspectives of cognition and discourse. Section 3 is a brief description of the data and methodology adopted for this study. Section 4 specifically conducts a corpus-based analysis of 'war' and 'journey' metaphors in order to highlight the linguistic expressions dominating COVID communication in the media and how they can be perceived by readers. Section 5 draws some conclusions on the role of metaphor as a way of framing the ideas, attitudes, and values of discourse participants. These conclusions should function as a set of recommendations for journalists and reporters, whose linguistic choices and patterns in metaphor use may have an inevitable impact on citizens' behaviour in general and on COVID patients in particular.

2. Frame and framing

'Frame' and 'framing' are two widely discussed notions in a variety of fields, from sociology (Goffman 1974; Gamson and Modigliani 1987) to discourse analysis (Semino et al. 2018). According to Goffman (1974: 21), 'frames' enable individuals "to locate, perceive, identify, and label" occurrences or information. Similarly, Gamson and Modigliani (1987: 143) claim that a 'frame' is a "central organizing idea or story line that provides meaning" to events related to an issue. In particular, in line with Entman (1993) frames involve 'selection' and 'salience':

To frame is to *select some aspects of a perceived reality and make them more salient in a communicating text, in such a way as to promote a particular problem definition, causal interpretation, moral evaluation, and/or treatment recommendation* for the item described. (Entman 1993: 52, italics in original)

Accordingly, framing foregrounds some aspects of a perceived reality and backgrounds others, thus being associated with particular lexical choices in language, and generating expectations and inferences in communication and action. Among the "symbolic devices" that signify the use of frames, Gamson and Modigliani (1987: 143) identify metaphors, exemplars, catchphrases, depictions, and visual images. More recently, framing theory has been expanded by introducing figurative framing (Burgers et al. 2016, 2018), including figurative language types like metaphor, hyperbole, and irony, as well as their combinations considered as complex figurative frames. Frames and framing have been associated to metaphor both in cognition and in discourse, which are the two approaches adopted in this study.

2.1. The cognitive approach

Within the cognitive approach, Lakoff and Johnson's (1980) Conceptual Theory of Metaphor (CTM) considers metaphors as pervasive in language. Expressions such as 'He *attacked every weak point* in my argument' or 'He's without *direction* in his life' reflect conventional patterns of thought, known as 'conceptual metaphors'. Conceptual metaphors are defined as systematic sets of correspondences, or 'mappings', across conceptual domains, whereby a 'target' domain (e.g. our knowledge about arguments or life) is partly structured in terms of a different 'source' domain (e.g. our knowledge about war or journeys), such as, ARGUMENT IS WAR and LIFE IS A JOURNEY. These conceptual metaphors involve the mapping of aspects of the 'source' domain of WAR and JOURNEY onto aspects of the 'target' domain of ARGUMENT and LIFE. For example, the ARGUMENT IS WAR conceptual metaphor involves correspondences between participants in arguments and opponents or enemies, strategies in arguments and attack or defence, the outcomes of arguments and victory or defeat, and so on. Similarly, in the LIFE IS A JOURNEY metaphor, people correspond to travellers, actions to forward movement, choices to crossroads, problems to impediments or obstacles to travel, and purposes to destinations.

In CTM, Lakoff and Johnson (1980: 10-13) point out that the choice of a source domain highlights some aspects of the target domain and hides others. This bias in the process of conceptualisation is what constitutes the 'framing' power of metaphor. For example, ARGUMENT IS WAR highlights the competitive aspect of arguments, and hides their potential collaborative aspects. Metaphors are therefore regarded as crucial because they reflect and influence how we think about different things or experiences, and how we consequently act.

Moreover, cognitive metaphor theorists emphasise that target domains typically correspond to areas of experience that are relatively abstract, complex, and unfamiliar, such as time, emotion, or life, whereas source domains typically correspond to concrete, simple, and familiar experiences, such as motion, physical objects, and so on. This clearly applies to the LIFE IS A JOURNEY conceptual metaphor, where the target domain (life) is relatively more abstract and complex than the source domain (journey) having its basis in the simple experience of moving along a path from one location to another.

In the version of CMT proposed by Grady (1997), conceptual metaphors such as LIFE IS A JOURNEY are seen as the result of the combination of several more basic conceptual mappings (called 'primary metaphors') such as PURPOSES ARE DESTINATIONS and ACTION IS SELF-PROPELLED MOTION (Grady 1997). In other words, the LIFE IS A JOURNEY conceptual metaphor is claimed to derive ultimately from basic experiential correlations between performing actions and moving, reaching destinations and achieving purposes, and so on. Analogously, the conceptual metaphor ARGUMENT IS WAR, where the source domain (war) is rather complex, can be seen as arising from the basic experience of physical struggle amongst individuals with contrasting goals (Lakoff and Johnson 1980). In the present study, the 'war' and 'journey' conceptual metaphors and their implications in healthcare communication will be explored in the context of COVID-19.

2.2. The discourse-based approach

In discourse-based metaphor studies, public discourse is often analysed in relation to different figurative communicative frames and the related rhetorical effects. These studies inspect specific communicative domains, such as politics (e.g. Musolff 2004) or healthcare (Semino et al. 2017, 2018), where metaphor is used to express personal beliefs or attitudes towards common issues.

For this discourse-based approach, Musolff (2006) even introduces the more specific notion of 'scenario', which he defines as:

a set of assumptions made by competent members of a discourse community about 'typical' aspects of a source-situation, for example, its participants and their roles, the 'dramatic' storylines and outcomes, and conventional evaluations of whether they count as successful or unsuccessful, normal or abnormal, permissible or illegitimate, etc. (Musolff 2006: 28)

This definition emphasises the fact that scenarios are extracted from authentic discourse, thus showing how the cognitive and the discourse-based approach to metaphor can be combined in order to inspect the influence of figurative language on people's reasoning and behaviours.

Recently, Wicke and Bolognesi (2020) have described how the discourse around COVID-19 is framed figuratively on Twitter. The results emerging from their corpus-based analysis show that the WAR framing is used most frequently, especially to talk about the virus treatment, but not about the effects of social distancing on the population. Alternative figurative framing used in tweets includes STORM, TSUNAMI and MONSTER frames. In particular, words falling in the STORM and in the TSUNAMI frames relate to events and actions associated with the arrival and spreading of the pandemic (e.g., "wave", "storm", "tsunami", "disaster"); whereas words within the MONSTER framing talk about the behaviour of the virus in a rather personified way (e.g., "devil", "demon", "monster", "killer"). By contrast, from a diachronic perspective, Wicke and Bolognesi (2021) have shown how the WAR frame in COVID discourse has changed over the last two years. Their diachronic analysis indeed demonstrates that, while at the beginning of the pandemic war-related terms, such as "fight" or "battle", were used figuratively, more recently words within the WAR frame, such as "riots", "violence", or "soldiers", are used in their literal sense, thus referring to real riots and fights discussed on Twitter.

In this study, I will use evidence from the *Coronavirus Corpus*, with authentic texts such as media (newspaper and magazine) articles that are concerned with communication about the COVID-19 pandemic, to investigate conventional linguistic metaphors and underlying conceptual metaphors. The use of large updated collections of genuine data can allow a systematic analysis of actual metaphor use by members of specific discourse communities, and show the importance of a definition of framing which considers all locations of the communication process (i.e. the communicator, the text, and the receiver, see Entman 1993: 52) and also includes aspects such as agency, evaluation, and emotion (see Semino et al. 2018: 625).

3. Data and methodology

Relevant data for my analysis were selected from the *Coronavirus Corpus*. The *Coronavirus Corpus* is designed to be a fundamental record of the social, cultural, and economic impact of the COVID-19 pandemic in 2020 and beyond. It collects authentic texts drawn from online newspapers and magazines in 20 different English-speaking countries. The corpus, which was first released in May 2020, is currently about 1,492 million words in size, but it continues to grow by 3-4 million words each day. My collection of 'war' and 'journey' metaphors was made between November 2021 and July 2022. The examples selected for the analysis belong to the timespan from May 2020 to July 2022.

For the data selection, I first looked at collocates with the key terms *Covid*, *Covid-19*, and *Coronavirus* by using the tools available on the corpus platform. Since this automatic search only yielded results related to 'war' metaphors (esp. *fight* and *battle*), I also manually searched the collocations of the above-mentioned key terms with the words *journey* and *road* (*map*). The results obtained from this supplementary search were related to 'journey' metaphorical expressions, which were the second domain I wished to investigate. The quantitative data stemming from the *COVID-19* and *Coronavirus* collocates search are reported in the analysis conducted in Sections 4.1-4.2. For all collocates in the analysis both the raw and the normalised frequencies are reported in round brackets. For war-related collocates also the Mutual Information (MI) score, i.e. the strength of association between the word and its collocate, is indicated.

A close reading of the pertinent examples in larger contexts was then necessary to establish more specific sets of correspondences between the PANDEMIC and the WAR/JOURNEY domains, and to investigate the role of such frames in healthcare communication with COVID-affected patients, as well as all citizens who run the risk of being infected and testing positive to the virus. Relevant findings on the use of the inclusive pronoun "we" and of the possessive adjective "our" also emerged from the qualitative analysis.

4. Framing and metaphors for COVID-19

This Section analyses the framing effects of 'war' and 'journey' metaphors for COVID-19 with the purpose to show that metaphors can have a crucial, and potentially beneficial, role in the experience of people with the disease, as well as in people's behaviours and practices. In relation to this, some scholars claim that war-related metaphors can turn out to be dangerous, especially with patients suffering from serious illnesses such as cancer (see Semino et al. 2017; Semino 2021 for an overview). However, studies investigating the framing effects of 'war' metaphors in various contexts (from climate change to cancer) have identified both potential strengths and weaknesses of such metaphors (Flusberg et al. 2018; Wicke and Bolognesi 2020). Similarly, studies of 'journey' metaphors for cancer have found that they can be used in a variety of different ways, including to express positive views and emotions, and to suggest different degrees of encouragement on the part of patients (Semino et al. 2017, 2018). However, 'journey' metaphors may also have negative aspects, since they can suggest a long and difficult process with an uncertain conclusion. In line with those perspectives, the analysis conducted in Sections 4.1-4.2 aims at showing which metaphors should be preferred in communication about Coronavirus and which metaphors should be avoided, especially with citizens and infected people.

4.1. 'War' metaphors

From a quantitative corpus-based analysis of the words *COVID*, *COVID-19*, and *Coronavirus*, the most common collocates triggering a metaphorical interpretation have to do with 'war': e.g.,

- *COVID/COVID-19* + *fight* (17,167 occurrences, 11.50, 3.39)[2], *combat* (9,032, 6.05, 3.16), *warriors* (618, 0.41, 4.98), *combating* (124, 0.08, 3.01), *warrior* (92, 0.06, 4.03), *casualty* (72, 0.04, 3.18), *conquered* (49, 0.03, 4.80);
- *Coronavirus* + *fight* (11,630 occurrences, 7.79, 3.26), *combat* (8,705, 5.83, 3.54), *battle* (3,840, 2.57, 3.20), *task-force* (25, 0.01, 3.72).

The raw and normalised frequencies of the collocates show the relevance of the WAR domain to the pandemic and the MI score confirms that war-related metaphors are pervasive and ubiquitous (Garzone 2021). Collocates related to the military domain which display an apparently low frequency in the corpus (e.g. *conquered*, *task-force*) actually have a strong association with the terms *COVID* and *Coronavirus*, as their high MI score demonstrates, and are useful to represent the various aspects of the pandemic.

In particular, from this preliminary investigation of the collocates it is possible to draw a series of correspondences between the conceptual domains of WAR and PANDEMIC, including the following:

---

[2] The numbers in brackets show the raw frequency, the normalised (pmw) frequency and the Mutual Information (MI) score of the collocates with *COVID-19* and *Coronavirus* in the corpus.

- THE VIRUS IS AN ENEMY/AN INVADER
- TREATMENT FOR THE VIRUS IS FIGHT/COMBAT
- HEALTH PROFESSIONALS ARE WARRIORS/TASK-FORCE
- SICK/DEAD PEOPLE ARE CASUALTIES
- ELIMINATING THE VIRUS IS VICTORY/CONQUEST

Several examples extracted from the *Coronavirus Corpus* can illustrate these correspondences. For instance, the conceptualisation of the virus as an "enemy" or an "invader" is shown in (3)-(4):

(3) Thanks to the leadership of President Trump and the courage and compassion of the American people, our public health system is far stronger than it was four months ago, and we are winning the fight against the invisible *enemy*. (*The Hill*, 22 June 2020)

(4) It goes without saying, this SARS-CoV-2 virus is one complicated *invader* for sure, in terms of how it affects us Homo sapiens when infected: some of us show no symptoms; many show mild symptoms; many show severe symptoms; and unfortunately, a large number also die. (*Caledonian Record*, 22 June 2021)

where COVID-19 is described as our *invisible enemy*, alluding to the difficulty of preventing or identifying it, as well as *one complicated invader*, suggesting that a collective action is necessary to face it.

Moreover, in the 'war' frame, dealing with the virus is described as "war", "fight", "combat", or "battle":

(5) Authorities are alarmed and declared "a state of *war*" in the *fight* against the virus. (*Daily Mirror*, 8 January 2021)

(6) Advisers to the U.S. Food and Drug Administration this week recommended changing the design of booster shots for this fall – an effort to *combat* variants of the coronavirus that are circulating. (*News Yahoo*, 30 June 2022)

(7) Biden calls authorization of vaccine for children ages 5 to 11 a "turning point" in COVID-19 *battle*. (*CNN*, 17 November 2021)

'War' metaphors were dominant at the beginning of the pandemic, on the one hand, to show the need for a collective sacrifice and effort, and, on the other, to legitimise authoritarian procedures. Lockdown, stay-at-home or shelter-in-place orders, face-covering, physical distancing, restrictions, closures, isolation, quarantine are all measures adopted to "fight" the pandemic (*declared "a state of war", the fight against the virus*). Vaccination is ultimately described as *an effort to combat variants* and *a "turning point" in COVID-19 battle*.

In the battle, health professionals are described as "warriors" or "task force":

(8) This year's edition honors and celebrates the undefeated spirit of COVID-19 frontline *warriors* who have courageously led the battle against the pandemic. (*Business Wire India*, 14 August 2021)

(9) Indian-American physician Dr Vivek Murthy on Monday was named one of the three co-chairs of the COVID-19 *task-force* that will guide President-elect Joe Biden on dealing with the coronavirus pandemic that has claimed over 236,000 lives in the country. (*IN News Yahoo*, 9 November 2020)

Doctors, physicians, nurses, and other people working in the health system are regarded as *COVID-19 frontline warriors* or even as an army, a *task-force* with a common military aim. Like soldiers, they have experience and skill in fighting, especially on the front line, like a task force they are guided by a common goal, i.e. defeating the enemy.

Analogously, people who suffered from COVID-19 and eventually died of this virus are viewed as "casualties":

(10) On Friday, the United States exceeded 495,000 COVID-19 *casualties*, according to health tracker Johns Hopkins University. (*New York Daily News*, 19 February 2021)

They are described as *COVID-19 casualties* or victims who succumbed to COVID-19, as many of them were badly affected and died after fighting against the virus.

On the other hand, eliminating the virus is metaphorically regarded as "victory":

(11) Africa and China fought side by side until the *victory* against the virus was *won*. (*Ipp Media*, 26 April 2020)

(12)   South Korea reveals how to *win* Covid-19 war. (*Dhaka Tribune*, 28
       March 2020)

Victory may be long-term (*until the victory against the virus was
won*), or desirable (*how to win Covid-19 war*) but cannot be achieved
if not through a joint effort (*fought side by side*).

4.2. 'Journey' metaphors

Compared with 'war' metaphors, 'journey' metaphors are much less
frequent in the corpus, as shown by the collocates with *COVID*,
COVID-19, and *Coronavirus*: e.g.,

- *COVID/COVID-19* + *peak* (399 occurrences, 0.26)[3], *navigate*
  (359, 0.24), *journey* (164, 0.10), *road (map)* (46, 0.03);
- *Coronavirus* + *peak* (260 occurrences, 0.17), *navigate* (152,
  0.10), *road (map)* (17, 0.01), *journey* (15, 0.01).

These quantitative data suggest that non-war alternative
metaphorical expressions are less common and appear far more
sporadically than war-related ones in discourses about Covid-19
(Garzone 2021). These collocations followed by close reading of
the related contexts suggest that a set of correspondences between
the conceptual domains of JOURNEY and PANDEMIC can be
established:

- RECOVERING FROM THE VIRUS IS A JOURNEY
- PROGRESS IN RECOVERY IS MOVING/STEPPING
  FORWARD
- PLAN FOR RECOVERY IS ROAD MAP
- SICK PEOPLE ARE TRAVELLERS/CLIMBERS
- FULL RECOVERY IS A MOUNTAIN PEAK
- VACCINATION IS LIGHT AT THE END OF THE
  TUNNEL

---

[3] In most of cases, journalists refer to *peak* as the highest level of contagion, hence
the high frequency of the collocation *Covid-19* + *peak*. However, on some occasions
(see, e.g., (20)), when sick people are regarded as climbers, the peak is viewed as
full recovery.

These correspondences are illustrated by examples manually selected from the *Coronavirus Corpus*. For instance, dealing with the virus has been often described as a "journey", as shown in (13)-(14):

> (13) Europe is about a month ahead in the COVID-19 *journey*, and the soft reopening there will no doubt provide useful lessons and experiences that can be leveraged in the U.S., such as effective social distancing and sanitising protocols. (*Seeking Alpha*, 10 June 2020)
>
> (14)   Loneliness is a big factor during your COVID-19 *journey*. Two weeks might not seem long, but confined to your bedroom or only certain parts of your home, this can be become a very long and lonely *journey*.

The journey may be described by policymakers as collective travel (*Europe is about a month ahead in the COVID-19 journey*), but has also been perceived by individuals as *a very long and lonely journey*. Hence, isolation in this journey may be felt by sick people as abandonment.

Each progress in the recovery of specific patients as well as of the whole community are conceptualised as a "step forward":

> (15) After 12 days of Phase 2, he had the confidence to *move forward*. "Our COVID-19 journey continues today," Mr McGowan said. (*Herald Times Reporter*, 28 May 2020)
>
> (16)   "This is one of those moments during our COVID-19 journey at WellSpan Waynesboro Hospital where we can pause for a minute and celebrate a huge, positive *step forward* for one of our patients." (*Public Opinion*, 11 May 2020)

In direct speech, the use of the inclusive pronoun "we" or of the possessive adjective "our" (*Our COVID-19 journey continues today, our COVID-19 journey at WellSpan Waynesboro Hospital, we can ... celebrate a huge, positive step forward for one of our patients*) shows that all communicators, from health professionals to policy makers, adopt an empathetic attitude towards (both actual and potential) patients. The metaphors of "movement" or "stepping forward" can be regarded as encouraging to receivers and as a reward for their sacrifices and efforts.

In the media, the government's plan for recovery is often positively conceptualised as a "road map", including all public measures adopted to face the pandemic:

(17)   Later this week another Covid-19 *road map* will be announced by the government. (*Sunday World*, 1 May 2021)

A less reassuring metaphor, conversely, is shown in (18):

(18)   Like the US President Donald Trump, who recently tested positive for COVID-19, Wilson said she is also on a Coronavirus journey but there is no *roadmap*. (*International Business Times*, 5 October 2020)

where the absence of a "road map" (*she is also on a Coronavirus journey but there is no roadmap*) suggests uncertainty and lack of hope.

Sick people, in their turn, are viewed as "travellers" along a "road":

(19)   On her seventh day in confinement, she began to feel better and craved for food, her brother-in-law, Jojo, brought her danggit and pusit, as her request, and started her *road* to being Covid-free. (*International Business Times*, 5 October 2020)

or even as "hikers" who are "climbing" to the "mountain's peak":

(20)   Like so many *hikers* who *climb* to a mountain's *peak*, I feel a sense of both joy and accomplishment, especially when I can look down into the valley, see the twists and turns on the path, and remember the ascent. (*The Boston Globe*, 3 May 2020)

When people reach the *peak*, they can decide to look back at the *ascent*, remembering how difficult it was, or to look forward, towards the valley, which, despite the arduous path, can be regarded as a kind of rest in tranquillity (*look down into the valley, see the twists and turns on the path*). Similarly, the *peak* can be found to be *a long plateau*:

(21)   And though we are increasingly recognizing that the COVID-19 *peak* is, unfortunately, *a long plateau*, we can at least take this

moment to see just how far we have come on this journey. (*The Boston Globe*, 3 May 2020)

and yet looking back at the long journey made may be equally reassuring and encouraging.

Even more reassuring is the metaphor of "light at the end of the tunnel":

> (22) The well-established Elmcroft community at 11246 Fallbrook saw *light at the end of the tunnel* for their coronavirus journey last Saturday, Jan. 16, when they each rolled up their sleeves and received the first round of two vaccinations to ward off the COVID-19 virus. (*Houston Chronicle*, 23 January 2021)

Vaccination is indeed described as a possible solution, as the light that people see at the end of darkness, the final destination being the complete end of the COVID-19 pandemic.

4.3. 'War' and 'journey' metaphors: cognitive and discourse-based approaches

From a cognitive perspective, the analyses conducted in 4.1-4.2 show two different but consistent frames of the experience of illness. However, in order to link cognitive and discourse-based approaches to metaphor, in this Section I will use Musolff's (2006) notion of 'scenario', allowing us to capture the implications of 'war' and 'journey' metaphor patterns in authentic datasets. The term 'scenario' will be used here to refer to a particular setting, which includes participants, their roles and actions, possible goals, and emotions.

From a discourse perspective, in the 'war' metaphors highlighted in (3)-(12) the government or the community are placed in the role of fighters, the disease is placed in the role of enemy or invader, healthcare professionals are explicitly placed in the role of frontline soldiers, being cured, or living longer is construed as winning the fight, while not recovering or dying corresponds to losing the battle. More generally, these expressions suggest difficulty, danger, and the need for bravery, both on the patients' and on the healthcare professionals' parts.

Nevertheless, there are also differences among the examples, which could result in different framings. While example (3) expresses positive emotions and places the government in an empowered position of being able to win the fight against the virus, example (4) describes a different scenario with some patients winning the battle and others losing it. Similarly, in examples (5)-(7) different scenarios are presented: an alarming scenario in (5), with the declaration of a state of war, and reassuring scenarios in (6)-(7), with vaccination being described not only as a way to combat the virus, but even as a turning point in this battle. Hence, expressions such as a *"turning point" in Covid-19 battle* or *we are winning the fight against the invisible enemy* are used to emphasise the government's agency and determination in difficult circumstances, and suggest a sense of pride in collective efforts.

In addition, examples (8)-(9) present scenarios in which doctors, nurses, and healthcare professionals show their bravery, valour, and strength to combat the virus, but above all their need to act together, as a task force, a military group having a common aim: i.e. defeating the virus. Finally, examples (10)-(11) present two contrasting outcomes: in (10) the battle is concluded with numerous victims, who represent people's impotence in front of the opponent, whereas in (11)-(12) the war ends with victory or hope that one day the virus will be overcome.

Analogously, the 'journey' metaphors highlighted in (13)-(22) present different scenarios involving positive and negative emotions. They present COVID-19 as a journey, with some people having similar experiences to others on that journey, but not all going the exact same route. Patients are here depicted in the role of participants, recovery as a final destination, but some being alone on their path, while others having a road map leading their collective walk towards the end of the journey.

The scenarios presented involve different actions and emotions. In (13), for instance, the common journey of all Europe can be used by other countries to invoke people's sense of responsibility and encourage them to persevere in adopting the appropriate measures to contrast the virus' spread. Similarly, examples (15)-(16) present positive scenarios of a collective journey with no impediments to move forward, or even the personal success of a COVID patient, and the pride of doctors having helped him/her to proceed in his/her journey.

Conversely, in (14) the personal experience of a COVID-19 patient is described as a very long and lonely journey, which suggests negative emotions and a sense of abandonment when people test positive and are confined to their own homes.

Having a clear plan is another fundamental factor which should be stressed in 'journey' metaphors: for instance, in (17) the government announces a new road map for their journey, whereas in (18) the absence of a road map is not encouraging, as citizens need to know their destination and the path to reach it.

Finally, in this same frame, the journey may be presented as a road with twists and turns, as a mountain's peak to achieve, or as a tunnel to pass through, as in (20)-(22). These different scenarios imply difficulty, commitment, sacrifice, but also pride, joy, and accomplishment when people have succeeded in climbing the mountain and can finally look down into the valley, or when they can at last see the light at the end of the tunnel.

5. Conclusions

This study has focused on the 'framing' function of metaphor and on its relevance from the different perspectives of cognition and discourse. For the analysis, I have used data extracted from a corpus of articles from online newspapers and magazines as a case study to demonstrate the value of an integrated approach to labelling and analysing patterns of metaphor in use, and accounting for their potential framing effects. This integrated approach reveals that war and journey-related conceptual metaphors can present different scenarios depending on the context in which they are used.

On the one hand, 'war' metaphors make the virus into an enemy to be confronted and people as its victims. These violent metaphors can increase people's perception of the pandemic as serious and urgent, and strengthen their motivation to modify their behaviours to limit its dangerous effects. On the other hand, a more positive scenario may also be presented, having potentially more productive framing effects. For example, in the context of Coronavirus prevention, 'fight' metaphors can increase hope and people's willingness to engage in self-limiting behaviours to lower COVID-19 risk, such as wearing facemasks and being vaccinated. Moreover, framing the collective action against the virus as victory and health professionals as heroes who struggle on the front line may encourage citizens to abstain from their normal activities, and to contribute to the general triumph with their individual sacrifice. Unlike 'war' metaphors, 'journey' metaphors do not involve an opponent, but other negative scenarios with impediments to moving forward, the absence of a road map, and even a long and lonely path. These conceptual metaphors may have implications on the emotive reaction of patients and the general public, in that they entail paralysis, impotence, disorientation, and even loneliness. However, the journey may be also positively depicted in such ways as to see steps forward as achievements, the end of the tunnel as success, the peak of the mountain as a reward for the common sacrifices and efforts, after twists and turns along the path.

Another fundamental factor in framing the pandemic as a journey is the idea of a common road map guiding citizens along their paths. If policymakers have a plan in their minds, people are encouraged to follow restrictions and regulations to attain their destination.

From the theoretical viewpoint, this study emphasises the need for a more precise definition of framing, including more specific scenarios and aspects such as agency and emotion.

References

BURGERS, CHRISTIAN, KONIJN, ELLY A., STEEN, GERARD J., 2016, "Figurative framing: shaping public discourse through metaphor, hyperbole, and irony", *Communication Theory* 26 (4), pp. 410-430. DOI: 10.1111/comt.12096.

BURGERS, CHRISTIAN, RENARDEL DE LAVALETTE, KIKI Y., STEEN, GERARD J., 2018, "Metaphor, hyperbole, and irony: Uses in isolation and in combination in written discourse". *Journal of Pragmatics* 127, pp. 71-83. DOI: 10.1016/j.pragma.2018.01.009.

CAMERON, LYNNE, LOW, GRAHAM, MASLEN, ROBERT, 2010, "Finding systematicity in metaphor use", in L. Cameron and R. Maslen (eds), *Metaphor Analysis: Research Practice in Applied Linguistics, Social Sciences and the Humanities*, Equinox, London, pp. 116-146.

Coronavirus Corpus, 2020-present, Available at https://www.english-corpora.org/corona/, last accessed 19 June 2022.

ENTMAN, ROBERT M., 1993, "Framing: Toward clarification of a fractured paradigm", *Journal of Communication* 43 (4), pp. 51-58.

FLUSBERG, STEPHEN J., MATLOCK, TEENIE, THIBODEAU, PAUL H., 2018, "War metaphors in public discourse", *Metaphor and Symbol* 33 (1), pp. 1-18.

GAMSON, WILLIAM A., MODIGLIANI, ANDREW, 1987, "The changing culture of affirmative action", in R. G. Braungart and M. M. Braungart (eds), *Research in Political Sociology*, JAI Press, Greenwich, CT, pp. 137-177.

GARZONE, GIULIANA ELENA, 2021, "Re-thinking metaphors in COVID-19 communication", *Lingue e Linguaggi* 44, pp. 159-181. DOI 10.1285/i22390359v44p159.

GOFFMAN, ERVING, 1974, *Frame Analysis: An Essay on the Organization of Experience*, Harper & Row, New York.

GRADY, JOSEPH E., 1997, *Foundations of Meaning: Primary Metaphors and Primary Scenes*, Unpublished PhD thesis, University of California.

LAKOFF, GEORGE, JOHNSON, MARK, 1980, *Metaphors We Live By*, University of Chicago Press, Chicago.

MATTIELLO, ELISA, 2022, *Linguistic Innovation in the COVID-19 Pandemic*, Cambridge Scholars Publishing, Newcastle-upon-Tyne.

MUSOLFF, ANDREAS, 2004, *Metaphor and Political Discourse. Analogical Reasoning in Debates about Europe*, Palgrave Macmillan, Houndmills, Basingstoke.

MUSOLFF, ANDREAS, 2006, "Metaphor scenarios in public discourse", *Metaphor and Symbol* 21 (1), pp. 23-38.

RITCHIE, DAVID L., 2013, *Metaphor*, CUP, Cambridge.

SARANGI, SRIKANT, 2004, "Towards a communicative mentality in medical and healthcare practice", *Communication & Medicine* 1 (1), pp. 1-11.

SEMINO, ELENA, 2008, *Metaphor in Discourse*, CUP, Cambridge.

SEMINO, ELENA, 2021, "'Not Soldiers but Fire-fighters' – Metaphors and COVID-19", *Health Communication*, 36 (1), pp. 50-58.

SEMINO, ELENA, DEMJÉN, ZSÓFIA, DEMMEN, JANE, 2018, "An integrated approach to metaphor and framing in cognition, discourse and practice, with an application to metaphors for cancer", *Applied Linguistics* 39 (5), pp. 625-645.

SEMINO, ELENA, DEMJÉN, ZSÓFIA, HARDIE, ANDREW, PAYNE, SHEILA, RAYSON, PAUL, 2017, *Metaphor, Cancer and the End of Life: A Corpus-based Study*, Routledge, New York.

WICKE, PHILIPP, BOLOGNESI, MARIANNA M., 2020, Framing COVID-19: How we conceptualize and discuss the pandemic on Twitter, *PLoS ONE* 15 (9): e0240010. DOI: 10.1371/journal.pone.0240010.

WICKE, PHILIPP, BOLOGNESI, MARIANNA M., 2021, COVID-19 discourse on Twitter: How the topics, sentiments, subjectivity, and figurative frames changed over time, *Frontiers in Communication* 6: 651997. DOI: 10.3389/fcomm.2021.651997.

Framing the Pandemic in the UK and in the US: The War, the Science and the Herd

Denise Milizia

Abstract
This research looks at the frames British and American leaders have chosen to refer to the COVID-19 crisis. After a short description of the black swan metaphor to prove that the coronavirus pandemic was not an unexpected event, but rather predicted and foreseen, the paper first illustrates how politicians found themselves using a military language when discussing such a 'crazy and horrible plague', as bellicose rhetoric serves special and legitimate purposes, thus communicating the sense of urgency and emergency. Then, I look at two frames which have come to characterize the pandemic: 'the' science and the myth of herd immunity. I first show how leaders claimed to "be guided by the science", thus causing the frustration of experts who were held responsible for all decisions made by politicians, and then I illustrate how the 'herd immunity' myth is managed in the UK and in the US, with a special focus on the idiosyncratic use Donald Trump makes of the word 'herd', which takes on an altogether different meaning from the scientific original frame.
Key-words: coronavirus, metaphor, war, science, herd.

1. Introduction

This paper presents results from a comparative analysis of speeches delivered by the British and American leaders during the COVID-19 pandemic.

The data are drawn from a corpus that consists of spoken data delivered by the then British Prime Minister, Boris Johnson, and the two presidents of the United States, Donald Trump and Joe Biden, who both found themselves in office during the coronavirus crisis. When the virus started to spread in early March 2020, the incumbent American president was Donald Trump, with Joe Biden taking over in January 2021. Boris Johnson's corpus includes speeches from

Textus 1-2023, pp. 281-308

ISSN 1824-3967

March 2020 to June 2022, totaling 2 million tokens. On July 7, 2022, Johnson announced his pending resignation, but he remained in office until September 6, when a new party leader was elected. The American corpus includes 4 million tokens altogether of spoken data, with 3 million words uttered by Donald Trump (January 2017-January 2021) and 1 million words by Joe Biden (January 2021-June 2022) respectively.

The article is divided in two parts: after a brief description, in section 2, of the black swan metaphor to prove that the coronavirus pandemic was not an unexpected event, and that indeed the reality of a global pandemic was a question of when, not if, in section 3 I analyse why war metaphors are ubiquitous and pervasive in language in general, and in the description of this extraordinary global crisis in particular, and I provide examples of how and when politicians inescapably found themselves using a military language when discussing such a 'crazy and horrible plague', to borrow one of Trump's frames.

In this study I agree with Musolff (2021) that, despite the 'blanket' criticism, the pandemic as war metaphor is multi-functional, as it fulfils different rhetorical and argumentative purposes. I also agree with Garzone (2021) that, since the war rhetoric dies hard, its entailments are virtually omnipresent, so the ongoing pandemic will, inevitably, always be framed and remembered as a war.

In the second part of this paper, in sections 4 and 5, I provide an in-depth investigation of two frames that will always be remembered in the debate of the Coronavirus pandemic: 'the science' and 'herd immunity'. I provide examples of how the British and American leaders claim to be "guided by the science", and "follow the scientific advice", and how the 'herd immunity' myth is managed in both the UK and the US. Interestingly, some idiosyncrasies are analysed in Donald Trump's usage of the word 'herd', which takes on an altogether different meaning from the canonical one. In section 6 some conclusions are drawn.

The software I rely on to interrogate my data is *WordSmith Tools* 7.0 (Scott 2017).

2. Was the coronavirus pandemic a black swan?

The metaphor of the black swan has recently been used quite regularly to refer to the coronavirus pandemic, as the world was turned upside down, causing a sudden inversion of the normal order

(Charteris-Black 2021: 2). Yet, we wonder whether the event was really as unpredictable, unexpected, and extreme as it is often being said. The metaphor of the black swan usually refers to high-impact, random and unforeseen events which are difficult to predict: these events of massive scale are considered outliers, because there is no past data which can point towards its occurrence in the foreseeable future. Yet, if the unpredictable is increasingly probable (Taleb 2010), the coronavirus pandemic had indeed been foreseen, and according to Bill Gates, among others, it was wholly predictable. In fact, in 2015 Bill Gates issued an alert about the fear of microbes, as opposed to the fear of missiles. In a TED talk he said:

We are not ready for the next epidemic. [...] We need to do simulations, we need to do germ games, not war games, to see where the holes are. The last time a germ game was done in the US was back in 2001, and it didn't go that well. So far, the score is: germs 1 people 0. [...] There is no need to panic, but we need to get going, because time is not on our side. If there is one positive thing that can come out of the Ebola epidemic, it's that it can serve as an early warning, as a wake-up call, to get ready. If we start now, we can get ready for the next epidemic.

In this speech, delivered in Vancouver in April 2015, Bill Gates cautioned world leaders and businesses that the next global catastrophe would be "a highly infectious virus" more devastating than any natural disaster or war. He warned that a pandemic was on the horizon and that we were not ready for it. Seven years later, in April 2022, two years after the pandemic started to sweep the globe, he gave another speech in Vancouver spurring his audience to pay closer attention to his advice about how to prevent another pandemic wreaking similar havoc on society.

   For years western scientists had warned about the possibility of a serious pandemic, but it was thought that any infection would be restricted to South-Asia, China or Africa, just like previous infectious pathogens such as Ebola, bird flu, SARS or swine flu (Charteris-Black 2021: 1). Few believed that the transmission of a virus from animals to humans could threaten all of humanity. Indeed, with the benefit of hindsight, the reality of a global pandemic was a question of when, not if (*ibid.*). The black swan metaphor, just like the boiling frog metaphor (Nerlich 2020), refers to the poor ability of humans to take action in the case of threats and events of high magnitude that build gradually rather than suddenly. Thus, I argue here that the coronavirus pandemic, despite undoubtedly being an extreme event with severe consequences and severe impact, was not a black swan, since it was not unique and was instead predicted and foreseen: in other words, it was prospectively unpredictable, yet retrospectively predictable. Indeed, the scientific community had many indications that it would come, that it could be catastrophic, yet it was ignored altogether. It seems instead that the metaphor of the grey rhino is, very likely, more appropriate than the one of the black swan, since the crisis had long existed and threatened us, but we had not paid attention.

Whether the virus was a black swan or a grey rhino, along with Levenson (2020) this paper argues that representing the pandemic as an out-of-the-blue emergency displaces the blame from governments who have failed to take the right coping measures and the adequate prevention.

3. Metaphor and COVID-19

From its very beginning, the global understanding of the coronavirus disease was a metaphorical one, as "metaphor uses the better known to elucidate the less known" (Black 1962). Popularizing medicine is a difficult task in itself (Garzone 2006), and explaining a complex and extraordinary phenomenon such as a global pandemic to the general public is especially problematic (Garzone 2021). Thus, when a new invisible virus arrived that was responsible for illness, death and unprecedented disruption, it made sense that metaphors were relied on to turn something incomprehensible into more familiar, accessible and predictable terms (Semino 2021b).

It cannot be denied that, even though there have been famous warnings against their use, e.g. by Thomas Hobbes and John Locke (Musolff 2017), metaphors have helped us understand the pandemic, even though they can also create confusion and complacency (Semino 2021b). Aristotle, unlike the two British philosophers, argued that we are metaphorical animals, and considered metaphors as a means to achieve conceptual clarity, serving mainly to elucidate "where the intellect of the hearer is a little behind", highlighting the importance of metaphor to present arguments so that they are vivid and succinct. It is argued here, though, that metaphors have the power to elucidate as well as confuse, and hence, as Semino (in Semino et al. 2020) suggests, they should be chosen carefully, i.e. governors should be able to find the right metaphor, and govern the phenomenon, because metaphors show some things and hide other things. There is nothing worse than a bad metaphor in a crisis; one may think, for instance, of the 'war on terror' metaphor, initiated by George W. Bush in the wake of 9/11 (Lakoff 2001).

Metaphors are ubiquitous and pervasive in language, and they are also unavoidable (Lakoff and Johnson 1980), as we cannot help using them, consciously or unconsciously, when talking or thinking about complex, abstract and sensitive subjects. Used sensitively and appropriately, they can help individuals and societies overcome overwhelming problems, but used insensitively and inappropriately, metaphors can add to confusion and disillusionment, making problems harder to overcome, thus becoming a double-edged sword (Semino 2021b).

Just like Daniel Defoe and Albert Camus, who framed the plague as "the terrible enemy", the coronavirus was framed first as an enemy to fight, an invisible enemy, then a mugger, a tsunami, a storm, a raging fire, a rising tide, a race, a marathon, and even a glitter that gets everywhere, or a game or match that would be difficult to win (Brandt and Botelho 2020; Costa 2020; Koller 2020; Semino 2021a; Wodak 2021). The pandemic was also framed as a zombie apocalypse threatening humans, even though it is easier to imagine killing a zombie than suppressing an infection (Charteris-Black 2021: 97).

Echoing Defoe and Camus, the former president of the United States of America chose the word 'plague' as his favourite word to frame the SARS-CoV-2, which is the official name of the virus. In line with his scapegoating rhetoric, which constitutes an important feature of right-wing populist parties' discourse (Wodak 2017), Donald Trump, whilst trying to talk about racial equality, calls the virus 'the China plague', 'the Chinese plague', 'the plague that came from China', and "these scapegoats have to be punished and suffer the consequences of their actions, you watch".

FIGURE I. CONCORDANCE LINES FOR *PLAGUE* IN DONALD TRUMP'S SPEECHES

As Figure 1 shows, the China virus, or the China scourge, or the China plague, which is 'crazy', 'deadly', 'horrible', 'rough', 'ugly', can be addressed in several ways, and with many different names (line 29), "but we always call it the invisible enemy". The verbs Donald Trump uses to say that the virus came from China are many and from different source domains: "we had the plague flow in from China", "when the plague floated in", "when the plague flew in", "the plague pouring in from China", "when the plague struck", "the plague ushered in", "the plague set in".

Enlarging the context in line 25, we read as follows:

The supply changed rapidly with COVID-19, or whatever you want to call it. I had never heard so many names. You have about 30 names you can call this thing. (Laughter.) All I – I call it "the plague from China." (Laughter.) "The plague." (Laughter and applause.) And it's not good. And it's not good. And it's – it could have been stopped. It could have been stopped in China, but they decided not to do that. And we'll have to figure that one out, won't we? You watch.

Interestingly, but not surprisingly, Donald Trump calls the virus "this thing", or "whatever you want to call it", emphasizing the fact that he had never heard so many names to describe a disease, as there are about 30 names "you can call it". Thus, in the attempt to abdicate responsibility, he typically frames the debate in antagonist terms, through representations of "us vs them", e.g. "*You* have about 30 names *you* can call this thing" vs "*I* call it the plague from China". He then adds, in line with his conspiracy theories, that "It could have been stopped in China, but *they* decided not to do that".

3.1. The war: the inevitable and inescapable frame

It is hardly surprising that war metaphors were dominant at the beginning of the pandemic: the European civilization is based on the idea of war. Europe starts with the Iliad, the story of such a beautiful war that all generations talk about (Semino et al. 2020). In Homer's poem, all the gods fight together with men to decide on the destiny of humanity. Thus, we cannot blame all those who have spoken of war when the coronavirus started to spread, even though most of the people who have done so have not even experienced war personally. Sometimes, in some phases, it has also been argued that evoking the war, while sitting on the couch, was somehow offensive (Briguglia, in Semino et al. 2020). Coronavirus has often been defined the Third World War against an invisible enemy, except that in this case, as Bill Gates observes, we are all on the same side. Typically, a war involves an enemy, an overseas enemy, or another nation state, but this is more a health catastrophe, a health disaster, literally, one of the worst health crises of all time, which has put to test our health facilities that we thought to be efficient.

The war metaphor, whether we have experienced war personally or not, may have been appropriate at the onset of the pandemic, but subsequently it became "potentially counterproductive" (Semino 2021b). As a matter of fact, research shows that the metaphors we are exposed to affect how we think and feel about problems and their solutions (cf. Panzeri et al. 2020). Sontag (1978), in her seminal work about the language used in medical discourse to describe illnesses and people affected by diseases such as cancer and HIV, argues that the military rhetoric contributes to stigmatize a disease as well as its bearers, inciting violence and encouraging fatalism, while justifying sweeping measures (Semino and Potts 2019). In her book, Sontag suggested that she was looking forward to a time when cancer would be talked about entirely literally, but we wonder whether the British government's messages, which were in competition with the hyperbole and metaphor of the British media, would have been listened to, had the language been more literal and had metaphor been avoided.

It is argued here that the war frame was the inevitable and inescapable frame, as the sense of crisis that enveloped everybody when the pandemic broke out made war the natural way to frame the experience. The military frame is an effective way of grabbing people's attention, and the fear evoked by bellicose language can motivate people to pay attention, change their beliefs, and take action about important issues (Charteris-Black 2021: 33). War metaphors indicate that the situation is very serious, very dangerous, and that there is a need for collective sacrifice and effort, encouraging an 'all-in-this-together mentality' (Garzone 2021), thus echoing the Pope's homily that "we are all in the same boat". Pope Francis, in fact, likened the coronavirus pandemic to a storm, which can be overcome only by coming together in faith, realizing that we are all on the same boat, all of us fragile and disoriented, but at the same time important and needed, all of us called to row together, and each of us in need of comforting the other. This very same spirit, this spirit of togetherness, "when we all pulled together", was very often compared to the 'Blitz spirit' (see Musolff 2021), the legendary sense of solidarity that saw Britain through adversity in World War II. Yet, the Blitz metaphor has been regarded as questionable and annoying in several respects, even though the deeper meaning of the Blitz spirit is that "we must stay resilient, not give up, and remember that all this will pass" (Charteris-Black 2021: 41). Indeed, when people who had experienced the Second World War were asked how the pandemic compared to the war, they said that, socially and psychologically, the coronavirus crisis is nothing like the Blitz, it is indeed far worse, as the war brought people closer together whereas the pandemic forced them further apart (*ibid.*).

It is true, though, that when language becomes inflammatory, fear mongering and emotive, with references to war, we all feel that it is a community effort, that everyone is in it together. This is mainly due to the fact that war metaphors are persuasive, and metaphors affect largely at the unconscious level (Charteris-Black 2014). Framing the pandemic as war certainly raised the awareness of danger and the fear of death or, to borrow Wodak's (2021) words, the terror/dread of death.

The recourse to the war rhetoric at the onset of the pandemic was almost natural, just like in earlier health crises such as AIDS, Ebola, SARS, bird flu, etc., which were also perceived as warfare. One of the main reasons why the war frame was necessary when the virus started to spread was to legitimize the excessive clampdowns imposed by governments, who increasingly emphasized that there was no alternative to their draconian measures. Thus, the TINA-argument (There Is No Alternative) was used as rationalization legitimation (*ibid.*). Nations started to close down their economies and their borders, even the Schengen Area was suddenly suspended in response, in order to "keep the virus out" (Wodak 2020). Usually, borders are closed to keep the enemy out, e.g. the migrant, the foreign, the refugee, the Other, now the enemy to keep out is the virus. The tendency of the 'nation state', of 'renationalizing', specifically visible in the EU, became thus very strong, as was later visible also in the vaccine nationalism.

Let us now look at my corpus and see whether and to what extent the previous and the current governors have compared the pandemic to a war both in the UK and in the US.

Boris Johnson and Donald Trump both contracted coronavirus, respectively in April and in October 2020. Two years later, in July 2022, also Joe Biden caught a highly contagious COVID-19 strain.

FIGURE II. CONCORDANCE LINES FOR *WAR* IN BORIS JOHNSON'S SPEECHES

Concord

File Edit View Compute Settings Windows Help

N	Concordance
82	will only grow larger and more indelible every day this war continues.? ? But don't just take my word for it. ? All
83	to my Russian friends: [In Russian] I do not believe this war is in your name. It does not have to be this way. This
84	war, an absolutely inexcusable and unnecessary war. But having been here in Kyiv for just a few hours, I
85	its own people an unacceptable cost for an unnecessary war – a war of choice - that should end as soon as
86	help to create so you deal with terrorism and with war and extremism, and you help people to tackle climate
87	Kingdom in a display of solidarity not seen since world war two and so today we must combine that energy and
88	contact – steps that are unprecedented since World War 2. They will have an effect on the spread of the
89	in Harrogate, re-presented with his Second World War Defence Medal which he had previously misplaced
90	together to rebuild the world following the Second World War, so too will we apply our combined strength to the
91	people in this country to have served in the second world war at Cape Matapan, where he was mentioned in
92	of our planning system since the end of the second world war Yes, we will insist on beautiful and low carbon homes
93	service in the Royal Navy in the Second World War; his commitment to young people in setting up The
94	the nation's biggest challenge since the Second World War and the worst pandemic since 1918, any
95	catastrophic attack on its people since the Second World War, in which 67 British citizens also lost their lives at the
96	the 75th anniversary of victory in the Second World War. And in times of trial, our tributes matter even more.
97	the foundation of the UN at the end of the Second World War. In fact it was far bigger: there were more than 120
98	career in the Navy. When he served in the second world war, he was mentioned in despatches for his "alertness
99	just as we forged new institutions after the Second World War. And I believe this concept of coalitions coalescing
100	paid a price. For the first time since the second world war, the largest western democracies were left behind in
101	going during our biggest crisis since the Second World War. We will commemorate the small acts of kindness,
102	us in the gravest crisis since the Second World War, resolving to go forwards together, Mr Speaker, and
103	. Heroes like George Arthur Roberts. In the First World War he would literally pick up German bombs with his

concordance collocates plot patterns clusters filenames follow up source text notes

103 Set

In his first speech after he left intensive care, Boris Johnson, channeling his hero, Winston Churchill, started to bring in new measures "unprecedented since the Second World War", saying that "we must act like any wartime government".

Interestingly enough, never does Boris Johnson collocate the word 'war' with the pandemic, rather he likens it to World War II in order to communicate the sense of urgency and emergency, heightening alarm and instant awareness.

In June 2021, Boris Johnson and Joe Biden met in-person for the first time to agree on a new 'Atlantic Charter', modelled on the historic joint statement made by Churchill and Roosevelt in 1941, setting out their goals for the post-war world order that led directly to the creation of the UN and NATO. Even though they compared the COVID-19 crisis to the Second World War, they acknowledged that the world today is a very different place to 1941, and yet the values that the UK and the US share remain the same. Enlarging the context in line 48 (not reported here), we read Boris Johnson's statement that "while Churchill and Roosevelt faced the question of how to help the world recover following a devastating war, today we have to reckon with a very different but no less intimidating challenge: how to build back better from the coronavirus pandemic".

The word 'war' occurs on 103 occasions in Boris Johnson's corpus: its high frequency is not due to the pandemic, but rather to the "inexcusable, unnecessary and unacceptable war" in Ukraine, as we read in lines 84 and 85. After boasting for being the first nation in the world to administer a vaccine[1], the fastest in Europe to roll it out, the country that delivered the fastest booster campaign in Europe, and the first to start "to see the light at the end of the tunnel", Boris Johnson acknowledged that the British NHS moved 'to a war footing', and that this was the nation's biggest challenge since the Second World War and the worst pandemic since 1918.

---

[1] Matt Hancock, the British Health Secretary, announced that the approval of the first vaccine against the virus, produced by Pfizer-BioNTech at the beginning of December 2020, was owed to the fact that, because of Brexit, the government could make a decision on their own and not go at the pace of Europeans. The first day of vaccination was labeled V-Day, reminiscent of VE Day (Victory in Europe), to remind everybody of the end of WW II (Musolff 2021).

Interestingly, but not surprisingly, *fight against the pandemic/ covid-19/covid/the virus/the pandemic* is instead fairly frequent, as Figure III illustrates:

FIGURE III. CONCORDANCE LINES FOR *FIGHT* IN BORIS JOHNSON'S SPEECHES

Unlike Boris Johnson, both the previous and current president of the United States clearly call the pandemic a war, as Figures IV and V show (divided in IV A and IV B and V A and V B for the sake of clarity and convenience):

FIGURE IV A. CONCORDANCE LINES FOR *WAR* IN JOE BIDEN'S SPEECHES

FIGURE IV B. CONCORDANCE LINES FOR *WAR* IN JOE BIDEN'S SPEECHES

FIGURE IV B. CONCORDANCE LINES FOR *WAR* IN JOE BIDEN'S SPEECHES

The evidence of the data shows that "We still are in a war with this deadly virus" (line 1), "I said we ought to treat this like a war" (line 4) "we are on a war footing" (line 3 and lines 6-9), "We're in the middle of a war with this virus" (line 5). Joe Biden's scenario is made even more warlike when he says that "You're the Coast Guard. I really mean it. This is a war. You are the frontline troops" (line 2). He insists that his language is literal, that he is not exaggerating, "It sounds like hyperbole, but it is not" (line 8). He repeats on several occasions, as Figure IV B illustrates, that "This is a wartime undertaking, it's not hyperbole", and that COVID-19 has taken more fellow Americans than the Vietnam War, 9/11, World War I and World War II combined".

Along the very same lines, Donald Trump, labelling himself a wartime president, reiterates that "in a true sense, we are at war", and this invisible enemy has inflicted a steep toll on the American nation, killing more people than Pearl Harbor and 9/11 (line 30). He explains that this enemy, in many ways, is a different enemy than anybody has ever fought before, is a tougher enemy, is a much more dangerous enemy, precisely because it is invisible, as opposed to a visible enemy, because "We do very well against the visible enemies". To communicate the scale of the crisis, Donald Trump highlights that "it's not a battle, it's a war" (line 32), and it is a different war, as it is not a financial war, it is a medical war, and "we have to win this war" (line 23). It is an all-out-war against this virus, against this terrible virus, this horrible, horrible virus (lines 184-185). Figures V A and V B illustrate some examples:

FIGURE V A. CONCORDANCE LINES FOR *WAR* IN DONALD TRUMP'S SPEECHES

FIGURE V B. CONCORDANCE LINES FOR *WAR* IN DONALD TRUMP'S SPEECHES

Martial rhetoric is inherently divisive and, when the pandemic is described with a bellicose language, the "us versus them" framework is inevitably set up. In the passage below, Donald Trump presents the American people as warriors, vaunting that "nobody is like us, nobody is tough like us", and that, supplying "the weapons, the armor, the sweat", his country will defeat the new invisible enemy.

Now it is one more time for the men and women of Honeywell who are supplying the weapons, the armor, the sweat, and the scale in a war to defeat the new invisible enemy – a tough enemy, a smart enemy. But nobody is like us, and nobody is tough like us. And I said it before and I'll say it again: The people of our country are warriors.

To conclude this section on the omnipresence and inevitability of military language when speaking of the COVID-19 pandemic, I argue here that "the war on war metaphor" (Panzeri et al. 2020) is far from won, and never will be, since the war frame inevitably serves different purposes, despite the 'blanket criticism' of being misleading and/or counterproductive (Musolff 2021).

As Hanks (2006) argues, some metaphors are less metaphorical than others, being frequent and well established, thus requiring little effort to be interpreted. It cannot be denied, though, that using the war as the source domain and the pandemic as the target domain helped to conceptualize complex and invisible processes. War-related metaphors, being dominant and pervasive, are by now conventional, worn-out and familiar, hence predictable and less resonant than novel and unusual metaphors (Black 1977), like some sort of cliché and like an elastic band that has lost its tension through overuse (Charteris-Black 2021: 40).

Hence, even though the SARS-CoV-2 disease will always be perceived and remembered as a war, in the second part of this paper I discuss two frames for which the pandemic will also be remembered, i.e. 'the science' and 'herd immunity'.

4. 'The' science

"Fighting against coronavirus was like fighting in the dark against a callous and invisible enemy, until science helped us to turn the lights on and to gain the upper hand", Boris Johnson said, in an official statement, on March 23, 2020, the day after the United Kingdom was put under lockdown due to the COVID-19 pandemic. A few days before, on March 17, 2020, he claimed that "Yes, this enemy can be deadly, but it is also beatable – and we know how to beat it, and we know that if as a country we follow the scientific advice that now is being given we know that we will beat it".

The reliance on 'science' and 'the scientific advice' that the Prime Minister invoked when the virus started to spread in March 2020 and which continued throughout seems to suggest that, after the recent wave of populism, experts were now, in times of fear and despair, as well as of uncertainty, back in fashion. Suddenly, appeals to the wishes 'of the people' were replaced by those based on the authority of 'science', which now formed the main argument for the legitimacy of their decisions (Charteris-Black 2021: 14). In June 2016, when the UK succumbed to the populist virus by deciding to apply for the most powerful tool in the populist box, i.e. the referendum, Michael Gove, a staunch supporter of leaving the EU, famously said: "I think the people in this country have had enough of experts with organizations from acronyms saying that they know what is best and getting it consistently wrong". Populist parties usually offer solutions, promise change, and seem quite proud not to need any experts, not to need knowledge, thus endorsing the "arrogance of ignorance", appeals to common sense, intuitions, and anti-intellectualism (Wodak 2016). It is worth remembering, in fact, that both the British and the American leader understated the extent of the virus, respectively boasting of shaking hands with people (thus not adhering to the advice of experts), and promising that "by Easter, and with the warm weather, this will be gone", and that "we are rounding the corner", or even "we are turning the tide".

Yet, with the arrival of the pandemic, governments everywhere could not help relying on the authority of experts in molecular evolution, epidemiology, statistics, virology, microbiology, social science, social psychology, economics and other disciplines (Charteris-Black 2021: 14). Any decision governments would take, they would justify it with the claim that they were based "on what science has advised".

Figures VI and VII illustrate how Boris Johnson heavily relied on science and scientific advice.

Since early on in the pandemic, the British government, and the Prime Minister in particular, claimed that their approach to the coronavirus was guided by "what the science tells us". Thus, the refrain "follow the best scientific advice" (line 8), "based on the best scientific advice" (lines 7-11), "guided by the science" (lines 73-

78), "driven by the science" (line 79), became the common refrain that governors used to justify their decisions, mainly those related to severe constraints on personal freedom. It is worth noticing that the use of the passive voice removes agency from the Prime Minister altogether, handing it over to the Chief Scientific Advisor, Sir Patrick Vallance, in particular, and to the Chief Medical Officers, more generally, as we can see in Figure VI.

FIGURE VI. CONCORDANCE LINES FOR *SCIENTIFIC ADVICE* IN BORIS JOHNSON'S SPEECHES

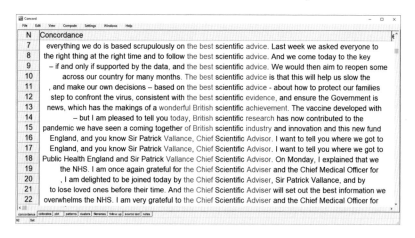

FIGURE VII. CONCORDANCE LINES FOR *THE SCIENCE* IN BORIS JOHNSON'S SPEECHES

Rarely was this expression used prior to the pandemic and, needless to say, experts did not hide their frustration at being held responsible for all decisions made by politicians, mainly because it was regarded as a way to abdicate responsibility for political decisions and as an attempt to avoid blame. Criticisms grew even more because paying tribute to 'the science' (Figure VII), with the definite article, rather than 'science', was perceived as a way to signal unanimity of scientific opinion. Rarely is scientific opinion unanimous, hence this oversimplification sounded somewhat annoying and dishonest (*ibid.*: 125).

Let us now look at the American corpus, which includes both Donald Trump's (2020-2021) and Joe Biden's (2021-2022) data.

It was perhaps quite surprising to find out, at first, that, in the corpus of the former President of the United States, 'scientific experts' and 'science' were in fashion, as well. Yet, as Figure VIII shows, while bragging about America's scientific brilliance, Donald Trump was also showing off his relentless self-promotion and the promotion of his country, for the way the US has been able to tackle the pandemic: "There is nothing like us. There is nobody like us. Not even close" (line 12).

FIGURE VIII. CONCORDANCE LINES FOR *SCIENTIFIC* IN DONALD TRUMP'S SPEECHES

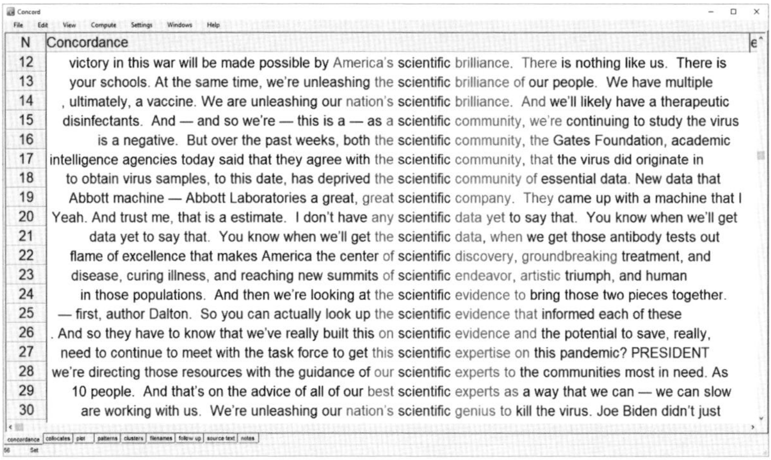

N	Concordance
12	victory in this war will be made possible by America's scientific brilliance. There is nothing like us. There is
13	your schools. At the same time, we're unleashing the scientific brilliance of our people. We have multiple
14	, ultimately, a vaccine. We are unleashing our nation's scientific brilliance. And we'll likely have a therapeutic
15	disinfectants. And — and so we're — this is a — as a scientific community, we're continuing to study the virus
16	is a negative. But over the past weeks, both the scientific community, the Gates Foundation, academic
17	intelligence agencies today said that they agree with the scientific community, that the virus did originate in
18	to obtain virus samples, to this date, has deprived the scientific community of essential data. New data that
19	Abbott machine — Abbott Laboratories a great, great scientific company. They came up with a machine that I
20	Yeah. And trust me, that is a estimate. I don't have any scientific data yet to say that. You know when we'll get
21	data yet to say that. You know when we'll get the scientific data, when we get those antibody tests out
22	flame of excellence that makes America the center of scientific discovery, groundbreaking treatment, and
23	disease, curing illness, and reaching new summits of scientific endeavor, artistic triumph, and human
24	in those populations. And then we're looking at the scientific evidence to bring those two pieces together.
25	— first, author Dalton. So you can actually look up the scientific evidence that informed each of these
26	. And so they have to know that we've really built this on scientific evidence and the potential to save, really,
27	need to continue to meet with the task force to get this scientific expertise on this pandemic? PRESIDENT
28	we're directing those resources with the guidance of our scientific experts to the communities most in need. As
29	10 people. And that's on the advice of all of our best scientific experts as a way that we can — we can slow
30	are working with us. We're unleashing our nation's scientific genius to kill the virus. Joe Biden didn't just

FIGURE IX. CONCORDANCE LINES FOR *SCIENCE* IN DONALD TRUMP'S SPEECHES

In Figure VIII, Donald Trump is highlighting that "you can actually look up the scientific evidence" (line 25), "with the guidance of our scientific experts" (line 28), "on the advice of all of our best scientific experts" (line 29), "We're unleashing our nation's scientific genius to kill the virus" (line 30), seemingly showing that in these fraught times reliance on experts is natural and inescapable. In Figure IX, he goes on claiming that the US has the best science, the best researchers, the best talent (line 16), the best common sense (line 17), the best modeling, and the best medical experts (line 18). Besides, he insists on saying that his administration is pursuing a science-based approach that protects the most vulnerable, and that the reopening his government has planned is science-based.

On reflection, and as the evidence of the data shows, Trump's communication is characterized as the extreme personalization of American diplomacy, and, despite a massive use of the pronoun "we", he remains the ultimate authority as regards the management of the crisis (Saltykov 2022). Indeed, on several occasions he had shown disdain for the scientific community, calling, for example, Dr. Anthony Fauci, the head of the National Institute of Allergy and Infectious Diseases, "an idiot", "a disaster", and other medical experts "a bunch of thugs"[2]. In an interview with Fox News, he disowned Dr. Fauci and said:

I get along with him very well, I agree with him on a lot of what he says, but I inherited him, I found him here, he's been here since 1984, he is part of this huge piece of machine, I don't agree with him that often.

It seems worthwhile remembering, however, that in March 2020 Donald Trump declared that the United States would be terminating its relationship with the WHO (World Health Organization), and this decision was somehow immoral, encapsulating his utter contempt of science and experts.

Thus, it appears clear that Trump's appeal to expertise does not aim to justify restrictive measures, unlike what we have seen for Boris Johnson in the UK and what we shall now see for Joe Biden in the US.

Figure X clearly shows the belief of the current President of the United States in science.

Unsurprisingly, Joe Biden's argumentative strategies resemble Boris Johnson's in many respects. First, the "follow the science" refrain is omnipresent, and it appears clear that its main purpose is to legitimize the authoritarian measures imposed, urging the people that this must be a whole-of-society effort. Science, or indeed 'the' science, is really a metonym for "what scientists believe" (Charteris-Black 2021: 125), indicating that the government claimed to be heeding the advice of scientists. More specifically, Joe Biden argues that by following the science, washing our hands, staying socially distanced (line 68), wearing a mask, getting tested, getting vaccinated (line 72), in other words "sticking with the science" (line 86) and abiding by "what the science tells us" (lines 84-85), we shall overcome this deadly virus, because the science is "clear and overwhelming" (line 77), as well as "unmistakable and undeniable" (line 83).

---

[2] Dr. Anthony Fauci and New York Governor Andrew Cuomo are often referred to as the most trusted leaders in the battle against coronavirus. They are both communication experts and rely very often on metaphor to talk about science to the general public, simplify complexity, and explain what is at stake. Dr. Fauci advised seven Presidents on HIV/AIDS, respiratory infections, diarrheal diseases, tuberculosis, malaria, as well as Ebola, Zika and COVID-19.

FIGURE X. CONCORDANCE LINES FOR *SCIENCE* IN JOE BIDEN'S SPEECHES

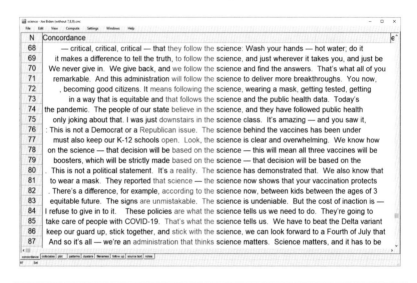

We conclude this paragraph saying that the 'science' trope, i.e. "follow the science", "follow the scientific advice", "guided by the science", whose criticisms grew extensively with its constant repetition, was initiated by politicians, and then reverberated in the media to the extent that it became a cliché. The 'science' metonymy, playing a key role in framing the debate around the pandemic, and reducing the agency of those living through it, is surely a frame for which the COVID-19 crisis will be remembered, together with an immunity-related metaphor that we shall consider next.

5. Herd immunity

In March 2020, UK pandemic adviser Graham Medley said: "We are going to have to generate what we call herd immunity", which would require "a nice big epidemic". Needless to say, the idea received furious criticisms, and British officials denied that herd immunity had ever been part of their plan. A few months later, in August, the White House started to ponder a policy of immunity, but again, also in the US, officials issued a prompt denial (Jones and Helmreich 2020).

The appeal of herd immunity is obvious, in that if it is reached, the epidemic ends. But, in order to achieve it, about 60% of the people would need to get infected. Thus, it is easy to understand why there was an outraged response to the concept that, because of its widespread use, from being a scientific concept, became an everyday expression.

The phrase 'herd immunity' was first coined in epidemiology in 1923, and even though it enjoys scientific status, it became a controversial expression, mainly because the word 'herd' usually refers to domesticated animals, especially livestock, like cows, goats, or sheep, usually sacrificed for human consumption. Few humans would like to be part of that kind of herd, as the inference of behaving like sheep is not appealing. Furthermore, the word 'vaccination' comes from the Latin 'vacca', i.e. cow, and much of the early resistance to vaccination comes from moral feelings about the threat to the sanctity of the human body posed by injecting animal products into their bodies. Unconsciously, the animal frame triggered a negative response and was more likely to encourage anti-vaccination sentiments (Charteris-Black 2021: 134-135).

Given the negative semantic prosody that 'herd immunity' took on, and given its controversial impact, the British government switched away from this metaphor. In Boris Johnson's corpus we find no instance of 'herd immunity', but 4 instances of 'the wall of immunity' and one of 'a huge wall of an immunity".

Jonathan Van-Tam[3], the former Deputy Chief Medical Officer for England, given the controversy around the 'herd immunity' concept, aptly avoided it, replacing, in a surreptitious manner, 'herd' with 'community'. Its alternative, 'community immunity', sounds like a very clever linguistic techinque, and it is also acceptable and persuasive (*ibid.*).

Let us now look at the American corpus and at the way the current and the previous leaders of the US have managed the 'herd immunity' concept:

---

[3] Professor Jonathan Van-Tam was Deputy Chief Medical Officer for England from 2017 to 2022. He is well-known for his ability "to turn medicine into stories". JVT was nicknamed Mr Metaphor and was the master of the metaphor when making the case for the vaccine. He put his pandemic point across using analogies about trains, penalties, hosepipes, planes and yoghurt.

FIGURE XI. CONCORDANCE LINES FOR *IMMUNITY* IN JOE BIDEN'S SPEECHES

	Concord − □ ×
	File Edit View Compute Settings Windows Help
N	Concordance
1	to be well on our way to heading toward herd immunity and increasing the access for people
2	while we're getting to this point, we get to herd immunity. MR. COOPER: You've made —
3	to take that vaccine so we can reach the herd immunity? THE PRESIDENT: We are. We are
4	so we can get to the point where we reach herd immunity in a country of over 300 million people.
5	, when do you think the U.S. will reach herd immunity? When do you believe the U.S. will
6	When do you believe the U.S. will reach herd immunity? THE PRESIDENT: I think, by the
7	got to reach the point where we have herd immunity — meaning where we have a vast
8	— there's a debate on what constitutes herd immunity. "Is it 70 percent of the population?
9	considerably because of what they call "herd immunity." And now they're saying somewhere
10	. Q Mr. President, (inaudible) end qualified immunity? That's one of the hang-ups in
11	also eliminate gun manufacturers from the immunity they received from the Congress.

| concordance | collocates | plot | patterns | clusters | filenames | follow up | source text | notes |
| 11   Set |

Of the 11 instances displayed in Figure XI, Joe Biden utters the phrase on 6 occasions. Interestingly, in line 8 he is wondering what really constitutes herd immunity, whether 70% of the population, or 68% or 81%? In line 9, he adds that herd immunity, they say, constitutes 60% or even 50%. He then goes on that "the disease is going to diminish considerably because of what they call 'herd immunity'", thus giving scientificity to his claims, because it is 'they', 'the experts', 'scientists', who say so. It is clear, as we also saw in the previous paragraph, that for the current President of the United States 'science matters'.

The word 'herd' in English frequently co-occurs with both 'mentality' and 'behaviour'. It is perhaps because of the confusion between 'herd immunity' and 'herd mentality' that Donald Trump claimed that "herd mentality could make the coronavirus disappear with or without a vaccine".

Figure XII illustrates the usage of the word 'herd', that, interestingly, the former US Presidents employs in an idiosyncratic manner.

The phrase 'herd immunity', as we can see in Figures XII A and XII B, occurs in the corpus in lines 14-18, and on all five occasions the metaphor is uttered by scientists, i.e. Dr. Fauci, Dr. Birx and Dr. Slusher. Never, in fact, does Trump use the word' herd' with 'immunity', but only with 'mentality' (lines 8-9), spelling out what is meant with 'herd mentality' – or 'herd concept' – (lines 24-25):

[…] The herd concept of opening up and stay open. […] So we've really done it right. But now it's time to be open, it's time to stay open. And we will put out the fires as they come up, but we have to open our schools. It's so important to open our schools. And when you said, from a psychological standpoint, with respect to staying home any longer, you can't do it. You can't do it.

FIGURE XII A. CONCORDANCE LINES FOR *HERD* IN DONALD TRUMP'S SPEECHES

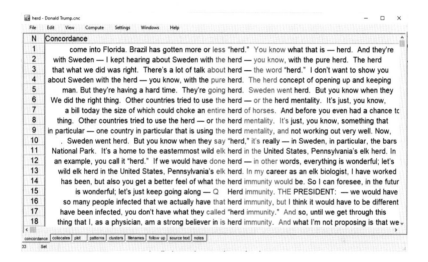

FIGURE XII B. CONCORDANCE LINES FOR *HERD* IN DONALD TRUMP'S SPEECHES

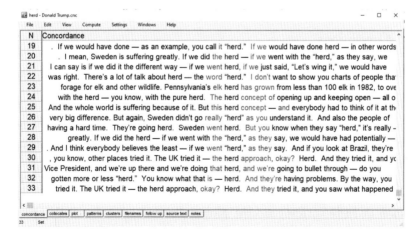

It appears clear that the herd mentality and the herd concept have no semantic relation with herd immunity, since it refers to the idea of opening up and keeping open, in particular schools, shops, bars and restaurants, in other words the economy, according to what is usually referred to as the "Swedish model" (Wodak 2021: 14). The 'Swedish way', the 'Swedish trust', or the 'Swedish model' differed from that of all other liberal democratic countries: Sweden, in fact, never introduced a complete lockdown. A few rules were introduced but mostly the government decided to propose recommendations that experts believed to be relevant and effective in order to contain the spread of the virus, hence the people trusted the government and the government trusted the people (*ibid.*).

Thus, it seems that Donald Trump is attempting to promote and export the Swedish way, asking the American people for trust and collaboration. One of the best ways to go back to normality is re-opening, or 'to go herd' (lines 5, 21, 26, 27, 29) and 'to do the herd' (lines 12, 20, 31). The UK, Trump goes on, tried the herd approach (line 30), and in the first phase of the pandemic 'they went herd', 'did the herd', and 'went with the herd'.

In Figure XII the word 'herd' appears in speech marks 8 times, thus indicating that it is very likely a novel metaphor. Ironically, though, despite the highly idiosyncratic use of the word, he tries to abdicate responsibility, e.g. "*they* say herd" (line 10), "if we went with the herd, as *they* say" (lines 28-29), thus passing the buck to some other agent and, in a way, shifting the blame and the accountability of his words.

6. Conclusions

Starting from the assumption that metaphors contribute to the moral framing of a situation in such a way that we become biased towards one form of action over another, providing insight into the moral framing of our actions (Charteris-Black 2021: 5), this research was an attempt to discuss some of the frames to the numerous aspects of the pandemic.

We started with the pandemic-as-war metaphor, which has been especially pervasive and frequent since the beginning. In fact, when in early spring 2020 the global dimension of the COVID-19 pandemic became clear, many leaders in the world declared "war" on the pandemic. Earlier health crises such as AIDS, Ebola, SARS, bird flu, were also perceived as warfare, but also in the medical and in the political sphere we hear about the war on cancer, drugs, alcohol, and on terror. Recourse to the war rhetoric seems to have become almost unavoidable, in that it serves several special, and arguably, legitimate purposes (Musolff 2021). Military jargon is by now entrenched in discourse and plays a significant role in framing.

Our quantitative analysis has shown that, even though the British governors have likened the pandemic to the Second World War, and have used bellicose rhetoric to communicate the sense of urgency and emergency, their linguistic favourite way of addressing the coronavirus crisis is 'fight', e.g. "our fight against COVID is by no means won". Conversely, the American government has repeatedly declared to be "at war", claiming that "we are on a war footing", "we are in the middle of a war with this virus" and "we have to win this war". Both the previous and the current US president reiterate that this war has taken more fellow Americans than all previous wars, when the enemy, though, was a visible enemy, unlike the current foe who is invisible.

Despite the several and successful attempts to frame the COVID-19 crisis with alternative metaphors (see Olza et al. 2021), we argue here that, even though they have lost their resonance and their potential impact (Garzone 2021), war-related metaphors will always be the inevitable and inescapable frame of the extraordinary global pandemic that has affected the whole world. However, there are also other frames for which the pandemic will be remembered, whether relatable, witty, emotional, or particularly interesting, as the pandemic has touched upon several social, political, economic, ecological, emotional, and epistemological aspects. Hence, I have focused on two frames in particular, the science and the myth of herd immunity, as employed by Boris Johnson in the UK and by Donald Trump and Joe Biden in the first and in the second phase of the pandemic respectively. I have put forward the hypothesis that the pandemic might have killed populism (Milizia 2023), given the strong reliance on 'the science' and on 'the best scientific advice', but I have also agreed with Charteris-Black (2021: 152) that this was, most likely, a strategy to abdicate responsibility for political decisions and justify the draconian clampdowns imposed by governments. Ironically, this (pseudo) appeal to expertise was yielded also in

Donald Trump's corpus, despite his well-known disdain for the scientific community and his contempt of experts. I have discussed also the herd immunity frame, which, despite enjoying scientific status, turned out to be counterproductive, to the point of being rarely used by Boris Johnson himself. The phrase was, instead, often employed by Joe Biden, who uses this frame, yet ascribes it to scientists – "what they call herd immunity" – thus confirming that, to him, science matters. I have concluded the paper looking at the idiosyncratic use Donald Trump has made of the word 'herd', and the phrases in which he embeds the word, i.e. herd mentality, herd approach, go herd, go with the herd, do the herd, thus creating an altogether new phrase, carrying no semantic relation, whatsoever, to the scientific original frame.

Further investigation of novel and creative metaphors, including also other countries, e.g. Italy, seems to be a particularly promising avenue.

References

BLACK, MAX, 1962, *Models and Metaphors. Studies in Language and Philosophy*, Cornell University Press, Ithaca.

BLACK, MAX, 1977, "More about Metaphor", *Dialectica* 31 (3-4), pp. 431-457.

BRANDT, ALLAN and BOTELHO, ALYSSA, 2020, "Not a Perfect Storm – COVID-19 and the Importance of Language", *The New England Journal of Medicine*, available at https://www.nejm.org/doi/full/10.1056/NEJMp2005032

CHARTERIS-BLACK, JONATHAN, 2014, *Analysing Political Speeches. Rhetoric, Discourse and Metaphor*, Palgrave Macmillan, Cham.

CHARTERIS-BLACK, JONATHAN, 2021, *Metaphors of Coronavirus. Invisible Enemy or Zombie Apocalypse?*, Palgrave Macmillan, Cham.

COSTA, PAOLO, 2020, "Emergenza coronavirus: non soldati ma pompieri", available at http://www.settimananews.it/societa/emergenza-coronavirus-non-soldati-ma-pompieri/

GARZONE, GIULIANA E., 2006, *Perspectives on ESP and Popularization*, CUEM, Milano.

GARZONE, GIULIANA E., 2021, "Rethinking Metaphors in COVID-19 Communication", *Lingue e Linguaggi* 22 (1), pp. 159-181.

HANKS, PATRICK, 2006, "Metaphoricity is gradable", in A. Stefanowitsch and S. Gries (eds), *Corpus-Based Approaches to Metaphor and Metonymy*, Mouton de Gruyter, Berlin, pp. 17-35.

JONES, DAVID and HELMREICH, STEFAN, 2020, "A History of Herd Immunity",

The Lancet 396, available at https://www.thelancet.com/journals/lancet/article/PIIS0140-6736%2820%2931924-3/fulltext?rss=yes

KOLLER, VERONICA, 2020, "A battle, a tsunami or a raging fire? Metaphors for COVID-19 and why they matter", available at https://www.westminster.ac.uk/events/a-battle-a-tsunami-or-a-raging-fire-metaphors-for-covid-19-and-why-they-matter-veronika-koller.

LAKOFF, GEORGE, and JOHNSON, MARK, 1980, *Metaphors We Live By*, Chicago Press, Chicago.

LAKOFF, GEORGE, 2001, *Metaphors of Terror*, available at https://press.uchicago.edu/sites/daysafter/911lakoff.html

LEVENSON, ERIC, 2020, "Officials keep calling the coronavirus pandemic a 'war'. Here's why", "CNN", 2 April, available at https://edition.cnn.com/2020/04/01/us/war-on-coronavirus-attack/index.html.

MILIZIA, DENISE, 2023, "Interview with Stanley Johnson", in D. Milizia and A.M. Silletti (eds), *L'Unione europea tra pandemia, nuove crisi e prospettive future*, LED, Milano, pp. 21-31.

MUSOLFF, ANDREAS, 2017, "Metaphors and persuasion in politics", in E. Semino and Z. Demjén (eds), *The Routledge Handbook of Metaphor and Language*, Routledge, London, pp. 309-322.

MUSOLFF, ANDREAS, 2021, "'War against COVID-19': Is the pandemic as war metaphor helpful or hurtful?", in A. Musolff, R. Breeze, K. Kondo and S. Vilar-Lluch (eds), *Pandemic and Crisis Discourse. Communicating COVID-19 and Public Health Strategies*, Bloomsbury, London, pp. 307-320.

NERLICH, BRIGITTE, 2020, *Metaphors and realities: Coronavirus and climate change.* Available at https://blogs.nottingham.ac.uk/makingsciencepublic/2020/09/18/metaphors-and-realities-coronavirus-and-climate-change/

OLZA, INÉS, KOLLER, VERONICA, IBARRETXE-ANTUÑANO, IRAIDE, PÉREZ-SOBRINO, PAULA and SEMINO, ELENA, 2021, "The #ReframeCovid initiative: From Twitter to society via metaphor", *Metaphor and the Social World* 11 (1), pp. 98-120.

PANZERI, FRANCESCA, DI PAOLA, SIMONA and DOMANESCHI, FILIPPO, 2020, "Does the COVID-19 war metaphor influence reasoning?", *PLoS ONE* 16 (4): e02250651.

SALTYKOV, MARIA, 2022, "A populist president in campaign: Donald Trump, or the management of the COVID-19 crisis", *Argumentation et Analyse du Discours* 28, available at https://journals.openedition.org/aad/6449.

SCOTT, MICHAEL, 2017, *WordSmith Tools* 7.0. Lexical Analysis Software Limited.

SEMINO, ELENA, 2021a, "Not Soldiers but Fire-fighters" – Metaphors and COVID-19", *Health Communication* 36 (1), pp. 50-58.

SEMINO, ELENA, 2021b, "Fire, waves and warfare: the way we make sense of COVID", available at https://www.theguardian.com/commentisfree/2021/jul/05/fire-waves-and-warfare-the-way-we-make-sense-of-covid.

SEMINO, ELENA, FLUSBERG, STEPHEN, BRIGUGLIA, GIANLUCA, PAULUS, DAGMAR, GARASSINO, MARINA CHIARA and VILLA, ROBERTA, 2020, *Guns, Germs, and COVID-19. Why science communication needs metaphors*, an online roundtable, available at bit.ly/45dbRzT.

SEMINO, ELENA and POTTS, AMANDA, 2019, "Cancer as a Metaphor", *Metaphor and Symbol* 34 (2), pp. 81-95.

SONTAG, SUSAN, 1977, *Illness as Metaphor and AIDS and Its Metaphors*, Picador, New York.

TALEB, NASSIM NICHOLAS, 2010, *The Black Swan: The Impact of the Highly Improbable. On Robustness and Fragility*, Routledge, London.

WODAK, RUTH, 2016, "The language of walls – Analyzing Right-Wing Populist Discourse", available at https://www.youtube.com/watch?v=aWa3T_6FNOQ

WODAK, RUTH, 2017, "The "Establishment", the "élite", and the "People". Who's who?", *Journal of Language and Politics* 16 (4), pp. 1-15.

WODAK, RUTH, 2020, "What future for the EU after COVID-19?", available at https://www.opendemocracy.net/en/pandemic-border/what-future-eu-after-covid-19/

WODAK, RUTH, 2021, "Crisis communication and crisis management during COVID-19", *Global Discourse* 11 (3), pp. 329-353.

'Living with Covid': Boris Johnson's Communication in Post-Pandemic Times

*Maria Cristina Paganoni**

Abstract
This article investigates Boris Johnson's COVID-related communication during the final part of his term, spanning from January to September 2022. Taking into account a data set of thirteen scripted texts, the politician's stance is scrutinised with the toolbox of Critical Discourse Studies to identify the salient turning points and the ideological thrust of his post-pandemic health policy announcements. While the military narrative previously adopted by the government is downplayed, the long shadow of the pandemic introduces a new scenario, timescale and metaphorical framing. Now Johnson rhetorically shifts from fighting the common enemy of disease to restoring liberties and lifting restrictions to keep the country open and its economy going, often sidelining experts on preventive measures. This way, a morally responsible behaviour is discursively prioritised over political responsibility, which is in fact abdicated to the British people. Despite an ongoing inquiry, no admission is made of his government's poor performance of the public health crisis and the exit from the political stage is delivered in self-aggrandising tones. In conclusion, the prime minister's post-pandemic COVID-related communication appears to largely ignore the complexity of the new normal, in and out of metaphor.
Key-words: Boris Johnson, COVID-19, Critical Discourse Studies, framing, metaphor, political communication, public health.

1. Background

This study aims to add to the discursive investigations of how Boris Johnson articulated the UK government's response to the pandemic, focussing on his 'living with Covid' plan before his resignation

* The author would like to thank the two anonymous reviewers for their insightful comments on an earlier version of this paper.

ISSN 1824-3967
© Carocci Editore S.p.A.

on July 7, 2022. On that occasion which saw him forced to step
down in a heap of ethics scandals,[1] the embattled Conservative
prime minister claimed to be proud of "getting us all through the
pandemic, delivering the fastest vaccine rollout in Europe, the fastest
exit from lockdown" (Johnson 2022l), although a public inquiry into
his government's (mis)handling of the health crisis is currently in
train. Despite Johnson's claims, the sad truth is that in the UK the
mortality rate from COVID-19 is, "per capita, one of the highest
in the world" (McVittie 2021: 1), leading British scientists and war
strategists like Sir Lawrence Freedman to denounce the country's
poor performance (Freedman 2020b; Scally, Jacobson, Abbasi 2020;
Horton 2021).

The privileged field of analysis is therefore the discursive framing
of Boris Johnson's COVID-related public health decisions in the last
months of his tenure, at the nadir of his political trajectory, before
he was ousted by his own party, a rebellion labelled by opposition
Labour Party leader Keir Starmer as "the first recorded case of the
sinking ship fleeing the rat" (Wheeler 2022). Intrinsic and extrinsic
factors explain this approach. To begin with, a wealth of linguistically-
informed studies dealing with COVID-19 communication during the
pandemic peaks quickly emerged over a short-time span (Garzone
2021; Semino 2021; Coupland 2022; Liégeois and Mathysen 2022;
Pérez-Sobrino et al. 2022). Quite expectedly, several contributions
to this impressive scholarly output have placed critical attention on
communication from political leaders and elites to citizens (Drylie-
Carey, Sánchez-Castillo, Galán-Cubillo 2020; Islentyeva 2020;
Hancock 2021; Kirk and McDonald 2021; Lilleker and Stoekcle 2021;
Warren and Loftstedt 2021; Lorenzetti 2022; Power and Crosthwaite
2022).

With regard to Boris Johnson, in addition to these critical
insights, journalists and academics alike have expanded on his
rhetoric of British exceptionalism in general and on the use of
metaphors to justify the extraordinary measures undertaken in

---

[1] Most noticeably, the Partygate scandal, whose evidence was collected in a report
by civil servant Sue Gray. It showed that Boris Johnson breached COVID-19
regulations holding lockdown parties at government offices. Johnson addressed
the report in an oral statement to the House of Commons on January 31, 2022
(Johnson 2022d).

response to the COVID-19 public health emergency. After initially belittling the threat in March 2020 and hoping that the British people would acquire 'herd immunity' by natural infection, in turn Johnson framed the pandemic as 'a deadly/invisible enemy', 'an invisible killer/ mugger', 'a physical assailant', 'an alien invader', 'a tide', 'a tsunami', 'a tidal wave', at the same time foregrounding his political persona as muscular enough to squash the 'sombrero' of the epidemic curve after getting Brexit done (Demianyk 2020; Charteris-Black 2021; Lilleker and Stoekle 2021; Andrews 2022; Musolff 2022).

Now that the emergency has subsided and endemic COVID-19 beckons, political leaders need to reorient their messages and priorities. Governments "know that there will be a reckoning [...] and it is time to recover and rebuild" (Freedman 2020a). This change of discursive frames, which is the object of the analysis, is also observable in Boris Johnson's post-peak phase.

On February 21, 2022, he announced a "living with Covid" plan in Parliament, lifting all legal restrictions and saying it was time to finally move "from government intervention to personal responsibility" (Johnson 2022f). The decision was taken although public health experts had warned against an inadequate sick pay scheme and the risks of prematurely ending universal free testing in England, showing concern for the most vulnerable sector of the population (Scientific Advisory Group for Emergency 2022). On January 5, 2022, in his statement to the House of Commons, Johnson had already anticipated an easing of restrictions despite the Omicron wave in December 2021 that had urged the implementation of 'Plan B' (amounting to such measures as work from home, mandatory face masks in public indoor venues, self-isolation and daily testing for COVID-19). The aim was to slow the spread of the variant, relieve the pressure on the NHS and gain time for boosters.

Along this line, Boris Johnson's discourse on COVID-19 could be described as going from the overriding hypermasculine and martial frames adopted to describe the first pandemic waves (hence political muscle flexing, war metaphors and military terms) to a less inflated stance where other linguistic and discursive features appear more salient. In light of the above, this analysis posits two research questions that intend to describe Johnson's rhetorical attuning to the new normal. The first research question focusses on

Boris Johnson's framing of the post-peak phase of the pandemic, as conveyed in his parliamentary statements, press conferences, releases, interviews and comments, from January 5 to his final speech on September 6, 2022, his last day in office. The second research question discusses the prime minister's narrative against the social repercussions of the health crisis as portrayed in his own account of NHS difficulties, the country's economic challenges and the British people's uncertain morale. The aim of the analysis is to contribute to a wider investigation of how "executive political discourse relat[es] to the temporalities of the COVID-19 pandemic" (Jarvis 2022: 30).

2. Data and methods

The linguistic data examined here are drawn from a heterogeneous mini-corpus of thirteen scripted texts that announce Boris Johnson's COVID-related policies after the 2020-21 emergency or, at some point, make reference to his government's past, current and future actions. They comprise different genres such as written and oral statements to the House of Commons, an interview with the BBC, and press releases and conferences, all within the time span between January 5 and September 6, 2022, when Johnson gave his final speech as prime minister before leaving office.

This study adopts a qualitative approach that draws from the concept of framing to observe in what ways a specific interpretation or perspective in text is constructed by salient linguistic cues (Entman 1993). Framing is combined with the toolbox of Critical Discourse Studies to show how any communicative act conveys an ideological stance and is enmeshed in power dynamics, which are encoded in the selection of linguistic and discursive features, as well as textual inclusions and omissions (Hart and Cap 2014; Wodak and Meyer 2016). With regard to the coronavirus pandemic, a wide range of studies have explored how leaders, health authorities and the news media framed their messages to engage public opinion, justify the adoption of often unpopular health restrictions and encourage safety behaviours (Cap 2021; Andrews 2022; Jarvis 2022). Prominent are those that investigate how conceptual metaphors may influence health-related decisions (Scherer et al. 2015) and work as cognitive, discourse-based and practice-based devices (Chilton 2004; Charteris-Black 2014, 2019; Flusberg, Matlock, Thibodeau 2018;

Semino, Demjén, Demmen 2018; Islentyeva 2020): "each mapping between a particular target and source domain can emphasize a specific problem definition, cause, evaluation and solution for the same situation" (Brugman et al. 2022: 102).

In brief, politicians use metaphorical language to clarify their points, provoke emotional responses, enhance the communicative impact of the message, and avoid blame for unpopular choices. It explains why metaphors have abounded in COVID-19 communication since the beginning of the pandemic (Charteris-Black 2021; Garzone 2021; Kirk and McDonald 2021; Schönefeld 2021; Semino 2021; Musolff 2022), one reason among others being that "metaphor offers moral justification for their own policies" (Charteris-Black 2021: 284).

However, the complexity of post-pandemic contexts, in which citizens demand more thoughtful and less emotional answers, cannot be effectively conveyed by figurative language alone. Therefore, in examining Boris Johnson's construction of yet another narrative, following Brexit and the war on COVID-19, attention will also be given to the role of linguistic cues and discursive features beyond metaphor.

3. The long shadow of the pandemic

Boris Johnson's metaphorical flourishes are a defining trait of his bombastic communicative style (Charteris-Black 2019). During the peaks of the 2020-21 health crisis, it was observed that Johnson's communications "relied on three broad forms of talk: war metaphors, following the science, and concerned advice" (McVittie 2021: 2). In his own words, his government's handling of the emergency was explained and licensed by a variety of military, natural and spatial metaphors, such as "a call to arms" to "turn the tide around", "flatten the peak (*of infections*), squash that sombrero", just to name a few (Demianyk 2020; Landler 2020; Rawlinson 2020). Likewise, the successful vaccination campaign was announced by "the distant bugle of the scientific cavalry coming over the brow of the hill" (Charteris-Black 2021: 270), while the sudden spread of a new variant in fall 2021 was described as the "tidal wave of Omicron coming" (Gillett 2021). As for the rhetorical strategy of inviting the nation to "follow the science" and offering concerned advice, it was criticised as a form of "empiricist accounting" aiming to "avoid accountability" for one's leadership (McVittie 2021: 4), particularly when the advice provided was contradictory.

In the long term, the conventional war frame that was relatively effective in the early stages of the pandemic, partly due to the persistent myth of the Blitz in the nation's collective memory, has proven to be ineffective for psychological, epidemiological and political reasons. First, "it is offensive to suggest that those inflicted by the disease have been called to combat, as if their survival depends on inherent willpower rather than medical, social and economic factors far beyond their control" (Freedman 2020a). Second, post-pandemic times are negatively affected by *a.* endemic COVID-19; *b.* the post-viral chronic syndrome figuratively named 'long Covid' and first described in patient-based accounts of the illness (Callard and Perego 2021); *c.* the 'long shadow of the pandemic', an emergent conceptual metaphor in news and public discourse that aims to portray the social and economic impact of the pandemic, including overwhelmed public health systems (Christakis 2020; Rushforth et al. 2021). Finally, a real war, not a metaphorical one, is creating havoc in Europe.[2] All these factors introduce long-term timescales and prioritise new values beyond stamina, preparedness and resilience. In the long Covid context, an appeal to the 'Blitz spirit' as an apt model of national unity and heroic perseverance, such as that made by Johnson in March 2020, would fall flat.

As the prime minister begins to establish a 'living with Covid' rhetorical terrain "after two of the darkest grimmest years in our peacetime history" (Johnson 2022g), a change in the framing of political messages and the use of metaphors is perceivable. This turning point in discourse would seem to betray the need for more "adaptive policymaking" (Cairney 2021: 110), while the "production of COVID-19 as a moment of temporal discontinuity [*is*] completed, finally, with the imagination of the post-pandemic climate as a 'new normal'" (Jarvis 2022: 32).

---

[2] Boris Johnson did not waste time claiming that the UK has been "leading the west in standing up to Putin's aggression in Ukraine" (Johnson 2022l).

4. "Giving our NHS the funding it needs"

In Boris Johnson's own account, the first serious repercussion of the pandemic is represented by the extraordinary pressure on the NHS, resulting in record waiting times in hospital and secondary care and staffing shortages.

(1) I will make a Statement on the Omicron variant, and our measures to contain this virus, fortify our NHS and keep our country open. [...]
All of these measures are helping to [...] manage the immediate pressures on our NHS and buy time for the boosters to take effect. [...] faced with these pressures on our NHS. [...]
[...] this will continue to increase the pressures on our NHS.
This is the very best way to save lives, reduce the pressure on our NHS and keep our country open. (Johnson 2022a)

(2) There remain, of course, significant pressures on the NHS. (Johnson 2022b)

(3) Covid led to the longest waiting lists we've ever seen, so we will deliver millions more scans, checks and operations in the biggest catch-up programme in the NHS' history. We know this won't be a quick fix, and we know that we can't fix waiting lists without fixing social care. Our reforms will end the cruel lottery of spiralling and unpredictable care costs once and for all and bring the NHS and social care closer together. (Johnson 2022h)

(4) It is therefore right that this Government are now investing more in our NHS than any other Government in history, giving our NHS the funding it needs to help to clear the covid backlogs. (Johnson 2022i)

(5) We are tackling the covid backlogs – hiring thousands more doctors and nurses to speed up treatments. (Johnson 2022j)

In the above excerpts, figurative expressions drawn from the conceptual metaphors of COVID-19 as the enemy to fight ("contain this virus, fortify our NHS") and of confinement as imprisonment ("keep our country open") are intertwined. Containment measures and the vaccine booster campaign are set in place to "save lives". However, unlike the enforced lockdown, quarantines and restrictions of the pandemic peaks, current measures do not limit freedom of movement or close national borders. Confinement as a preventive public health intervention belongs to the past and any restrictions would now be intolerable.

Though in a cooling-down phase, the defensive war is still ongoing and impacting the quality and costs of healthcare services ("pressures", "covid backlogs", "waiting lists"). In response, the government pledges immediate and future support ("helping", "investing", "tackling", "we will deliver", "we will end"), while announcing reforms in health and social care that will take time to be implemented ("this won't be a quick fix") and will probably imply budget cuts to contain expenses ("the cruel lottery of spiralling and unpredictable care costs").

Despite Johnson's claim of unprecedented investment in public healthcare, critics object that the Conservative Party "does not believe in the NHS but does not dare to say so" (Savage 2022), partly because it is a national icon, though consistently underfunded.[3] After the government's initial hesitancy in March 2020, the lockdown was enforced in the spirit of "stay home, protect the NHS, save lives". The message was carried by the red and yellow lectern sign at the televised daily government press conferences held at 10 Downing Street. However, "[t]he simplicity of the slogan adopted by the government [...] hid a tension. Ensuring the NHS could cope might have been a necessary condition to saving lives, but it was not sufficient" (Freedman 2020b: 58). Although extra funding for the NHS had been promised during the 2019 election campaign before Johnson's resounding victory (Clarke 2020), "long-standing disinvestment in the public sector left the health system, and especially the public health system and social care, in particular jeopardy" (Horton 2021: 865). In addition, among the negative effects of Brexit there is the high number of EU health workers that have left the NHS since the referendum.

5. "We can live with Covid without letting our guard down"

The lifting of any remaining legal restrictions was anticipated in the two oral statements to the House of Commons, delivered on January 5 and 19 respectively.

---

[3] "We must be there for our NHS in the same way that it is there for us" (Johnson 2022h).

(6) [T]his government does not believe we need to shut down our country again. Instead we are taking a balanced approach, using the protection of the boosters and the Plan B measures to reduce the spread of the virus, while acting to strengthen our NHS, protect critical national services and keep supply chains open.
[…] Mr Speaker, our balanced approach also means that where specific measures are no longer serving their purpose, they will be dropped.
[…] Mr Speaker, all of these measures are balanced and proportionate ways of ensuring we can live with Covid without letting our guard down. (Johnson 2022a)

(7) […] we will set out our long-term strategy for living with Covid-19, explaining how we hope and intend to protect our liberty and avoid restrictions in future by relying instead on medical advances – especially the vaccines which have already saved so many lives. (Johnson 2022b)

Again, the metaphorical framing is recognisably that of a protracted defensive war ("long-term strategy", "keep supply chains open", "without letting our guard down", "saved lives") against the disease, represented as an active and aggressive force of nature ("the spread of the virus"). The binomial "we hope and intend", in which the feeling of hope works as a form of affective hedge to mere willpower, suggests that a positive outcome is still uncertain despite the successful vaccine and booster rollout. Saving human lives should not be decoupled from the protection of "our liberty" through "balanced and proportionate" measures, aiming to "avoid restrictions in future". Likewise, on January 31, at the launch of VisitBritain's campaign to attract international tourists, Johnson mentions "the phenomenal success of our booster campaign and the extraordinary efforts of the public", making the UK "officially one of the most open countries in Europe and ready to welcome visitors from across the globe" (Johnson 2022c).

In the oral statement to the House of Commons on February 21, the prime minister's position with regard to the end of all restrictions is fully articulated.

(8) Covid will not suddenly disappear.
So those who would wait for a total end to this war before lifting

the remaining regulations, would be restricting the liberties of the British people for a long time to come.
This government does not believe that is right or necessary.
Restrictions pose a heavy toll on our economy, our society, our mental wellbeing, and the life chances of our children.
And we do not need to pay that cost any longer.
We have a population that is protected by the biggest vaccination programme in our history.
We have the antivirals, the treatments, and the scientific understanding of this virus, and we have the capabilities to respond rapidly to any resurgence or new variant.
And Mr Speaker it is time to get our confidence back.
We don't need laws to compel people to be considerate of others.
We can rely on that sense of responsibility towards one another, providing practical advice in the knowledge that people will follow it to avoid infecting loved ones and others.
So let us learn to live with this virus and continue protecting ourselves without restricting our freedoms. (Johnson 2022f)

In this speech, Johnson's frequently repeated line of the war against the resurgence of coronavirus cases coexists with the overriding country-as-prison metaphor. With their "heavy toll on our economy, our society, our mental wellbeing, and the life chances of our children", restrictions are lethal to "the liberties of the British people" and accompanying "Brexit freedoms" (Johnson 2022i, j, m), a historical and political sign of that British exceptionalism his government has promised to protect. Second, as he had announced in a BBC interview in February 2022 in anticipation of the 'living with Covid' plan, "now is the moment for everybody to get their confidence back [...]. We think you can shift the balance away from state mandation" (Johnson 2022e). Third, trust in the British people's exercise of personal responsibility is prioritised over political responsibility ("We don't need laws to compel people to be considerate of others"), again the trademark of his right-wing populism (Lorenzetti 2022).

Later that day, the speech at the Covid press conference rephrases the same points, condensing the government's response to the post-pandemic context for the general public.

(9) Good evening, when the pandemic began, we had little knowledge of this virus and none about the vaccines and treatments we have today.

So there was no option but to use government regulations to protect our NHS and save lives.

[…] But those restrictions on our liberties have brought grave costs to our economy, our society, and the chances of our children.

So from the outset, we were clear that we must chart a course back towards normality as rapidly as possible, by developing the vaccines and treatments that could gradually replace those restrictions.

And as a result of possibly the greatest national effort in our peacetime history, that is exactly what we have done.

[…] And while the pandemic is not over, we have passed the peak of the Omicron wave, with cases falling, and hospitalisations in England now fewer than 10,000 and still falling, and so now we have the chance to complete that transition back towards normality, while maintaining the contingencies to respond to a resurgence or a new variant.

[…] In England, we will remove all remaining domestic restrictions in law.

From this Thursday, it will no longer be law to self-isolate if you test positive, and so we will also end the provision of self-isolation support payments, although Statutory Sick Pay can still be claimed for a further month.

If you're a fully vaccinated close contact or under 18 you will no longer be asked to test daily for seven days.

And if you are close contact who is not fully vaccinated you will no longer be required to self-isolate.

Until 1 April, we will still advise you to stay at home if you test positive.

But after that, we will encourage people with Covid symptoms to exercise personal responsibility, just as we encourage people who may have flu to be considerate towards others.

[…] Today is not the day we can declare victory over Covid, because this virus is not going away. But it is the day when all the efforts of the last two years finally enabled us to protect ourselves while restoring our liberties in full. And after two of the darkest grimmest years in our peacetime history, I do believe this is a moment of pride for our nation and a source of hope for all that we can achieve in the years to come. (Johnson 2022g)

The above excerpt illustrates the several layers of meaning and the ideological load of the 'living with Covid' frame. A statement ("today is not the day we can declare victory over Covid") emphatically concedes that the fight is not over ("this virus is not going away") and the present still uncertain. Meanwhile, the government's effort to "chart the course back towards normality"/"complete that transition back towards normality" is admittedly gradual. The metaphorical framing selected here is that of the nation-as-vehicle, guided through difficult times and brought to rescue by the Tory government, making "possibly the greatest national effort in our peacetime history". Moreover, Johnson insists on repeating that legal restrictions should be lifted since they constrain "our economy, our society, and the chances of our children". Opening up the country is the right way to protect the national economy in the true spirit of British liberties and Brexit freedoms. Personal responsibility and mutual consideration are invoked, using "moral coercion where legal coercion [is] no longer deemed necessary" (Charteris-Black 2021: 201). This stance, however, is problematic in so far as the emphasis is mostly placed on "what individuals should do to the exclusion of what government should do, and serves to justify government inaction" (Reicher, Michie, West 2022: 1). Lastly, in a widening focus that embraces the entire country, British exceptionalism – the driving force behind Brexit – is trumpeted ("this is a moment of pride for our nation").

Johnson's Loyal Address speech of May 10, which takes up the main points of the 2022 Queen's Speech, i.e. his own government's programme, adds further interesting touches to his post-pandemic narrative.

> (10) Let me send a clear message from this House today: this Government will tackle the post-covid "mañana" culture. We will take whatever steps are necessary to deliver for the British people, because the British people are not prepared to wait, and we share their impatience.
> We will get through the aftershocks of covid, just as we got through covid, as I have told you, Mr Speaker, with every ounce of ingenuity, compassion and hard work. We will do so not by irresponsible spending that merely treats the symptoms of rising prices while creating an ever-bigger problem for tomorrow, but by urgently pressing on with our mission to create the high-wage, high-skilled jobs that will drive economic growth across the United Kingdom – the whole United Kingdom. That is the long-term, sustainable solution to ease the burden on families and businesses. That is the way to get our country back on track after the pandemic, to unite and to level up across our whole country, exactly as we promised.

That is what this Queen's Speech delivers. I commend it to the House. (Johnson 2022i)

In Johnson's speech, a sequence of pledges "to deliver for the British people" ("this Government will tackle", "we will take", "we will get through", "we will do so") is followed by three marked declaratives that anaphorically refer back to the stated political agenda ("That is what this Queen's Speech delivers"). The "aftershocks of covid" phrase reiterates the conceptual metaphor of the disease as a force of nature, in this case an earthquake, whose rubble has placed a "burden on families and businesses" and tested the nation's resilience. The "symptoms of rising prices" phrase introduces the society-as-living-organism metaphor frame, representing the economic recession as an illness of the body politic and transferring the experience of disease from the individual to the whole country. The complex anthropological phenomenon of widespread social malaise after loss, trauma, enforced confinement, financial distress, and altered work and life patterns is simplified and stigmatised as "the post-covid 'mañana' culture". Borrowing the word for 'tomorrow' from Spanish, the 'mañana' culture stereotypically associates the attitude to procrastination with the south of Europe. For the prime minister, it is a deplorable, non-British trait that is dangerously permeating the civil service in the UK. Economic recovery will be achieved not by raising inflation ("irresponsible spending") but by driving the "whole United Kingdom" "back on track after the pandemic", where the country-as-vehicle metaphor frame is adopted. Such "a long-term, sustainable solution" – the use of the singular suggests that no other options are contemplated – includes upskilling ("high-wage", "high-skilled jobs") and "levelling up" the country.[4] Recovery plans should be carried out quickly, wasting no time (*fast*, *fastest* and *speed* feature among Boris Johnson's favourite words) and tackling inertia, a kind of long Covid of the social organism.

A combination of frames already encountered in this analysis appears in the Housing Speech of June 9, which provides a good

---

[4] 'Levelling Up' is a flagship policy first elaborated in the Conservative Manifesto 2019 before Johnson's landslide victory. A kind of soft populism, it aims to change the UK's economic geography and reduce inequality in wealth and income between different parts of the UK (Jennings, McKay, Stoker 2021).

example of the synergistic effects and polysemous quality of metaphorical language. Here Johnson represents the post-pandemic context as recovering from an exceptional catastrophe ("aftermath" may collocate with "war", "disaster" and "crisis"), refers to the long-term consequences of the pandemic as an illness of the body politic ("the lingering effects of Covid"), and elaborates on the country-as-ship and economy-as-engine metaphors.

> (11) The global headwinds are strong.
> But our engines – the great, supercharged, ultragreen marine propulsion units of the UK economy – are stronger, we will get through it.
> Today we are living in the aftermath of the worst pandemic for a century, and once again we are steering into the wind. We face global pressures on prices caused by the lingering effects of Covid and the shock of Putin's aggression in Ukraine. We will get through it, we will get through it just as we got through the far greater challenge of covid, and the colossal fall in output that entailed. (Johnson 2022j)

The country's progress through the adverse conditions of the post-pandemic rough sea ("the global headwinds are strong", "once again we are steering into the wind") is propelled by its stronger economic engine. To be noted, this engine is described as both "supercharged" and "ultragreen", thus implying its social sustainability. Under Johnson's energetic leadership – "we will get through it" is repeated three times – the UK's complete economic recovery is rhetorically foregrounded as real.

Delivered on the steps of 10 Downing Street on July 7, the prime minister's resignation speech is a self-congratulatory celebration of his commitment "to taking this country forward through tough times", from getting Brexit done to the fastest exit from lockdown and military support to Ukraine.

> (12) I am immensely proud of the achievements of this government from getting Brexit done and settling our relations with the continent after half a century reclaiming the power for this country to make its own laws in parliament getting us all through the pandemic delivering the fastest vaccine rollout in Europe the fastest exit from lockdown and in the last few months leading the west in standing up to Putin's aggression.

[...] as we've seen at Westminster, the herd is powerful and when the herd moves, it moves and my friends in politics no one is remotely indispensable. And our brilliant and Darwinian system will produce another leader equally committed to taking this country forward through tough times. (Johnson 2022l)

Worthy of note is the 'herd' metaphor to portray his detractors in the parliamentary party as animals moving in group to oust the isolated leader. The image ironically backfires on the false promise to achieve 'herd immunity' by natural infection that was advanced at the onset of the pandemic.

In his farewell speech as prime minister on September 6, 2022, Johnson extols the main achievements of his leadership – Brexit, the fastest vaccine rollout in Europe, early supplies of weapons to Ukraine, a recovering economy – granting "this government nothing but the most fervent support" (Johnson 2022m).

(13) [...] let me say that I am now like one of those booster rockets that has fulfilled its function and I will now be gently re-entering the atmosphere and splashing down invisibly in some remote and obscure corner of the Pacific.
And like Cincinnatus I am returning to my plough. (Johnson 2022m)

At the end of a scandal-ridden tenure, one might have expected Boris Johnson to describe his exit from the political stage as an anticlimax. In fact, his tones remain self-aggrandising. Two metaphor frames are here intertwined, that of the country-as-spaceship (a high-tech version of the country-as-ship) and that of himself as a booster rocket landing somewhere in the ocean after propelling the spaceship in outer space. Finally, after having impressed dynamism to the nation's recovery, the politician can retire like the Roman patrician and hero Cincinnatus.

6. Concluding Remarks

During the pandemic, Boris Johnson's "heroic leadership model, and its associated imagery, has been actively constructed through management of the Government's narrative" (Andrews 2021: 222) and supported by the Tory press. It is the war metaphor, with echoes of World War II, Winston Churchill and the Blitz, that acted as the main framing device of his COVID-19 communication.

In the post-pandemic context, however, as this analysis has illustrated, no definite victory or "armistice day" (Ball 2022) can be declared over the virus. Besides, the lingering effects of Covid in society (the overburdened NHS, delays in public services, people's lack of confidence) cast a shadow over full recovery. This affects the ways in which the prime minister discursively frames his government's decisions and communicates them to Parliament and the general public. While the warfare frame of the past two years is de-emphasised, the 'living with Covid' narrative is set against a changed background and a different timescale, with long-term sustainable solutions that require a fast implementation.

Johnson's rhetorical focus now emphasises the full restoration of civil liberties to keep the country and its economy open, often sidelining scientists and behaviour experts on COVID-19 measures. Despite an ongoing inquiry, no admission is made of his government's poor performance of the public health crisis. The plan to redress the structural difficulties of the NHS in fact anticipates cuts to spiralling public expenses. Lifting legal restrictions is possible as the trustworthy British people will be willing to adopt a morally responsible behaviour, although this amounts to abdicating political responsibility to the individual. Economic recovery is prioritised at all costs without taking stock of the nation's feeling of exhaustion. In conclusion, the prime minister's post-pandemic COVID-related communication appears to largely ignore the complexity of the new normal, in and out of metaphor.

References

Section A

JOHNSON, BORIS, 2022a, "PM statement to the House of Commons on COVID-19", oral statement to Parliament, January 5, https://www.gov.uk/government/speeches/pm-statement-to-the-house-of-commons-on-covid-19-5-january-2022, last accessed September 9, 2022.

JOHNSON, BORIS, 2022b, "PM statement to the House of Commons on COVID-19, oral statement to Parliament, January 19, https://www.gov.uk/government/speeches/pm-statement-to-the-house-of-commons-on-covid-19-19-january-2022, January 19, last accessed September 9, 2022.

JOHNSON, BORIS, 2022c, "Prime Minister Declares UK One of the Most Open Countries in Europe and Ready for an International Tourism Boom", press release, January 25, https://www.gov.uk/government/news/prime-minister-declares-uk-one-of-the-most-open-countries-in-europe-and-ready-for-an-international-tourism-boom, last accessed September 9, 2022.

JOHNSON, BORIS, 2022d, "PM Statement on the Sue Gray Report", oral statement to Parliament, January 31, https://www.gov.uk/government/speeches/pm-statement-on-the-sue-gray-report-31-january-2022, last accessed September 9, 2022.

JOHNSON, BORIS, 2022e, "Do Not Throw Caution to the Wind on Covid", BBC News interview, February 20, https://www.bbc.com/news/uk-60446908, last accessed September 9, 2022.

JOHNSON, BORIS, 2022f, "PM Statement on Living with COVID", oral statement to Parliament, February 21, https://www.gov.uk/government/speeches/pm-statement-on-living-with-covid-21-february-2022, last accessed September 9, 2022.

JOHNSON, BORIS, 2022g, "PM statement at Covid Press Conference", February 21, https://www.gov.uk/government/speeches/pm-statement-at-covid-press-conference-21-february-2022, last accessed September 9, 2022.

JOHNSON, BORIS, with SAJID DAVID and RISHI SUNAK, 2022h, "Health and Social Care Levy to Raise Billions for NHS and Social Care", press release, April 6, https://www.gov.uk/government/news/health-and-social-care-levy-to-raise-billions-for-nhs-and-social-care, last accessed September 9, 2022.

JOHNSON, BORIS, 2022i, "Loyal Address Speech", May 10, https://www.ukpol.co.uk/boris-johnson-2022-loyal-address-speech, last accessed September 9, 2022.

JOHNSON, BORIS, 2022j, "Prime Minister's Housing Speech", June 9, https://www.gov.uk/government/speeches/prime-ministers-housing-speech-9-june-2022, last accessed September 9, 2022.

JOHNSON, BORIS, 2022k, "Statement on COVID-19 Inquiry", written statement to Parliament, June 28, https://questions-statements.parliament.uk/written-statements/detail/2022-06-28/hcws152, last accessed September 9, 2022.

JOHNSON, BORIS, 2022l, "Prime Minister Boris Johnson's Statement in Downing Street", resignation speech, July 7, https://www.gov.uk/government/speeches/prime-minister-boris-johnsons-statement-in-downing-street-7-july-2022, last accessed September 9, 2022.

JOHNSON, BORIS, 2022m, "Final Speech as Prime Minister", September 6, https://www.gov.uk/government/speeches/boris-johnsons-final-speech-as-prime-minister-6-september-2022, last accessed September 9, 2022.

Section B

ANDREWS, LEIGHTON, 2022, "Mortality, Blame Avoidance and the State: Constructing Boris Johnson's Exit Strategy", in S. Price and B. Harbisher (eds), *Power, Media and the Covid-19 Pandemic: Framing Public Discourse*, Routledge, Abingdon-New York, pp. 220-235.

BALL, PHILIP, 2022, "Reaching for Military Metaphors Won't Help Britain Learn to Live with Covid", *The Guardian,* January 24, https://www.theguardian.com/commentisfree/2022/jan/24/britain-covid-how-pandemics-end, last accessed September 9, 2022.

BRUGMAN, BRITTA C., DROOG, ELLEN, REIJNIERSE, W. GUDRUN, LEYMANN, SASKIA, FREZZA, GIULIA, RENARDEL DE LAVALETTE, KIKI Y., 2022, "Audience Perceptions of COVID-19 Metaphors: The Role of Source Domain and Country Context", *Metaphor and Symbol* 37 (2), pp. 101-113.

CAIRNEY, PAUL, 2021, "The UK Government's COVID-19 Policy: Assessing Evidence-Informed Policy Analysis in Real Time", *British Politics* 16, pp. 90-116.

CALLARD, FELICITY and ELISA PEREGO, 2021, "How and Why Patients Made Long Covid", *Social Science & Medicine* 268:113426, pp. 1-5.

CAP, PIOTR, 2021, "Alternative Futures in Political Discourse", *Discourse & Society* 32 (3), pp. 328-345.

CHARTERIS-BLACK, JONATHAN, 2014, *Analysing Political Speeches: Rhetoric, Discourse and Metaphor*, Palgrave Macmillan, Basingstoke-London.

CHARTERIS-BLACK, JONATHAN, 2019, *Metaphors of Brexit: No Cherries on the Cake?*, Palgrave Macmillan/Springer Nature, Cham.

CHARTERIS-BLACK, JONATHAN, 2021, *Metaphors of Coronavirus: Invisible Enemy or Zombie Apocalypse?*, Palgrave Macmillan/Springer Nature, Cham.

CHILTON, PAUL, 2004, *Analysing Political Discourse: Theory and Practice*, Routledge, London-New York.

CLARKE, JOHN, 2020, "Building the 'Boris' Bloc: Angry Politics in Turbulent Times", *Soundings: A Journal of Politics and Culture* 74, pp. 118-135.

COUPLAND, NIKOLAS, 2022, "Normativity, Language and Covid-19", in J. Mortensen and K. Kraft (eds), *Norms and the Study of Language in Social Life*, De Gruyter Mouton, Berlin-Boston, pp. 211-232.

CHRISTAKIS, NICHOLAS, 2020, "The Long Shadow of the Pandemic: 2024 and Beyond", *Wall Street Journal*, October 16, https://www.wsj.com/articles/the-long-shadow-of-the-pandemic-2024-and-beyond-11602860214, last accessed September 9, 2022.

DEMIANYK, GRAEME, 2020, "UK Government Trapped in Metaphor Hell in Response to Vaccine Hope: Tooting on Bugles. Penalty Shoot-outs. Train Doors!", *Huffington Post*, November 9, https://

www.huffingtonpost.co.uk/entry/uk-government-metaphors-covid-vaccine_uk_5fa99134c5b66009569d403d, last accessed September 9, 2022.

DRYLIE-CAREY, LINDSEY, SÁNCHEZ-CASTILLO, SEBASTIÁN, GALÁN-CUBILLO, ESTEBAN, 2020, "European Leaders Unmasked: COVID-19 Communication Strategy through Twitter", *Profesional de la información* 29 (5), pp. 1-15.

ENTMAN, ROBERT M., 1993, "Framing: Toward Clarification of a Fractured Paradigm", *Journal of Communication* 43 (4), pp. 51-58.

FLUSBERG, STEPHEN J., MATLOCK, TEENIE, THIBODEAU, PAUL H., 2018, "War Metaphors in Public Discourse", *Metaphor and Symbol* 33 (1), pp. 1-18.

FREEDMAN, LAWRENCE, 2020a, "Coronavirus and the Language of War", *The New Statesman*, April 11, https://www.newstatesman.com/sciencetech/2020/04/coronavirusand-language-war, last accessed September 9, 2022.

FREEDMAN, LAWRENCE, 2020b, "Strategy for a Pandemic: The UK and COVID-19", *Survival: Global Politics and Strategy* 62 (3), pp. 25-76.

GARZONE, GIULIANA, 2021, "Re-thinking Metaphors in COVID-19 Communication", *Lingue & Linguaggi* 44, pp. 159-181.

GILLETT, FRANCESCA, 2021, "Covid: Boris Johnson Sets New Booster Target over 'Omicron Tidal Wave'", *BBC News*, December 13, https://www.bbc.com/news/uk-59631570, last accessed September 9, 2022.

HANCOCK, ALEXANDER, 2021, "The Language of War and Covid", *PI Media*, May 12, https://uclpimedia.com/online/the-language-of-war-and-covid, last accessed September 9, 2022.

HART, CHRISTOPHER and CAP, PIOTR (eds), 2014, *Contemporary Critical Discourse Studies*, Bloomsbury, London.

HORTON, RICHARD, 2021, "Offline: It's Time to Ask Questions and Learn Lessons", *The Lancet* 397 (10277), p. 865.

ISLENTYEVA, ANNA, 2020, "On the Front Line in the Fight against the Virus: Conceptual Framing and War Patterns in Political Discourse", *Yearbook of the German Cognitive Linguistics Association* 8 (1), pp. 157-180.

JARVIS, LEE, 2022, "Constructing the Coronavirus Crisis: Narratives of Time in British Political Discourse on COVID-19", *British Politics* 17 (1), pp. 24-43.

JENNINGS, WILL, MCKAY, LAWRENCE, STOKER, GERRY, 2021, "The Politics of Levelling Up", *The Political Quarterly* 92 (2), pp. 302-311.

KIRK, JESSICA and MCDONALD, MATT, 2021, "The Politics of Exceptionalism: Securitization and COVID-19", *Global Studies Quarterly* 1 (3), pp. 1-12.

LANDLER, MARK, 2020, "For Boris Johnson, and Maybe Trump, Covid as Metaphor Is Hard to Shake", *The New York Times,* October 20, https://www.nytimes.com/2020/10/10/world/europe/boris-johnson-trump-covid.html, last accessed September 9, 2022.

LIÉGEOIS, VINCE AND MATHYSEN, JOLYEN, 2022, "Frames Featuring in Epidemiological Crisis Communication: A Frame-Semantic Analysis of Pandemic Crisis Communication in Multilingual Belgium", *Lingue & Linguaggi* 47, pp. 297-329.

LILLEKER, DARREN G. and STOECKLE, THOMAS, 2021, "The Challenges of Providing Certainty in the Face of Wicked Problems: Analysing the UK Government's Handling of the COVID-19 Pandemic", *Journal of Public Affairs* 21 (4), pp. 1-10.

LORENZETTI, MARIA IVANA, 2022, "Dramatising Crisis: Rhetorical Responses to the COVID-19 Pandemic by Right-Wing Populist Leaders in the USA and UK", *Lingue & Linguaggi* 47, pp. 13-45.

MCVITTIE, CHRIS, 2021, "Shaping the UK Government's Public Communications on COVID-19: General, Follower, Other?", *Qualitative Research Reports in Communication*, online, pp. 1-8.

MUSOLFF, ANDREAS, 2022, "World-beating" Pandemic Responses: Ironical, Sarcastic, and Satirical Use of War and Competition Metaphors in the Context of COVID-19 Pandemic", *Metaphor and Symbol*, 37 (2), pp. 76-87.

PÉREZ-SOBRINO, PAULA, SEMINO, ELENA, IBARRETXE-ANTUÑANO, IRAIDE, KOLLER, VERONIKA, OLZA, INÉS, 2022, "*Acting like a Hedgehog in Times of Pandemic*: Metaphorical Creativity in the #reframecovid Collection", *Metaphor and Symbol*, 37 (2), pp. 127-139.

POWER, KATE and CROSTHWAITE, PETER, 2022, "Constructing COVID-19: A Corpus-Informed Analysis of Prime Ministerial Crisis Response Communication by Gender", *Discourse & Society* 33 (3), pp. 411-437.

RAWLINSON, KEVIN, 2020, "Bugles, Shootouts, Trains? Covid Vaccine Hopes Prompt Strained Analogies". *The Guardian*, November 9, https://www.theguardian.com/politics/2020/nov/09/bugles-shootouts-trains-covid-vaccine-hopes-prompt-strained-analogies, last accessed September 9, 2022.

REICHER, STEPHEN, MICHIE, SUSAN, WEST, ROBERT, 2022, "The UK Government's 'Personal Responsibility' Policy for Covid Is Hypocritical and Unsustainable", *British Medical Journal* 378:o1903, pp. 1-2.

RUSHFORTH, ALEX, LADDS, EMMA, WIERINGA, SIETSE, TAYLOR, SHARON, HUSAIN, LAIBA, GREENHALGH, TRISHA, 2021, "Long Covid – The Illness Narratives", *Social Science & Medicine* 286:114326, pp. 1-9.

SAVAGE, WENDY, 2022, "How the Tory Party Has Systematically Run Down the NHS", *The Guardian,* August 3, https://www.theguardian.com/society/2022/aug/03/how-the-tory-party-has-systematically-run-down-the-nhs, last accessed September 9, 2022.

SCALLY, GABRIEL, JACOBSON, BOBBIE, ABBASI, KAMRAN, 2020, "The UK's Public Health Response to Covid-19: Too Little, Too Late, Too Flawed", *British Medical Journal* 369, pp. 1-3.

SCHERER, AARON M., SCHERER, LAURA D., FAGERLIN, ANGELA, 2015, "Getting Ahead of Illness: Using Metaphors to Influence Medical Decision Making", *Medical Decision Making* 35 (1), pp. 37-45.

SCHÖNEFELD, DORIS, 2021, "Framing in American and British Governmental Discourse about Covid-19", in G. Kristiansen, K. Franco, S. De Pascale, L. Rosseel and W. Zhang (eds), *Cognitive Sociolinguistics Revisited*, De Gruyter Mouton, Berlin-Boston, pp. 97-106.

SCIENTIFIC ADVISORY GROUP FOR EMERGENCIES (SAGE), 2022, "SPI-B: Social and Behavioural Impacts for Lifting Remaining Restrictions", February 10, https://www.gov.uk, last accessed September 9, 2022.

SEMINO, ELENA, 2021, "Not Soldiers but Fire-fighters" – Metaphors and Covid-19", *Health Communication* 36 (1), pp. 50-58.

SEMINO, ELENA, DEMJÉN, ZSÓFIA, DEMMEN, JANE, 2018, "An Integrated Approach to Metaphor and Framing in Cognition, Discourse, and Practice, with an Application to Metaphors for Cancer", *Applied Linguistics* 39 (5), pp. 625-645.

WARREN, GEORGE W. and LOFSTEDT, RAGNAR, 2021, "Risk Communication and COVID-19 in Europe: Lessons for Future Public Health Crises", *Journal of Risk Research*, online, pp. 1-15.

WHEELER, RICHARD, 2022, "Starmer Brands Johnson a 'Pathetic Spectacle' in 'Dying Act of Political Career'", *The Independent*, July 6, https://www.independent.co.uk/news/uk/boris-johnson-government-labour-mps-chris-pincher-prime-minister-b2117003.html, last accessed September 9, 2022.

WODAK, RUTH and MEYER, MICHAEL (eds), 2016, *Methods of Critical Discourse Studies*, third edition, Sage, London-Thousand Oaks (CA).

Framing the COVID-19 Pandemic Crisis in Financial Discourse.
A Sentence Embeddings Approach*

Walter Giordano, Katerina Mandenaki

Abstract
This study aims at identifying and interpreting recurrent frames in corporate communication, and in particular in CEO Letters to Shareholders, sent in 2020, the first year of the COVID-19 pandemic crisis. The identification and analysis of discursive frames can shed light on the discourse strategies deployed by companies as a function of their performance, and in particular on how in their Letters CEOs accounted for unexpected positive or negative financial performance due to *force majeure* contextual events, i.e., those related to the pandemic, through the use of linguistic resources designed to convey specific interpretations and evaluations of situations and issues. To accomplish this, the study proposes a novel methodology of approaching text by implementing computer assisted text analysis and state-of-the-art natural language processing techniques. The research has been carried out from a quantitative point of view experimenting with state-of-the-art neural networks models in generating frames from textual corpora.
Key-words: natural language processing, topic models, sentence embedding, framing in financial discourse, CEO letters, strategic communication.

1. Introduction

The COVID-19 pandemic has entailed a massive change in many aspects of people's ordinary life. It has re-designed, re-mediated,

* This study falls within the scope of the scientific research activities of DAF (Digital Accounting and Finance). Part of Università degli Studi di Napoli Federico II's spin-off K-Synth, DAF conducts research in the field of quantitative textual analysis and text mining. The two authors are jointly responsible for the design of the study, the findings and the conclusions. Section 1 and Section 6 have been written by Walter Giordano; Sections 3 and 4 have been written by Katerina Mandenaki . The two authors are jointly responsible for Sections 2 and 5, with Subsections 2.1, 5.1 and 5.2 being written by Walter Giordano and Subsections 2.2, 5.3 and 5.4 being written by Katerina Mandenaki.

ISSN 1824-3967

re-shaped and re-framed communication at all levels, from signs at hospitals to institutional corporate communication. The unprecedented magnitude of the change can be gauged both in terms of spread of new means of communication and in the content of the message. In particular, institutional corporate communication worldwide has experienced a necessary transformation, as companies had to cope not only with more demanding consumers, but especially with deeply changed business practices. Some industries were on the verge of a crash: companies with a flourishing business history in industries like tourism or HORECA (*Hotels, Restaurants and Catering*) had to reinvent themselves to survive; others, like logistics or consumer electronics, thrived in a brand-new business paradigm. The difficult task to communicate this historic earthquake in the global economy was entrusted not only to news and press releases, but also – strategically, and in a way that implied personal involvement – to CEOs, in their Letters included in companies' Annual Reports. The year 2020 was a turning point for many companies worldwide: most CEOs said it was "a difficult year". Not surprisingly, this assessment takes on a different underlying meaning whether stated by a CEO after a negative financial performance or by a CEO after a positive financial performance.

This paper aims at investigating on a comparative basis the corporate institutional communication of CEOs Letters immediately after the outbreak of the COVID-19 pandemic. The study is part of a much broader research project based on a comprehensive corpus consisting of the Annual Reports of 998 companies listed in stock indexes like Eurostock600, Standard&Poors500 and Nikkei225. The main comparative classification of the texts relies on the companies' reported yearly performance in these stock indexes: a company with a negative index is classified as a "loser", and a company with a positive index is classified as a "winner".

The main aim of the project, therefore, is to compare the discourse of losing and winning companies and study their differences, as well as the predictability in their communicative strategies in periods of global crisis, using natural language processing tools and computational methods. To do so, a first effort to identify the sentiment behind the narrative and the strategic tools used to convey meanings will be followed by the identification of the possible frames used in the Letters via statistical text analysis tools.

The investigation will try to answer the following research questions: what communication strategies are adopted by CEOs in the midst of the pandemic crisis? Is it possible to detect one or more recurrent frames in such historic institutional business communication?

After these introductory remarks, Section 2 contains a literature review of institutional business communication, as well as a theoretical background on the notion of framing and its role in discourse. Section 3 provides a detailed description of the corpus, while Section 4 contains the methodology we have used to analyse the corpus. In Section 5 we interpret and discuss the results. The conclusions are drawn in Section 6.

2. Theoretical background

2.1. Framing in financial discourse

Institutional business communication in modern economies is usually addressed through press releases, interviews to corporate representatives, or in special sections of companies' websites. While these texts provide information on specific aspects of corporate operations, strategy and performance, the document that is comprehensive of all the information on sustainability, strategy, financial position and reputation of a company is the Annual Report. Financial reporting has been studied extensively, either in the form of the Annual Report or in the form of the CEO Letter (also Chairman Letter, Chairman Statement or Letter to Shareholders). Studies have been carried out from a functional perspective (Malavasi 2005; Nickerson and de Groot 2005; Rutherford 2005; Amernic and Craig 2007; Garzone 2004, 2008; Breeze 2013; Giordano 2019, 2020), as well as from a diachronic or diatopic comparative perspective (Ruiz-Garrido, Fortanet-Gomez, Palmer-Silveira 2012; Palmer-Silveira and Ruiz Garrido 2014; Conaway and Wardrope 2010). In much of the existing literature, the communication conveyed via Annual Reports is seen as highly significant and a reliable source of information for what concerns identity construction, stance and strategic focus. It is worth pointing out, in this respect, that the generic structure of annual reports has undergone some change over time (Giordano 2020: 20), and so have the form of the message, the audience and the "moves" which make up this form of communication (Gillaerts

1996; Garzone 2008). This has implied a renewed concern and attention on the part of CEOs aimed at exploiting any possible communicative strategy to provide the external world (customers, stakeholders, financial analysts, banks, etc.) with a well outlined disclosure of information.

This concern was the cornerstone of financial communication in the COVID-19 era. In 2020 – a year marked by an unprecedented and unforeseeable crisis – regardless of whether they had profited from the pandemic (winners) or experienced losses (losers), all players had to make sure that their CEO Letters depicted the company's work in the best possible light. With reference to crisis communication, the strategic moves of companies and their public relations departments in times of crisis have been extensively studied (Kim, Avery, Lariscy 2009; Ingenhoff and Sommer 2010; Valvi and Fragkos 2012; Giordano 2019), but mostly with reference to scandals or wrongdoings, with crises arising from events out of the control of companies and on a scale such as that of the COVID-19 pandemic being markedly absent from current scholarship. The present investigation aims to fill this gap by shedding light on the framing strategies detectable in corporate information issued in the immediate aftermath of the COVID-19 pandemic and the consequent unprecedented financial results.

Framing is a well-established discourse analysis tool especially suited to studying people's understanding of ordinary life events through the identification of the schemata used for their interpretation (Goffmann 1974: 21). A comprehensive definition of framing is provided by Entman in the following terms:

To frame is to select some aspects of a perceived reality and make them more salient in a communicative text, in such a way as to promote a particular problem definition, causal interpretation, moral evaluation, and/ or treatment recommendation for the items described. (Entman 1993: 52)

Hallahan claims that framing is used to make the meaning of a message more directly accessible, and to lead the audience to concentrate on particular portions of the message in order to generate a favourable response (Hallahan 2005: 340). Hallahan further stresses the importance of the psychological component in this process, as framing operates at both the conscious and subconscious levels. Consequently, framing guides the way people are expected not only to receive the message but also to make inferences about events and to impute meaning not manifested in the message itself via association and expectation (Hallahan 1999: 208). This suggests that frames play a key, albeit subtle, role in fostering preferred interpretations of events. In this respect, for instance, Kapranov claims that in foregrounding some aspects and backgrounding others, frames are an effective tool for making the narrative context clearer and suggesting possible solutions to problems (Kapranov 2018: 56). Fiss and Hirsch give even greater emphasis to the strategic role of framing by making a distinction between framing and sensemaking: in their view, sensemaking is the internal process of meaning construction upon the "raw world", and provides the background against which an "account of what is going on" is discursively constructed at a structural level, while framing is the external strategy whereby meanings are functionally created to serve specific purposes (Fiss and Hirsch 2005: 31).

These characteristics make the notion of framing highly relevant for the field of corporate communication and may be expected to play a key role in areas such as impression and reputation management. Indeed, this has been recognized in scholarly literature on the topic. For instance, Maier and Ravazzani have highlighted how by organizing, assembling and downplaying meanings and experiences in particular ways in discourse, in order to represent some as more prominent compared to others (2018: 466), it is possible to shape public perception of business practices, ethics, reputation and responsibility.

2.2. Topic models and sentence embeddings

In this study, we have attempted to identify frames from our texts implementing two main techniques: topic models and sentence embeddings. Topic modeling is a broad name for a set of approaches and algorithms that detect clusters of words (topics) occurring frequently in document collections, thus revealing latent thematic organization and discursive clusters. For example, if a cluster of words such as "business", "investment", "stock", "financial" is assigned to an unknown news item, one can infer that the text is a business news story.

Furthermore, the semantic fields of any given word, as well as their closeness with other linguistic entities including verbs, nouns or bigrams, may be investigated using analytical techniques such as word embeddings for vector space models, i.e., vector-based representations of words that capture key aspects of semantic meaning. Rather than simple collocations of terms appearing together, word embedding models produce vectors, namely numerical representations of words based on their context (defined as a predetermined set of words before and after a nodal term). The result is a framework that makes it possible for computers to 'understand' word semantics by looking at how words cluster together in a high-dimensional vector space, thus producing what could be considered their semantic fields. For instance, in our corpus the embeddings for the term "COVID-19' were *'coronavirus'*, *'virus'*, *'COVID-19_pandemic'*, *'pandemic'*, *'disruption'*, *'lockdown_ measure'*, *'immune'*. Although it is beyond the scope of this paper to provide a thorough technical analysis of vector space models, it is worth noting that such models have been successfully implemented to study the evolution of cultural meanings and gender, race, and ethnicity stereotypes, to explore migration discourse, and to analyze and classify ideologies.

Furthering the affordances of word embedding algorithms, sentence embeddings encode the whole meaning of a sentence in a vector space by calculating several features of the words composing the sentence such as semantic meaning, syntactic structure and topic. More specifically, a computer can encode the existence or non-existence of a word in a sentence by simply assigning it the number 1 (exists) and 0 (does not exist). That is what is called one "hot encoding" which allows computers to simply calculate frequencies of words.

Embedding algorithms assign long and complex arrays of numbers to each word. Such numbers represent much more than its mere existence – namely, its position in the sentence, its context as well as its grammatical and syntactic characteristics. Embeddings have been known to be effective in disambiguating word sense (Sousa et al. 2020, Iacobacci et al. 2016) by distinguishing e.g., the use of the word *apple* as the fruit and as the company Apple©. More specifically, Conneau et al. (2018) examined what sentence embeddings actually capture as features, and according to their results these models take in surprising amounts of information (Arora et al. 2017; Adi et al. 2017) such as sentence length, word content, verb tenses, subjects and objects, as well as part of speech sequences. When used as a feature for other tasks, the information encoded in word embeddings was found to be particularly valuable in sentiment analysis (Le and Mikolov 2014) and paraphrase detection (Socher et al. 2011).

3. Data and corpus description

Our official sources of data were three main world stock indexes: Eurostock600 (Europe – 506 companies), Nikkei225 (Japan – 140 companies) and Standard&Poor's 500 (USA – 352 companies). We turned to a professional financial analyst[1], who provided the full set of companies listed in the indexes. We then retrieved their Annual Reports from their websites and extracted the CEO Letters. After "cleaning" the retrieved texts and removing non-values, we ended up with a corpus consisting of 998 Letters. Based on the companies' stock performance from 12/31/2019 to 12/31/2020, we created two subcorpora: companies that had reported a positive performance (winners – 504 Letters) and companies that reported a negative stock performance (losers – 494 Letters). This distinction was the hypothesis of our research, which aims to investigate the management communication behaviour following a positive or negative performance in a very peculiar year like 2020.

We point out that it is important to consider that the distinction was based upon the stock market performance of the companies considered. We could have adopted the fiscal year results (profit or loss), but we decided to adopt the stock index parameter by reason of its reliability, as indexes are the expression of a number of contextual, quantitative and external variables that truly express the state of a company. This parameter cannot be influenced, at any rate, by the company's management.

4. Methodology

4.1. Preliminary analysis

We conducted an initial empirical overview of the texts by implementing a topic modeling algorithm to empirically categorize

---

[1] We thank dr. Alessio Garzone for providing the complete list of all the companies and their performance in 2020.

the texts and investigate clusters of words that occurred frequently together in our texts. Topic modeling may be accomplished using a variety of methods. We chose the Latent Dirichlet allocation (LDA) model (Blei et al. 2003) as it has been successfully applied to a variety of problems in the digital humanities, literature studies, political science, and discourse analysis (Grimmer and Stewart 2013; Törnberg and Törnberg 2016; Mohr and Bogdanov 2013). This first step in the analysis revealed a large theme related to the COVID-19 impact, with words such as *COVID-19*, *pandemic*, *coronavirus* and *COVID-19_impact* dominating the generated topics and indicating extensive framing. To extract framing sentences from our texts, we then conducted an exploratory analysis through which certain seed words, i.e., words which can be considered as cues for identifying specific topics or aspects of a topic (including its framing), were identified following well-established corpus linguistics techniques relying on word frequencies, collocations and concordances (Gabrielatos and Baker 2008; Sinclair 1991; Stubbs 1996). Since our analysis focuses on the pandemic crisis, for the sake of readability we narrowed the cohort of seed candidates to the terms *impact, _ COVID-19, pandemic, human, diversity* and *positive*, which lead to the next step in the analysis.

4.2. Sentence vectors as frame detectors

The purpose of the analysis was to identify recurring frames. While single terms can indeed cue frames, considering words in context can provide a more robust method for frame identification. We therefore expanded our analytical query from single terms to whole sentences in order to perform a sentence similarity analysis, i.e., an analysis aimed at identifying sets of sentences semantically similar to a given one, with similarity scores providing an indication of the degree of similarity. The underlying idea is that the presence (generally, across the corpus, or limited to one of the two subcorpora) of semantically similar (though obviously not identical) sentences conveying representations of COVID-related issues could be interpreted as an indication of the existence and regular use of shared frames.

To identify similar sentences and calculate their similarity score, we implemented sentence embedding techniques to represent entire sentences and their semantic information as vectors to guide our algorithm into 'understanding' context as well as additional tones and subtleties in the corpus, and to detect homogenous statement representations, i.e., recurring ideas and arguments. Our purpose was to examine if the algorithm can detect recurring patterns and ideas in the form of similar sentences. At this stage of the analysis, we extracted all the sentences both from the "winners" and from the "losers" subcorpora. We preprocessed the texts (we removed punctuation, special or random characters, URLs, hyphens, etc. and lowercased the texts) and separated the sentences[2] thus creating a list consisting of more than 131,000 sentences. We then introduced them to the Universal Sentence Encoder model (Cer et al. 2018) to convert them in a series of numbers (representing several attributes of the text as discussed in section 2) and calculate their sum. At this point, it was necessary to set the measure according to which we could detect how similar two or more sentences were. To do that, we defined a function to calculate the cosine similarity metric, one of the common metrics implemented in natural language processing[3]. This function compares the numerical identity of a *query*, namely a selected sentence, with the whole list of sentences and generates the most similar ones based on their similarity score. The information and terms obtained by our preliminary exploratory analysis provided the basis for several types of *queries*. Finally, we specified the lowest similarity score required for a sentence to be considered at >0.4 (>40%).

5. Discussion of findings

Drawing from the extensive literature on frames and framing effects (Edelman 1993; Entman 1993; Goffmann 1974; Iyengar 1991; Neuman, Just and Crigler 1992; Price, Tewksbury and Powers 1997) we searched for generic frames, i.e. "aspects of perceived reality" (Entman 1993: 52) that are "broadly applicable to a range of different topics, some even over time and, potentially, indifferent cultural

---

[2] We implemented the Sentencizer component of the Spacy library in Python c.f. https://spacy.io/api/sentencizer, last accessed September 2022).
[3] The cosine similarity metric represents the angle between the vectors of words in a two-dimensional space. The smaller the angle, the higher the similarity (c.f. Ristanti, Wibawa and Pujianto 2019).

contexts' (De Vreese et al. 2001: 108) such as *conflict, morality, human factor* (Semetko and Valkenburg 2000) as well as thematic frames such as *attribution of responsibility* (Iyengar 1991) and *opportunity*.

5.1. Conflict Frame (COVID-19 impact)

Of the words identified in the preliminary analysis as being potential cues of frames, *impact* appeared to occur in contexts where conflict (i.e., a situation involving some kind of struggle) was featured. We therefore introduced the lemmas *pandemic* and *impact,* and we went through the generated concordance lines. We extracted the following two sentences from our concordance lines and introduced them to our sentence embeddings model: query= '*it will take some time to eliminate the impact of the pandemic*' and query = '*the economic downturn that occurred due to the COVID-19 pandemic dramatically impacted market*'.

The data retrieved suggested that the "winners" were mostly framing their struggle with COVID-19 as a global problem in which they also participated, whereas the "losers" steered their discourse towards a 'safety' frame, emphasizing the ways they ensured their personnel safety or the opportunities to reduce costs and promote workplace advancements. The term *impact* appeared strongly correlated to a general "global COVID-19 impact" discourse for the winner companies and a "despite the COVID-19 problem" frame for the loser companies, which opted for a discursive future-oriented narrative of the pandemic as an opportunity to either present other achievements such as reducing costs and ameliorating safety conditions or to comment on humanity's efforts to overcome the crisis, as can be seen in the following losers' examples with similarity scores ranging from 0.46 to 0.61 (on a scale of 0=totally dissimilar to 1=exact match):

- the COVID-19 pandemic continues to have a tremendous impact on the lives of people all over the world and i sincerely wish nothing more than to see this pandemic brought to an end at the earliest possible date but i am also encouraged to see humanity pooling its wisdom and using innovation to minimize economic disruption while controlling the spread of the virus; similarity = 0.51219803[4]

---

[4] Similarity to both queries with minimal difference.

- while we expect for fy 2022 the final year of the mediumterm management plan to be impacted to a certain degree by the COVID-19 pandemic I am confident that we can overcome the negative impact by accelerating the above strategies and focusing very closely on opportunities to reduce costs; similarity = 0.61167645

- the pandemic has led us to pay closer attention to detail and we are convinced this has had a positive impact on safety; similarity = 0.5228065.

The strategic aim of such framing might be the attempt on the part of CEOs to partially distance themselves from the effects of the pandemic. On the one hand, the crisis was unforeseeable; on the other hand, companies usually have a buffer plan to face unexpected positive or negative dramatic changes in ordinary business life. If the buffer plan fails, the impact of a crisis can be devastating. In this view, emergency, crisis and uncertainty have to be managed. A company's management has to be able to smoothen the effects. We stress once more that the winner or loser classification comes from stock indexes; it is the financial market that determines whether the company is successful or not. This result is obviously dependent on the company's strategies and ability to survive crises. More specifically, and in relation to further investigation of the impact framing, the query *the economic downturn that occurred due to the COVID-19 pandemic dramatically impacted market* generated 31 utterances from the "winners" subcorpus and 51 from the "losers" subcorpus. In this specific query, the global dimension of the pandemic was intensely highlighted by both "winners" and "losers". However, "losers" tended to frame the catastrophe in a more social or regional manner, as can be seen in the extracted utterances below, whereas "winners" tended to comment on the impact of the pandemic on a business, market, or economic level, in what can be seen as a slight variation to the "global catastrophe" frame: the problem for the "winners" was the overall impact of the pandemic on the economy and the market, but for the "losers" it was its effects on society, which suggests an external attribution bias (El-Haj et al. 2016) along the line of "this was everybody's problem":

- the outbreak of the coronavirus pandemic has had an extremely strong impact on society and on global stock markets and unfortunately we have not seen the end of it yet; similarity = 0.53622943 (loser)

- the spread of the COVID-19 pandemic quickly came to negatively impact societies economies and financial markets globally; similarity = 0.53588986 (loser)

- this past year was no different as we witnessed the significant impact of the COVID-19 pandemic resulting in depressed economic activity and the heavy toll this has taken on society; similarity = 0.52788544 (loser).

Furthermore, the global impact of the pandemic was outlined quite starkly by the winning companies. They produced several utterances outlining the *volatility, ambiguity* and *uncertainty* of the market environment which put companies (and the market) under tremendous strain (see examples):

- the current operating environment is characterized by volatility uncertainty complexity and ambiguity making it difficult to project the future of society and business and this environment is becoming increasingly opaque due to the global COVID-19 pandemic; similarity = 0.7489477

- the global COVID-19 pandemic has brought with it economic stagnation and changes in consumer behavior which is increasing the uncertainty of the future; similarity = 5340057

- as of today demand has become highly volatile as a result of the global COVID-19 pandemic; similarity = 0.45856893

It is interesting to observe that both categories used the terms in the same manner, either as a triad (*uncertainty, ambiguity* and *volatility*) or as a dyad (*uncertainty* and *volatility*), indicating an extensive use of fear metaphors (Ho 2016). However, the same framing served as a ground for losers to elaborate on other issues that outline the ambiguity of the global situation with multiple utterances on digitalization, climate change, even ageing populations:

- although the COVID-19 pandemic continues to reap havoc around the world vaccinations are steadily progressing and customers and smbc group are using digital technology to adapt our corporate activities to the current business environment; similarity = 0.5484737

- in the meantime climate change continues to generate growing risks around the globe while japan is confronting problems arising from an ever lower birthrate and a rapidly aging society; similarity = 0.487889

- with global warming and disasters becoming more and more serious in recent years it is becoming more crucial than ever for companies to act in harmony with the environment; similarity = 0.5896668

Loser companies appear to counteract the 'ambiguity and volatility' frame by generalizing on well-known current problems as 'opportunities' that will establish the company's value and contribution to the resolution of the problems.

5.2. Morality frame: involvement with social issues

In the losers' discourse we detected a socially oriented moral framing. The sentence *"morally bound to support society's digital shift and contribute to solving social issues"* that was generated in previous similarity queries was reintroduced to the embeddings model and generated 6 utterances by the winner companies and 24 by the loser companies, which appear to pursue the moral framing of the pandemic consequences and to steer discourse towards their participation in 'solving social issues':

– to achieve that we will continue to solve social issues through our business activities; similarity = 0.4099568

– by helping resolve social issues through business and innovation; similarity = 0.41986397

– our priority themes in resolving social issues; similarity = 0.40944907

– it also contributes to the resolution of social issues by providing environmentally sound products and creating a recycling based society; similarity = 0.5208542

5.3. Human factor frame

Another frame which appeared to recur in the corpus is the human factor frame. This frame, however, has been salient for quite some time in corporate reporting, with companies increasingly recognizing the importance of giving adequate consideration to the needs and expectations of all stakeholders, including employees.

In order to properly assess the incidence of this frame in the CEO Letters published in the wake of the pandemic, a comparison with Annual Reports from previous years would be necessary, particularly in order to identify signs of continuity with already established frames. Such comparison was beyond the scope of our research. We did, however, locate significant utterances and different framing strategies regarding the human element in both categories of Letters, some of them suggesting that the human factor was already a point of focus before the pandemic, but became even more relevant as a result of the specific challenges posed by COVID-19. In investigating the human factor framing, we opted for a query that would exploit the human capital utterance detected in our collocations inquiry and introduced the query = '*until now too we have advanced workstyle reforms to create more active workplaces and had worked to implement telework and work from home since before the COVID-19 pandemic in order to make maximum effective use of human capital*'.

Although the co-occurrences of the term *human* generated by the loser companies had a more sensitive tone, with bigrams such as *human_tragedies* and *human_touch* appearing more prominently within their discourse, both company categories elaborated over the human factor, focusing on working conditions and their labor productivity. Notably, the winner companies were promising 'vibrant' and 'innovative' workplaces:

– the comsys group has been promoting workstyle innovations for some time now and as a result we have been successful in making a smooth transition to remote working in the midst of the pandemic; similarity = 0.47535425

– the pandemic served as another reminder of this and we are implementing various measures to create a vibrant workplace for all of our employees; similarity = 0.41488525

The losers emphasized their effective human resources departments, their diversity and their inclusivity strategies as effective tools of advancing their personnel's efficiency and satisfaction.

– in order to make maximum effective use of human capital we are advancing HR strategies such as diversity and inclusion work life balance and HR development; similarity = 0.6915907

- however we have taken steps to broaden the experience of employees though for example cross departmental and international assignments and as a result our human resources have significantly strengthened in each of the businesses and communication in every division has improved largely contributing to the groups growth; similarity = 0.43111318

- the group has worked on developing global human resources in expanding its business areas focusing on the pacific rim region and we must further promote the effective use of their capabilities; similarity = 0.40108806

Further delving into the human factor framing, we looked more closely at the *diversity* theme, and queried our texts with the following sentence extracted from our collocations: *'we have established a special task force to examine our culture and make sure that it is one that supports diversity, inclusion and equality'*.

We found that the 'diversity/inclusion' frame cued by this and similar sentences was more widely implemented in the winners' discourse, with the query producing 30 utterances (see samples below):

- interpump promotes a culture based on training diversity inclusion and safety for all employees; similarity = 0.52583694

- championing diversity and inclusion through the year we ramped up our focus on diversity and inclusion with particular focus on gender diversity an issue that many consumer tech firms grapple with; similarity = 0.5991696

The losers subcorpus, on the other hand, generated 11 utterances cueing the diversity/inclusion angle:

- our approach to diversity and inclusion which entails the creation of unique added value through interaction among our diverse employees is without doubt part of our dna; similarity = 0.5009831

- we have identified targets for gender and ethnicity representation our leaders have completed diversity and inclusion training and all of our employees complete mandatory diversity e-learning as part of their induction; similarity = 0.6079282

As other frames in this study, the 'diversity and inclusion' frame provides a way-out for CEOs to shift attention away from the main problem, the pandemic crisis. Issues like diversity, inclusion and equal opportunities are current discussion topics in modern societies. As the 2018 Edelman Earned Brand (Edelman 2018) study showed, 64% of consumers around the world value firms which they perceive as being socially active and engaged. As a matter of fact, there are several examples of companies and CEOs taking advantage of such trends to catalyze the audience's attention. An example of this is NIKE's choice to employ American football star Colin Kaepernick for the 30th anniversary of the iconic "Just Do It" campaign. The athlete became a symbol in 2016, after having had his contract with the San Francisco 49ers rescinded, for protesting against police brutality towards African-Americans in the USA by kneeling instead of standing during the national anthem before a NFL match. Despite the resulting protest, boycotts and the eventual fall of NIKE's shares in the aftermath, the company's CEO, Mark Parker declared his pride in the new campaign as it "strongly resonated with customers around the world and drove a record engagement on social media" (Thomas 2018).

5.4. Opportunity frame

As mentioned earlier, our preliminary analysis generated the term 'positive'; therefore, we opted to investigate whether there was a 'silver lining' or an 'opportunity' frame present in our corpus.

Query = 'one of these positives is the rapid progress of digitalization that has occurred due to self-quarantine practices'.

This query generated multiple utterances from the losers subcorpus, highlighting positive outcomes deriving from the pandemic, such as direct2customer (d2c) business or digitalisation:

- as for iwg this fundamental shift in the way people work is clearly an enormously positive step over the medium and longer terms; similarity = 0.45920333

- people told us they were more engaged than before which is a positive step; similarity = 0.43290773

- expanding direct to consumer our dtc business has seen a positive uplift from COVID-19; similarity = 0.38117257

- COVID-19 has sped up so many changes digitalisation is advancing apace; similarity = 0.37142107

- the COVID-19 pandemic created a need and an opportunity to accelerate our transformation; similarity = 0.44863898

This is consistent with the previous finding of losers counteracting the *ambiguity* and *volatility* of the market with a forward-looking promise of how the company (or group) will enhance its value via its mobilization and its engagement to tackle global problems such as climate change. In the 'opportunity' case, novelties such as digital transformation were presented as the "success story" that emerged from the lockdown disadvantage. To further investigate the 'opportunity' frame we introduced the queries = *'the COVID-19 pandemic is causing more difficulties than we ever imagined still i take it as an opportunity to reform the group'* and *"viewing the COVID-19 pandemic as an opportunity to look back on the past analyze the present and contemplate the future'*.

The queries generated only one related utterance from the winners subcorpus:

- however I would like to view our crisis management in response to COVID-19 as an opportunity to thoroughly eliminate waste and i have instructed the entire group accordingly; similarity = 0.41912514

On the other hand, several utterances were returned from the losers subcorpus, indicating that the 'opportunity' frame was more intensely implemented by the losers discourse, as can also be seen in the examples below:

- in so doing we will need to overcome the scourge of the pandemic and approach it as an opportunity for growth; similarity = 0.45896977

- the COVID-19 pandemic created a need and an opportunity to accelerate our transformation; similarity = 0.44863898

- umicore adjusted with agility to the challenges caused by the pandemic; similarity = 0.4853001

These examples represent, for the CEOs, a way out of the difficult position the company finds itself in through a recasting of the problem as an opportunity for change. This strategy may help CEOs reposition the company's current situation, suggesting the idea that crisis may generate sound recovery.

This query also produced two positive self-attribution sentences within the opportunity framing indicating an interesting transfer of meaning executed by the algorithm:

- the response of our colleagues to the challenges of the pandemic has been outstanding; similarity = 0.5168563

- our operations have proven to be robust in the face of the pandemic; similarity = 0.45777413.

This latter result gives the CEOs a chance to highlight and give credit to the effort of the company's representatives to tackle an exogenous problem (as in the 'human factor' frame). In terms of corporate unity, this move appears to be really powerful.

6. Concluding remarks

This study is a small part of a much broader research project aimed at studying financial institutional communication of the world's major companies in the aftermath of the COVID-19 pandemic and its impact on the global economy.

In this study, we limited the discussion to the identification of the communicative strategies, and more specifically of the frames used to encourage preferred interpretations of events, used by CEOs to discuss, justify and inform stakeholders (customers, investors, financial analysts) of their performance in 2020 and also of the situation of their company after the shakedown that the pandemic inflicted on global economies. We studied companies reporting both positive and negative stock index results in 2020.

We found that the communication conveyed by CEO Letters featured some recurring framings: conflict, morality, human factor and opportunity. The results are differentiated and particularly interesting if filtered for losers and winners: losers, for instance, tend to bend their communication towards morality, typically by making references to the sad moral consequences of the pandemic, human factors, with sensitive compassionate depictions of the reality; and the world of opportunities that this crisis may have generated. We interpret this as descending from the CEOs' need to minimize their role and to represent the responsibility for the negative performance as a shared one, thus treading on safe ground while framing the crisis in commonly recognized and accepted moral themes. This decision may help give the audience the impression that the company, even while being forced to cope with a crisis, did not abandon the tracks of modern governance, thus presenting an image of soundness.

Winners do not seem to exploit as extensively as losers the 'opportunity' frame, possibly because they prefer to show themselves as sympathetic to the situation, having scored positive results in 2020. As regards the 'human factor' frame, winners take a more optimistic stance than losers, promising a "vibrant" future.

As regards the 'conflict/impact of the pandemic' frame, both winners and losers represent the pandemic as a global problem; however, winners tend to highlight the scale of the pandemic and its overall impact worldwide, whereas losers tend to claim credit for having ensured safety in spite of the crisis. What emerges clearly is that both winners and losers use framing strategies extensively in their communication, thereby providing clearly accessible preferred pathways for interpreting their overall performance. We interpret this trend as resulting from the need to represent reality in the best possible light, in an attempt to convey a more palatable message to the audience. Framing becomes, then, a tool to channel more convincing, effective and impressive communication.

As for our computational approach, in spite of its inevitable limitations[5], it has shown a potential for increasing the robustness and reliability of research findings by providing an approach to the analysis of a given corpus of textual data less dependent on the subjective choices of the researcher. This approach can be helpful to detect recurrent discursive patterns. Sentence embedding techniques appear to be a promising and adaptable strategy for pattern identification and demonstrate how the advancement of numerical representations and statistical techniques in language may result in

---

[5] In our future work we aim to extract more detailed data-driven markers, such as grammatical and syntactic markers that could steer the analytical stages to more focused queries.

the ability to recognize and "understand" recurring patterns in all types of conversation, and in broadening the researcher's scope of analysis. As mentioned repeatedly in this article, this is only a first step in a much larger research project. In the further stages of the research, we will advance the extraction of information from the corpus via emotional analysis of the texts and feature extraction for machine learning methods. The goal is to further operationalize corporate discourse and highlight its multiple characteristics, thus achieving a more comprehensive idea of corporate communication during the 2020 crisis.

References

AMERNIC, JOEL H. and CRAIG, RUSSEL J., 2007, "Guidelines for CEO-speak: editing the language of corporate leadership", *Strategy & Leadership*, 35 (3), pp. 25-31.

ADI, YOSSI, KERMANY, EINAT, BELINKOV, YONATAN, LAVI, OFER, GOLDBERG, YOAV, 2017, "Fine-grained Analysis of Sentence Embeddings Using Auxiliary Prediction Tasks". In: 5th International Conference on Learning Representations, ICLR 2017, Conference Track Proceedings. Published online: https://arxiv.org/pdf/1608.04207.pdf, last accessed June 15 2022.

ARORA, SANJEEV, LIANG, YINGYU, MA, TENGYU, 2017, "A simple but tough-to-beat baseline for sentence embeddings", in *Proceedings of International Conference on Learning Representations (ICLR)*. Published online: https://oar.princeton.edu/bitstream/88435/pr1rk2k/1/BaselineSentenceEmbedding.pdf, last accessed June 17 2022.

BLEI, DAVID M, NG ANDREW Y, JORDAN, MICHAEL I., 2003, "Latent dirichlet allocation", *The Journal of machine Learning research*, 3, pp. 993-1022.

BREEZE, RUTH, 2013, *Corporate Discourse*. Bloomsbury, London.

BRUCHANSK, CHRISTOPHE, 2017, "Political Footprints: Political Discourse Analysis using Pre-Trained Word Vectors", *ArXiv*, abs/1705.06353.

CER, DANIEL, YANG, YINFEI, KONG, SHENG-YI, HUA, NAN, LIMTIACO, NICOLE, ST. JOHN, RHOMNI, CONSTANT, NOAH, GUAJARDO-CESPEDES, MARIO, YUAN, STEVE, TAR, CHRIS, STROPE, BRIAN, KURZWEIL, RAY, 2018, "Universal Sentence Encoder", *ArXiv*. 1803.11175.

CONAWAY, ROGER N. AND WARDROPE, WILLIAM J., 2010, "Do their words really matter? Thematic analysis of U.S. and Latin American CEO Letters", *Journal of Business Communication,* 47 (2), pp. 141-168.

CONNEAU, ALEXIS, KRUSZEWSKI, GERMAN, LAMPLE, GUILLAUME, BARRAULT, LOIC, BARONI, MARCO, 2018, 'What you can cram into a single vector:

Probing sentence embeddings for linguistic properties", *ArXiv*: 1805.01070.

DE VREESE CLAES, JOCHEN PETER, SEMETKO HOLLY, 2001, "Framing Politics At The Launch Of The Euro: A Cross-National Comparative Study Of Frames In The News", in *Political Communication* 18 (2), pp. 107-122.

EDELMAN, MURRAY, 1993, "Contestable categories and public opinion", *Political Communication*, 10, pp. 231-242.

ENTMAN, ROBERT, 1993, "Framing: Toward clarification of a fractured paradigm", *Journal of Communication*, 43 (4), pp. 51-58.

EL-HAJ, MAHMOUD, RAYSON, PAUL, E., YOUNG, STEVEN E., WALKER, MARTIN, MOORE, ANDREW, ATHANASAKOU, VASILIKI, SCHLEICHER, THOMAS, 2016, "Learning tone and attribution for financial text mining", in *Proceedings of LREC 2016, Tenth International Conference on Language Resources and Evaluation. European Language Resources Association* (ELRA), pp. 1820-1825.

FISS, PEER C., AND HIRSCH, PAUL M., 2005, "The discourse of globalization: Framing and sensemaking of an emerging concept", *American Sociological Review*, 70 (1), pp. 29-52.

GABRIELATOS, COSTAS AND BAKER, PAUL, 2008, "Fleeing, Sneaking, Flooding. A Corpus Analysis of Discursive Constructions of Refugees and Asylum Seekers in the UK Press, 1996-2005", *Journal of English Linguistics*; 36, p. 5.

GARZONE, GIULIANA, 2004, "Annual company reports and CEO's letters: Discoursal features and cultural markedness", in C. Candlin and M. Gotti (Eds.), *Intercultural Aspects of Specialized Discourse*. Peter Lang, Bern, pp. 311-341.

GARZONE, GIULIANA, 2008, "Letters to shareholders and Chairman's statements: Textual variability and generic integrity", In P. Gillaerts and M. Gotti (Eds.), *Genre Variation in Business Letters,* Peter Lang, Bern, pp. 179-204.

GILLAERTS, PAUL, 1996, "The address to the shareholders in annual reports. A genological approach", in *1996 European Writing Conferences. Barcelona: Institut de Ciencies de l'Educació* (CD-ROM: EARLI Special Interest Group Writing).

GIORDANO, WALTER, 2020, *Investigating the discourse of financial reporting: communicative strategies and problems of translation*, Editura Politehnica, Timisoara, Romania.

GIORDANO, WALTER, 2019, "Communication Strategies and Crisis Management in 2015-2016 Volkswagen CEO Letters to Shareholders", in Maci S., Sala M., *Representing and redefining specialised knowledge: variety in LSP,* CERLIS Series Vol. 8, Università di Bergamo.

GOFFMAN, ERVING, 1974, *Frame analysis: An essay on the organization of experience*, New York, Harper & Row.

GRIMMER, JUSTIN and STEWART, BRANDON M., 2013, "Text as data: The promise and pitfalls of automatic content analysis methods for political texts", *Political Analysis* 21 (3), pp. 267-297.

HALLAHAN, KIRK, 1999, "Seven models of framing: Implications for public relations", *Journal of Public Relations Research* 11 (3), pp. 205-242.

HALLAHAN, KIRK, 2005, "Framing theory", in R.L. Heath (ed.), *The Encyclopedia of Public Relations*, Sage, Thousand Oaks, CA, pp. 340-343.

HO, JANET, 2016, "When bank stocks are hobbled by worries: A metaphor study of emotions in the financial news reports", *Text & Talk. An Interdisciplinary Journal of Language Discourse Communication Studies* 36 (3), pp. 295-317.

IACOBACCI, IGNACIO, PILEHVAR MOHAMMED T., NAVIGLI, ROBERTO, 2016, "Embeddings for Word Sense Disambiguation: An Evaluation Study", in *Proceedings of the 54th Annual Meeting of the Association for Computational Linguistics*, pp. 897-907.

INGENHOFF DIANA AND SOMMER KATHARINA, 2010, "Trust in Companies and CEOs: a Comparative Study of the Main Influences", *Journal of Business Ethics* 95 (3), pp. 339-355.

IYENGAR SHANTO, 1991, *Is Anyone Responsible? How Television Frames Political Issues*, The University of Chicago Press, Chicago.

KAPRANOV OLEKSANDR, 2018, "The framing of climate change discourse by Statoil", *Topics in Linguistics* 19 (1), pp. 54-68.

KIM, SORA, AVERY, ELIZABETH J., LARISCY, RUTHANN W., 2009, "Are crisis communicators practicing what we preach? An evaluation of crisis response strategy analyzed in public relations research from 1991 to 2009", *Public Relations Review* 35 (4), pp. 446-448.

LE, QUOC AND MIKOLOV, TOMAS, 2014, "Distributed representations of sentences and documents", in *Proceedings of the 31st International Conference on Machine Learning* (ICML-14), pp. 1188-1196.

MAIER CARMEN D. AND RAVAZZANI, SILVIA, 2018, "Framing Diversity in Corporate Digital Contexts: A Multimodal Approach to Discursive Recontextualizations of Social Practices", *Journal of Business Communication* 58 (4), pp. 463-489.

MALAVASI, DONATELLA, 2005, "Banks' Annual Reports: An Analysis of the Linguistic Means Used to Express Evaluation", in *Proceedings of the Association for Business Communication, 7th European Convention*, May 2005, Association for Business Communication.

MOHR, JOHN W. and BOGDANOV, PELKO, 2013, "Introduction – Topic models: What they are and why they matter", *Poetics* 41 (6), pp. 545-569.

NEUMAN, W. R., JUST, M. R. and CRIGLER, A. N., 1992, *Common knowledge*, University of Chicago Press, Chicago.

NICKERSON, CATHERINE and DE GROOT, ELIZABETH, 2005, "Dear shareholder, dear stockholder, dear stakeholder. The business letter genre in the annual general report", in P. Gillaerts and M. Gotti (Eds.), *Genre Variation in Business Letters,* Peter Lang, Bern, pp. 225-246.

PALMER-SILVEIRA, JUAN AND RUIZ GARRIDO, MIGUEL, 2014. "Examining US and Spanish Annual Reports: Crisis communication", in *Business Professional Communication Quarterly*, 77 (4), pp. 409-425. https://doi.org/10.1177/2329490614543176

PRICE, VINCENT, TEWKSBURY, DAVID, POWERS ELIZABETH, 1997, "Switching trains of thought: The impact of news frames on readers' cognitive responses", *Communication Research* 24, pp. 481-506.

RISTANTI PUTRI Y., WIBAWA AJI P., PUJIANTO, UTOMO, 2019, "Cosine Similarity for Title and Abstract of Economic Journal Classification", *5th International Conference on Science in Information Technology (ICSITech)*, pp. 123-127, doi: 10.1109/ICSITech46713.2019.8987547.

RUIZ-GARRIDO, MIGUEL, FORTANET-GÓMEZ, IMMACULADA, PALMER-SILVEIRA, JUAN, 2012, "Introducing British and Spanish companies to investors: Building the corporate image through the Chairman's Statement", in J. Aritz and R. C. Walker (Eds.), *Discourse Perspectives of Organizational Communication,* Fairleigh Dickinson, University Press, Plymouth, pp. 159-178.

RUTHERFORD, BRIAN A., 2005, "Genre Analysis of Corporate Annual Report Narratives: A Corpus Linguistics-Based Approach", *Journal of Business Communication* 42 (4), pp. 349-378.

SEMETKO, HOLLI And VALKENBURG PATTI M., 2000, "Framing European politics: A content analysis of press and television news", *Journal of Communication*, 50 (2), pp. 93-109.

SINCLAIR, JOHN M.H., 1991, *Corpus Concordance Collocation*, O.U.P., Oxford.

SOCHER, RICHARD, PENNINGTON, JEFFREY, HUANG, ERIC H., NG, ANDREW Y. AND MANNING, CHRISTOPHER D., 2011, "Dynamic pooling and unfolding recursive autoencoders for paraphrase detection", in *Advances in Neural Information Processing Systems*, 24, pp. 801-809.

SOUSA, SAMULE, MILIOS EVANGELOS, BERTON LILIAN, 2020, "Word sense disambiguation: an evaluation study of semi-supervised approaches with word embeddings", *International Joint Conference on Neural Networks*, pp. 1-8, doi: 10.1109/IJCNN48605.2020.9207225.

STUBBS MICHAEL, 1996, *Text and Corpus Analysis: Computer-Assisted Studies of Language and Culture*, Blackwell, Oxford.

TÖRNBERG, ANTON and TÖRNBERG, PETTER, 2016, "Combining CDA

and topic modeling: Analyzing discursive connections between Islamophobia and anti-feminism on an online forum", *Discourse & Society* 27 (4), pp. 401-422.

VALVI, AIKATERINI. AND FRAGKOS, KONSTANTINOS, 2013, "Crisis communication strategies: a case of British Petroleum", *Industrial and Commercial Training*, 45 (7), pp. 383-391.

Websites:

EDELMAN EARNED BRAND, 2018, "Brands take a stand", https://www.edelman.com/sites/g/files/aatuss191/files/2018-10/2018_Edelman_Earned_Brand_Global_Report.pdf, last accessed April 8, 2023.

THOMAS, LAUREN, 2018, "Nike CEO Mark Parker says he's 'very proud' for the Kaepernick Ad Campaign", CNBC, 25 September 2018, https://www.cnbc.com/2018/09/25/nike-ceo-mark-parker-says-hes-very-proud-of-kaepernick-ad-campaign.html, last accessed April 8, 2022.

CONTRIBUTORS

Jacqueline Aiello is Assistant Professor in the Department of Political and Communication Sciences at the University of Salerno, Italy. She earned her doctorate in Multilingual and Multicultural Studies from New York University. She is the recipient of a Fulbright ETA grant and two NYU Global Research Initiative Fellowships. She is the author of *Negotiating Englishes and English-speaking Identities* (2018, Routledge), winner of the 2019 AIA Junior Book Prize, and *The Discursive Construction of the Modern Political Self* (2023, Routledge).

Alessandro Aru is a PhD student in his third year at the University of Pisa. His research project focuses on analysing the cognitive complexity of compound figures of speech. These complex non-literal expressions result from the interaction of two or more tropes, such as ironic metaphor, ironic hyperbole, and hyperbolic metaphor. The study specifically analyses the compounds' logical, temporal, and psychological order of interpretation. The research includes an experimental section examining participants' ability to process meanings across multiple dimensions. Recently, he has published various works, including a chapter on irony in Professor Marcella Bertucelli Papi's collection "Lecture notes on irony and satire"; an article on extended metaphor and the conceptual structures which explain the interactions and the relationships of the multiple micrometaphors contained within the extended metaphor; and an article on the irony markers in British newspapers and tweets concerning climate change.

Textus 1-2023, pp. 355-364

ISSN 1824-3967
© Carocci Editore S.p.A.

Lorenzo Buonvivere is a PhD Student in Foreign Languages, Literatures and Cultures at "Roma Tre" University. He is currently working on a doctoral project that focusses on the identification of recurrent framings of nature in ecotourism discourse. His main research interests include ecolinguistics, cognitive linguistics, and Critical Discourse Analysis.

Paola Catenaccio is Full Professor of English Linguistics and Translation at Università degli Studi di Milano. Her research interests lie primarily in the field of discourse analysis, which she applies to a variety of domains (legal discourse, business communication, professional discourse, ELF communication, the discourse of science and of scientific popularisation) in combination with other methodological perspectives (most notably corpus linguistics), adopting a multi-methods approach to linguistic research, especially in an intercultural perspective. She has authored numerous articles which have appeared in international journals and edited collections. She has also coedited several volumes on various aspects and domain-specific discourse and authored two volumes on the interface between corporate communication and the media (*Corporate Press Releases. An Overview*, 2008) and on emerging paradigms in business discourse (*Understanding CSR Discourse: Insights from Linguistics and Discourse Analysis,* 2012), as well as one (with Giuliana Garzone) on *Ethics in Professional and Corporate Discourse: Linguistic Perspectives* (2021). She is Co-Editor in Chief of the journal *Languages, Cultures, Mediation*.

Stefania Consonni is Associate Professor of English language and linguistics at the University of Bergamo. She specializes in textual paradigms; narratology; the semiotics of visual vs. language; resemiotization and multimodality; the history and theory of spatialization; specialized communication in a discourse-analytical and culturalist perspective; the semiotics, pragmatics and epistemology of traditional and new genres within academic, artistic, aesthetic, scientific, entertainment and media discourse. A member of the CERLIS Research Centre and the Eye Tracking Lab team (both based in Bergamo), as well as of the CLAVIER-Corpus and Language Variation in English Research consortium, she is on the editorial board of *JCaDS-Journal of Corpora and Discourse Studies*

(University of Cardiff), the *CERLIS Series* and *Ibérica* (European Association of Languages for Specific Purposes). Since 2006 she has been involved in PRIN projects, funded by the Italian Ministry of Education, on social/cultural studies and on specialized language and discourse.

Giuliana Elena Garzone is *Professore Onorario* (Professor Emeritus) of English, Linguistics and Translation at IULM University, Milan. She formerly taught at Milan State University where she directed the PhD Programme in Linguistic, Literary and Intercultural Studies. Her research has mainly focused on two main areas: English linguistics, and especially the textual and pragmatic aspects of specialised communication, and Translation and Interpreting Studies. She has published over a hundred and fifty book chapters and journal articles and has authored or (co-)edited more than fifty books, focusing in particular on legal, business, scientific and media discourse, and on translation and interpreting. She has coordinated various local and national research projects. She is Co-Editor in Chief of *LCM Journal*, which she founded in 2014, and of the book series "Lingua traduzione didattica" (Francoangeli). She sits on the Advisory Board of various international journals, among them the *Journal of Applied Linguistics and Professional Practice* (Equinox), *Journal of Multicultural Discourses* (Francis & Taylor) and *Lingue e Linguaggi*. In 2018 she received the Francis W. Weeks Award of Merit from the Association for Business Communication, and in 2019 she was awarded a Doctorat ès Lettres honoris causa by McGill University, Montréal.

Walter Giordano has held the position of Chair of Business English at the Università degli Studi di Napoli "Federico II" since 2007. His primary research interests lie in the field of Language for Specific Purposes (LSP), with a particular focus on business communication, financial discourse, advertising, translation studies, discourse analysis, and genre variation. His most recent publications include: "Scripting the Communication Strategy for Mineral Water Advertising in the USA: A Multimodal Textual Analysis" (2023, co-authored with E. Ammendola), "Textual and Visual Catalysts/ Distractors in Advertising" (2022), and "Translating Financial Statements from Italian into English: Strategies, Issues, and Semantic

Aspects" (2022). In addition, he works as a business consultant and specializes in providing training for business professionals and corporate personnel.

Maria Grazia Guido is Full Professor of English Linguistics and Translation at the University of Salento (Italy), where she is the Director of the Department of Humanities. She holds a PhD in English Applied Linguistics at the University of London Institute of Education. Her research interests are in cognitive-functional linguistics applied to ELF in intercultural communication, cognitive stylistics and specialized discourse analysis. Her monographs include: *English as a Lingua Franca in Migrants' Trauma Narratives* (Palgrave Macmillan), *English as a Lingua Franca in Cross-cultural Immigration Domains* (Peter Lang), *Mediating Cultures* (LED), *The Acting Translator* and *The Acting Interpreter* (Legas).

Pietro Luigi Iaia is Associate Professor of English Linguistics and Translation in the Department of Humanities at the University of Salento. He holds a PhD in "Linguistic, Historical-literary and Intercultural Studies" from the same university. His research interests focus on the cognitive-semantic, pragmatic and socio-cultural dimensions of the translation of multimodal texts; game localization; English uses as a Lingua Franca in cross-cultural audiovisual discourse and in online communication among video-game players. His publications include: the monograph *Analysing English as a Lingua Franca in Video Games* (Peter Lang); "Creativity and Readability in Game Localisation" (*Lingue e Linguaggi*); "Towards a 'COOPING' Model for the Investigation of Gamers' Online Conversations in English" (*Iperstoria*); and "Multimodal Strategies of Creation and Self-Translation of Humorous Discourse in Image-Macro Memes" (in *Humour in Self-Translation*, ed. by Margherita Dore).

Katerina Mandenaki is a graduate of the Department of Communication and Media Studies at the National and Kapodistrian University of Athens Greece, Master of Arts in Communication and Mass Media – Digital Media and Interaction Environments. The subject of her dissertation was "Text Analysis by Automatic Extraction of Arguments from Physical Language Texts Using

R-Studio Text Extraction Tools". Since 2017, she has been a research associate of the Laboratory of New Technologies in Communication, Education and Media at the National and Kapodistrian University of Athens within the framework of Digital Humanities, Text Mining, Machine Learning, Neural Networks for text analysis and classification, Sentiment and Emotional analysis as well as Data Journalism techniques. She is currently working on her PhD in Algorithmic Discourse Analysis and Ideology and has published research on Populism, Neural Networks and Discourse Analysis, Machine Learning, as well as Data Privacy and Surveillance. She has extensive professional experience in journalism and is currently Director of Communication and Marketing in the tourism industry.

Elisa Mattiello is Associate Professor of English Language and Linguistics at the Department of Philology, Literature and Linguistics (University of Pisa). She holds a PhD in English Linguistics from the same University, where she teaches courses of ESP and English linguistics. Her research focuses on English word-formation and lexicology, with particular attention to the creative mechanisms used to coin new words in English. In these areas, she has published extensively in leading journals and volumes. She authored the monographs *An Introduction to English Slang* (Polimetrica, 2008), *Extra-grammatical Morphology in English* (De Gruyter, 2013), *Analogy in Word-formation* (De Gruyter, 2017), *Linguistic Innovation in the Covid-19 Pandemic* (Cambridge Scholars Publishing, 2022), and *Transitional Morphology* (Cambridge University Press, 2022). She serves as reviewer for numerous international journals and is currently a member of the Editorial Boards of the *International Journal of English Linguistics*, *International Journal of Language and Linguistics*, and Cambridge Scholars Publishing.

Denise Milizia is Associate Professor at the Department of Political Science at the University of Bari Aldo Moro. Her research interests are in the field of ESP, Corpus Linguistics, political phraseology in American, British and Italian cultures, and legal phraseology, in particular in European documents. She has published several works in which she analyses the relationship between the UK and the European Union, with a special focus on the role of metaphor in

European politics. Her most recent interests lie in the study of new crises, in particular the COVID-19 pandemic and climate change and the global warming challenge, both in Europe and in the U.S. Her recent publications include *"Britain was already cherry-picking from the European tree without bothering to water the soil or tend to its branches". A metaphorical study of the UK in Europe* (John Benjamins, 2023). She has recently edited *The European Union between the pandemic, new crises and future perspectives* (LED, 2023). She is co-editor of the international journal *ESP Across Cultures.*

Anna Mongibello, PhD, is Associate Professor of English Language and Translation at the University of Naples "L'Orientale", and currently Visiting Professor at the University of Toronto. Her research focuses on the analysis of communication in digital environments; digital activism; deepfakes and Political Discourse; News Discourse; the intersections of Language, Ideology and Identity, with an emphasis on issues of representation and self-representation explored through the lens of Critical Discourse Analysis and the tools of Corpus Linguistics. She has also worked on eLearning, virtual worlds, and innovative models for teaching/learning in digital environments. She has published two books and several book chapters and articles in national and international journals, including "#alleyesonwetsuweten: An Analysis of the Wet'suwet'en protest on Twitter" (2022) and "Supporting EFL learners with a Virtual Environment: A Focus on L2 Pronunciation"(with Jacqueline Aiello, 2019). She co-edited with Bronwyn Carlson (Macquarie University, Sydney) a special issue of *Anglistica* on "Indigenous Resistance in the Digital Age: The Politics of Language, Media and Culture" (2022).

Francesco Nacchia is a Research Associate at the University of Naples 'L'Orientale'. He holds a PhD in (Euro)languages and Specialised Terminology from the University of Naples 'Parthenope', where he researched on Agribusiness Terminology with a specific focus on wine-tasting language and alternative/innovative eating habits. He is currently working on a project concerning sustainability in the wine sector and metaphorisation dynamics in specialised discourse.

CONTRIBUTORS

361

His major research interests include Corpus Linguistics, Critical Metaphor Analysis, Multimodal Critical Discourse Analysis and Specialised Discourse.

Jekaterina Nikitina is a Research Fellow in English Language and Translation at the University of Milan, where she lectures in linguistic mediation and discursive practices in legal and international settings. She holds a PhD in Linguistic, literary and intercultural studies in European and extra-European perspectives from the University of Milan. Her academic interests include specialised discourse and translation studies. She works on LSP theories and applications, knowledge dissemination dynamics, legal discourse, discourse of healthcare, medicine and bioethics. In her research, she applies qualitative and quantitative, specifically corpus linguistics, analytical approaches. Her published academic work includes publications on legal translation, discourse of human rights, dissemination of bioethical knowledge, popularisation of scientific topics through a range of channels, with a focus on medically assisted procreation and gene editing. She is a member of the Corpus and Language Variation in English Research Group (CLAVIER) and of the Italian Association of Translators and Interpreters (AITI).

Maria Cristina Nisco, PhD in English for Special Purposes, is an Associate Professor of English Language and Translation Studies at the University of Naples 'Parthenope', where she is also a Board member of the international PhD programme in 'Linguistic, Terminological, and Intercultural Studies'. Her research areas include identity and diversity in news and legal discourse, through the lens offered by CDA and corpus linguistics. She has published extensively on the linguistic and discursive construal of ethnic and gender diversity, migration, and disability. Among her recent publications, the *International Journal of Language Studies* special issue on "Disability, Shame and Discrimination" (co-edited with Hughes, 2022, 16/4), "Online Abuse and Disability Hate Speech" (2020), "Disability in the Populist Press: An Investigation of British Tabloids" (2019), *Agency in the British Press: A Corpus-based Discourse Analysis of the 2011 UK Riots* (2016), *Languaging Diversity* (co-edited with Balirano, 2015). She is also the co-editor in chief of the international peer-reviewed *I-LanD Journal* (with Caliendo), and the Deputy Director of the I-LanD Research Centre.

Maria Cristina Paganoni (PhD) is Associate Professor of English Language and Translation at the University of Milan. Her research approach falls within the methodological frameworks of Discourse Analysis, Critical Discourse Studies and social semiotics. With Palgrave she has published *City Branding and New Media: Linguistic Perspectives, Discursive Strategies and Multimodality* (2015) and *Framing Big Data: A Linguistic and Discursive Approach* (2019). She is the author of several peer-reviewed book chapters and journal articles. Discourses of tourism and mobility, gender violence and media coverage, and public health issues in legal and political communication, especially in response to the pandemic, are her current research focus. She has recently edited a special issue on COVID-19 communication across contexts and media for *Languages, Cultures, Mediation (LCM Journal)*.

Sergio Pizziconi is Researcher of English at the University of Calabria, Italy, and has taught in secondary schools for thirty years. With an Italian doctorate in Linguistics and Teaching Italian L2/FL and an American PhD in English and applied linguistics, he has taught linguistics-related courses in Italian and American universities. His research interests cover cognitive linguistics, pedagogy and languages for special purposes.

Martin Reisigl is Associate Professor at the Department of Linguistics at the University of Vienna. His research interests include (critical) discourse studies, text linguistics, sociolinguistics, pragmatics, politolinguistics, ecolinguistics, rhetoric, language and history, linguistics and literature, argumentation analysis and semiotics. Recent co-edited publications include *Diskursanalyse und Kritik* [Discourse Analysis and Critique] (with Antje Langer and Martin Nonhoff, 2019), *Discursive Representations of Controversial Issues in Medicine and Health* (with Giuliana Elena Garzone and Maria Cristina Paganoni, 2019), *Sprache und Geschlecht. Band 1: Sprachpolitiken und Grammatik. Band 2: Empirische Studien* [Language and Gender: Volume 1: Language Policies and Grammar.

Volume 2: Empirical Studies] (with Constanze Spieß, 2017), and *Diskurs – semiotisch. Aspekte multiformaler Diskurskodierung* [Discourse – semiotically. Aspects of multiformal discourse coding] (with Ernest W. B. Hess-Lüttich, Heidrun Kämper and Ingo H. Warnke, 2017).

Eric Louis Russell is Full Professor of French & Italian and courtesy professor in Linguistics, Gender, Sexuality & Women's Studies at the University of California, Davis. He is the author of *The Discursive Ecology of Homophobia* (Multilingual Matters, 2019), *Alpha Masculinity* (Palgrave, 2021), and *Redoing Linguistic Worlds* (Multilingual Matters, 2024), as well as the forthcoming *Transgressive Language* (Routledge), in addition to numerous journal articles and chapters.

Michele Sala, PhD (University of Bergamo), MA (Youngstown State University, Ohio), is an associate professor in English Language and Translation at the University of Bergamo (Department of Foreign Languages, Literatures and Cultures), where he teaches English linguistics and translation at graduate and undergraduate level. He is a member of AIA (Associazione Italiana di Anglistica), CERLIS (Centro di Ricerca sui Linguaggi Specialistici), CLAVIER (Corpus and Language Variation in English Research Group) and a member of the scientific and editorial board of the CERLIS Series (international peer-reviewed volumes on specialized languages). His research activity deals with language for specific purposes and, more specifically, the application of genre and discourse analytical methods to a corpus-based study of specialized texts in the domain of academic research, law, medicine and applied linguistics, as well as digital humanities. He has also dealt with text linguistics in cognitive terms.

Piergiorgio Trevisan is Associate Professor of English Language and Linguistics at the University of Trieste, Italy. His research interests include Stylistics, Critical Discourse Analysis and Systemic Functional Linguistics with a special focus on experimental stimulus design. Some of his latest publications include the monograph *Characterisation through Language* (2019), the volume *Cultures on the Screens* (edited with Leonardo Buonomo, 2022), the essays

Character's mental functioning during a 'neuro-transition': Pragmatic failures in 'Flowers for Algernon' (2022) and *'You don't know nothing about me': Ideology and Characterisation in* When They See Us (2022).

TEXTUS
ENGLISH STUDIES IN ITALY
STYLESHEET

1. *Submission of manuscripts*

Please submit:
- an electronic version (RTF or Word) as an e-mail attachment;
- a printout of the paper;
- a suggested running head;
- a brief description (max. 6 lines) of current and past teaching/research positions, main research interests and publications;
- an abstract (12-14 lines), which should come before the main text.

2. *Style*

a) Formatting
- use font 11;
- use single line spacing;
- number pages progressively (top left corner);
- indent paragraphs (0.5 cm) except the first in each section or after a line space;
- the standard page is 38 lines x 68/70 characters including spaces (approx. 2,600 characters per page)
- use italics for emphasis or for non-English words;
- use British English spelling conventions (such as 'analyse' and not 'analyze', 'specialise' and not 'specialize') in your text, though it might include American quotations which of course you will quote as published.

b) Footnotes
- use footnotes, not endnotes; they should be used only when strictly necessary for explanatory purposes and be as brief as possible;
- in the main text the footnote number should be directly after the word in question and before any punctuation marks, with the exception of question marks in which case it comes after; there should be no space between numbers and punctuation marks; the footnote should be full line.
- use font size 9;
- no line spaces between footnotes.

c) Quotations in the text
Short quotations (2-3 lines) should run on in the main text; use rounded double quotation marks (" ").
Longer quotations should have a line space before and after the quotation; do not use quotation marks; use font size 10; quotations should be full line with no indenting left or right. E.g.:

said of English speakers:

we are more apt to make a grasping gesture when we speak of grasping an elusive idea than when we speak of grasping a door knob. (Whorf 1956: 157)

Use single quotation marks for quotes within quoted passages. E.g.: "the so-called 'campus novel'".

d) Citation in the main text
The sequence should be author's surname, space, year, colon, space, page number; use 'f' or 'ff' to indicate subsequent pages, as follows:
- one author: (Buxton 1967: 59ff) or .... Buxton (1967: 59ff);
- for two authors separate surnames with *and*: (Chouliaraki and Fairclough 1999: 16);
- for three or four authors, separate surnames with commas: (Baker, Frances, Tognini Bonelli 1993: 12);
- for five or more authors use *et al.* after the main author: (Pollard *et al.* 1923: 43);
- separate works by different authors and more works by the same author with a semicolon (Bay 2000; Chomsky 2001) (Hansen 2002; 2010);
- use italics for play or poem titles. E.g.: Tennyson (*The Lady of Shalott*, ll. 10-14)
- citations of plays should include act, scene and line number. E.g.: Shakespeare (*The Tempest*, I.ii.323-26);
- for omitted text use three dots between square brackets. E.g.:

When it first appeared in 1975, *After Babel* created a sensation, quickly establishing itself as [...] a seminal study of literary theory.
- always give the full author-date citation: do not use "op. cit", "loc. cit", or "*ibidem*".
- When many quotations from the same work follow in little space, you just need to insert page number preceded by p. or pp. in brackets.
- Example:
- Says Murphie, "magic had always been [...] as well" (Murphy 2006: 114). [...] He goes on to argue [...] (p. 114).

e) Tables and graphs
IMPORTANT! graphs should be black and white and submit in Word, RTF or Excel.

Graphs, line drawings, photographs and the like should be labelled as "Figures" and numbered consecutively. A brief description of the figure is to be added above it. Information presented in rows and columns should be labelled as "Tables" and numbered consecutively, with text ranged left and numbers ranged on the last figure as follows:

TABLE I
This is the caption for Table 1

Verb types	*Occurrences*
Auxiliary verbs	131
Modal verbs	25
Other verbs	3

f) Examples and lists
All examples should be numbered progressively. Items in lists should be numbered or be introduced by a), b), c) etc. or i), ii), iii).

g) Acknowledgements and appendices
Permission acknowledgements should go in a footnote at the beginning of the article.
Other acknowledgements and appendices should go at the end of the main text before the References section.

h) References (bibliography)
Check that all citations in the main text have a reference.
List references alphabetically at the end of the article.
Format references in accordance with the examples below; please pay attention to the following:
–   single author or editor: surname followed by a comma followed by full first name;
–   two authors or editors: as above; separate names with "and";
–   three or more authors or editors: as above; separate names with commas;
–   put the date of the first edition in square brackets followed by the date of the edition used. Example: POE, EDGAR ALLAN, [1840] 1984, "The Man in the Crowd", in P. F. Quinn (ed.), …
–   if you are using the English translation of a foreign text, the note and

bibliographical record must refer to both the original (with date of first publication) and to the translation.

Example: SCHLEIERMACHER, FRIEDRICH, "Über die verschiedenen Methoden des Übersetzens", 1813, Italian trans. "Sui diversi modi del tradurre", by G. Moretto, in G. Moretto (ed.), *Etica ed ermeneutica*, Bibliopolis, Napoli, 1985, pp. 85-120.

- use (ed.) for singular, (eds) for plural; vol. for singular and vols for plural;
- when referencing online publications, please include the most recent access date as follows: http://..., last accessed May 12, 2011.
- when you are quoting publications by University Presses please use U.P. (Manchester U.P., but for ex. the abbreviation of Oxford University Press usually used is O.U.P.)
- if there are two towns (as in John Benjamins, Amsterdam-Philadelphia) please unite them with a hyphen, not with "and" or other solutions.

i) Books
VAN DIJK, TEUN A., 1993, *Elite Discourse and Racism*, Sage Publications, Newbury Park (CA).
CHOULIARAKI, LILIE and FAIRCLOUGH, NORMAN, 1999, *Discourse in Late Modernity*, Edinburgh U.P., Edinburgh.
BAKER, MONA, FRANCES, GILL, TOGNINI BONELLI, ELENA (eds), 1993, *Text and Technology: in Honour of John Sinclair*, John Benjamins, Amsterdam-Philadelphia.
POLLARD, ALFRED W., GREG, WALTER W., THOMPSON, EDWARD M., WILSON, JOHN D., CHAMBERS, RAYMOND W., 1923, *Shakespeare's Hand in the Play of Sir Thomas More*, C.U.P., Cambridge.
HOLDSWORTH, ROGER V., [1990] 1991, *Three Jacobean Revenge Tragedies*, Macmillan, London.

ii) Articles in books
SCHLEIERMACHER, FRIEDRICH, "Über die verschiedenen Methoden des Übersetzens", 1813, Italian trans. "Sui diversi modi del tradurre", by G. Moretto, in G. Moretto (ed.), *Etica ed ermeneutica*, Bibliopolis, Napoli, 1985, pp. 85-120, and in S. Nergard (ed.), *La teoria della traduzione nella storia*, Bompiani, Milano, 1993, pp. 143-79.
HILL, LESLIE, 1990, "The Trilogy Translated", in L. Hill (ed.), *Beckett's Fiction: in Different Words*, C.U.P., Cambridge, pp. 59-78; also in J. Birkett and K. Ince (eds), *Samuel Beckett*, Longman, London-New York, 2000, pp. 99-116.

iii) Articles in journals
ULRYCH, MARGHERITA and BOLLETTIERI BOSINELLI, ROSA MARIA, 1999, "The State of the Art in Translation", *Textus* 12, pp. 219-41.
ELLIOTT, WARD and VALENZA, ROBERT, 2010a, "Two Tough Nuts to Crack", *Literary and Linguistic Computing* 25 (1), pp. 67-83.
LEPPIHALME, RITA, 2000, "The Two Faces of Standardization. On the Translations of Regionalisms in Literary Dialogue", *The Translator* 6, pp. 247-69.

iv) Films, video, TV series, movies
Information and data to be provided and order: *film title* (in *italics*), Dir. (followed by a full stop), production and distribution company, country, year. For TV series or series in general, "episode title/season" in rounded letters between double quotation marks, *series title* in italics; episode writer/screenwriter should be listed as well as the director.

Examples:

(L')Auberge Rouge, Dir. Jean Epstein. Pathé-Consortium-Cinéma, France, 1923.
Borderline, Dir. Kenneth Macpherson. The Pool Group, Great Britain, 1930.
Thaïs, Dir. Anton Giulio Bragaglia. Novissima Film, Italy, 1917.
Voyage dans la lune, Dir. Georges Méliès. Star Film, France, 1905.

Scooby-Doo and the Witch's Ghost. Dir. Jim Stenstrum. Warner Brothers Animation, USA, 1999.
Scooby-Doo! Legend of the Phantosaur. Dir. Etan Spaulding. Warner Brothers Animation, USA, 2011.

"Asylum". *Supernatural*. Dir. Guy Bee. Writer Richard Hatem. Season 1, Episode 10, 2005.
"The French Mistake". *Supernatural*. Dir. Charles Beeson. Writer Ben Edlund. Season 6, Episode 15, 2011.